D1293795

PSYCHOANALYSTS TALK

PSYCHOANALYSTS TALK

VIRGINIA HUNTER

Foreword by LEÓN GRINBERG

THE GUILFORD PRESS
New York London

A Division of Guilford Publications, Inc.
72 Spring Street, New York, N. Y. 10012

Printed in the United States of America

This book is printed on acid-free paper.

Last digit is print number: 9 8 7 6 5 4 3 2 1

Library of Congress Cataloging-in-Publication Data

Hunter, Virginia, Ph.D.
Psychoanalysts talk / Virginia Hunter
p. cm.
Includes bibliographical references and index.
ISBN 0-89862-373-1
1. Psychoanalytic interpretations—Case studies.
2. Psychoanalysis—Psychology. 3. Psychoanalysts—Interviews. 4. Borderline personality disorder—Diagnosis—Case Studies. 5. Borderline personality disorder—Treatment—Case studies. I. Title.
[DNLM: 1. Psychoanalysis—methods—interviews.
2. Psychoanalyic Therapy—methods—interviews.
3. Borderline Personality Disorder—diagnosis.
4. Borderline Personality Disorder—therapy. WM 460 H947p 1994]
RC509.8.H86 1994
150.19'5—dc20
DNLM/DLC
for Library of Congress

93-40502
CIP

If you observe a really happy man, you will find him building a boat, writing a symphony, educating his son, growing double dahlias in his garden or looking for dinosaur eggs in the Gobi Desert. He will not be searching for happiness as if it were a collar button that has rolled under the radiator. He will have become aware that he is happy in the course of living life twenty-four crowded hours of the day.

—W. B. WOLFE

Such a man is my husband, Phillip Redding, to whom this work is dedicated, and without whom it would not have been possible.

About the Author

Virginia Hunter, L.C.S.W., B.C.D., Ph.D., a training and supervising psychoanalyst, practices in Long Beach, California, where she sees children, adults, couples, families, and groups. She has served on the faculty of the Department of Social Work at California State University, Long Beach. Before she focused her practice on individual analysis, family, and group therapy, she had extensive experience in child welfare and outpatient mental health clinics. Dr. Hunter was the nonmedical director of the Psychiatric Clinic for Children in Long Beach. She has presented her work at major conferences in the United States and Latin America and has published numerous articles in psychoanalytic and social work journals. She has also produced numerous video tapes of leading psychoanalysts worldwide. She is currently working on her second book, *Treating Blocks to Learning and Creativity in Children and Adults.*

Foreword

For centuries man has argued about the origin of the universe. At a time when most people believed in a static and immobile universe, the question posed was whether or not it has a beginning. This question gradually evolved into a complex subject with metaphysical and theoretical implications, as Stephen Hawking points out in his book, *A History of Time*. Some scholars maintained that the universe has existed since time immemorial. During the decade of the 1920s, however, scientists observed that the more distant galaxies are moving away from us, giving rise to a new theory which suggested that the universe is expanding, and that there was a time when the universe was infinitely small and dense until an enormous explosion—the "Big Bang"—occurred, causing the beginning of the expansion of the universe.

But, as Hawking maintains, any physical theory has always been provisional; it can never be proved conclusively. If it agrees with our predictions after submitting it to experimentation, then the theory will survive and our confidence in it will increase. If, however, a new observation arises to contradict it with convincing arguments, it is then abandoned or modified. This is what happened when Einstein's theory of relativity modified or completed earlier theories which had existed for centuries.

At the present time, however, many physicists believe that, in spite of its extraordinary and revolutionary advances, the theory of relativity is still only a partial theory which needs to be complemented by another partial theory such as quantum mechanics. In other words, we must leap from the theory of the extraordinarily immense to the theory of the extraordinarily minute. But, undoubtedly, all those previous theories were valuable in that they contributed elements and concepts which facilitated the rise of new theories which developed those concepts and, in turn, led the way to new discoveries.

These reflections do not necessarily imply an extrapolation, but rather a metaphorical comparison to suggest that something similar is occurring in the realm of psychoanalysis. The psychoanalytic universe is also expanding with the addition of important theories that are being incorporated into the basic preexisting theories. Anna Freud, Hartmann, and Melanie Klein could not have developed their ideas if it had not been for the fundamental bases laid down by Freud's discoveries. Winnicott, Bion, Kohut, and many others, in turn, drew upon the theories of their teachers to develop productive ideas for the understanding of how the mind functions. Theories involving original elements are constantly arising, some of which can open for us "new frontiers toward the hitherto unknown within ourselves," as analysts such as Schafer and Bernardi have affirmed.

But how are these ideas formed? How do they arise and on what do they depend? What are the essential factors that influence their gestation?

Virginia Hunter attempts to respond to these questions in her meticulous and rigorous study based on direct interviews with eleven prestigious psychoanalysts who were presented with clinical material that consisted of a single analytic session with a borderline patient. Furthermore, in addition to seeking commentary on her patient, Dr. Hunter also conducted personal interviews with those analysts in order to learn about details of their childhood history and the influences of their culture and milieu that could have existed in the choice of their vocation and their allegiance to theories they have adhered to throughout their professional careers.

Her main aim was to attempt to demonstrate her hypotheses about the gravitation that certain factors could have exerted on the creation of their respective theories and interpretive modalities. These factors, according to the author, are the following: (1) transference to theory; (2) personal myth; (3) personal history; and (4) cultural, social, and political events.

Undoubtedly, some of the aspects making up those factors are enormously important, especially if we take into account, for example, the cultural milieu in which psychoanalytic training took place and the transferential relationship that the analyst has had in his personal analysis. It is not surprising, then, that there exist what we might call "psychoanalytic families" in which theories and ideologies are transmitted through tradition from psychoanalytic "grandparents" to "parents" and from "parents" to "children." For many years these traditions have been staunchly maintained and the diverse geographical regions seem to have held on at all costs to a particular theory that characterized that region in a particular way. Nevertheless, parochialism and the dogmatic attitude of certain sectors were responsible for pernicious factors that acted against the progress of psychoanalytic theory, thereby hindering genuine communication between analysts and sterilizing the possibility of bringing to light the hitherto unexplored riches of psychoanalysis.

I should like to emphasize the merit of Virginia Hunter's experiment, in that she has chosen to investigate the bases for those differences existing between the various analysts in relation to their respective theories and modalities of interpretation in psychoanalytic practice. Of course, hers was not the first experiment of this type. There have been others who sought similar goals by sending identical clinical material to several analysts in order to compare their responses. They tried to corroborate the idea that it would be possible to reflect the theoretical differences between the analysts who participated in those experiments by analyzing the nature of the therapeutic interventions and clinical interaction. They found evidence that previously fixed theoretical positions did, in fact, influence their clinical evaluations. In most cases the data were distorted by the analyst's bias.

In my opinion, Virginia Hunter has done something different and much more complete because it has been enriched by her personal face-to-face dialogue with each of the discussants of her clinical case. Her interviews were like direct supervisions in which she was able to extend her data and inform her material with more detail regarding her transference and states of mind, according to the comments she received. It was possible for her to transmit nonverbal aspects of the exchange with her patient and describe her own emotional reactions to specific attitudes of the analysand. This nonverbal communication conferred greater value on the gathering of data. Moreover, her interviews were recorded and filmed on video. In addition, she was able to research the personal background of the analysts interviewed, their milieu, and their theoretical and professional background and development, all of which she used to support her hypotheses.

The project in which she has been involved is praiseworthy for the constancy and courage with which she carried out her work, as well as for the value of an investigation that enables us to better understand the close relationship between a theoretical frame of reference and psychoanalytic practice and the factors influencing them.

The author emphasizes in one of her chapters that, in her study of the responses of the eleven analysts, there was a consensus of opinion in regard to the basic diagnosis of the clinical case as a "borderline personality disorder," and that the treatment would have to be an extremely long-term one. She adds, however, that there were marked differences in emphasis, focus, aims, and the nature of the treatment itself; in other words, whether it was a matter of analysis or of psychoanalytic psychotherapy.

I believe, in effect, that there are similarities and differences between analysts of different theoretical tendencies. In this sense, I agree with Wallerstein when he refers to the notion that "our common ground" resides in sharing the theory of transference and resistance, conflict and compromise. For him, all our general theories are like explicative metaphors. He admits that there are differences, but he holds that these differences are merely in style and form and that they are compatible with a common and shared conception of approach to the basic analytic task. In my opinion, however, these differences continue to be important and must be taken into consideration.

From the commentaries of the analysts participating in this experiment, the differences in focus and clinical and technical criteria in regard to the understanding of material and the intervention of the therapist are clearly evident. In some cases Hunter received explicit criticism in relation to specific interpretations or attitudes and behavior, pointed out as actings of the analyst. But it is significant to emphasize that these very same attitudes and interpretations were praised and supported by other analysts interviewed. It is interesting to note that in both the study that I am commenting on and in other experiments I have mentioned, each analyst expressed his opinion according to the theoretical frame of reference to which he or she belonged. Nevertheless, it should be recognized that each contribution added something more to the comprehension of the patient, in spite of the fact that the theoretical contributions were sometimes apparently incompatible.

The choice of clinical material was not left to chance. The author admits that she specifically chose a session which she called "The Hour" and a "Piece of an Hour," with a long dream whose content appeared associated with the subject of a story, "Rappaccini's Daughter," by Nathaniel Hawthorne. The tale clearly reflected the main problem of the patient, who felt herself to be poisoned, trapped, isolated, incapable of trusting her parents, and incapable of escaping her fate. In this session several of Roslyn's most important symptoms appeared: her fear of falling into a limitless space; her sensation of lacking a skin to contain her; the feeling of "imploding" or bursting inward; experiencing herself as a brittle crystal, formed in a chaotic world and exposed to the danger of fragmentation.

Virginia Hunter holds that this material can demonstrate the analyzability of borderline patients who, in spite of the seriousness of their symptoms, can still present sensible, creative aspects in greater contact with reality. Often these patients behave as "false selves" and suffer from what André Green has termed "private madness." According to Dr. Hunter, this study can be enriching in that it enables us to think about those technical problems that must be taken into account in order to treat those patients who present oscillations between their pregenital and psychotic structure and their neurotic part, and that many times it will depend on the personality and style of each analyst whether or not to decide to analyze this type of patient. One of the most valuable aspects of this book is the fact that it clearly points out that psychoanalysis is not a monolithic construction, but that it contains a great variety of possibilities for individual creativity.

As I have pointed out earlier, the author emphasized the influence of four factors on the incorporation and development of the theories held by analysts. The first is the Transference to Theory factor, based on a quotation from Leo Rangell, in which he points out that the association of an analyst with a psychoanalytic group has a profound influence on the adherence of that analyst to a specific theory. That influence is reciprocal, and it may be the case that a theory can lead an analyst to join a particular group. The training analysis and the idealization or deidealization of the analyst towards his training analyst or his institution can influence and be transferred to the theory, albeit accepting or rejecting it.

The second factor, the Personal Myth, refers to personal recollections and autobiographical images of the analyst, as well as to conscious and unconscious fantasies of his childhood with respect to what he aspires to be as an adult. The presence of the analyst's personality is undoubtedly an integral part of the analytic process, beyond the transference–countertransference relationship. The influence of that personality, with its specific characteristics, can, for example, eventually hinder the development of a useful regression in the patient. There are authors who include the importance of personal factors such as professional competence, educational level, customs, and ideals that may influence the functions of the analyst so that certain characteristics predominate over others, for example, warmth versus distance, rigidity versus flexibility, aggression versus passivity, and so on. The third factor, Personal History, will also have important repercussions on the behavior, knowledge, ideas, and emotional life of each analyst.

The fourth factor, Cultural and Sociopolitical Influences, is one that weighs heavily on the analyst in regard to his preference for certain theories, as we have already pointed out. The author cites, among others, Riccardo Steiner (see Chiarandini, 1992), who warns us against the risk of indoctrination when only one single theory is taught. Steiner states that the analyst does not separate his ideas as a citizen from his ideas as a psychoanalyst. Periods of crisis, such as in wartime, or under the domination of totalitarian regimes, produce profound impacts not only on the analyst but on the patient as well. The same is true of different types of economic or social problems.

I should like to give special mention to the excellent summary that the author has compiled in her Synoptic Chart, in which she compares the interventions of the analysts interviewed through different points of reference classified in different columns. Each column has a specific heading corresponding to the content and objectives of each commentary. These headings are as follows: Main Focus, Genetic Focus, Dynamic Focus, Comments on Dream, Comments on Transference, Comments on Countertransference, Treatment Recommendations, and the Expected Audience for the Comments. In a clear and concise manner, Virginia Hunter sets out the theoretical and clinical positions of each one of the analysts interviewed—all of whom, as she emphasizes, are "respected, honored, and senior clinicians"—in separate boxes and in relation to the various items characterized by the titles of the different columns. Thus, it is easy to trace the points of coincidence and divergence among those analysts who participated in the experiment. I should especially like to point out that this table constitutes an eloquent sample of the different psychoanalytic theories that underlie the statements and points of view of the analysts consulted, in spite of the similarity of many of their comments.

Returning to the metaphoric comparison of the expansion of the universe to which I referred at the beginning of this Foreword, I believe that it can be a useful model for a better understanding of the emergence of psychoanalytic theories. One of the models developed by Bion in his trilogy, *The Memoir of the Future* (1975–1979), is that of the origin of the universe as produced by a great explosion (the model of the "Big-Bang"), causing the expansion of the universe. Bion thinks that psychoanalysis itself is undergoing a similar process, expanding constantly in many areas and generating different theoretical possibilities. Moreover, this process, which is happening at an extremely rapid pace, gives rise to what Bion calls the loss of "lateral communication" (communication between peers). It would be useful for the new theories which have arisen from the expansion of the psychoanalytic universe to find at least some elements that would favor a lateral communication that would be comprehensible and accessible to all psychoanalysts. This book can furnish one of the means to achieve this goal.

LEÓN GRINBERG

Acknowledgments

It seems impossible to express the gratitude I feel to the 11 analysts who generously participated in this study. They are André Green, Hanna Segal, Frances Tustin, John Bowlby, Ernest Wolf, Peter Giovacchini, Arnold Goldberg, Rudolf Ekstein, Robert Wallerstein, Arnold Modell, and Jacob Arlow. They were all generous in the gift of their time and the sharing of their minds. I gained more than I could ever put into words from their acquaintances, correspondence, the time I spent studying their writings and their work, and the hours I spent in discussion with them.

Interviews which I have done for inclusion in other formats or other publications, especially those with Clifford Scott and Joseph Natterson, also helped me to form my ideas about the relationship between transference to theory, personal myth, personal history, cultural and sociopolitical factors I have outlined, and clinical interpretations. These interviews, too, have been extremely helpful in getting a perspective on the interviews presented in this book.

This work could not have been written without the knowledge, generosity, and trust of Roselyn. I am indebted to her for all she has shared with me and taught me. She, too, hopes that sharing our work may be of help to others. After all, this is also her book.

It may seem strange, but I must also thank Margaret Little for her own courage and many contributions to the literature. She was my inspiration and was to have been the first participating analyst in this study. Because of increasingly poor health, she had to cancel our time together only a few days before it was to have taken place. However, the work she and Winnicott did together was never far from my mind. Roselyn has read their work, and it gave her hope and supported her will to try.

Marcy Schott of Menninger Clinic, Topeka, Kansas, Professional Information Services, was of invaluable help as my bibliographical researcher. Having struggled with many of the usual problems of dyslexia until my second analysis, I often relied upon her for aid in research. Paula Wood's work as secretary has always been excellent. Her ability to read my writing was a miracle.

The training and ideals I acquired at Reiss–Davis Child Study Center are a part of this work. The center itself was a special world. Ruth Bro, my social work supervisor, especially deserves my gratitude for all the interfering transferences she contained during that period of my life. Others who have supervised my analytic work—Lillian Weitzner, Morton Shane, Robert Stolorow, Martin Grotjahn, Tom Mintz, William Brooks, and Louis A. Gottschalk—have all been valuable resources, and many of their ideas and beliefs are surely blended somewhere in this work. I would like to thank Lawrence E. Hedges. His careful reading of the first draft of the case responses was invaluable to me. His generosity to me, at a time when he was completing a book of his own, can never be repaid. Joseph Natterson and Michael Russell were also supportive and encouraging regarding the earliest draft. Special thanks to Tim Lockwood, a writer of many technical books and a patient friend who read this "one last time" before typesetting. I am grateful for the editing skills of Jodi Creditor, Production Editor at the Guilford Press. She was "right on." Thanks, too, to Kitty Moore, Senior Editor at Guilford, for her enthusiasm about this book. Kitty took me by the hand and led me right in. I am grateful to Jay Martin, without whose mentorship and friendship this book would not have been created. Ann Link graciously gave the manuscript one last reading.

Thanks to my mother, Theo P. Deason, who, though far away and in her 80s, has always been a constant source of encouragement and proud. I appreciate her allowing me the guilt-free freedom to pursue my dream of making a contribution in my chosen field. Before her retirement, she, too, was a social worker, and she has always provided a model of caring and commitment. I regret that my father, Archie K. Deason, did not live to share in my accomplishment. He was a university professor in chemistry and physics. I hope he knows and is smiling.

The quality of my life has been enhanced by the love and generosity of my dear friends Elaine Bunzel and Ed Nevin for their frequent loan of their home on the ocean, which provided an inspirational and creative space in which to write and paint. Clark Garen, a true friend, has supported me in too many ways to list.

The dedication of this work to my husband, Phillip Redding, expresses my most profound and heartfelt debt.

Contents

PSYCHOANALYSTS TALK

Author's Notes

I entered the world of psychoanalysis through the doors of a postgraduate fellowship at Reiss–Davis Child Study Center in 1967. Psychoanalysis has never ceased to educate, intrigue, excite, and occupy me. It is a world full of never-ending ideas, challenges, increasing knowledge, and questions. As a movement, psychoanalysis had stressed the primacy of the medical profession and gave little credit to the contributions of social workers. After completing training at Reiss–Davis, a personal analysis, a group psychoanalytic experience, and many more years of individual supervision with psychoanalysts, I had proclaimed myself to be a psychoanalyst and practiced child and adult psychoanalysis. Much of my extensive supervision was not institutionalized. In the 1960s in the United States, this was the path of many nonmedical clinicians who became psychoanalysts. In the 1980s, I belonged to a Freud Study Group that later evolved into one of the first nonmedical psychoanalytic schools in California. Yet, after graduating from that school, having undergone yet another psychoanalysis, more supervision, and having received a Ph.D. in psychoanalysis, I still do not belong, as yet, to an institute affiliated with the International Psycho-Analytical Association.

Many of the nonmedical psychoanalysts in the United States say it does not matter to them if they are outside the main body of psychoanalysis. But it has mattered and still matters to me. I would envision that the psychoanalytic movement should develop in a way that will allow it to comprehend and include practitioners whose origin of training is not only in psychiatry but also in psychology, the humanities, the sciences, and social work. In short, I want to see develop what Freud himself hoped for: psychoanalysis suffused with the intellectual disciplines of our time.

I began this study out of the desire to have discussion and dialogue with other analysts. I videorecorded all the interviews and case discussions because I hoped future researchers and students might enjoy them. Unfortunately, I had problems with my camera during my time with Wallerstein; only the written account remains. Being on the outside has some advantages as well as disadvantages. I wanted to know to what degree personal history, myth, transference to theory, and cultural and sociopolitical influences might have influenced each analyst's choice of theory and response to a single case. I could ask direct questions others might have hesitated to ask—questions about the politics of psychoanalysis, clinical practice, personal history, and other elements important in clinical practice, but not ordinarily discussed openly. Contemporary psychoanalysis is quite different from classic psychoanalysis.

Long ago I accepted that I did not know enough, and probably never would, in my own eyes; but I did know that I loved learning. I had not been forced to adopt only one school of psychoanalytic thought. Both Reiss–Davis Child Study Center, in my day, and my nonmedical institute, at its inception, were accepting of many listening perspectives and did not discourage me from considering each analyst–therapist dyad in the context of multiple theoretical frameworks. Granted, it is always easier to have only one theory of psychoanalysis, but it is also intellectually limiting. We are all theorists. That is, we all have our own theories about personality, development, relationships, and treatment. Stolorow and Atwood (1979, p. 167) may well be correct in asserting that all theories of personality are structured by the formative experiences in the theorist's life.

In 1985, another very positive experience spurred my imagination. I had the opportunity to present a borderline case, in Paris, to one of several well-known analysts. This was at a conference sponsored by the University of California, Los Angeles. Rumor had it that André Green would be the most exacting of the respondents. I, therefore, felt I would learn the most by choosing to present to him. He proved kind and generous, as well as thoughtful, regarding the case I presented to him: He was deeply respectful, and he liked my work. The conference in Paris was videotaped. Later, he agreed to come to my institute to present his work to us and agreed to give me an interview for publication. The conference in Paris was also videotaped.

Another element in my personal history has had a special influence on me. During my many years of practice, I have shared a suite and practice with Menninger-trained psychiatrist, Dr. Arthur Nickerson. We shared many cases—one of us treating the presenting patient, often a child, and the other treating the parents or family. We do not usually accept cases for treatment unless we can treat the entire family. Many of these cases originally presented because of school and learning problems. I, myself, was dyslexic until I worked through a great many of the related problems in my second analytic experience. Through the years I have learned a great deal about treating learning difficulties and creative blocks of all kinds. Earlier, however, decoding the written word and writing were especially difficult for me. Yet I loved auditory learning and learning through visual perceptions. Thus, creating the videos, as well as this book for others, was a natural extension of my wish to share my rich learning adventure with others. André Green and the French school place particular stress and value upon the examination of language use in individual psychology. Although I did not think so at the time, I now know that Green's positive response to me and my work helped free me to risk sharing written language with others.

The experience of presenting the same case to a series of analysts and publishing the responses has been done previously (Silverman, 1987). Like Silverman, I found value in each response, and I am convinced that readers will also profit by the variety and richness of the responses contained in this book. My dialogic investigation of one case by a number of clinicians makes for a unique contribution to the literature. But I find that the closer this book gets to publication, the more anxiety I have. It takes an act of will to leave the text unaltered and unchanged. Presenting a patient with borderline structures creates special concerns.

Contemporary analysis must concern itself with many different kinds of patients. There has long been debate regarding the question "What is psychoanalysis?" in contrast to "What is psychotherapy?" My own view has always been that if one seeks to make what is unconscious conscious, uses dreams and free associations, and forever seeks to understand the transference–countertransference symbols and meaning, *that* is psychoanalysis. None of the psychoanalysts in this book took exception to my treating the patient Roselyn psychoanalytically. Perhaps because, historically, the American Psychoanalytic Association requires that cases accepted for training be neurotic ones, many psychoanalysts regard work with more troubled patients in a less than favorable light. In addition, I believe that there is good evidence that many training analysts focus so intently upon the didactic aspects of training that institutionalized psychoanalytic education often deemphasizes examination of primitive structure. My own conviction is that working with such patients as Roselyn requires the ability to move rapidly between neurotic and psychotic structures and associations. It is difficult work for which the ability to tolerate threats of loss of life and terrible responsibility is necessary. Winnicott, Margaret Little, and many others have reported that the ability to adapt to the patient's needs is crucial. Little (1990) points out that intuitive behavior and management, not verbal interpretation and technique, are indicated.

It may be that regression to dependency is essential to achieving "good-enough" basic trust. This state of trust may come only after having been allowed to fall, while helpless, and face the dread of annihilation. As Little says:

> The analyst has to be able to give up his defenses against the same anxiety, the dread of annihilation, of loss of identity, both for himself and for his patient. At the same time, his own identity must remain distinct and his reality sense unimpaired, keeping awareness on two extreme levels, reality and delusion. He is in the position of a mother vis-à-vis her infant, but where neither he nor his patient is in fact in that situation. (1990, p. 90)

For the patient to disclose, or for the analyst to experience, such states of mind, is not easy. It is not possible for me to hide behind a professional role and also accept the direct relationship required in treating such patients. I believe the analytic frame, here, has to fit the patient, not the other way around.

Often professionals speak of borderline patients as though they are always desperate, chaotic, and feeling or thinking really "crazy" thoughts. There are such patients. But just as frequently in my own experience with patients with borderline bits or fragments, they are "false selves." By this I mean they may appear very sound, creative, high functioning, and calm to friends, colleagues, and relatives; but inside they indeed suffer from what André Green and I call "private madness." This may even include somatization that contains the madness of overwhelmingly chaotic feelings. Others may not realize they are depersonalized and feeling very unreal. Even the children of a currently "fashionable group"— adult children of alcoholics—may have areas in their psychic structure that are encapsulated. Many patients who were battered, abused, or suffered unbearable psychological abuse or neglect have disavowed or disconnected feelings that, when connected or freed, may seem overwhelmingly "mad" for a time. As these patients regress, in the service of being able to risk feeling their real selves again, they need acceptance, calm, a firm commitment, and the courage to risk bearing terrible disturbances in the analysis or treatment. Many patients are like Margaret Little. She was a competent practicing physician long before her treatment with Winnicott. They need confidentiality, secure holding, and perhaps, as Winnicott has suggested, a quality of maternal preoccupation in the psychoanalyst.

Clearly this book represents work in progress. During the period of my research and interviews, I, of course, developed considerable insight and considerable understanding. This book is meant to assist clinicians in their own thinking. One of its values for me, and possibly for others, is that it allows us to see that psychoanalysis is not a monolithic construct; rather, it has a great deal of variety and individual creativity. Each analyst, it is hoped, allows himself or herself to take the shape needed by the individual patient, individual consultee, or the person being supervised, at the same time the primary tenets of psychoanalysis are maintained.

Beyond the examination of the varied perspectives that these twelve analysts, including myself, have placed upon the case, it would also be useful, I think, for the reader who is a theorist or clinician to ask himself or herself what perspective he or she would have stressed, missed, or touched on differently than those included in this book. I would hope this work would be used as a continuing way of examining one's own special perspectives, special emphasis, lacuna, and special forms of originality and creativity. This book, therefore, should assist the clinician in examining what theory or theories one has aligned with and in questioning its limitations and advantages relative to the many varieties of clinical work.

The excitement of what I learned both from my work with Roselyn, the subject of these pages, and the analysts' comments upon it, with their disclosures regarding the personal backgrounds upon which *they* work, provided me with a special kind of experience in psychoanalysis. This experience has achieved for me, now, exactly what I had always aimed for: the feeling of oneness with the psychoanalytic aim, its importance, and its value. Different as the analysts were, as different as their interpretations of the case may have been, each one welcomed me and took Roselyn seriously, although she was a borderline patient. Without question, all exhibited the seriousness of the commitment of analysts of all kinds to the psychoanalytic quest.

Personal Factors Subjectively Influencing Interpretation

The foundation of this chapter is the idea that psychoanalysis is based on epistemological assumptions; that is, that the human mind is able, subjectively, to comprehend ideas and feelings that are "transcendental," imprecise, or what Christopher Bollas calls the "unthought known" (1987). But clearly, such comprehension is individual, not mechanically duplicable, even as wide disagreement would exist in the listening process. Psychoanalysis relies heavily upon the analyst's mind as the instrument of investigation. From mind to mind, no perfect identity exists, and no mental investigation will be precisely duplicated when conducted by more than one mind. This study of the response of eleven analysts to identical case material, which was elaborated upon individual request or in spontaneous dialogue, exhibits consensus concerning the basic diagnosis of borderline personality disorder and the belief that treatment will be long term. There are striking differences in emphasis, focus, goals for treatment, and questions about the nature of treatment—even whether I was doing psychoanalysis or psychoanalytic psychotherapy. There are even differences of opinion as to whether these questions actually matter or are worth discussing. There are striking differences in suggestion for treatment plans and recommendation for technique.

All of the respondents are respected, honored senior clinicians. I am grateful for their candid responses. Each adds something of value to one's consideration of the world Roselyn and I have created and share together.

Psychoanalysis serves many different kinds of analysts and patients. The patients may range from those presenting with diagnoses that are neurotic to those that are borderline or even pyshotic. Today, as in the early history of psychoanalysis, a psychoanalysis may also be sought by a "well person" who wishes to better understand his own mind and the mind of others—including the minds of politicians, writers, physically ill persons, gang members, and so on, extending, I hope, to interest in the mind of the species in general.

Historically speaking, psychoanalysts themselves have biased analysis toward treating the neurotic. Contemporary psychoanalysis—learning from research in many fields—has made appropriate adjustments and accommodations to today's body of knowledge and today's patients. No longer are tripartite models or drives forced to occupy center stage. More likely, today, dominating the psychoanalytic dialogue are: basic faults; developmental issues; early rejection and trauma; specific areas where traces of parental deficit remain; such issues as soothing, calming, mirroring, psychosomatics, animated responsiveness, and enthusiasm; learning; creativity; and intimacy. All are central to discourse in contemporary psychoanalysis. Today, even more than in the past, the area of conflict the patient chooses will be followed by the analyst, who is ever more committed to listening acutely and knowing as much as possible, even while minimizing his own memory and his own desire.

What, then, makes for normal and even expected differences in the approaches of psychoanalysts to the same case material? There is general agreement that subjectivity is the major source of difference. Subjectivity will influence technique, interpretation, focus, activity, gratification, responsiveness, empathy, the way defenses are analyzed, and countertransference. It causes each psychoanalytic dialogue to be unique. Subjectivity, which gives each individual analysis its special power, is also the major reason for the differences among psychoanalyses.

No one would deny that analysis of the ego and understanding of the unconscious, dreams, free associations, defenses, transference, and countertransference are essential in any treatment. Yet it remains true that there are many different analytic approaches and experiences. In this chapter, I describe four subjective factors which have emerged in my study as those which most centrally influence analysts.

All analysts are influenced, more or less, by one of many subjective factors or by a combination of them. The subjective elements I believe to be the most important are "transference to theory," "personal myth," "personal history," and "cultural and sociopolitical influences," both past and present. Although there are undoubtedly many others, I believe these to be among the most significant and most frequently occurring influences in introducing divergence of interpretation. I have not mentioned genetics or intelligence. While I can think of cases where these were, for special reasons, unusually important factors, we do have to separate these from the most frequent factors causing divergence.

I have not assumed that these differences are usually negative. These generous master clinicians show us, very soon, how stimulating, exciting, enriching, challenging, and fun playing with the differences can be. I found their variety of responses both freeing and demanding.

My purpose is to show the uniqueness, the special influences of personal or theoretical biases, of cultural and historical background, and of personal myth on these clinicians, all of whom I chose because of my personal admiration for them and because of their contributions to the literature that had already helped me with understanding myself or patients. These subjective, personal factors are operative in us all; they represent those parts of our personality and character that are always in operation in the individual alone or in the interaction of any dyad. We are all theorists. That is, we all have our own theories about personality, development, relationships, and treatment.

Each of these outstanding individuals has a personal history and personal integrity that necessarily mark his or her works. Each has a personal way of working, of evolving an analytic relationship, and of stimulating the emergence of analytic and other interpersonal relatedness. The frame I presented, although left as open as possible, was still mine. The video camera was mine; the final editing, although mine to complete, had to be approved for publication by each subject. This mode of response to analytic material was not as easy for some as for others, since people obviously relate, think, and present in their own special ways. Time and many other factors may have influenced in the light in which some are seen. It may be that the light cast on some was a result of the nature of the study and the case chosen. Several participants were frank in saying they generally do not treat patients as disturbed as they have diagnosed Roselyn to be for various objective reasons such as time, or for subjective reasons such as unwillingness to deal with the extra demands and needs of such patients. Some simply stated that they were not referred such patients even though they might wish to treat them. None canceled or withdrew from participation after receiving the case material, which is, perhaps, why they are considered special in their field. All possessed that quality of mind that is necessary to engage undefensively in sharing and exploring the study of the human mind and heart.

Transference to Theory

During training, a powerful relationship develops between the analyst and psychoanalytic theory. Leo Rangell (1982) has written a persuasive article showing that the association of the analyst to the psychoanalytic group with which he or she affiliates has a profound influence in attaching the analyst to a theory. "The two are reciprocal. Being part of a group can determine one's theory, and a theory can cause one to become part of a group" (p. 29). His argument is that the theory that one adopts, with its concomitant impulse to stay true to and to remain a part of the group, influences how one must hear material.

Transference to psychoanalytic theory occurs from a variety of sources. It may be displaced from the training analysis. Unanalyzed "dissatisfaction in the personal analysis [may] lay down the initial and probably basic seeds for a negative transference to psychoanalysis itself" (Rangell, 1982, p. 35). Narcissistic hurts during the analysis, which are not analyzed, may later be displaced onto the theory of psychoanalysis. Unresolved idealization and other impulses and struggles against them may affect choice of theory and rejection of theory. The possibility of overidealization of the analyst also exists and may lead the candidate to try to duplicate his or her analyst in him- or herself.

Not only is the experience of the training analysis vital, but that of the institute of training is crucial as well. The psychoanalytic institute as well as the student group may have a need, for example, for passivity versus activity, for dependency versus independence and autonomy, or for masochistic submission or sadistic attack. Attachment of man to groups is a ubiquitous factor in human life with sociological and biological determinants (Hartmann, 1939). Milgram (1975) has demonstrated the extent to which an average person can subvert his or her will in obedience to the authority of the group. These can range from small, insignificant collusions to the most violent and dangerous acts. "An individual could not espouse the new idea without the strength of a group to support him. And a group could not form around such concepts without individuals who wish to group toward this end" (Rangell, 1982, p. 31). The type of group adherence that Rangell describes typically results in global defenses, a composite of such mechanisms as repression and denial, splitting, idealization, and rationalization. "Massive inconsistencies exist unchallenged with a dominance of primary over secondary process thinking. What is normal in the unconscious becomes operative in the preconscious–conscious. Contradictions exist side-by-side, and incompatibilities uttered in quick succession escape the critical faculty of the individual ego" (Rangell, 1982, p. 32). This is not to say that it is not possible to achieve object relations while resisting their pathological effects. It is possible to retain individual ego and superego functioning under the pressure of forces emanating from the group. Nor is this to say that a rational process of evolution and change cannot be important in modifying, adding to, deleting, or reshaping changes in theory according to scientific standards. It is not always easy to determine if a theory is chosen because of clear, autonomous thought or because of a wish to adhere to a group. Once one has chosen, or once one is identified with a theory, it may become difficult to listen objectively.

In essence, Rangell is arguing that the normal wish or tendency to idealize or devalue mentor figures and to adhere to supportive groups may affect individual psychoanalysts. The need to belong to a group and to honor the analyst can place theory before active, suspended listening. When this occurs, the treatment and its interpretations may result not so much from *listening to* the patient as from *hearing in the patient's associations confirmations of one's own theory* and support of one's group.

Personal Myth

Personal memories, autobiographical image, and private personal myth affect patient and analyst alike. Kris (1975) describes the problems presented by personal myth which may screen, distort, and cause omissions in the patient's material. Analysts have self-representations or self-images that may affect hearing, listening, or being objective. Analysts have secret scripts, some conscious, some unconscious. Personal analysis brings many of these to awareness and light. Analysts, when they were children, have all entertained secret fantasies of who they were and would become. Life experiences tend to support or destroy these hopes and beliefs. Stolorow and Atwood (1979) assert that the theorist's "vision of the ideal human state will represent a solution to his own most central problems and conflicts" (p. 168). As Kris observes, "A coherent set of autobiographical memoirs, a picture of one's course of life as part of the self-representation has attracted a particular investment" (p. 294). Personal myth may give pleasure throughout life. "The dynamics of memory function suggest that our autobiographical memory is in constant flux, is constantly being reorganized, and is constantly subject to changes which the tensions of the present tend to impose" (Kris, 1975, p. 299). Personal myths affect personality and style.

The strong presence of the individual personality of the analyst is an integral part of the analytic process beyond the transference–countertransference continuum. Chrzanowski (1989) posits that the analyst's internal personality permeates all interchanges in the therapeutic field. Adler (1981) discusses the ways in which analysts may inadvertently impede the development of a useful regression in patients, often related to unconscious personality traits and values of the analysts as well as to their theoretical positions and technical handling of clinical situations. These may profoundly affect factors involving assessment of treatability. There is also status assigned to treating some types of patients and loss of status assigned to treating others. These and other aspects of personal myth in personality have not been sufficiently studied, especially in relationship to their influence on such issues as who is deemed treatable and who is not.

Baudry (1991) points out:

> The personality of the analyst has a far greater impact on the course of treatment than our theory allows. This is in part because a theory, due to its general nature, cannot take into account individual differences. Normally one does not think of the character of the analyst as a component of analytic technique. Perhaps it is relegated to the "art" part of psychoanalysis, those subtle, unfathomable, intuitive aspects of the professional behavior of an analyst that provide much of the frame and background of the analytic relationship. (p. 917)

He defines the analyst's character as the "complex organization of stable recumbent traits, behavior and attitudes which define him" (p. 918). These shape the analyst's perception and influence his or her view of the world and therefore personal style. Some are verbal and some nonverbal.

Ticho (1966) includes such elements as professional competence, commitment, values, range of education, language, interests, customs, ideals, physique, and residues of life experience. Certainly the application of the rule of abstinence is colored by many of these. The analyst's personal need for emotional distance or uninvolvement or the opposite are influenced by personality as well as by scientific theory.

Baudry says we are all aware of the myriad of general ego and self-syntonic beliefs and attitudes that permeate all aspects of the analyst's function, both personal and professional: warmth versus distance, rigidity versus flexibility, pessimism versus optimism, aggression versus passivity, authoritarian versus dependent, and so forth. We are also aware of "aspects of the style of the given analyst—tone, manner, verbosity, use of humor, degree of irony" (Baudry, 1991, p. 922). All of these personal qualities of the analyst form a backdrop to the conduct of the analysis. Even charm, frankness, capacity for enthusiasm and the tendency or comfort of seeing oneself as an authority play into the analytic capacity.

Gedo (1983) considers that Hartmann's (1958) claim of "scientific objectivity" is a fiction and that the criteria for analyzability suggested by Freud, based on the "epistemology of positivism" and the assumption that the analyst and patient share all values are untenable. Gedo has described the influence of the analyst's personal values on his or her individual preferences and choice of theory, interpretation, and technique in psychoanalysis.

Personal History

The analyst's choice of theory or even creation of theory may be affected by the analyst's personality and history. The stance any analyst conceives of as appropriate, therapeutic, and comfortable in his or her work, aside from the intrinsic technical merits and limitations inherent in each approach, reflects that specific analyst's history. This includes his or her personal history, personal analysis or analysts, as well as training. Choice of technique may also be reflected in the place in history from which the analyst has emerged.

This relationship seems so self-evident, so logical and obvious, it appears almost needless to elaborate this basic assumption of psychoanalysis that one's personal history and development will have very important effects on one's behavior, ideas, and emotional life. Allport (1961) defines personality as "the dynamic organization within the individual of those psychophysical systems that deliver his characteristic behavior and thought" (p. 28). This definition would lead us to understand that psychophysical systems respond to biological, psychological, and sociocultural influence. "The organization of the personality is always dynamic" (Knobel, 1990, p. 59).

Knowledge of one's self is crucial in an analysis; how one's history has affected one's knowledge is of equal importance. In making referrals to others, we always ponder how we feel certain therapists and patients will "match." Even what we know about the analyst's history and ideological values may affect our choice.

Cultural and Sociopolitical Influences

In a recent interview article (Chiarandini, 1992), Riccardo Steiner took up the "myth of analytic neutrality" in a way that resembles Rangell's approach; he called it "indoctrination" to theory. Steiner said, "If you teach only North American psychoanalysis, you are indoctrinating; if you teach only Kleinian analysis, you are indoctrinating. Theories have to be deconstructed, brought out with all their implications. In this way we will indoctrinate less" (p. 29).

When Chiarandini, in this same interview, said, "It seems then, that you don't think it possible for the analyst to separate his ideas as a citizen from his psychoanalytic ideas," Steiner replied,

> Of course not. All those people used their psychoanalytic knowledge as citizens—Bowlby, Susan Isaacs, Donald Winnicott, following the British democratic tradition, and Anna Freud, following the tradition of others like Aichhorn and Bernfeld, who in Vienna were deeply interested in social issues during the thirties. They were not so successful as they wished, but they were successful, and they had a profound impact on the community, through education and on hospitals. Of course, they could not have been at all influential under a totalitarian regime. Psychoanalysis cannot develop under totalitarian regime. (p. 30)

He went on to say that psychoanalysts can be extremely authoritarian in their institutions. Psychoanalytic institutions can work like political parties.

Times of life or death crisis, as in wars, dangerous regimes, famines, or the AIDS crisis, cannot help but have a profound impact on the analyst and patient alike.

Since values are influenced by morals as well as finances, analysts are influenced personally and professionally by the divorce and property laws of various lands. In relationship to divorce, what might be considered by an analyst in one culture as masochistic and a failure to resolve a destructive attachment, might be considered financially sensible and self-protective in another.

Some feminist analysts involved in a feminist culture may have profound attitudes toward male and female relationships. Those involved in a heterosexual or homosexual life style will be affected by their life choices. I have not even touched on superego as related to gender development and its effect on interpretation or values.

We are all affected by swings in cultural values, for example, the dichotomy between the value of the individual versus the value of the group. In the United States, we have recently watched an increase in interest in the positive value of support and dependency, both for children and adults. Changes in sexual mores and attitudes, drug use, use of alcohol, and so forth that are passed through in our culture affect us all. We are currently experiencing in the United States the promotion of "quick fixes" in mental health that are made to sound possible and desirable, even if there exists evidence that these do not last. The social and financial problems of our medical system encourage treating patients with drugs rather than prescribing costly psychotherapy. The abortion issue, with all its medical, ethical, and philosophical concomitants, is another sociopolitical issue that has enveloped our national psyche. Many other such cultural areas exist. I hope the mention of these few will stimulate readers to think about the cultural and sociopolitical influences that have affected them.

I will now turn to the eleven analysts and their interviews and case discussions. You may speculate how transference to theory, personal myth, personal history, and cultural and sociopolitical influences may have impacted their responses. Clearly, my own responses to my encounter with these various clinicians were also influenced by many reactions, both conscious and unconscious, in me. You may want to consider what factors influenced you in choosing your own particular supervisor, therapist, or analyst.

The interviews are presented in the order in which they took place.

The Case Summary

The patient is a bright, 45-year-old, married, educated, career woman who came to treatment because of her wish to die. She felt she did not exist and could think of no reason to continue her life. She is an only child. Her earliest memories (age 2) are of her mother's bloody attempt to kill herself and of ambulances coming for her father who chronically suffered from bleeding ulcers and nervous breakdowns. She remembered hiding in closets, hoping somehow to be protected during these episodes. Very early, she felt that her mother wanted her dead and that she and her mother despised each other. The mother, who was a functioning psychotic, would alternately shower the child with presents in order to take photographs and then physically and verbally abuse her.

Roselyn felt suspended in "unreal space" where the danger of annihilation was always present. She created a world of "little people" who kept her company and were like parts of herself until about the age of 7. She was never quite sure, nor is she now, what is real and what is fantasy. In relationship to her mother, she still isn't certain. Her father was basically uninvolved and passive. Despite the chaos in the home, Roselyn was an excellent student. She felt that she was two selves—one trying to learn, live, and create, and another begging for her dismal unreal life and self to end. She feels humiliated that she often begged her mother to stop hitting her and wishes she had just died with dignity. She is deeply distressed and only recently has begun to share any of the details of her real childhood and current feelings with anyone except me. She often suffers from migraines and hides them unless they necessitate a trip to the emergency room for an injection.

Roselyn has had two brief psychotic episodes, when I have felt it necessary to become involved in her physical and mental survival. On one occasion, there was an emergency call from the referring physician, at a hospital where my patient needed emergency surgery. (Roselyn was outwardly calm and inside desperately convinced that the surgeon meant to kill her or that her mother would somehow see that she died while she was under sedation.) The physician felt it risky to proceed until Roselyn had a chance to sort this out, no matter how briefly. My presence reassured her, at least consciously, and the surgery proceeded. On another occasion, when burglars, for the second time, had vandalized her home and emptied every closet, container, and drawer, her husband called asking me to come. The patient was huddled on the floor of her closet in a psychotic state. Again, my presence or containing seemed to help her reconstitute herself within an hour or so.

Roselyn, who is usually well-oriented in time and space, still often asserts that her mother, who died some years ago, is present and is still trying to kill her. She knows that these thoughts and feelings are not correct, but the feelings themselves are still very real and powerful to her.

I have been seeing her four times a week for 9 years.

An Hour (1985)

The patient comes in her usual way, reclines on the couch, and says she had a dream. She describes, "The dream occurs in a maze-like place with bushes all around, too high—you can't see over them—like in an early English garden. It is a constraining place that one could not easily exit. Nearby, in the maze, near the exit, is an old crone lady selling things from a black container, like a chute for coal, slanted down and caged over with wire. In this slanted black cage are kittens and little chickens, two animals that do not get along, and the crone is selling them. Her price is too high, and no one will buy them. The chickens and cats are picking and scratching and sliding down to the bottom of the caged chute and scratching and pecking back to the top. It is all useless. The toothless crone is all in black, wearing a black babushka, like a witch. The chute has wheels and rests on gravel. There is no grass or any softness anywhere. The crone is under an overhanging roof, and there is no light except the moonlight. The kittens are grey. The moonlight and bushes make me think of Japan, a Japanese garden. You remember how the Japanese gardens looked, kind of grey and black in the moonlight? I like them. It also, oh, it reminds me of a Hawthorne Garden . . . what was the name of that story? Nathaniel Hawthorne's Garden. 'Rappaccini's Garden' or 'Rappaccini's Daughter.' This doctor had moved into this house and had a daughter; and then a medical student moved in above the garden and fell in love. The daughter lived on poison that she had been given by her experimenting father. The daughter is so used to it that it had no effect on her, but she had had so much poison that it would poison the medical student. It was a death garden. (*The patient begins to sob for some time.*) The parent poisoned her so no one else could get close or live with her, ever. (*The patient sobs some more.*) That's what I feel like . . . like a fairy tale. The crone, sleeping beauty, and apple."

At this point, the patient sits up slightly, turns her head toward me, and says, "You wanted death—you got it." She whispers softly, "I am convinced I will alienate anyone I love, and they will let me do it. In the story, she does not have to say she is doing it—she just does it. It makes me think of those one-celled animals that have these stinging capsules all over and all around them—it's a defense system. They are called paramecia and anything in the world can trigger that defense. They can even sting themselves or another one. Sometimes when I hurt myself, it feels like I am hurting my mother. Sometimes when I feel hurt, I really feel unhurt. (*The patient sits up with her feet still on the couch, crying.*) I must have been destined . . . it's like it was the first thing that happened after I was born, the poison. The defense system. The lady in the dream was like a flower lady I remember in Asia, when I lived there. There they sold puppies in cages; so futile because there was no end to it. You would have bought the puppies. In that country, they ate young puppies and when they discovered that the Americans felt bad about it, they would take the puppies to the church where the Americans went on Sunday and sell the puppies to the Americans. Of course, it was futile because they just made more puppies. You don't think people should eat young things. I remember my mother's mouth. I was so afraid. I was so squirmy. I felt like somehow her mouth was going to get me. I always felt that. Sometimes I feel that way here, so unreal. (*She begins to cry again.*) You know, it is really a horror, that feeling of being poisoned by your own parent. It is really a horror. The other thing that you don't know, and that I haven't told you much about, is that the painting there is like a mirror, and when I feel I need protection, or when I feel I cannot stand reality, I go into the painting and move behind it, and you don't know I'm there. I feel torn between the real world and the temptation of an unreal world." (*The patient continues to cry, alternatingly softly and loudly and is dreadfully distressed.*)

As the patient comes out of her state, she turns her head toward me and says, "This is not my Catholic stuff. (*She continues weeping.*) I feel poisoned; I must keep talking. If I don't keep talking, I lose it all, and you won't know. The problem is how I got here and where I want to go. Do I want to live, or do I not? How did my conscience get here? Can someone be born poisonous? Can someone be born poisoned? Do you know? I wanted to talk about yesterday. Is there time? When I think about falling off the earth, or falling off, I think about running into a barrier like the painting. I want to disappear. I want to not have to be real and deal with these real feelings. Have you noticed that the wooden pattern on your door has a big cow on it? The wood grain makes a cow. I could disappear there, too. . . . Oh God, it makes me think of Solomon, the story of Solomon where they couldn't decide who should get the baby, so the plan was to cut the baby in half. That's good, but it was also bad. I feel that way. I don't know whether I have to stay poisoned, with my parents, or if there is some way you and I can get me out of this. It's hard to know. I want to believe there is a way, but it is so hard to believe. The other thing it makes me think of is my little people. My little people can go back and forth into the mirror or the painting or into the world. Some of them, when I was a child, wanted me to go into the unreal world and live, and some of them also, in my own mind, wanted me to stay in the real world. There has always been this conflict."

A Piece of an Hour (1990)

Roselyn: I feel so terrible.

Virginia Hunter: (*After several minutes silence*) Physically or mentally?

R: Both. I have a headache. (*More silence*)

VH: It seems difficult for you to talk today, and I am unsure if my silence is helpful or not.

R: I know what I must work on, but I am terrified to. (*Breathing is gasping and in little puffs.*)

VH: And yet the silence may feel something like it felt when you were very small and overwhelmed with so many feelings, and no one was there to contain you. [I wish I had said "hold you" instead of "contain you."]

R: But if I think, I feel everything is whirling. Things like tiny pins are attacking and pricking. I am in space. (*Tears run down her face as she holds onto herself.*)

VH: (*Breathing and silent as I think how to respond.*) The pain of feeling so alone and in danger must have felt unbearable.

R: (*Intellectual and somewhat excited*) But yesterday, I felt I had a glimpse of something about the migraines. It seems like when I get closer to expressing my real feelings, I get migraines. You remember my talking about implosions—holes in the universe where stars exploded inward? A black hole—containing all my "back into myself-self." Words seem inadequate.

VH: (*Softly*) They are what you have—words and feelings.

R: The migraines feel like they are me in a container inside my self, of pain, and pain that would destroy me if it came outside. It would explode my mind, my self. I'd be like little molecules going any and everywhere.

VH: If you feel your real feelings and trust me with them, you are afraid you will go mad and cease to exist?

R: Couldn't I?

VH: (*Silence as I try to respond*)

R: I told you once about crystals being formed in a centrifuge. They whirl around and make beautiful shapes, but since they are formed in a violent and chaotic environment, they are always brittle and lack what's needed to hold them together and help them be resilient and survive. They can be demolished and annihilated very easily.

VH: You want me to share your fear that our analytic world will not contain you safely and that you will die in feeling all your feelings.

R: I am so terrified.

André Green

Dr. Green is a well-known French analyst who is noteworthy for his important contributions to psychoanalytic literature. He is especially interested in language and attended Lacan's seminar for some years before he and Lacan went their separate ways. His concepts of "red anxiety" and "white anxiety," as well as "private madness," are well known to psychoanalysts.

This interview with Dr. André Green was conducted in November 1986 during his 4-day visit to southern California. He spent 2 days at the Newport Center for Psychoanalytic Studies in Orange, 1 day at the University of California, Los Angeles, Continuing Education Seminar in Westwood, and a night at a combined meeting of the Southern California Psychoanalytic Society and the Los Angeles Psychoanalytic Society and

Institute in Los Angeles. Dr. Green presented a total of five papers and a case; in addition, he responded to five case presentations. We were not strangers, as I had had the pleasure of presenting a case to him in Paris in July 1985 and had communicated with him by letter and phone regarding this California visit. He graciously fit this interview in at various times in an impressive, yet fatiguing, professional, and social schedule. His words reveal that in addition to being a creative genius, Dr. Green is a warm, candid, and extremely generous man.

Interview

VIRGINIA HUNTER: What I want to do today is simply have you talk about the path you traveled from Cairo to becoming a world famous author and French psychoanalyst.

ANDRÉ GREEN: I was born in Cairo in 1927. I was the fourth child of the family. I have two sisters and an elder brother, 3 years between each. I was born 9 years after my brother, who was the third child in the family. My parents belonged to the Jewish community of Cairo, and during that time the great division was between the Arabs and the so-called European community, of which the Jews were a part. The common language of the European community, which was very cosmopolitan, was French, and we spoke French at home. We only spoke Arabic with the servants. But all the people who were there—Italians, Greeks, Armenians, and so on—all the people belonging to the European community had, as a common language, French which was at that time the diplomatic language; so French is really my maternal tongue. Going to the Lycée Francais in Cairo exerted an enormous influence on me because the cultural life in Egypt was not very rich. Or so I thought then. In fact, when I left, I realized it was richer than what I had supposed, but since I left at the age of 19, that was probably the age in which I would discover it. So I had decided very early on that I would leave Egypt to go to France, not only to study but to live. Oddly, I knew very little about Egypt when I lived there. I knew much more about France. Yet, I foresaw that this very happy life that we had in Cairo would probably cease one day because the Egyptians would take the destiny of their country into their own hands, and there would be an awakening of nationalism. This started 2 years after I left the country in 1946. So, if I hadn't exiled myself, essentially I would have lost my home there anyway.

VH: You arrived in Paris in 1946, then?

AG: Yes, I arrived in Paris in 1946 and that coincided with the start of my medical training. Of course, it was difficult in the beginning because I had no family living in France, no friends. I experienced a rather long period of solitude before getting in touch and establishing relationships with French comrades, on the faculty or elsewhere. It was a rather solitary time.

I think that the great change in my life occurred when I started my training in psychiatry. My intention in starting medical training was to become a psychiatrist so I had to wait for a long time, practically 6 years, my whole training in medicine, before I could really be interested in what I was doing. Even now I have very strong feelings, which grew all the stronger when I became a psychoanalyst, because I realized the terrible loss of time it had been studying disciplines that proved to be of absolutely no use for me. I was really bored, not so much with medicine itself, but the way medicine was taught. Even now I regret and deplore that a young man who wants to become involved in the psychiatric field—either as a psychiatrist or a psychoanalyst—must train in medicine. Medical training is probably one of the best ways to obscure the mind—I mean as far as psychiatric matters are concerned—and, to learn, as a young man, how to think about the mind in an entirely distorted way. I had to struggle for years before I could get rid of the conventional ways of thinking which are operating when you study medicine. The trouble with medicine is that it is not a science: In its higher forms of knowledge, it is an art, though it relies on fundamental sciences. Unfortunately, doctors do not have the openness and the wide vision that is truly scientific, such as a physicist might have. It is in the fields that are the closest to the study of the mind (neurophysiology, neurology, biology) that the communication with psychoanalysis is the most difficult. The situation is quite the same with the subsections of psychology that are close to psychopathology.

So, the study of medicine gave me little preparation for the study of psychiatry in its truly scientific and artistic aspects. I had to wait a long time to begin my real professional life. For the same reason, my life truly changed when I started my residence in psychiatry.

VH: Things have changed.

AG: Of course, now things are different in France and in America. A psychiatric residency in France gave at the time a very special direction to one's life. It was an all-encompassing activity, and this is not the case in America. In France, to be a resident in psychiatry meant that you had to win a scholarship and spend 4 years of residence which in most cases implied that you had to live in the hospital and not only work in it. In turn, the fact that you belonged to that special community as a young doctor created friendships and exchanges with some people who are still my friends some 40 years later. The fact that we used to spend all our time at the hospital, not only to share work there but to live there—that also meant to entertain together—to have a sort of community life for 3 or 4 years brings one's life and work together in a very special, very satisfying way. I consider those 3 years I spent in St. Ann's Hospital during my training to be probably some of the richest years I ever lived.

VH: You had also married, as I recall, at age 23 in 1950.

AG: Yes, we had four children. I began my residence 3 years later.

VH: Those must have been very stimulating years at St. Ann's.

AG: Certainly. Psychiatry in France at that time was quite apart from the rest of medicine. We psychiatrists spent long, intense times with each other—we ate together and celebrated together and, more importantly, had permanent intellectual exchanges—and not only about psychiatry. We used to stay there until very late in the evenings endlessly discussing the problems of the body–mind and all the great theories that lay behind psychiatry. This was a very, very stimulating experience. I was very lucky because I really had the opportunity to have the best masters one could ever dream of in those years—I mean, during the years of 1953 to 1958. We did our work for 2 hours in the morning and that was the end of our obligation. All the rest of the time, at least some of us, those who really wanted to work and to think and to become really involved in the psychiatric life at the time, we consulted with the other masters who were not running the psychiatric wards but who came from outside as consultants. At St. Ann's Hospital in those times, we had a lot of really extraordinary people. For instance, I was the pupil of the person whom I believe was the greatest psychiatrist of his time—Henri Ey.

VH: How did Ey influence you?

AG: He was remarkable. He was very affectionate to me and, when he decided to retire, asked me to continue his teaching. Henri Ey used to practice far from Paris—130 kilometers at a very ancient abbey in Bonneval, near Chartres, which became a psychiatric hospital. Henri Ey was famous to all of us French psychiatrists, and he was really a kind of Pope of French psychiatry. He was not a professor, but he was a fantastic teacher and organizer. He organized the first Psychiatric World Congress in 1950. He created the French Encyclopedia in psychiatry. He created the Bonneval meetings, which are famous in the history of psychiatry, between 1945 and 1970. All sorts of people participated. Lacan used to go there because of his close relation to Ey; their friendship lasted throughout all their lives.

All the great topics of psychiatry served as themes for controversial debates between psychiatrists with different approaches: Some, of course, reflected an organic point of view; others were more inclined toward psychopathology. Beyond the traditional opposition, which one can find anywhere else, others could be found related to a more immediate context. Some of them were psychoanalysts; others were of Marxist trend; others were more influenced by philosophy, mainly phenomenology, enlisting the banner of powerful authors such as Hegel, Husserl, Heidegger, Sartre, and Merleau-Ponty. At the time, in the psychoanalytic approach, the fight was between the two giants—psychoanalysis and phenomenology. Lacan was the main figure for the first party and Ey represented the second. It is only later in the mid-1960s that another partner joined the field: structuralism. We were prepared for the discussion because of our earlier training.

It is interesting to note that the birth of psychopharmacology (a French discovery) in the early 1950s did not, in any respect, quench our passionate need to discuss other theories. And no one at the time would have paid the least respect to any clinical approval of the DSM-III type.

Around the same time, I was also associated in St. Ann's with several excellent neurologists—brain neurologists—whose names are not very known here: Aguriaguerra and Henry Hecaen, whose contributions on brain functions were highly valuable.

VH: And, of course, psychoanalysts were also there.

AG: Yes, there were also a lot of psychoanalysts who came to St. Ann's: Lacan did, and also Francis Pasche and Pierre Marty, and many others. They used to have public interviews with patients, and we attended these consultations so that we could have a very open view about what psychoanalysis was because they expressed different viewpoints there. And, at least as far as I am concerned, I learned very early on that there was no such thing as one psychoanalysis, but that each psychoanalyst, even if he revered, say, Freud, or Melanie Klein, or anybody else, would necessarily understand psychoanalysis in a way that was uniquely his own. I think that this experience taught me to form my own independent judgment.

So I consider that these years of training were very important to me as a resident in psychiatry for all the varied influences that they gave me.

VH: Did you start training in psychoanalysis very soon?

AG: On the contrary, I didn't come to psychoanalysis immediately. At first, I was convinced that the secret of mental diseases was in the brain, and I was even very strongly against psychoanalysis because it didn't seem to me scientific enough.

The year I won my scholarship to St. Ann's was a very important year for France and even for the history of psychiatry because that year was 1953. This year is a landmark in the history of French psychiatry because it was the year that drugs were introduced in psychiatric treatment.

I worked in the service where the first experiments were conducted at that time. And so, I could see the difference—I had the chance to see that difference in the atmosphere in the services where the drugs were used and the services where the drugs weren't used. This was something new. Some physicians were afraid of the new medications. They were not immediately convinced by the experiments that were being made. As for me, even now I keep in mind the difference between the services that I saw then. I was one of the witnesses of a crucial time in the history of psychiatry. I saw shock treatment, insulin treatment, and all those other treatments which are now, if not obsolete, at least far less employed. Moreover I visited services where even these treatments were not used, or were used on a very restricted basis. So I have seen more psychiatric wards that look exactly as you could see them in movies that represented them in the 19th century. It was really horrible. No one could appreciate what I mean who hasn't seen these people in states of extreme anxiety, agitation, fury, and confusion. It was really hell. But, in the services where drugs were being used, it became more quiet, and more peaceful—though that too sometimes had a really deadly atmosphere, which could not be taken as an ideal of cure, but whose effect could be used to approach yet unapproachable patients.

VH: But obviously, you saw that psychoanalysis, or a dynamic approach in general, was also needed: Medication couldn't do everything.

AG: Later, I realized that in the long run drugs couldn't really help people in solving their problems and being able to live, I would say, a real, ordinary life—not past the appearance of a normal life but a reasonable expectation in social life for independence, choice, and a minimum of personal satisfactions.

Actually, in my training, I became interested in some patients whom I had seen for many, many hours without the benefit of a psychoanalytical approach or any training on my part in psychoanalysis. At that time, psychoanalysis was not as popular as it is now and not many of us—I mean at St. Ann's—not many of us were analysts or candidates. It took time for me to get started in proper analytic training. What brought me to it was a dawning understanding of the transferential relationships that were being established between the patients and me. I realized that this was something I couldn't handle with the psychiatry I knew. So I had the choice. Either I would take no interest in the patients, prescribing drugs or treating them very coldly, not really talking to them and with them, and, of course, that would be a way of remaining personally uninvolved. Or else, I could try to get in touch with them, establish a contact and a lengthy, long contact. For the latter, I needed psychoanalytic training. I remember talking to patients for hours—not 1 hour but 2, 3, 4 hours—trying to do something, trying to give them assistance that they could get only in this way. Of course, this created transferential reactions that I was not ready to handle. Needless to say, there were also personal problems that I had to confront. So, finally I decided to train in psychoanalysis.

VH: Deciding to train in psychoanalysis must have brought you into the middle of the divisions over psychoanalysis that were occurring in France around that time.

AG: Precisely. Now I told you that 1953 was a very important date, and this was especially so because it was also the date of the first splitting between the Paris Society and another faction, among which the most important people were Lacan and Lagache. Thus, when I arrived at St. Ann's, I arrived right in the middle of the struggle, or at the end of the struggle, at least the end of one phase of the struggle, which finally resulted in the first division between the Paris Society and the group that was going to create the French Society of Psychoanalysis.

VH: Lacan was at the center of the struggle?

AG: Lacan, at the time, was a dominant figure because he used to have his seminars at St. Ann's, and his public seminar attracted many people. At the time most of the participants came from the psychiatric world—and also from philosophy or letters, and humanities. As I had chosen the Paris Psychoanalytic Society for training, I did not attend Lacan's seminar until 1960. I had my training in the Paris Society and had chosen the Paris Society because, in spite of Lacan's immense prestige and the fact that I was impressed by his lectures or talks, I was reticent about some aspects of his personality that I was afraid could also influence his ideas, in the sense that these could be less true than attractive for dubious reasons which I was too young to explain but that I could already feel. Later on, I found myself able to really analyze, understand, and communicate what I had only felt at the beginning as being wrong in his conceptions. I trusted the Paris Society because I found that the Paris Society (this was true then and is true now) had one enormous advantage over Lacan's group. Maybe the people who were there were less brilliant than Lacan, but they afforded a diversity of opinions, which enables everyone to think about the problems in their widest scope. Lacan was really the only one of the *Société Francaise de Psychanalyse* who had an outstanding talent (with the exception of the much less interesting Lagache). I said to myself that if I trained in the Societé Francaise I would have Lacan and Lacan alone, whereas in the Paris Society, I would have many good teachers. If none were as brilliant as Lacan was, there were many of them, and they could teach me something that Lacan couldn't in terms of learning my profession. That's why I went for training at the Paris Society.

VH: Can you tell me something about your training there?

AG: My analysis, of course, was of fundamental importance. I was analyzed by Maurice Bouvet who was, at the time, the most brilliant mind of the Paris Society. He died in 1960 at the age of 48. That is quite young, terribly young. The last time I saw him was at my last session in analysis. I terminated. We were planning to meet at the conference in Rome in which he was supposed to present an important work. But he fell ill before; he couldn't come to that conference, and he died 3 months later. From 1956 until 1960, I completed my training, and at the time I still was part-time psychiatrist and psychoanalyst.

Then in 1960 a very important event occurred. Henry Ey organized, in Bonneval, one of these huge meetings—in which he would gather all the people who wanted to attend—a symposium on the unconscious.

VH: The Lacanians were there too?

AG: It was the first time, 7 years after the 1953 split, where people from the two societies could meet and discuss. But there were not only psychoanalysts present. There were also psychiatrists, philosophers, professionals, and followers of all orientations; some neurophysiologically oriented, some philosophically oriented, some more or less inclined to a sociological approach, and so on. This was an historic event. It was one of the symposia that represents a sort of a dream come true, because in one place, you could find prominent people from different fields of knowledge who were interested in all the problems of the unconscious. We would discuss together for 3 days, with very articulate papers, divergent points of view, and so on.

It was on that occasion that Laplanche and Leclaire presented a paper on the unconscious that reflected, in large measure, the point of view of Lacan. I must say that this event was a total shock for me because the analysts who were representing my Society gave papers that were very weak compared to those of the pupils of Lacan. This was a disaster. We tried to save the honor of the Paris Psychoanalytic Society, my friend Conrad Stein and I, and we both were very young analysts.

VH: And Lacan himself was there?

AG: Lacan came to that meeting and gave an extraordinary demonstration of his talent. From that time I decided to follow Lacan's seminars which I had avoided until now, wanting to be faithful to my camp. I attended Lacan's seminars from 1960 to 1967, while continuing to belong to the Paris Society. The fact that I went to Lacan's seminars raised problems for me. People in my institution tried to exercise pressure on me not to go there any more because the feeling was that if I went to that seminar other candidates would go and that would create some disturbances in the society because of Lacan's influence on them. I resisted the pressures because I have learned in my life that you are only respected if you resist these kinds of pressures. I also resisted Lacan's pressures because, of course, Lacan wanted me to join his school. I was, in short, a "fellow traveler" of Lacan's for 6 years, and I had a very good personal relationship with him. He used to invite me for dinner—of course, there was a lot of intellectual seduction in what he tried to do, but I have one thing to say about Lacan. Lacan was ready for work anytime. You could phone him and tell him: "I want to see you because I have a new idea I would like to discuss with you." He would say, "Well, come, we'll have dinner together." He was intensely excited by ideas. Of course, he knew what transference is and if one called him to ask him to discuss with him, he knew that this was not only a purely intellectual matter, but also involved a sort of transference to him; and he exploited this to some extent. But, if you could keep your mind clear and see what was going on, you could benefit from these exchanges.

So I started attending his seminar in 1960, and his seminar was really something very extraordinary. Of course, he had wonderful charisma, as is well known. He was extraordinarily gifted. He went far beyond all the others in terms of thinking and in terms of being able to formulate things in a manner which was not academic and which was not . . . well, let me put it this way: We have an expression in France that is "*la langue de bois*," wooden language, that is, the official vocabulary of a party or a community. It was first used for the language of the Communists. It is kind of stiff language, like someone who would not be given the opportunity to open a discussion anyway, but now it has expanded from the initial use about Communist language and has extended to all language in which there are marks of rigidity. Lacan was extraordinarily gifted in speaking another language. Of course, there were obscurities in his language and vocabulary. If there were, let's say, three or four sentences during which you would not understand what he was trying to say, the fifth one would be brilliant and illuminate everything. That fifth one clarified what you had been unable to understand in the four previous ones.

I never attended Lacan's school but had a special relationship with him. He was generous enough to give me the opportunity to speak at this seminar. The seminar was open to the public and the seminar had moved from St. Ann's Hospital to the *École Normale*. There were also some sessions that were closed sessions, to which Lacan admitted people by invitation only. He selected the people to attend these seminars, and two times, in 1965 and in 1967, as I had objected to what he was saying, he gave me the opportunity to lecture and discuss what he said. He was very agreeable in that because I was really the only one at the time who had that privilege, not being of his school, nor having beem analyzed by him.

We all know that Lacan's way of analyzing his candidates created and maintained a dependent relationship—really these people, for the most part, couldn't say a thing. It was terrible, because if they expressed a divergent point of view, Lacan would call them on the telephone or communicate in other ways to tell them how much he had been "worried" by what they had said and that they had no gratitude for him or for what he did. So he used to make them feel quite guilty.

VH: You are suggesting that he had a lot of narcissism tied up in his special position of preeminence?

AG: Yes, I was the only one in the special position of having a very good relationship with him, but I was totally independent, and I could freely express my point of view without retaliation of any kind. And I think he was happy about that. I think I am not wrong that Lacan had affection for me and also, I think, esteem. This relationship ceased in 1967 because it was as if Lacan had waited all this time, hoping that one day my attachment to him and his seductive approach would lead me to leave my society and take part in his own program. I didn't.

VH: So I gather that you and Lacan also came to take separate paths?

AG: On one or two circumstances, as he used to do with everybody, he started making very nasty, but veiled, allusions. That was the method he used. Lacan never attacked someone, I mean, one of his people, openly and directly. He openly attacked his enemies, but as far as the people of his herd were concerned, he used to make allusions and afterward the seminar people talked together, "Who do you think he meant?" "It is probably Mr. So and So." And I reacted to this very vigorously. I told him, "If you object or disagree with anything I say or write, you are perfectly right to do so, but you name me and you say exactly what you are against. And you give me the opportunity to reply." But that was not his way, and finally I decided not to go to his seminar any more. Six months after I stopped going he came to my home and asked me to come back to his seminar, but I said, "No, I can't do that. Because, if you attack me viciously, hiding yourself, I can't come and attend the seminar as if nothing had happened." And that was the end of my fear.

VH: What did he attack you viciously about? Did you ever know for sure what it was about?

AG: I think I know. It was about an important paper I had published on primary narcissism—a paper that I considered one of the most important that I had written on the subject. In my paper I did not refer to his work. Lacan was interested in you as far as you referred to his work, quoted him, or showed that he was the one who understood more profoundly about things more than anyone had previously. In that paper, I was oriented otherwise. I didn't feel the necessity to refer to him. I had in the past referred to him on other occasions, but for that book—that particular paper—his work was not relevant to my approach. I say "that book" because it was a huge paper that has been subsequently edited as a book in South America. So it was not by neglect that I left Lacan out. It was because my discussion didn't lead me to mention him or his work. That's all. So, I stopped seeing Lacan at that time. But, of course, I kept my interest in his writings. To tell the truth, though, I think that after 1967 Lacan really did not add anything essential to the body of his thought. Now I am very critical of his work, although it was the work of an outstanding personality.

VH: But it is clear from your work that you were not only influenced by French psychoanalysis. I think that the British object-relations school had a big impact on you. How did that come about?

AG: The year of 1961 was very important for me because it was the year of my discovery of British psychoanalysis. In 1961, there was an International Congress in Edinburgh, and, for the first time, the British Psychoanalytic Society organized a pre-Congress Conference. I think it was planned for the foreigners and mainly for the Americans who would come to Edinburgh and stop first in London. This meeting was completely apart from the Conference and gave an opportunity to psychoanalysts of all countries to get a taste of British psychoanalysis. I attended the pre-Congress in London, and that's where I personally met some people who were to become very important influences for me—especially Winnicott.

I still remember the seminar he gave on that day of July 1961. It impressed me a lot. It was unforgettable because he was extraordinary. He talked on the squiggle technique and it was wonderful. I also listened to Herbert Rosenfeld and to a presentation by Sidney Klein about a psychotic case, which was very impressive. I also attended a seminar by the late John Klauber, who became one of my friends. So, the discovery of the English psychoanalysts, who were so different from the French ones, opened my eyes and opened perspectives that have had a considerable influence on my work. The English school was entirely clinical and far less concerned with theoretical debates around the work of Freud. In France, we worshipped Freud, and we made a great distinction between Sigmund and Anna.

In London I had my first meetings with the Kleinians. I admired their work—Hanna Segal's and Rosenfeld's above all. They had an impressive skill in clinical work. I might not have shared their understanding of the unconscious, but I was sure that their understanding related to the unconscious in some other way, especially in the cases of very disturbed people.

VH: Did you know Bion then?

AG: No, I studied him in the 1970s and met him in 1976 when I came to the Menninger Symposium to present a paper on borderline personalities. Our friendship lasted until his death.

VH: The influences upon you were enormously varied, and this has been a major factor in the originality of your work, I think.

AG: I have been working in an intellectual climate made by the influence of French analysis, British analysis, and nonpsychoanalytic thought. So, eventually, I felt as if I were continuing my years of residency, because when I was a resident I used to work in the library and study there, but I didn't study psychiatry alone. The writings of Merleau-Ponty and Sartre were important for me. The writings of the philosophers were as important as the writings of the psychiatrists. I have also read the work of the old psychiatrists, the psychiatrists of the 19th century, in order to get a view of the history of psychiatry and to put the history of psychiatry inside the greater realm of the history of ideas. That had been the general atmosphere in St. Ann's where we learned how to work with patients. At the same time, we had, as I told you, passionate debates on philosophical and psychiatric problems. I guess I have, all along, been following out the implications of my earliest education as a resident. But this also is a characteristic of French psychoanalysis, which tries to link up clinical problems to broader concepts concerning the human mind. Was this not Freud's inspiration?

VH: I'd like the readers of this interview to see what the intellectual development of yours has led to in practice. I wonder if you would give a brief example of how you actually work in a psychoanalytic hour?

AG: Let me try. The first thing is to listen exactly to what the patient says and never jump to conclusions, never—as I say—go to the general store of psychoanalytic interpretation and pick up the most obvious, general, intellectualized interpretation you can find. Recently, a patient came to her hour and began to give details about all the bits and pieces that were in front of her. She has the sleeves, and she has the waist, and she has all the parts of the garment, but she cannot put them together. She says, "My thoughts are linear, like the string in the necklace." It's totally useless to say to the patient immediately, "You're angry because I'm going to leave you and abandon you for 10 days" because the answer will be, "I know. You're the third person to tell me. I had two analysts before. What can I do about it? Nothing. What can you do about it? Nothing." The patient is right. You are not going to stay with her and give up your projects or holidays, and it's totally useless to say that.

But the first thing, when you listen to patients, is to listen exactly to the words and listen to what I call the implications of what they say. Patients do not use just *any* language, they do not use just *any* material, *any* complaint, or *any* memories; they say specific things. Even if these things seem very banal, these things are specific; the words patients use are specific. The first thing when I, for instance, pour over very familiar material . . . I have to represent to myself what it means for a patient to tell me this or that. I have to represent; I have to figure out in what way his psychic apparatus is functioning and how this is reflected by what the patient is talking about.

Imagine this female patient. She gives details about all the bits and pieces that are there in front of her. She has the sleeves, waist, she has all parts of the garments, but she cannot put them together. And I ask myself what does it all mean? And then she gives me the image of the necklace. Now I notice that for the first time in the session she wore a necklace, and a real one, and a beautiful one, which was very unusual. So what is that image of the necklace implying? She has already said it, "My thoughts are linear, like the string in the necklace." That is the way we come to know a *specific* patient, not just *any* patient, but *this* woman who is wearing a necklace in this hour.

The string ensures the continuity between the pearls in the necklace. This is a condensed representation of our bond, our object relationship, which is always fragile, always on the verge of breaking off to one or the other side. It is a kind of minimal symbolization that refers to a body image of the self. The string foreshadows the dress of her feminine identity. So even in her state of sadness and eventually of despair, there still remains an unconscious fantasy seduction. The interesting thing is that in her case the seduction is not based on the positive wish to be attractive (to prevent me from leaving) but on the contrary, on the fantasy of breaking into bits and pieces, which would scatter in the consultation room. This does not raise, as one would think, a particular anxiety. Winnicott would say, I suppose, that it would express the desire to return to an unintegrated state rather than a fear of disintegration. But things may be a bit more complicated. The unintegrated state is a regression, sometimes accompanied by feelings of pleasure, to a certain extent, if the object is available and distant enough. But it can also raise a feeling of fear and resourceless dependence. Also, in regressing to such a state, she would succeed in avoiding all the anger linked with my leaving. Maybe we could even say that she would be able to transform that object loss into a loss of the unity of her self to resolve the hostile feelings which could endanger the existence of the object.

But I would not interpret what was happening only in terms of primitive anxieties or archaic object relationship because it took me many months before I could understand that the most desirable and most feared condition for her was the feeling that together we composed a dyad in the session. Sometimes in a state of confusion and extreme anxiety she would say to me that I did not exist, that she could not even see me in a three-dimensional space (a statement she would occasionally say about herself). All this meant, in fact, in her mind, that I did not have a palpable body.

To put it in more general terms, I remain convinced of the importance for mental functioning of its grounding in a theory of drives. This implies that it is not so much a question of giving up one theory in favor of another, than our necessity to reformulate theories. But the fecundity of the psychoanalytic experience is to bring to the fore this base functioning through the most sophisticated relationship, that is, the highest from the point of view of integration—mental communication. Everything that lies between these two extreme poles constitutes the scheme of psychic experience. To me, object relationships are not opposed to drives, because the object is the revealer of the drives. It is what compels the drive to a tremendous work of transformation. We can only witness the byproduct of such a work.

The extreme heterogeneity between drives and language is paralleled by internal and external representation. These apply to the inside and outside, and to the levels of representation both from the body to reality and of the body as reality. All this seems to sustain a basic heterogeneity of the mind in search of incomplete unity, building by incessant forms of compromise that can only exist in a continual state of unbalance that enhances progress and evolution. We always struggle against excessive unbalance that would lead to disorganization or excessive balance that would mean the risk of rigidness or utter stillness.

I suppose that the function of representation is the best safeguard against these opposite dangers and that it constitutes the central aim of psychoanalysis. To that extent representation applied to the specificity of the relationship between drives and language is equivalent to symbolization because it separates drives and language on the one hand and also relates them to the object.

VH: After all these remarkable influences on you that you've talked about, I have the distinct feeling that you have brought them together in a way just as remarkable as your own. What marks your work, I think, is your attention to detail. That talent derives from your freedom from dogmas of any sort. It is your great achievement, as your work and this interview shows, that you really do listen to the specific, the detail, the person. Thank you very much for listening to me on this occasion and allowing me to ask you questions, and thank you too for your illuminating answers.

Case Discussion

In his case comments, Dr. Green focuses on the patient's splitting between her external and her internal worlds. He points out that she has extreme pain and anxieties from a violent "real" and dead "white" mother and has no psychic formations to express her painful affects.

I presented this case to Green in Paris, France, in July 1985, at a University of California, Los Angeles, Continuing Education Conference. Green began by asking what my feelings were about the case. I said I felt good about the way the case was going; however, Roselyn continued, at times, to have psychotic transferences. She could appear perfectly rational and in touch with reality when she arrived at my office and yet would soon regress and believe I was a great danger to her physically and mentally. During these times, her feelings of danger were very real to her. He began, "What I wanted to emphasize is that splitting between external reality and her inner world because, of course, when you get this type of material and these types of regressions, you would suspect that the patient could or should be hospitalized for severe psychotic regression. And it isn't the case here, I assume. It isn't the case because these patients not only show a false self personality which, of course, they have; but they also display what I call 'private madness.' What I mean by 'private madness' is that the madness is contained and limited to the significant people around her, her husband, her mother, and her analyst. As a patient of mine said, 'Thank God I have my analysis, this place of mine.' And that wasn't only because she had an analyst who could understand her. She said, 'At least there is a place where I can live my madness, live it out.' And it seems that the analyst and the analysis is used as such a space and time, to live out one's madness. Now, of course, you will not be surprised that this patient couldn't lie down on the couch and that it needed 3 years for her to accept not seeing the object, not having control over the analyst through sight because of this state of anxiety and terror, which she experienced in solitude. One thing interesting is her migraines, very severe migraines, if I understand, which led her to the hospital which is rather unusual."

I said, "Particularly if I go on vacation."

Green replied, "Particularly if you go on vacation. Now this is a typical psychosomatic symptom. But what is the interpretation of migraine here? Of course, it is easy for an analyst to understand the symptom of migraine as an expression of terrible anger, frustration, violence, and pain, and even an internal destruction of the missing object. But it is not so simple—the fact is that the patient doesn't bring up those fantasies to the analyst. She has migraines *instead*, which means that she has no psychic formations to express that anger, and the migraine here stands as a painful inhibition of thought processes. It is as if the fantasies are so violent and so cruel that they have to be completely split off and have no psychical expression whatsoever. Instead we have the migraine and the pain. It is as if the psychosomatic symptom served as a sort of acting in—'in' meaning in her body out of reach of her mind."

I said, "That's what she has always said. She has said, 'It is so powerful and so big that it would destroy the whole office or me.' There are no words. She lets you know she can't even imagine expressing it without there being total destruction of everything—me, the room, herself."

Green said, "It reminds us of these children who bang their heads on the wall."

I said, "She did that as a child."

Green continued, "She did that. Because what happens then, of course, is that these children are in so much despair that, in such times of feeling of loneliness and solitude and bereavement, it was the only way for them to feel their body. And also to feel their own uncontrollable defenses against the awareness of their anger and what caused it. This is not only a projection, but a provocative maneuver to include some kind of representation of the object's response. Not necessarily in terms of hitting but mainly, I would say, to invite us to find behind the protest the object's deafness. A stumbling block. It is not only a projective identification, but the pain helps to feel that there is a body there. So she's giving herself a pain, maybe to counterattack her psychotic fantasies that she would otherwise have at that moment."

I said, "You're absolutely right. She took a file once in my office and began to scratch her arm to the point of bleeding because, she said, 'Now I know I'm here.' It also represented her memory of terror concerning her mother's attempt at suicide."

Green replied, "No, not only. Because in the way you told us about it, there was the bleeding and there were the white walls. In a paper I wrote about narcissistic anxieties, I opposed red anxieties and 'white' anxieties. What I call 'red' anxieties are anxieties which are linked with violence, body hurt, and bleeding. You can even label castration anxiety as a red anxiety. You also have, what I call, white anxieties. In fact, in French, I said *blanche*. If I want to convey it in English, I would say 'blank' anxieties. Now the red anxieties are connected with the drives directed toward the object. Red anxieties are linked, for me, to the drives in some representational form. The red (anger, violence, excitation) drives are associated with defined objects.

"On the contrary, the blank anxiety is, for me, related to narcissism, which to some extent expresses the fact that representations are unfit to cope with narcissism. Here I must point out a possible misunderstanding. It is common to see in the analytic literature an allusion to self-representations (as opposed to object representations). This view is a post-Freudian one and should be scrutinized because behind its clinical claims to be accepted, it is more a phenomenological feature than a truly psychoanalytic one. It is totally absent from Freud's work, and one should ask oneself why. It is not the result, in any way, of a kind of neglect. In fact, Freud did not believe in the possibility of self-representations—only in object representations, although he himself introduced the concept of narcissism, which is different from the idea of self-representation.

"We can also draw the comparison between the paranoid anxieties and the depressive anxieties. The paranoid anxieties are linked with violence and destruction. The depressive anxieties are linked with blankness, emptiness, nonexistence, and so on. Of course, we know that aggression plays a major role in depressive states. But, first, it remains to be shown that it is of the same nature as when it comes into play, some violent behavior is being expressed. And, second, should this be the case, one has to think about the transformations that occur when its outcome is depression rather than direct expressions of an aggressive nature. Now, of course, in the parameter figures of the internal world of this young woman, both mother and father are bleeding. The mother is bleeding because of her suicide attempt, and the father is bleeding from his ulcer. But we have to represent what the situation of that child was before the mother committed the suicide attempt. We have to represent what traits remain in the material of the depressed mother, the mother before committing that act of violence, the suicide attempt.

"I have written a paper which I entitled 'The Dead Mother.' By the dead mother, I am not alluding to a mother who is dead but, rather, a mother who is alive but depressed and presents the child a blank face, making the child to feel meaningless to the mother, making the child to feel himself or herself as if he had a mirror that reflected an image of himself, as if it were a lifeless child. This contrasts with the child's own experience of vitality, which, being not reflected in the mother, is transformed into violence and the impossibility of expressing the feeling of meaninglessness, generating anger, which, if it were expressed, would destroy more of the already half-destroyed mother. So the only recourse for the child is not only to split off his violent fantasies but, to some extent, to deconnect himself, as if he meant, 'I do not exist for my mother. I do not exist myself.'

"It's the basic dilemma, either it's my fault, or it's her fault. If it is her fault, she is the worst, the most despicable thing. If it is her fault, she is the worst, the most abominable, dreadful, witch mother. Of course, these thoughts do not happen in the mind through these expressions but in some unthinkable way for us ('Here comes the worst, the despicable, the dread . . . ') indistinctively applying both to the object and to the immature ego—and mobilizing all the hatred, with only a partial achievement in discharging it or projecting it outward. It is very interesting to think of Roselyn's methods of survival—using the little people who drove her to unreality or the closing off and the showing of the facade. So if she is there in the external world, she's closed off inside and will not show anything of what she really feels or experiences. If she wants to express something that is inside, then she has to be in the unreal and to deny the existence of external reality. There's no way of sharing anything.

"It is interesting to see that you have chosen two episodes of her decompensation. The first episode resulted from something that happened to her from the inside when she had to undergo an operation. In the second episode, it was something that happened to her for which she was not responsible. She was burglarized. She was deprived of her privacy in her space, with a situation of chaos or upside down, and she had an immediate regression. And this brings us to the point brought up by James Grotstein—the identification—with this outside space, which has been so disturbed. But, of course, it was also linked with an extraordinary state of anger of having been intruded, violated, abused, forced in such a way that she had to defend against the invaders by destroying herself, becoming also the cause of chaos."

I said, "I could have killed the mother myself many times."

Green said, "That's good. I could have killed her myself too. Not that it would have helped a lot but because these feelings of the patient could be sheltered in you. Because what you say is probably what the child has felt but couldn't afford thinking. She had a migraine instead."

I said, "When her mother died she, later, was able to say, 'I'm glad she's dead.' "

Green said, "Yes. You can say that when you're over 30, and also if you have other rooms in your psychic space for other feelings which will appear, for instance, in dreams, not when you are a 12-month-old baby.

And then we have that dream. Of course, it's a very interesting dream. Obviously the dream is about childbirth because also one very important thing about this patient is that she has no children. Was it on purpose?"

"Yes," I replied.

Green went on, "I believe that she didn't want to kill the children if they came to life."

I agreed, saying, "She says it's cleaner."

Green said, "It's a clean death. Of course, this dream about childbirth is also a very compensated dream because it's also the problem of the fantasy about her own childbirth; and it is also the problem of how to expel the bad mother out of herself. How can she 'excorporate' the mother? I would say by a situation of witchcraft, of being possessed by such a witch that she has inside of her and of whom she is, at the same time, possessive. Bewitched by the mother and becoming herself a witch. It's about, of course, this poisonous plant. Now, of course, it is very important that in a dream she could represent this lady, this witch; and I believe also the fact that she represents the children as kittens and little chickens is an indication of some kind of devouring process between the two. Like kittens, little chickens, well you can expect what is going to happen when they grow up. And it's all a matter of holding or leaving it out.

"Now what is the problem for her if she really separates from her mother? What is the problem for her if she gives up the fantasy of that bad mother? The problem is that she will find herself again in a state of emptiness—void and nonexistent. It's better to have a bad mother than no mother at all. Of course, this is being worked out in the transference, and I think that some work should be done about what happens during the separation because there is an allusion to separation when she speaks of Japan—you're going to Japan, she's going to Japan. In that material there's something that gives us a hint about her state of mind. I mean, how the depression can be mixed up with paranoid anxieties. I mean, in that kind of transference she not only projects but *does* to her analyst; that is, she hurts her after her analyst says, 'I can't stand your wounding yourself.' And, of course, one can expect that the analyst would say, 'I can't stand you committing suicide or wanting to die.' "

I said, "She's taught me not to say that one."

Green went on, "Because at a certain moment the idea of death and suicide becomes the only weapon, not only in terms of revenge, but in the illusion that it is an act of individuality and freedom. In this distortion death is not only a revenge, it is considered that at least *this* is mine. This is mine, and don't take it away from me."

"Well," he continued, "I've acted quite differently with a patient who threatens suicide, but she never went so far as yours. But one day I said to the patient, 'You know, if you really want to commit suicide, I won't be able to prevent you from doing it. If you want to make it a struggle for power, you'll always be more powerful than I am, and I won't be able to do anything about it; and I can admit in advance that I shall be defeated.' The patient was completely amazed because I didn't appear as omnipotent any more or wanting to be all powerful and trying to control her entirely. I said, 'I think we could have better choices than that.' I think that in such a situation it would be quite legitimate to interpret to the patient the feelings of anger that she wants to instill in the analyst because she is unable of tolerating them herself. She fears that the analyst may be destroyed by this anger; so he's supposed to experience it—but not be the victim of it.

"About the relationship between the pre-oedipal and the oedipal in that dream—the dream is overtly pre-oedipal with these childbirth fantasies and the children, the lady, the witch, and so on. But when she comes to the conclusion it's Rappaccini's daughter and the mother is, of course, present in the dream through the poisonous plant. There is the bad father who is the scientist who nourishes, in close alliance with the mother, the daughter who is also a poisonous plant. But there is the young man, still. There is a charming prince, somewhere, who falls in love with her, and here we have a passage to an oedipal situation. But the whole thing seems fabricated from some fairy tale at hand and does not seem to show a real working through. It's a kind of ready-made fantasy. Anyway, it is wrong, in my mind, to split off too severely the pre-oedipal and oedipal, because they are mixed up in the material; and when we speak of pre-oedipal fixations, and when we say that the psychotic has no oedipus complex, I think this is totally wrong. I think that everyone has an oedipus complex, but of course, each one has a unique pattern. Of course, it has no reliability; it has no strength; it is weak; it is precarious; but it exists, and we mustn't forget that it exists and must avoid being tempted to dig right to the supposed 'deeper' layers.

"So our conclusion today is linked with what I say. 'You, Hunter, are the mother talking to the father André Green to say, 'Look, what can I do with this child? It is difficult to hold her.' "

Hanna Segal

Perhaps the best known of the living Kleinians, Dr. Segal is famous for her original work with psychotic patients and her writings concerning the confusion such patients have in using symbols. She has written a number of books regarding Klein's work and the Kleinian perspective.

This interview with Dr. Hanna Segal was conducted on December 28 and 30, 1989, and February 17, 1990, in her London apartment, where she and her husband live and where she sees patients. Her office is spacious and is furnished with beautiful, carefully selected antiques. A crystal vase of fresh, casually arranged tulips graced the antique table in front of a tall window opposite her chair and the analytic couch. She treasures a small well-crafted desk she has had since her childhood in Poland.

Dr. Segal is known for her work in the Kleinian tradition. She has written two books concerning Klein: *An Introduction to the Work of Melanie Klein* (1978) and *Melanie Klein* (1979). Her own original papers are collected in her third book, *The Work of Hanna Segal* (1981). Her most recent book is *Dream, Phantasy and Art* (1990).

To start our conversation, I asked Segal to see the Hunter watch she had inherited from Melanie Klein. Alas, it had been stolen in a burglary. Her husband explained that a "Hunter watch" was not a brand of watch, but a mechanical system before the balancing of wheels became standard on timepieces.

Interview

Hanna Segal: The watch was lovely. It was a little pendant watch with an enamel case. Beautiful little jewel. It was a very beautiful piece of jewelry, and it was heartbreaking when they stole it. I am not very fond of possessions. I'm from a part of often ravaged Europe where you traveled and moved and lost things. It can affect you two ways. Either you get very possessive about things, or your treasure is where you heart is and you don't care very much. But I did miss that watch. And I'll show you something else which I treasure. I had my 70th birthday a couple of years ago, and various ex-analysts and students gave me a party and presented me with this brooch, dating from about the same time as Mrs. Klein's watch. It must be Edwardian or Victorian.

Virginia Hunter: It is beautiful.

HS: It is beautiful, isn't it? So nicely chosen because they know I like rather discreet jewelry, and this I can even wear for work. It is not a very dress up thing. And I would like to arrest any gossip, which you told me about, that I only dress in black and don't allow anybody, even myself, to wear any jewelry.

There is one other thing I would like to correct and that is the impression left by the Grosskurth book on Klein. The book describes that Mrs. Klein's housekeeper said that a patient, Dr. W., whom Mrs. Klein transferred to me, rang up Mrs. Klein every night threatening suicide. She suddenly stopped calling, and Mrs. Klein told the housekeeper she had killed herself. The book makes it sound like Mrs. Klein transferred her to me with coldheartedness and the patient killed herself. That puts Klein and me in a very bad light with Klein's absolute coldheartedness not to see this person ringing her every day, and me, not being able to handle the transfer. Dr. W. *did* commit suicide, but 5 years after stopping her analysis with me and 6 years after Mrs. Klein's death. It is a very different story, isn't it? She couldn't ring Mrs. Klein in heaven!

VH: Yes, quite different. Was she a borderline patient?

HS: Yes. She was one of those people who was extremely schizoid and withdrawn. As soon as she got into an analysis she started into a manic–depressive swing.

VH: But not one that would be treated with lithium?

HS: There was no lithium in those days. I think probably not. At some point her family had sent her for an interview with Dr. William Gillespie who was quoted in his review of Grosskurth's book as saying: "Whatever you do for this patient, she will end in suicide." What happened, actually, was this. When I got pregnant with my last child, she just could not acknowledge, in the slightest, that I was pregnant. I have never had an experience like that. I interpreted that she obviously noticed changes and she would respond, "Yes, I have a fantasy you are pregnant." I even told her. I had a rather flowery skirt, the kind pregnant women wear in the summer, and she had a dream of a flower pot with paper, one of those papers with a pattern. I interpreted that she noticed my maternity skirt and obviously there was a plant growing. I never, before or since, had resistance of that kind. She broke off her analysis when I interrupted to give birth. I meant to resume with her a very short time after birth. I think, following a disappointment in a love affair, she committed suicide. Grosskurth will correct this in the next edition. She also should not have divulged the patient's name, in my opinion.

VH: Is that kind of depression treatable?

HS: I don't know. I am very much more experienced now. I think probably I may have done better now. We know more now about the psychotic mechanisms—but one doesn't know. One thing I do know, that children who are sent to boarding schools at the age of 3 or 4, as she was, will obviously experience a severe trauma at that young age. People make a wrong assumption if they believe that Kleinians think only the first year is important. It is not true. They think the basic personality patterns are based on the first year.

VH: I am noticing in my practice, which is basically an upper-middle-class practice, that more and more women feel entitled to have children despite their primary commitment to their work. They have a child, and they get a housekeeper and off they go. And the housekeeper may change many times. They think nothing about the child having a loss.

HS: That is right. My parents were very enlightened parents—

excellent parents—from about the age of 6 or 7 onwards, but my early nannies kept changing every few months or every few years. It was very common then too. And the problem was not working mothers. My mother was a lady of leisure; many children today see more of their working mothers!

VH: How do you feel it affected you?

HS: Well, like everybody else. A depressive streak, not anything damaging. I remember my father playing with me and my mother was around, but she wouldn't wake up until 11:00 or 12:00, midday—still there was the framework of home. They would go away on long holidays without me until I was about the age of 7.

VH: Coming back to Dr. W., I'd imagine that your own experience of loss would have given you a special awareness of the impact on her of your interrupting analysis for the birth of your child. You would have had to have been more profoundly aware of how a separation might affect her.

HS: Well, it is all a question of what goes into making a psychoanalyst. I think that one of those things that makes a psychoanalyst is a variety of experiences. But a uniformly depressed, abused childhood would, of course, not be a very good preparation. I suppose being familiar, in oneself, with many different states of mind, helps though.

VH: How did you become an analyst?

HS: I am one of those few people who started wanting to be an analyst very early. I think it was most unusual in the culture I came from in Poland before the war. We had only two analysts. Bychowski, who became quite a famous American analyst, and another one whose name I don't remember. I probably went into medicine mostly because I was interested in analysis. I read a lot in adolescence, and then it was quite a sort of marathon run. I went to Bychowski when I was a 3rd-year student and asked him, "How does one become an analyst?" He said, "You have to go to Vienna." That wasn't on my agenda at all. Austrian culture had no attraction for me. Then, when the war broke out (I was in Paris, in 1939), I knew the name of one French analyst, so I rang him and asked him how one becomes an analyst. He said, "Sorry." He was leaving Paris that day, being evacuated. I'm very glad I didn't get any other response from him. Maybe that is why I forget his name. One thing I found out, subsequently: He used to take his patients and family swimming in his swimming pool every weekend and things like that, which I don't hold to at all. And at that time I didn't know any better. I could have been pulled into anything. The other is that he is the only French analyst who has not been readmitted to the society because of suspected collaboration with Nazis. So maybe I forgot his name now not to be open to a libel suit.

Then, after the fall of Paris I came to England and eventually landed in Edinburgh in the Polish medical school. I started working as a volunteer in a child guidance clinic there and, through the staff, I found out that Dr. Fairbairn was there. He was the first analyst I met professionally. So I went to Dr. Fairbairn, and I owe a great deal of gratitude to him. First of all, he told me how to become an analyst. One had to go to London, which I was going to do anyway as soon as I finished my studies. He said, "There is an institute and one has to apply." I was very grateful to him and to my luck, because Wilfred Bion told me that he had wasted, I don't know, 10 or 12 years when he was a young doctor wanting to become an analyst, in some poor psychotherapy, because he had never even heard that an institute for training existed. Our institute has so little public face. Bion met analysts working in the Tavistock, and he applied for training. I don't know how old he was, but certainly he must have been in his late 40s if not early 50s when he started. He wasted all that time. Fairbairn told me that there were two different developments at the time—Anna Freud and Klein—and he gave me Anna Freud and Klein to read.

What I knew about analysis was whatever was translated from Sigmund Freud into Polish or French. When I came to England, I didn't read too much Freud—I was too busy getting my life together and finishing my medical studies. Fairbairn gave me Anna Freud's *The Ego and Mechanisms of Defense* (1937) and Mrs. Klein's *Psychoanalysis of Children* (1932). He didn't tell me which side he was on, so to speak. But he gave me the literature, and, of course, I was very fascinated. It was the first time I had heard the name of Klein, my first contact with her work. And then I came to London and went through analysis with Mrs. Klein. But before that, Fairbairn did another thing for me that was very good. I had no money at all, a pittance of 2 pounds a week, 30 shillings for a bed and breakfast. So I had little money for analysis. But Fairbairn told me in Edinburgh there was a Dr. Matthew, who had been analyzed by Mrs. Klein, an associate member. He took me over for a nominal fee while I was waiting to go to London. It was quite a colorful beginning!

VH: What about that year with him?

HS: That was very interesting. One thing I learned from him was very good, for it contrasted with what I saw later in the practice of many analysts. He had disseminated sclerosis and was quite obviously limping a bit, and his hand was deformed. He never let me get away with not speaking about it. He was immediately onto what I noticed and my anxieties about it and so on, without allowing me any denial of the fact or my fantasies. I say that this contrasts with other analysts. I remember, when I was in training, there was an analyst who was completely disabled, walking with a stick. And the only interpretation he gave was that the patient was envious of the stick, which represented his penis. All the anxiety about the health, the collapse of the analyst, the imperfections, wasn't touched.

VH: Does that seem a strange interpretation to you that someone would envy a disability?

HS: Oh no, I'm sure there is penis envy in the potency of the analyst, however disabled he is. But never to mention the other side! Yes, it did seem strange to me. But in those days some of the candidates of the classical tradition were given that kind of interpretation—the stick equals the penis. The actual appearance of the analyst, things like that, were not taken up so much. That came much later. Now, of course, in all schools of thought this kind of thing would be taken up. There are other behaviors of the analyst that may impact the patient; for instance, Freud's smoking.

VH: I understand that you yourself used to smoke quite heavily?

HS: Yes.

VH: And that patients were aware of it?

HS: Yes, and Mrs. Klein smoked.

VH: During the hour?

HS: Yes, lots of analysts did. In the culture of our day smoking was so common that it didn't really come into associations much. There was a joke among the candidates, when I was young, that you distinguish a Kleinian from an Anna Freudian because the Kleinians, irrespective of sex, smoke, and the Anna Freudians, irrespective of sex, knit—because a couple of young, male Freudians knitted. Mrs. Klein stopped smoking about halfway through my analysis. She told me later she had no difficulty with it. She also told me, after my analysis, she was very sorry that she never really analyzed, much, my smoking because it was so common. She would analyze my turning to my dummy when I was dissatisfied with her or something like that. But never very much the self-destructive aspects of it, because it just wasn't known.

VH: When did you stop?

HS: I never thought of stopping smoking because of the nicotine complication, because my heart was always in good condition and also I never had a smoker's cough, which suggested my lungs were cleaning themselves. Well, there was Swedish research that people who don't have smoker's cough are not very much at risk. But, a combination of two factors changed my mind. One was I was pregnant with my third child. I was about 40 then, and the statistics came out about the link between cancer of the lungs and smoking of cigarettes. I didn't stop smoking, but I shifted to cigars and pipes in private. For a time, it was very interesting because there was a fashion for women's pipes. It makes very good sense, and, in fact, it's a much more feminine smoke because you could use an elegant pipe for decoration. I had lovely pipes, but it never caught on. Many of my colleagues started, nobody persisted—I did. That lasted me, happily, until about 4 or 5 years ago when I started getting a precancerous change on my palate from pipes and cigars, and then I stopped. I found it very hard. I have become more irritable.

VH: Do you have any interpretations for that?

HS: Yes, but I won't tell you.

VH: Really?

HS: I was a very frustrated infant in the early phases. Also, I come from a heavily addictive family. My grandfather smoked about 80 cigarettes a day. He died at the age of 84. My father was a heavy smoker. And I started early. I will tell you something—how little was thought of cigarettes! When I was a child, I was puzzled when I was reading Tom Sawyer about chewing gum because we had no chewing gum. At some point he gives his chewing gum to his little girlfriend. In Polish it was translated "his rubber sweet." I kept wondering what was a "rubber sweet?" And then, when I was in my very early teens, we were on holiday in the south of France, and I had three little friends who were half American and half French, and they introduced me to chewing gum. I was, of course, delighted and was chewing gum all the time. But my father hated it. He said, "Look, you look like a cow chewing his cud. If you've got to have something in your mouth, have a cigarette." Now can you imagine today an intelligent, concerned father telling a child, "Have a cigarette because chewing gum is disgusting?" It was a completely different culture.

VH: Can you go back to the year you had with Dr. Matthew? And then the move of changing analysts? It seems strange to me to start an analysis with someone when you would be leaving the city in 1 year.

HS: That's right. One wouldn't do it nowadays much. I think my year with David Matthew wasn't really necessary—I was in no immediate therapeutic need, but you know, it was an offer. In those days, analyses weren't so long. So to be offered a year was good luck. I am very thankful. He was the first one to put me on to manic aspects of my character, things I was proud of, which were nothing to be proud of.

VH: Like what?

HS: Oh, I would be describing something to him. I was a stiff-upper-lip kind of person. I was describing the first day of war, when Poland, my country, was invaded, and I was very upset. But when I went to the hospital I made sure no one noticed my anxiety. Matthew questioned, "Well, what is that to be proud of?" I started questioning it. Everybody around me was anxious and here was I, pretending I was not. What does it imply? One is the denial of my anxiety which was stronger than my colleagues because it was my country that was invaded at that moment, and what does it mean? I'm pretending I'm not affected. I'm bloody superior to the others. But, after all, I was amongst colleagues. They were anxious. It was bloody right to be anxious.

VH: So he was questioning the need to be superior.

HS: Right. But that is only part of my response. He was questioning. But he obviously knew me. I was a cocky postadolescent, you see. But the point I want to make is that one has to know the context. It is always a problem, for example, responding to a case presented of another clinician. The clinician's interpretation will always be better because he or she knows the patient. It is difficult to interpret out of context. The point I want to make is that one has to know the context. In other circumstances the interpretation could have been, "You managed to contain your anxieties, not let them invade." I also remember another manic thing. I got a shock when I decided to take a week off to bicycle in the mountains, and I just sent him a telegram, "Sorry I will be away for a week." I was shocked when he charged me for those missed sessions. It sort of gave me a taste of an analytic relationship. But, I think I never developed a deep transference because I was all set to go to London. I had made up my mind, and it took some doing, to have Klein as an analyst.

VH: Does it seem ordinary to you that someone would not have discussed that parameter, if you were away you would pay? You sound as though it was a surprise to you.

HS: Yes, I think he hadn't discussed it. Nowadays, I think it is discussed. Possibly he could have said it, but I didn't take it in.

VH: How did you feel about it?

HS: Shock, chastened, and feeling he was bloody right. You don't treat people like that.

VH: But also he shouldn't do it without saying ahead of time.

HS: I don't know.

VH: How do you handle it now?

HS: How do I handle it and how do I advise candidates to handle it? I don't always advise them to tell it because it almost sounds like putting the idea into the patient's mind that he can take off. Usually for the clinic patients, you say you are responsible for all sessions that are booked—sometimes you don't, but when it comes up, when a patient says he wants to take off and he wants to be away, then you discuss it.

VH: Do you remember your first meeting with Klein?

HS: Yes. She was a bit older than I thought. She had a very characteristic walk, sort of slightly bent and very, you could sort of see, very intense. On coming in she didn't ask me any searching questions, anything like a psychiatric interview.

VH: I remember reading that somewhere.

HS: Yes, there was an interview I did at the Tavistock regarding Klein. We discussed sort of general things, my interest in analysis, times, fees, which were still a problem. My income was 10 pounds a month.

VH: How do you feel your work differs from Klein's? What influences do you feel she gave you that were most important to you and where have you gone on your own?

HS: I learned from her not to break the parameters. Analysis is about analyzing. Analysis is not about helping, not about reassuring, and not about advising. You know, something we wrote, Bion and I, in the obituary for Klein, was a quotation from Johnson, Samuel Johnson, something that goes like this: "If truth will be of any comfort to you I don't know, but what I do know is that whatever comfort you derive from falsehood is bound to be false and impermanent, and the comfort you get from truth, if any there be, like truth is permanent" (Bion, Rosenfeld, & Segal, 1961, pp. 4–5). And we said that all science is concerned with the search for truth. But that is not new. What is new about analysis is that it is the only discipline that considers that the search for truth is in itself therapeutic. Not a truth with a capital "T" because you can't find that, and it changes. But the fact is that the search for truth, for psychic truth, is the therapeutic factor. This was something that I felt I was looking for all my life and that I got with Klein. Now about what struck me about her technique—it is in contrast to what people think. The sort of idea that she overinterpreted the negative isn't at all so. It was just that when she wrote *Psychoanalysis of Children* aggression was so new! Probably, in her description of a new thought, it sounded as though she was centered on the negative. She wasn't at all. It's not that she didn't talk or make comments about other things. But one knew that it was the evolving transference that was really the process. Now in what ways do I differ? One is probably I do less frequent links with reality events of the past and childhood.

VH: Why?

HS: So as not to divert the transference. I do make reference to childhood, but I make it in the punch, when I know it is "hot stuff" in the transference. The other thing, which we all do, is interpret unconscious fantasy less directly. It is not that we don't see them. I think we are much more concerned with the levels of communication and in not being drawn into too much participation in the patient's fantasy. We pay much more attention to the subtleties of acting in. Not only just what the patient shows of the fantasy, but how he tries to actualize it in the transference. So, in that way, we pay more attention to minutes of silence, tone of voice, and things like that. So I think it makes less of a good story, in a sense.

VH: It's more subtle?

HS: Yes.

VH: Don't you think that the effort to get to deeper levels that are preverbal and somatic have been influenced by many analysts?

HS: Yes. With the Kleinians, it starts with the concept of projective identification and extends in the area of symbolism and, by Bion, in the area of "container and contained." I think the modern Kleinian movement is following my work on concrete symbolism—the difference between concreteness and communication.

VH: Can you say more about that?

HS: Well, it was hard analyzing the schizophrenic, the first one, and mine is the first analysis of an acute schizophrenic without parameters. It's true, Herbert Rosenfeld wrote a paper before, but that would now be called more a borderline case, or a sort of chronic, very schizoid case.

VH: Your case just amazed me in that he seemed to go from really psychotic to functioning pretty well.

HS: In a 4-year analysis!

VH: He got out of the hospital.

HS: He was out of the hospital, that was a big thing, because it wasn't like one of those acute schizophrenics we talk to. He'd been hospitalized for 18 months—with shocks and drugs. I think he made a very good contact with me.

VH: He must have.

HS: And with the new tool, projective identification, I was seeing how everything that was in his mind immediately became a perception of me. It was never felt as a fantasy, it was felt as *there*. It really gave me the first clues of the difference between an object that is symbolized and an object that is equated with the primary object. It opened up a completely different method of communication and method and possibility, or impossibility, of thinking, because concrete things you can throw out, but you can't think about them—work them through.

VH: Where does that come in in terms of the real relationship versus the transference relationship? Does that play in there anywhere in terms of the analyst as a real person?

HS: I think, that in a sort of acute, projective identification stage, a real person is obliterated, that's the difference. For neurotic patients you represent the mother, but they are very aware of your analytical function. With massive projective identification, the other's personality, in the patient's perception, is totally, almost totally obliterated. But gradually it comes through—in bits. But it takes a long time. You see, I think in America you speak a lot of the therapeutic alliance, and some people think it has to be built up before you start analysis.

VH: Some people think that is all there is!

HS: Some people think that is all there is. I think the therapeutic alliance is forged in the process of analysis. There must be some corporative part of the patient, some striving for something or the patient wouldn't start. But the real alliance, it's forged through the work and through the patient's becoming more and more aware of your functioning and what it is about. It fluctuates. It is never a permanent thing. That is why I seldom use the term because it has acquired this technical meaning, and we have an ordinary old word for it—cooperation. Unconscious cooperation. There are times when it's more, times when it's less.

VH: You had a special relationship with Klein. We talked about the timepiece she left you in her will. Of course, that was after the analysis ended. Certainly many patients long for something concrete to keep, and you got it. But during the analysis with her, were there things like papers or even the slightest things like paper clips?

HS: No. Never.

VH: Will you leave gifts to some of your former analysands also?

HS: I don't think so.

VH: It seems such a touching, wonderful thing to do to me.

HS: Yes, of course. But it wasn't to me as an analysand. It was to somebody who worked with her many years after, and it was very, certainly, very precious to me.

VH: But you must have students or analysands who have worked with you for many years, too. I guess I wanted to hear you talk about concreteness in terms of the prohibitions. These issues of concrete contacts come up so often.

HS: The prohibition of concreteness. I think we should talk about Bion's container and contained. Although Klein intuitively followed Freud's ideas about the transference, Freud himself didn't quite apply it.

VH: Yes, he gave soup and money.

HS: I think that the point is this: Even a patient who is functioning on a good depressive level, in analysis, does project very concretely. That is all our work on countertransference, isn't it? They communicate by making the analyst feel it or very often leading him to subtle acting out or acting in. Now, the analyst's task is what Bion would call "to convert Beta into Alpha." To enable the mentalization of that process.

VH: So the mental representation!

HS: That's right. I think whenever you do something like holding hands or giving milk—I don't mean, you know, small things that we all do that are breaches of technique such as saying something unanalytic, laughing at a joke, which you shouldn't, but you can't always not do.

VH: If a patient was coughing, coughing, coughing—would you offer him a drink of water?

HS: No.

VH: Never—even if you thought he or she was really in trouble?

HS: If they asked for it. I would say, "I always have water in the bathroom." Now I won't say I never intervene. I once took a patient, by taxi, to the hospital when it was a matter of life and death. I would hospitalize a patient. But generally I think not. However, breaches do sometimes occur, and you have to recognize them as breaches—not as a therapeutic instrument. This is what is important. Because the patient wants you to act out certain roles, and once you start acting them out you can interpret until you are blue in the face, and it's a wink between the patient and you. That goes for things like hand holding or confessions of any kind. Now, I have given extra sessions, over the weekend, for very anxious patients. But this is putting myself out and offering analytical help, which is something a bit different.

VH: Have you never had patients you couldn't contain without doing something like touching them to aid them in leaving your office?

HS: That is something I always dreaded happening, but it never did—not even with schizophrenics. I think that the patients quickly caught on to what is on and what is not. I'll tell you what my schizophrenic patient Edward told me. I think he was afraid I would overstep a session because he came late, and he said, "There is nothing I dreaded more. You are my clock, and if you don't clock right, the world will go to pieces."

VH: Do you accept any gifts from patients—flowers, drawings?

HS: I try not to, it is not always possible. I certainly would not accept any sort of gift of monetary value, but if a patient brings flowers or something like that I usually behave neutrally and try to analyze it and after a time they stop. I tell you why—because I said something traumatic to a patient once. It was one of my very first patients. He brought me a small box of cigarettes for Christmas and I said, "I am sorry, I don't accept presents from patients." And it was such a trauma for him. And I thought later, such an unnecessary hurt.

VH: Humiliation.

HS: Yes, a humiliation.

VH: You accept them now, but try not to encourage them.

HS: And analyze pretty thoroughly why they have to, want to, what they give things in place of, and its invasive quality—something like that. And it usually stops very soon.

VH: Can you go back to talking more of where your work differs from the work of Melanie Klein?

HS: As I say, in a way, it has become more technical. I pay more attention to minute splitting, to acting in, to the sort of whole area that was opened by Bion's container and contained. I am sure Klein used the countertransference a lot, intuitively, as Freud did. I think Paula Heiman, in her paper, said Freud discovered repression and resistance by countertransference. He felt something was opposing him. Klein was extremely sensitive, so she must have used countertransference a lot, but she didn't like talking about countertransference. When a supervisee would start talking about his feelings, she would tell us, "Tell that to your analyst, I want to hear what the patient has said."

VH: How do you feel about the use being made of it now as a tool?

HS: Positively and negatively.

VH: Both.

HS: Yes. I once said countertransference is the best servant and the worst master. I think that I do use my countertransference consciously, probably more than Klein did. If I become aware I am feeling irritation, seduction, I try to trace where it comes from. But I can see what Klein was about. I remember a story. A very nice young analyst said his patient had put confusion into him. Mrs. Klein said to him, "No, dear, she didn't put confusion into you—you were confused." She was afraid of countertransference being made an excuse. If somebody tells me they do this or that because the patient projected it, I say, "Look, countertransference is not an excuse."

VH: Yet, one must be aware of countertransference.

HS: To be aware—not to talk about it with the patient or act on it! The more aware you are, the less likely you are to be confused. But it is so, people take it as sort of a universal excuse. They don't stop to think: "Am I confused? What is going on? Did I get up on the wrong side of the bed?" I think that, to me, the worst danger threatening an analyst is omnipotence and arrogance. Any number of gifted analysts, in one way or another, have gone astray. It's always connected with some kind of omnipotent arrogance or narcissism.

VH: Could you say more about that? To me, analytic work seems to be such a humbling experience—hour after hour, with people searching for truth.

HS: That is the problem, you see, it is a very humbling experience and therefore difficult to bear.

VH: But it also has more love, more aliveness, than almost any profession you could have.

HS: You are quite right. Nevertheless, we know how frequently it happens that analysts, particularly in the later part of their lives, go sort of off analysis in various ways.

VH: Who are you thinking of?

HS: Well, Lacan was one, with the combination of the sort of omnipotence, narcissism, and arrogance. You are right that being an analyst is a very humbling experience, but on the other hand, after all, you are such a center of attention! It is very easy to abuse that attention. I don't mean consciously, but unconsciously to mistake the idealizing transference for qualities in yourself. There is something else: It is the relative slowness of the analytical process; not impressive, showy, with great improvements. People want something quicker, better, more "happening." I find, as you say, there is nothing more exciting than doing analysis. But as I say, it is humbling. It is a great strain—the deeper you go, the greater the strain. I'll tell you another joke, an old joke about the Freudians and Kleinians. There was an Old Freudian analyst practicing in a building and a young Kleinian starting his practice. And the young Kleinian sees this old man coming cheerfully down in the evening. The young Kleinian is exhausted, sweaty, and he says, "Tell me, colleague, how do you manage to work all those hours with all those projections, all this tension, all of this confusion that they bring and not be exhausted at the end of the day?" And the old Freudian says, "Er? Er?" He is hard of hearing. So, in a way, you've got two problems because if you don't work on a deep enough level, you don't know what hits you and you are more likely to act out. On the other hand, if you are conscious of those projections and follow the nonverbal communications leaving yourself open to the countertransference and yet watching not to act on it, it is very strenuous work.

VH: I love the work. It is scary to hear that maybe someday I won't. I feel very grateful to have the work. You know what I am saying?

HS: Yes. I don't think that many analysts go wrong, but if they do go wrong, nearly always it's from some sort of what you would call arrogant egotism.

VH: So does that mean, then, that you believe there is a basic narcissistic flaw in many of us who begin this work?

HS: Yes, but I think also that the nature of our work is most antinarcissistic and puts a great strain on us. And yet it gives narcissistic opportunities—to become idealized by your patients, have a following—this kind of thing. There is something else that comes to mind about that. Obsession with originality! Little discoveries get blown up, and our sources don't get acknowledged. You are original when you are not thinking about it. The obsession with finding something new is, in itself, a very destructive thing.

VH: Analysts work awfully hard to try to find new words to describe the same things.

HS: Exactly. The number of times the "depressive position" was discovered under other names is amazing.

VH: Even "fictive" personality, "as if" personality, you yourself called it something else—but perhaps these all mean nearly the same thing.

HS: Yes. "As if" personality—fictive personality—the false self—everything and everybody. In part, they are all variances of the borderline states, which are very different. But the trouble is that with each description goes a theory. I don't use the concept of false self. Winnicott gives a splendid description of the syndrome. But if you say "false self," you accept all his theory of how it's formed, which would be very different from mine.

VH: Tell me how it would be different.

HS: Well, basically Winnicott calls a false self a compliant self. When the maternal sort of thing fails, your own self fakes to fit in with mother. Now, there are many other possible mechanisms.

VH: Winnicott doesn't take account of the fact that in the face of great stress, one might also look to fictions, like characters in novels, to acquire a false self.

HS: To comply with mother and to go to a play or book to get a self are different. I don't know if the latter comes under false self. We would see that much more as an aspect of projective identification. To get inside mother and take over her function, which may be because of maternal failing, or because of envy, or a combination of the two.

VH: What about a search for an identity?

HS: What does it mean "search for an identity?" Somebody reviewing a book by an American novelist said, "Here is another American in search for identity. Every analysis has a search for identity?

What am I? What are my objects? How did I come to be?" Certain descriptive theories belong. In order to agree with the description, one must agree with theory. In fact, originality works very differently. You take in what you can, you work with it, you put things together, and a third new thing appears. While you're in search of being original, the only true original thing, I think, is shit—the original thing that the body produces. And even that isn't original. You have to eat first. Originality comes when you can acknowledge a good internal object. When you can allow your parents to come together to produce a baby. Allowing two items to come together—then a third appears! People obsessed with having to be original usually are much more narcissistic. "I do it all by myself." Sucking my own thumb, putting your own thumb in your own anus. So that's another thing, which I feel pesters some analysts. They have to be original, they have to make new theories with new languages.

VH: In child analysis, what new directions or new theories are being incorporated into Melanie Klein's theory?

HS: In child analysis, like other analysis, we are much more concerned with the sort of mental function in itself. When is the child playing? Communicating? When is he or she acting out? What part is acting out? What's the way the child wants to involve the analyst? More along those lines.

VH: Have the infant researchers brought anything to you that was helpful?

HS: Not much really. We have, as part of our curriculum, baby observation once a week. People, of course, read Stern. I'm not very much into it—I did follow some of the cognitive stuff. It was always a complaint that Mrs. Klein attributed too much individuality to the child, too much perception. I think, from the modern research, if anything, she really attributed too little.

VH: In America now "the self-regulating other" has become a catch word. There are some very interesting studies, I think, coming out about the way married couples impact each other's health organically.

HS: Of course. Of course.

VH: It would be interesting to hear your views.

HS: Yes, well, I don't do much of this work, but as you know, there is extensive work by Bion on groups, and certainly it's applied to couples and other systems of mutual projective identification. But, I wait for fashions to pass a bit. I am actually interested in Noam Chomsky and his work in linguistics. I think there is much to his idea that there is an internal, universal, prelinguistic structure and that grammar and language develop through external interaction with this matrix. I am told that

Chomsky was much more influential in the United States as an opponent of the behaviorists than analysts were. He also showed the importance of the internal. Basic fantasies—of basic functions, you know like feeding, intercourse, childbirth—would interact with the environment at various stages of maturity, and the fantasies would influence the perception of reality.

VH: Can you elaborate on that? I am not sure I understand what you are saying.

HS: Kyrle said, in essence it is strange that children have every considerable theory of parental intercourse except the right one. There is something internal which "knows," like internal grammar, how relationships start. But this is what is under attack by all forms of behaviorism and "reality"-oriented therapies.

VH: Many analysts who followed Mrs. Klein helped to develop and extend her work, particularly with regard to preverbal and somatic structures. Can you comment on these developments?

HS: Yes. That is right. And all of that is very much an extension of projective identification as described by Klein—but as extended by Bion in a very important way—because Mrs. Klein's projective identification refers to an omnipotent fantasy in the child's mind. The child thinks he's entered mother, or possessed her, or something like that. Bion says, "Not quite so. It's not just a fantasy. It's a fantasy that gets implemented." In a sense, the mother's state of mind is influenced by the child by feeling or not feeling, screaming, and the same happens in analysis.

VH: But that's real.

HS: That's right, but this is a real mental interaction. Of course, Klein used to take it up a lot, "You're doing that because you think that would anger me," and probably she would be aware she was getting angered. We see it all over the place. We do things to other people to make them react. Betty Joseph's technique is very much refined in various ways. She always asks, what are the patient's communications supposed to do to you? What is starting to happen? The patient is bringing me her distress. Interpretation of this depends where you are in the analysis.

VH: Some patients are afraid to need, want, or connect and to take the "good milk."

HS: Yes, this is the area we work in more. The point is that the patient projects into you, but you mustn't act out the projection. You must understand what patients are projecting and show them how they are doing it and then gradually *why* they're doing it. Was it because the stress was too great or is it an envious attack? And then gradually you come to it.

VH: Can you give me an example?

HS: A young supervisee of mine, with his second patient, had a very unpleasant experience. A young man with homosexual anxieties asked for a clinical analysis, but he had to wait 2 years. We picked him up from the waiting list. We didn't know that in the meantime he had become psychotic. In the first session, the patient sat on the couch and said, "I'm not going to lie down. I've laid down enough for that man," and all sorts of paranoid stuff. Now, what my clever supervisee said was, "You feel afraid that I will not know the difference between analytic treatment and buggery." He didn't interpret to him, "You're confused between buggery and analysis," because that would be felt as an attack. He was right. The patient was convinced that it was the analyst who did not know the difference between buggery and analysis. Then the patient relaxed and in the next session he did lie down. Gradually, it came out that the enormous resistances were because he had had anal intercourse, which he hated and wanted. But he acted so projectively that the analyst always had to think first, what is his perception of the object?—and gradually bring this understanding back to the patient. I was very impressed. That was an interpretation that was just at the right level. Not what any analyst may have said, "You're afraid to lie on the couch because you're afraid that I'm going to invade you," or whatever. That wouldn't be enough. But he hit it just right: "You think I'm confused between what is mental and what is physical."

VH: He learned how to do that from you—or your example.

HS: You interpret it in its projective form. In some patients it's very important to understand those things—words you use and how they're experienced by the patient. I had a patient who was going into a manic episode. He rang me in the evening to reassure me that he was all right, that he wasn't going mad and things were better. I had to say something, and I wanted to take the positive side because he was sort of reassuring me. I said, "You wanted to ring me to reestablish some contact between us." I didn't say, "to get in touch with me," because I knew if I used the words "to get in touch," it would create an erotic image in his mind. It might play into his erotomania. But it turned out "contact" was the wrong word, too. Because when he did go into a completely psychotic state, one of the most persecuting things was my word "contact." It became an electric wire burning in his mind.

VH: He must have heard it as a criticism.

HS: Yes, though it was meant as reassurance. He heard an erotic projection. He felt I had contacted him and invaded him in a hot, excited, sexual way. I don't know what word I could have used, I couldn't have been silent. I guess I could have tried not to give something half interpretive.

VH: You would never say, "It was nice that you thought to call."

HS: Oh Christ, no. I would never say, "It was nice," to a patient any more than, "It was nasty"—we're not here to pass judgment on whether it's nice or nasty. And with a patient with an erotomania to tell him he is nice! His whole psychosis is based on his delusion that I think that he's nice!

VH: So you try to keep very clearly to an interpretive word that's not at all emotional.

HS: No, I would be sure that what I said wasn't a value judgment. I could say, you felt it was a nice thing, or you felt this was a very nasty thing to do. I would never say it was a nice thing to do or a nasty thing to do.

VH: But if you said, "You felt," it would be okay?

HS: Yes. I had a patient who, in a very manic state, rang up Saturday morning, woke my husband, who was furious, just to say she had seen a play that was wonderful and that it was the last day to get tickets. I had to interpret to her that she thought she was doing a nice thing for me. It took a year before she could realize what an invasion her "kindness" was to my private life, an intercourse with me or my husband. With some patients you want to interpret it right away. With some patients you just have to say, "You thought you were doing a wonderful thing." And even formulating it like that, they will question, "Did I really?" I would never say, "It was *nice* of you to ring." I could say, "Thank you for ringing." A patient had a baby, in a difficult situation, and she rang the next morning, having gotten the nurses to take the phone to her to say she's had her baby and she's fine, and I said, "Thank you for ringing."

VH: Did you feel "thank you?"

HS: Yes, I did. She had a difficult birth, it was her first baby, she was young, with a difficult husband. Anyway, I'm sure that wasn't an intrusion. It wasn't the intention. But I wouldn't say, "How *nice* of you to ring." Of course, if the patient says, "I've got to go to the hospital" or something like that, I'd say, "Thank you for ringing. I'm sorry," or something like that.

VH: You gave a kind, courteous, human response.

HS: Yes, but you have to be careful. I think it's all right to say, "Thank you." So far as possible, outside the session I try to maintain ordinary courtesy.

VH: That makes sense.

HS: I mean I'm not a poker-faced analyst.

VH: That the patient wanted you to know about her baby clearly signalizes her attachment to you.

HS: Yes, of course.

VH: It's a positive thing. Isn't attachment, after all, a basic biological need?

HS: Yes—and no. There can be so many different kinds of attachment. They are not one thing. An attachment might be a projective identification. You put so much of yourself into the object, the object's tied to you because of the bits of you that are disappearing into it. It's what Professor Wollheim calls the "lure of the object." If it's you, you've got to control it, to be a completely different attachment than want, need, or dependence. You have to find out what the nature of it is. You're got many forms of attachment. If I know the form of a patient's attachment, if I know what form the oedipus complex takes, I know a great deal about the patient.

VH: How would you understand the patient's calling to say that her baby had been born?

HS: It depends on the attachment. It depends on the patient. With a neurotic patient, she may be very aware of her dependence. Now, with psychotic patients, it may be desperate because they may be falling to pieces.

VH: And in this instance projections will be crucial?

HS: With the patient mentioned before about "contact," in his mind I was so full of his projections, anything that came from me was projection. He wanted to keep in contact with me. He projected his violent desire to penetrate me and felt it as my desire to penetrate him, always chasing after a projective part of himself. You know, there is attachment and attachment. You spoke of biology. Biology is interesting, but I don't know what goes on in a little gosling's mind about the attachment. I'm concerned with the varieties of human attachment. What kind of attachment do we see? An attachment of dependence? An attachment of having projected such a marvelous part of oneself into me? A feeling he is nothing without me? An attachment because I have become such a persecutor you've got to keep an eye on me? Attachment and *attachment*.

VH: I wonder what Bowlby would say in response to what you're saying?

HS: Ask him.

VH: It would be interesting, wouldn't it?

HS: Interesting. When I was a student, Bowlby wasn't a training analyst, but he was, I think, secretary of the training committee. They were reorganizing. He had finished his analysis with Mrs. Riviere. He was the man who told me that he looks at everything from the point of view of fantasy! (*Dr. Segal chuckles.*)

VH: So you worked together at that point?

HS: Yes, he was ahead of me. He went more into applied psychoanalysis.

VH: He seems to have had a very different view of Melanie Klein than you have. Very different.

HS: Yes, very different. I met him a few times in later years, but since he went into the Tavistock I have had very little touch with him. Of course, we went two different ways. She was strictly analysis, and he went into family therapy and became involved in manipulation, I think.

VH: You don't do any supervision of family therapy or group therapy, even child therapy?

HS: I've done child psychotherapy supervisions for a very long time, and I still supervise child analysts. I wouldn't object to supervising someone who sees a child once or twice a week. I don't hold with family therapy actually, especially the way it's done in this country. I think it's like putting the child in a permanent, primal scene.

VH: The problem with your stance, it would seem to me, is that financially in most countries you have to find something that you can do.

HS: That's right. In child guidance centers and child guidance clinics in which the patient is seen once a week, the clinic can't provide more and the parents can't afford more. But in family therapy, often five people spend 10 hours a week discussing the case, and nobody gets to the child. The amount of time spent on that would be quite enough for intensive psychotherapy of the child. It's a matter of attitude more than of money. There are other ways of using limited resources.

I had a shocking experience in one of the psychiatric clinics at one of the big universities in America. There was a girl suffering from depersonalization. She was engaged in one of those community therapies where every passing person and every passing nurse would give you an interpretation. Everybody would discuss the patient. What's worse, they wanted me to interview the patient in front of 30 people. I put my foot down and said, "I will not." They decided to interview the poor psychotherapist. This poor intern was to interview the girl in the presence of 30 people. I was very critical. If that poor girl wasn't depersonalized before, she would be now. But I wanted to say something nice as well, so I said, "At least I envy you having the resources to provide that for a patient." But, I said, "I would organize it differently. I would have the nurses discuss things with her but not do any interpreting." They said, "Oh no, she pays tens of thousands of dollars at this clinic. Her father committed suicide because he was afraid he wouldn't be able to pay her fee." I said, "Do you mean that this person could have analysis, a good analyst, but instead attended this hospital at that price instead?"

VH: I would agree with you.

HS: So I think what method you use does not so much depend on the finances, but on what you think is best for the patient. I would arrange for the child, if I could, to have a psychotherapist and for the parents to have an analytically trained social worker. Now in consultation, I sometimes see the child and the parents together. I don't ask the parents about their sexual life or their interaction or what they feel about the child. I don't ask the child anything, because the child has a right to his privacy. I interview the child separately and the parents separately, a completely different attitude. Some family therapy would concentrate on the interaction. I'm not dismissing it. It's not the way you work with institutions. You only analyze the process.

VH: You may be right. Would you talk about your paper on symbolism? I think it's so wonderful and so rich.

HS: Yes, I could. That's my lasting contribution to psychoanalysis, but it's very difficult to talk about it without the complete background of what you think of object relations. My interest was drawn in that way because the first thing you're hit by with a schizophrenic is the difficulty of communication. You know how psychiatrists speak of concrete thinking. To schizophrenics, everything is so concrete.

One of my patients came to the session giggling, and eventually I found out that he was embarrassed because he was making a stool in the workshop, and he thinks the word "stool" is like bringing me a stool. He went home; he didn't allow me to talk about anything that happened in the hospital because that would "bite off" the people who were there. Talking about them was like biting them. On the other hand, I had some artists in analysis, and with them, the inhibitions always had to do with the difficulty of symbolizations. I had a patient, whom I quote in my paper on aesthetics, say, "I cannot use the words because it's like biting them into bits." It sort of hit me very early. The conclusion I came to is that there is a whole gradation of symbol formation, the symbol being totally equated with the object, like with the patient I quote—he cannot play the violin because he cannot masturbate in public. Or a completely different use of symbols where you can use the words freely, paint the canvas, you don't commit suicide because you've killed one thousand people symbolically.

I related the change in symbol formation to the whole idea of object relations. In projective identification, a part of the self is objects. A symbol is a three-way thing: the object, the symbol, and the connection in the self between the symbol and the object. There are no such things as symbols in the world. Nothing is a symbol of anything except in the mind of a person. In projective identification, the object becomes the self, there is no difference between the object and the subject. In the depressive position, it becomes a completely different thing—the symbol isn't the object that you possess. But the symbol is something in your mind that replaces the missing object, like having a photograph of a person. You could have the photograph of the person and masturbate with it, you know, if you have it as a concrete object. You could be aware that the object is distant, but thought replaces it in a symbolic way. In that situation, it is like a precept of mourning, internalizing the object. Then it becomes something that you can use freely. It's a fantasy of your mind. You can feel guilty about symbolic actions too. You could feel very bad if you tear a photograph; you could feel that tearing a photograph is killing a person. Of course to the artist, symbolism is crucial. Art is the creation of symbols. Technically, concreteness is linked with what I said about acting in. Concrete things can only be acted in. Action by concrete projection cannot be communicated in.

VH: Can you go back to your patient who was very concrete, therefore unable to represent the object, and talk about where that meant he was in terms of his primary object relations?

HS: Oh, I would have said, in the past, in the "paranoid schizoid position"—now I would say he is in a "pathological development, a paranoid schizoid position." There is this whole work of Bion, container and contained, in which he says that when the child has favorable development he projects into the mother, and she lifts it from what he calls Beta to Alpha. The child reintrojects a container capable of the containing functions of Alpha elements, of symbolism.

VH: Then you would say that with your patient the mother has been unable to contain.

HS: Either that or he was too envious to bear containment; possibly it was a function of both. In the normal paranoid schizoid position, you have the patient on the couch, and the patient can only communicate by making you feel. You interpret it, and the words become the container. They can take it, but you find, always, that if any of that happens, they smash it up because they can't stand it. Today, I wouldn't say it's a regression to the paranoid schizoid position. I'd say regression to a pathological position. Mrs. Klein, in her paper on "Paranoid Schizoid Mechanism," used to speak of excessive projective identification, excessive anxiety, giving rise to pathological development. Bion refined it very much with his work on the container and the contained.

VH: You speak very little about the Kleinian tradition in America, or about American Kleinians.

HS: I would like Americans to read more. The French read, they read English, they read American, they read everybody. I would like people to discuss more clinical material and clinical detail, to think of the specificity of psychoanalysis.

VH: I wonder if you could tell me of other Kleinian traditions of therapy that are important to you?

HS: I could not dismiss other therapies. When we undertake psychoanalysis we undertake something very specific, and indeed the science of all psychoanalytic therapies depends on the science of psychoanalysis developing.

VH: Our world is changing rapidly. Since I was here last, only a month ago, the Berlin Wall has come down, Mandela has been freed in South Africa. Perhaps you see some changes in psychoanalysis, too?

HS: Yes, yes. Today, we had our convention about nuclear war. They said that one has to look at everything that changes—the Russian threat has gone. For instance, the American Ambassador to Russia said he was amazed traveling through Europe that one always thought nuclear weapons were necessary because of the Russian threat. Now, he finds there is no Russian threat yet the nuclear weapons go on, because people could not visualize the world without. If you look, the Russian threat has gone, yet the British budget on nuclear armament has probably increased 2% in real terms. Americans cut down conventional weapons, but their nuclear weapons, they are probably 300% increased. There are other reasons.

VH: Psychological ones?

HS: Everything is in a point of turmoil. The situation was based on a sort of paranoid, "We're the goodies! They're the badies!" What does a paranoid patient do when the threat is withdrawn? I think our problem today is much like a problem with a drug addict because it's an addiction to the bomb. When psychotic patients lose paranoid delusion and when they become better, first, the family says, "Stop the treatment now." Another issue: You must not deny the improvement because it's very real, but you must be aware of what doesn't change and what other forms it takes.

VH: What other forms do you think it's going to take?

HS: I don't know. Analytically, I think this is the point, the sort of schizophrenic fantasies may turn into manic triumph. "Hey, look at us with our nuclear weapons. We won." We can project and exploit them like the Third World—we're on top.

VH: Yes, but they're also saying, "Feed us, feed us."

HS: Yes, it's true. Who is winning the battle?

VH: Perhaps it's a psychological stalemate.

HS: The same is true of Eastern Europe. That's also a manic structure. "We" think we should be the big father and mother, and "they" should be the despicable children. We have them feed from us, rather than seeing what we're doing to ruin them, and not allowing them to feed themselves. The point is that the addiction to the nuclear weapon is ongoing. Can we turn that around? I don't know. At the moment the world is in disarray. Someone told me I had lost a cause, and I said, "I wish I had."

VH: It's an exciting time to live in.

HS: Well, at the nuclear convention, one speaker reminded us of the Chinese. Deliver us from living in "interesting times." I'll be speaking of nuclear issues in America in May. You see, this is where I came out of the analytic closet, because I think that analysts have a contribution to make, that we can't make sense of what goes on unless people are more aware.

VH: I'm sure that with the splitting that's going on—the affluent, powerful, good white people and the impoverished, angry, bad black people—you would have a great many pertinent things to say about racial issues.

HS: Yes, yes, I have views on them, but I don't think the psychoanalytical movement should be committed to political causes, however valid. I made an exception in the case of nuclear weaponry because I think, after all, it is a matter of survival. I do think that analysts could write papers on the causes of racial discrimination, and other social issues. I think the movement itself should take a stance on this kind of thing. On nuclear issues, the American analysts are very good, better than ours.

VH: Do you have any psychoanalytic views on the way in which we are spoiling and destroying this earth beneath us?

HS: (*Sadly*) Yeah, it's a vicious circle of greed and envy.

VH: And exploitation.

HS: Unfortunately, the governments make it legal. We destroy ourselves. Behind that is the death instinct, too. It's not only being sadistic to others, it's destroying ourselves in the process.

VH: There's a lot of destruction, and it's very scary.

HS: I once heard a very nice, lovely paper presented long ago by Phyllis Greenacre, on the oral and anal routes of our economic destruction, something like that. It was written years before pollution became a fashionable subject. Greenacre is an analyst I respect very much. A beautiful paper. Mother Earth, it interests me very much. Phyllis Greenacre did it before any political movement. Let us finish. I hope you've gotten what you want.

VH: Yes, I did. Thank you so much for your time. It was especially generous of you to give me an hour beyond what I had originally requested. It's been a rare privilege.

Note. This interview originally appeared in Hunter (1993).

Case Discussion

Hanna Segal, a Kleinian, shows particular interest in the patient's attacks upon the functions of the analyst. She points out that Roselyn identifies with her destructive, suicidal mother, creating a split between idealization and cruelty. She further states that the patient lacks a container and is afraid of sanity and the realization of her mad mother.

This consultation took place in Segal's office in her London apartment on December 30, 1989. Segal felt she could talk about what she saw in the material, but she felt that the point lies in what to interpret here and now.

I wondered how she would handle Roselyn's wish that I should be responsible for her life. Segal replied that she had already made a note about that. "You do them damage because you allow them to project into you their own self-preservative instincts."

I said, "I interpret it over and over again that she is making me the good one, the carrier of life, herself the bad one who wishes her death; that she renounces these parts; that she is putting them unto me."

Segal responded, "You must find out why she does it."

Segal asked me to present the case, and I gave a long summary. Segal began, "Here I cannot operate the way I run a supervision, because in a supervision I see the person every week. But what I do at the seminar I will do here. First, we discuss the case in general, as we have done, and now we go to the session. What has struck me in this account—and I'll ask you questions, and then we see if your detail material confirms what I have said—is that the strain on your countertransference must be terrible, isn't it? Anxiety, the constant fear of her suicide, your guilt. Now one thing that immediately comes to my mind—that child had a mother who made constant suicidal attempts. The way I see it is what she projects into you are her own experiences as a child, and that is why you feel so helpless.

Not because you feel that you are mother to a child so much, but that you are put into a position of a 2-, 3-, 4-year-old who undoubtedly must be guilty when the mother commits suicide and you are left thinking, 'What have I done?', and are unable to do anything about it. So you are constantly put into a position of having the responsibility put into you. Which puts you in a state of 'What can I do?' She is your patient. You can't be with her every minute of the day. You make a wrong step. I remember when you told me about this patient, you said if you did this or you didn't, you worry she will commit suicide. Now picture to yourself what a 2- or 3-year-old, whose mother repeatedly threatened suicide, would feel. So it is projection.

"What does one do? In the past, I would have interpreted a lot, as I am sure you did, and I'm sure it's true I would still do it; that all suicidal attempts are an identification with her mother, and her internal mother turns bad and wants to kill her. I'm sure you have taken all that up. But I would also take up whenever she puts you in this anxiety state: how now she identifies with her mother not only because of those internal reasons, but to take it up; 'You want me to feel what you felt when your mother tried to commit suicide'—feeling responsible, guilty, anxious, and feeling like a little child being unable to do anything about it. Does that ring any bells, this use of countertransference?"

I said, "Yes, it certainly does."

Segal continued, "I do a lot more lecturing than I would during normal supervision. I wait for things to come up during the session and show them. I would watch for countertransference. And then when she does that, she's in a dilemma. Because one of her hopes is that you will succeed, but also the other is the hope that you will fail—partly because she wants to communicate her own feelings, the hopelessness of separation. And the other is out of spite and revenge. Because if you succeed where she hasn't succeeded, then she becomes envious. That is very important because we think, 'With such a bad mother, what is to be envious about?' But it isn't true. There is always something to be envious about, particularly if you become a more effective mother that can take all the projection of her despair and survive it and help her. Then you've become an object of envy because you have created the separation that she couldn't."

I said, "She is childless because she felt a child would destroy her, or she would destroy the child."

Segal replied, "So, you see, if you manage to help your analytical child survive, then you become an object of great hope because she is doing all this destruction in the projected part of her, wanting to project it all into you, because you are big and strong, so maybe you can deal with that despair. But at the same time, you know that she could want to destroy you because of what an enviable object you could become if she could subject you to all that and you continue functioning. Here we come to technique; because there is something very interesting. Winnicott says the important thing for those patients is that the analyst should survive as the analyst; and he was right. But it is not enough to survive physically. Her mother survived physically. I think an analyst must survive as an analyst, and that means not being pushed out of one's stance. Once she puts you out of your stance, she has you involved in her system, and as an analyst, you haven't survived."

Transcription follows:

VH: There are special circumstances in this.

HS: Yes.

VH: Because of her migraines and because of her long therapy she has exclusions for any mental illness on her medical policy. If she has to be hospitalized, her only choice would be a state hospital.

HS: It's this kind of thing; I am just trying to say if this kind of thing influences you, then you have already lost your stance.

VH: Well, it certainly does influence you in terms of if you had to hospitalize, I wouldn't want to hospitalize; but if it had to be, it would devastate her.

HS: I know, but you see, she knows it, too. She knows it, too.

VH: Yes. If you had a call, someone who was not normally psychotic, a patient of yours, who was having a psychotic episode, you would always say take her to the hospital?

HS: No. No. It is also not so that I never come out of my room. If somebody rang me that a patient is suicidal and won't come to the session, I might go there. I'm thinking of something else in the episode when her house was burglarized. No, before the operation, you sat hand in hand. I cannot visualize myself going to the bedside.

VH: Her blood pressure had dropped dramatically.

HS: I know. . . . But the point is, if your eyes are on the psychoanalytical process, I think in the long run, the survival of your patient depends on your survival as an analyst. Now, I would probably go to the hospital in such a situation, but I wouldn't hold her hand. Anybody can hold her hand. I would try to interpret to her without coming out of "I am the analyst; you are the patient."

VH: To do that, I would have to physically create a false distance because when she saw me, both arms went out; she was just hysterical.

HS: There is an enormous lot of pressure. I don't want to be critical of what you've done, but it is, you see, important. What Bion has said is,

"An analyst is like a field commander, and he doesn't have to think very well; but he must think under pressure." And, of course, I can see that the pressure this patient submits you to is enormous, particularly with the other historical element. But this is what I think. She does everything to put into you the responsibility and make it impossible for you to fulfill your responsibility.

I agree very much with you that she lacks a container. But the real container is fundamental. This container is understanding. For instance, if you are able to analyze her projections into you, the inducing of the despair, particularly how you have now become the despairing child who can't bear separation, then she will experience the container in Bion's terms. You know what Bion's terms are? The child or patient projects into mother unbearable things. In a very concrete way. Where feelings and thoughts and pieces and parts of the self are now indistinguishable. This is all shot into you by acting in. Now the understanding converts what he calls Beta elements into Alpha elements. So for me, I work very much in the "now." You asked about the new developments in Kleinian thought. We are very much concerned with the containing function. But we see that the containment is in being able to contain the despair, the anxiety, to make sense of it. If you step out of your role and start doing things of another kind, we would think it fails in containing. It means you feel overpowered by her projections and react to the Beta elements by giving her a Beta element.

VH: Certainly, in the early years when there were many dramatic threats of suicide, I would raise the question of hospitalization, but she said that prevented her from trusting me. So now we have an agreement: I won't suggest "hospitalize" again.

HS: I would never accept this agreement. I would say, "But how could you trust me if you think that when you actually try to commit suicide I wouldn't take steps to prevent it?" After all, she doesn't become psychotic. That means that you work well, that you contain it.

VH: Yes, but sometimes I've seen her 7 days a week to contain her.

HS: One patient, before starting, kept asking the analyst, "What would you do if I break down?" He came to me for a consultation. I said, "In your place I would say, 'If you break down and become a danger to others or to yourself, then I would hospitalize you.' " The analyst followed this advice. And suddenly, this patient, who made a condition of the treatment not to be hospitalized, became relieved. The patient's anxiety went down, and he simply said, "Okay," and they went on. His anxiety went down, and he said, "Okay." So one has to play it by ear. Never say, "Never," but I never promise a patient that I won't mention "hospital." I mention whatever is appropriate in the situation.

VH: The way she was doing it was making me terrified, and I needed to get distance.

HS: That is right. It is your life. It's your own. But then you don't follow the saying when you go to the hospital to hold her hand or when you worry about the financial affairs and who pays for her hospital.

VH: Or what it would do to her career?

HS: Or what it would do to her career.

VH: I don't think she'll have to be hospitalized.

HS: I was going to say I don't think so. Because this patient has quite a lot of ego strength, considering her pain.

VH: And she has built more.

HS: And she cannot make you responsible for her career. She can only make you responsible for her analysis. So long as she thinks she can blackmail you, and there's a strong hysterical element in that, she will use it. She is a clever cookie. That is one general thing. I don't want to persecute you with it. I just want to show how my attitude would be. Something else comes to my mind. I have a manic depressive patient who had a previous analysis. And his analyst said something I found very telling. It was the first holiday. My patient tells me and he told the analyst, "Even if I were to cut my wrists on your doorstep, you wouldn't stop your holiday." And the analyst, doctor-like, said, "I wouldn't stop my holiday." He said, "You would let me die bleeding." The doctor said, "Yes, but don't you think I would stop long enough to bind the wound and to call an ambulance?" And then the patient became calm.

Occasionally with those very psychotic patients, we have to say things that are not completely an interpretation but would state a certain reality. You are not an unfeeling crone that she could kill herself under your feet, and you do nothing. Nor are you blackmailed to give up your private life to her. You would do what was necessary. I was very impressed by this previous analyst. And this manic-depressive patient is the one patient with whom I had to take an action because he went into a high manic state. An elderly colleague of his went to visit him and asked, "Is there anything I can do?" And my patient said, "Yes, take me to my session." So this elderly colleague brought him, and I was in a session with another patient, and he was 20 minutes early. The manic patient was playing absolute havoc. There was no question he had to be hospitalized—he was in a very, very high manic state. So I interrupted the session, took them in the waiting room and then continued the session with this other patient. But in the meantime, fortunately, there was someone at home. I told them to call a cab to take the patient to the hospital. And when the cab came, I told him he had to go to the hospital; and he said,

"I'll go if you take me." And there was no way I could arrange it differently. I was afraid for the elderly colleague who was frail. The patient came out, and the cab was a private cab. And he said, "It's not a taxi." I said, "I'll take you." I canceled the next patient and took him to the hospital. But the moment he was in the hospital, I left him. I went out. So in a way, I did with him what the other analyst said. I did the minimum necessary, not to endanger the elderly colleague and the patient himself.

But I can sympathize with you because these hysterical psychotics, or the combination of psychosis with hysteria, are terrible because you never know how seriously to take them. If you interpret it as a manipulation, which it is, they become suicidal. If you take the real psychosis but don't interpret the manipulator, they twist you round their finger.

VH: She has manipulated me even through others. For instance, her husband and the doctor called, and another time the priest and husband called me, and they said they would feel very much better if I came. I went.

HS: I wouldn't give two hoots whether the priest sleeps better or not!

VH: What do you mean?

HS: You said the priest rang and said, "I'm a priest and would feel very much better if you came." Now, I wouldn't care two hoots if the priest feels better or not. He can go to his confessor. It's the priest's worry, her husband's worry, because they all know they have a nice, big, strong woman—they say, "Let Hunter worry, why should I worry?" Once you are drawn into their system, you are not you. You are not the you who analyzes. I see the pressures you are under. I wanted you to see theoretically how part of the pressure is to put you in the same impossible situation as she was in as a child—and secondly, to attack your analytical functioning because that links with something else, you see. I was thinking she is also holding onto her madness, that she is very afraid of sanity. And that links with my other point.

VH: All the pain of what she didn't get?

HS: The pain, it includes everything, the pain of what she didn't get, the realization of her mother's madness. After all, the child always projects into mother, and if the mother is a good mother, you know, she responds sanely. If the mother is a mad mother, the child always thinks he drove the mother mad.

VH: That is right. She thinks it was her fault.

HS: And she constantly projected that.

VH: That is what the mother frequently said.

HS: Of course. Of course.

VH: Always said.

HS: The question of love is this. Because in the Rappaccini story it is love that kills. Now I think that her position is something like that. I think that the little people have to do with her fantasy of destroying, to her fantasy of the uterus experience, not the reality, but the fantasy. I tell you why I think it is connected with that. She has the split between something totally idealized or totally cruel. And so long as that split exists, it is all right, she survives. Now, little people are also that because they go back into the ideal world. And she knows that. But as long as she keeps this split, she somehow survives.

VH: She said she was hiding pieces of herself.

HS: That is right. Hiding pieces of herself. If she comes together and recovers her love for her mother, that is where she is afraid of being suicidal, because she would be exposed to all the pain—the pain of seeing how ill mother is. The incapacity as a small child to make a separation. So one of the reasons she attacks your functioning—it is partly because she is envious—is that you've got sanity and she doesn't. You can create a healthy child if she becomes a healthy child, which she can't. But the other is her fear of sanity. If she becomes sane, which takes looking really at the self, at the destruction which she brought about, then she is afraid of being suicidal. Her fear of sanity is to see what damage she has done, not only to her mother, in her mind, but to her self. This is a very dangerous point in the recovery of real psychotics—of people who manage to survive with the hysterical defenses that when things come together, that is when there is real danger of suicide. So to obtain sanity is to get in touch with her grieving and her guilt, which can be unbearable. And that is where the real danger will be. But then there would be much less blackmail and persecution, and you would be able to cope with her. Now, before we get to the session and that sort of free association on my part, which I wouldn't do in a supervision, I want to tell you why I said what I did about the little people. Do you know the Piper story?

VH: The Pied Piper story?

HS: The Pied Piper story, the little babes going in. I think that this story is about the whole world inside mother's body. Because in the dream, she describes the Rappaccini thing. The Pied Piper story gives a horrible picture of a bad mother who is full of children who haven't come out—so both the good mother and the bad mother are filled with these babies. I would say that the little people and the Pied Piper are idealized equivalents of the horrible mother with the horrible children, because that bad mother is full of projection. She is full of small children fighting and being horrible inside her. She would get inside you and manipulate you to become this ideal womb in which the babies play, but she will not come and, as it were, take in the analytical food because that exposes her to the depressive position. I wanted to ask you about babies. She had no siblings?

VH: No.

HS: That is very important because she must have a fantasy then, obviously, that her mother was always pregnant. All the little children were inside her, and yet there was never a child. So she must also have the fantasy of having destroyed all the babies.

VH: She feels the mother somehow sadistically failed to destroy her along with the others.

HS: Yes, but that is keeping it on the destructive mother. What about her fantasies of her pregnant mother and provoking her? What does she know about your other patients? Does she even meet them?

VH: No. She has made fast friends with one of my colleagues' patients.

HS: If you look for it, you will see: She is full of fantasies—with the other patient, or whether you have children, or whether you are pregnant. You are a corpulent person, and she may see you as permanently pregnant. You are paradise. People who are very unhappy when they are babies have fantastic fantasies about how marvelous it is in the womb. Maybe everything good is in the womb. You know that is where babies are happy—little children who play and are never born and exposed to awful things.

VH: Whenever I say anything about her wanting mothering, she'll pop right up off that couch and look at me and say, "I didn't need a mother; I don't need a mother, and you are not my mother!"

HS: She is right in one way. See, you must remember there is a very psychotic element to a patient like that. You never say, "I am your mother." You can't even say, "I am like your mother" or do the mother's function. That would make her think that you don't know the difference between a mother and an analytical function. I wouldn't even interpret her concrete thinking but only her being afraid that you don't know the difference between being an analyst and a mother.

VH: So interpret it as a projection.

HS: Yes. Do you know Schreber? There is a magnificent passage in Schreber (1903) in which he complains, "The trouble with God is that He doesn't understand metaphors. He thinks that when I shit on people I actually do it with my feces." She projects her own concreteness into you. She gets panicky when you imply, "You needed a mother," or "Look for a mother in me." She thinks, "My God, my analyst is mad. She doesn't know the difference between a mother and an analyst." She continually pushes you not to act as an analyst but as a mother, but won't accept it if you do. I would also point that out to her. I would keep a very close eye on the concreteness and the projection of concreteness, and on her feeling that she has managed to make you think that an analytical function is to hold her hand. We need also to consider that you also need to represent a paternal function that she lacks. You are not only the maternal containing function, you are also the paternal interpreter, and part of the paternal function is to sort out mutual projective identifications between mother and child. You see, she thinks she is right inside mother driving her mad. But mother is right inside her, driving her mad. What is missing is a third factor, like a father's penis, saying, "You're there, mother's there; you're not getting inside mother. Mother is not getting inside you." And I emphasize that paternal function.

(*Continuing on about the paternal function*) Roselyn paid heavy in the dysfunction of the father. Now you see that is very important—what you said about the father, because, for instance, the kind of interpretation one could make would be something like this. Now you're back in a situation in which you feel you are both the child with the bad thoughts and the mother who wants to knock them out of the head. And you wonder if the analyst will be like your father—walking out and not doing anything to stop it. What you want me to give is an interpretation that would be like a perfect father saying, "You don't do it to one another. Stop it." That's what I mean about the father in the transference. Because you are left with this patient who is both the child and the mother. They both are against one another. When she says, "I am angry with my mother," that gets us nowhere. You know it's something else. What you could say and what you're missing is, "Like your father, who walked out of the room when you needed somebody to say something that would stop the child and the mother doing that to one another."

So when she goes mad into the other thing, you can interpret, for instance, that when she behaves in this and that way, she is afraid she wiped out your function as the one who interprets and brings thoughts out. Now she is left with you, the mother, as an analyst who she thinks is as mad as her mother and herself. But in your mind, the third person always exists. That is why I gave you this little book, *The Oedipus Complex Today: Clinical Implications* (Britton, Feldman, & O'Shaughnessy, 1989).

VH: To add the father?

HS: In very primitive situations, the role of the father is that factor which stops the endless thing of mutual projective identification. Because that's what goes on in the madness, isn't it? She drives mother mad, projects into mother her own mischievous ideas, and mother is mischievous and reprojects into her endless "You put it into me/I put it into you." A breath of sanity with something third, which is your interpretation. Let's say the maternal function gets interpreted because the father can be very containing too. And the mother can be very order-producing. But basically the breast contains, and the nipple feeds. But that experience, of on one hand having those things projected into you, then making a little order, and the containing—the interpretive function is the analytic function as well.

We talked about the recent death of Roselyn's father. Segal said that Roselyn hadn't dealt with the death of her father.

HS: When you remind her of that, she gets into a really psychotic state about the mother. Now, I think she is telling you, the diarrhea and constipation started because she felt that, after her father's death, now everything was in turmoil inside her. There was no father, no mother, only diarrhea and constipation; and she felt responsible, and she couldn't cope with it. I think that the disarray of the house and inability to cope with it is the same as the diarrhea and constipation. And then, when she speaks and you interpret to her, which is a good interpretation, she says, "Mother won't die; mother won't die; mother won't go away"—I would link that up. And you could possibly have linked that with 2 days you were away. She herself knows the connection. She is not as mad as she seems. But she seems to know no difference between herself and facts. And she thinks that this fantasy about her mother means that her mother is there. I would very much emphasize that. When I read the material, I thought she was afraid that you, also, don't know the difference between thoughts and fact. I would link it with her keeping her father's ashes. Because maybe she feels that having her mother's ashes is better, after all, than having thoughts. Because then you speak about attacking her mind, which is true. Because the point is, it's not her mother, as you so beautifully interpreted, that has no tense. It's a part of her that has no tense. But part of having no tense means no separateness and no separation.

VH: I am sure no one else ever hears this material.

HS: That is right. She's very split. There is a more healthy part operating. But, I would at some point also pick up, "When you say your mother has no past tense, it is something in you that has no tense." And I'd say, "You process a bad mother who exists in a thought. Tie the mother who is not there to the thought."

Segal then talked about a patient of her own. "There is also a constant testing out. I had a patient who was very good at that. She was also a borderline, was a very, very psychotic paranoid individual, and she would test me to the utter limit. But usually with sadism. If I withstood and could interpret and could contain it, then it meant to her, 'Well, I haven't done my worst.' So she tried me; that's why it will take such a long time. If you feel that you are succeeding in containing, then she feels she hasn't really communicated to you the despair of the child who says, 'I can't.' I'm not saying you should have done this or that, but I am trying to make you aware of the level on which you would reach her, and the concreteness, and the projections. Because so far you interpret the content perfectly correctly—you know her fear of her mother, her refusing to deal, her fantasies, but not the actual psychotic mechanism: how she deals with this. So she says, 'Yes,' and then she goes on, 'She wants to die; she feels so bad,' and so on.

"You are interpreting too generally. I think if you need a fast interpretation such as, 'There's something awful that the child and mother are doing to one another, and you want an analyst to say something that will disentangle it. Who's who?' Then stop. I think that might have got through. Or I would say, 'It seems to me that at the moment, you are enacting awful things that happened between a child and her mother, one having bad thoughts, the other wanting to knock those bad thoughts out.' And you feel you surrendered and so won because she does it to herself. But you would want an analyst to say something clarifying like a father who would step in and say, 'Stop doing it to one another.' I would take up, you see, not just the anger and the longing—those are feelings she's hardly aware of—but the complete entanglement of the two people who'd won. And even after that interpretation, if she went on and on, I would say, 'I would take it as a castration of you.' I would say, 'And it seems to me that you want to communicate to me that I am useless. Nothing I say or do will stop what happened between the part of you that's the child and the part of you that is mother.' I would interpret it simply as a castration attack or maybe, later, as, 'You want me to feel myself as a helpless, hopeless child who cannot stop what goes on. Like you couldn't stop your mother's madness.' Because I think you're really very, very in touch with her, but more with the content of the various fantasies than with the real psychotic way in which they express themselves."

Dr. Segal asked to hear a current hour.

HS: Now obviously, you have gotten through the psychotic thing because she started talking much more quietly, and she admits it was difficult dealing with the house because she doesn't know what's good, what's bad, and this is confusion. I would take from that that as much as she hates to think it, part of her reason for holding on to her mother and father, she is looking for something good. But she's afraid that it's combined with such pain that she can't bear it without going through the fantasy and the reality because what is the difference? It hurts just the same. And when you gave her the good interpretation that you thought, "I didn't want to have it in my office," she sort of protested that because she obviously doesn't like the idea that you want to contain it, that you can contain it. You give her this interpretation that when she was too little, it was too much for her as a child. Now we are two grownups, we can do it. And she responds by saying, "I'm so stupid, yuck, so humiliated." So, I would take on one hand she feels there is so much pain and horror, but she does need you to keep it in your mind, and on the other hand she finds it too humiliating that you should be able to do what she can't and immediately dismisses it as, "Oh, I'm just being silly." That's where the attack on you is, you see! After a very good interpretation, that she didn't want you to hold it in your office, all that's in your mind—that's a very good interpretation. She immediately states, "How silly can one be to sit on a staircase? How silly, yuck! Me? Good grief, it is vital to be the patient of you."

VH: She has good ego strength that you can see at times.

HS: I know, but this is part of the madness, you see. This is part of her madness.

VH: This is the part of her trying to keep me from helping her get well.

HS: Exactly. At that point, not out of fear of pain or anything, out of sheer envy. Sheer narcissistic need. To be so sure that she can contain something you can't. She seems narcissistic to me, so shrewd that she can contain—

VH: You seem to be using this in the same way that "object relations people" use fear of intimacy.

HS: Very broad—the fear of intimacy.

VH: But to me what you are saying sounds very broad too.

HS: Yes, well now they are about different things. One is about the fear of intimacy which we spoke about before the fear of love. Because it is love that will mobilize guilt and mourning and horror. Here, I'm speaking of something very narcissistic. It is unbearable to her that you should be able to do what she can't. There are other fears of intimacy, of being swallowed up, with the devouring that is projected into mother.

VH: I am being destroyed if she depends on me?

HS: Yes. But you know you can contain it. Suddenly she is very sane and very grande dame. How infuriating. That is my point. It is not all one thing. There is always a fear of a proper good object relation: either the fear you will let her down, or the fear she will damage you, or her fear of her own depressive pain. All that comes. But they are very different aspects, you see. She is afraid of love because that mobilizes guilt. With the terribly traumatized children, it's hard to get their pain because there is much pain, persecution, fear there; as soon as things begin to get better, she resists. I had a patient who had a very destroyed and destructive mother. . . . And now, she's just as ill as her mother was. Tremendous anger, ambition, always a rival to me to bring her down; and then she says, "You know, I didn't really know about anything. Everything was so overlaid by my mother's depression, my guilt, my fear. I didn't think there was anything to be envious of." But, of course, it isn't true. In a way, the mother is to be envious of the paradise of the Pied Piper. But it's only when they begin to feel how much analysis helps that the other side comes. Now, that patient had an association that she never pulls the widow's weeds from the garden and wondered why. And the conflict was very clear. It was before a holiday, and she would much rather kick me as a horrible depressed widow, persecuting her, demanding her presence, all these things, than let me go on holiday and become the oedipal couple. So there is the reality of the bad mother, but there is also the hanging onto that picture because it serves certain other purposes, you know, later, defensively.

Frances Tustin

Mrs. Tustin is probably the most well known of those clinicans who treat autism. She has written several books on autism and made numerous contributions regarding patients with autistic "bits."

Frances Tustin has contributed much to our knowledge and treatment of autistic children. Now retired, except for supervision, her fourth book on autism, *The Protective Shell in Children and Adults* (1990), had just been published. Other books include *Autism and Childhood Psychosis* (1972), *Autistic States in Children* (1992), and *Autistic Barriers in Neurotic Patients* (1986). She has also published 20 papers regarding autism. Mrs. Tustin has lectured in Great Britain, the United States, Italy, France, Monaco, Scotland, and Ireland. She has been invited to Australia, Canada, Argentina, and Brazil, but her failing health has made these long journeys impossible for her.

I had arrived in London on February 11, 1990, giving myself a day to organize before our first planned interview. I was surprised to hear the phone ring in my hotel room. It was Mrs. Tustin. With what I was to learn was her characteristic generosity, she called to tell me the route to her home and departure times for Amersham. She had arranged for her housekeeper to meet me at the station. She was only worried, she said, that her poor health might interfere with our interview.

She began our first session by saying that, despite setbacks to her health, wonderful things had been happening to her. She asked if I had seen the little book, *The Celebration of the Life and Works of Frances Tustin* (Winnicott Studies, 1989). She was delighted about its production by the Winnicott Society and proudly showed me her copy, bound in burgundy leather and stamped in gold. During our last session, she gave me a copy, inscribed.

Other honors she had recently received included being asked to contribute to a television program called "Key Figures in Psychoanalysis in England" to mark the 50th anniversary of Freud's death. Later, she showed me a 1984 letter from the British Psychoanalytic Society inviting her to become an honorary affiliate. The Classical Freudians, Kleinians, and Independents had voted unanimously in favor of her acceptance. She was pleased to be part of such a profession, she said, because she felt psychoanalysis makes important contributions to psychological knowledge.

I was somewhat surprised to learn that in England the prevailing view was that autistic children were untreatable. I asked her about that—and we began the formal interview.

Interview

FRANCES TUSTIN: It goes like this: The behaviorists say, "Autistic children cannot be treated successfully." I say, "I've treated some of them, and some of them have got better." Upon which they say, "Then they can't have been autistic" (*laughs*). Upon which I say, "But they were all diagnosed, apart from one, by Dr. Mildred Creak." Dr. Mildred Creak, who had an international reputation as a diagnostician of psychotic children, was the consultant psychiatrist at our well-known hospital for children in Great Osmond Street. When the questioners hear that the children I've treated have all been diagnosed as autistic by Dr. Mildred Creak, they are lost for words. The one who wasn't diagnosed by Dr. Creak was seen by Anni Bergman, who was Margaret Mahler's senior therapist. He was seen in this country when he was 3. Anni Bergman said that he was the worst autistic she'd ever seen. Many years after he had terminated his work with me, he wrote to me to thank me for "releasing him from the prison of autism," as he put it. It was a normal sort of letter from a university student who wanted a copy of one of my books. It's so generous that he thought of writing. He's doing well.

Many people, when they first see them, think that autistic children are impossible to treat because they don't talk, and they're so stiff and so withdrawn. They think the schizophrenicky ones will be treatable because they're sort of outgoing and they're warm and they're cuddly. But, in fact, they're much more difficult to treat—the schizophrenicky ones—because they're all over the place, a bit of them is in the table, a bit of them is in the chair, a bit of them is flying about on the ceiling. To get all these scattered bits together is very difficult. Whereas the autistic children, in a way, are much more intact, they're split into two halves, they're polarized. They're much more simple, whereas the schizophrenicky children are really very complicated, very diverse, very spread around. I find the autistic children much easier to treat than these schizophrenicky children. And I've found that other people have had the same experience, for example, the people at Rome University.

VIRGINIA HUNTER: You've talked about the need for parents to become aware they have something they can give to the autistic child and that they need to establish some sort of authority.

FT: I've been thinking a lot about the parents, particularly in my last paper. I've come to the conclusion that what has happened with the parents that I've seen and supervised is that many of the mothers have been extremely depressed. And because of that they've been in a state of pathological fusion with their baby. It's not that there is a normal autistic stage such as Margaret Mahler has proposed. That view was commonly held in the United States. I followed Margaret Mahler because she'd had such a lot of experience. However, such infant observers as Stern, Trevarthen, and Brazelton agree that from the word "go" the infant is alert and questioning and that they don't go through a primary autistic stage. I know that Margaret Mahler, in the last lecture that she gave in Paris when she was 80—I think it was just before she died—said she no longer held the view that there was this autistic stage in infancy.

I can understand why Margaret Mahler said there was an autistic stage. What I've seen is that in the cases I've treated, in early infancy, the mother and child had been in a state of fusion, but this was pathological, it wasn't a normal stage. The normal infant has phases of being differentiated to some extent, from the very beginning of life and has flickering awareness of the outside world. But in early infancy, because of the mother's depression, the mother and the later autistic child cling to each other. However, other infants can have a depressed mother but they don't become autistic. I think the child who becomes autistic has a depressive tendency. They feel vulnerable and seek the mother's protection, but this means that there's no space between the mother and the child.

VH: And that has very catastrophic consequences.

FT: Yes. If there's no space between the mother and the child, the children don't develop symbolic activities. They don't have memories because you only develop these symbolic things if you have a space between yourself and the mother and you have to do something about it. When she goes away, you miss her. This stimulates the making of a picture of the mother—a memory of the mother—something symbolic of the mother, and so forth. Thus, such fused children's cognitive and emotional development is very hampered. In infancy, mother and child were in this state of fusion and then suddenly something happened, or a series of things happened, that made them painfully aware of their bodily separateness. It's different things in different cases that do it.

VH: How is it different between the psychotic and the autistic child in the scenario that you're describing?

FT: Ah yes, thank you! What I've said applies to the autistic child. The more schizophrenicky child has experienced separateness from the mother. Mahler calls it a symbiotic psychosis, and I agree with her. In symbiosis there is a space between mother and child. They're not fused. They've developed to a state in which they are aware of their bodily separateness. They have used all sorts of ways to dilute the experience. One of these is confusion, so that the sharpness of the experience is modified. Their awareness is foggy and dimmed. But they have a confused awareness of separateness. Autistic children are different. Until they have the traumatic experience of awareness of their bodily separateness, they experience the mother as a limb, as a part of their body, or as a protective skin. And when they experience their bodily separateness, that is, when they are aware of it, suddenly, sharply, after their pathological state of fusion, they feel skinned alive, shorn of their skin, or they feel they've lost a supporting limb. The autism is a reaction to protect them from this terrible sense of having lost a part of their body.

VH: It's a terrible feeling of loss of something.

FT: Yes. And they're always trying to get that something back. They take your hand to open the door. They're always trying to get extra bits of their bodies that they feel they've lost. They're always wanting to be supported. For them, awareness of bodily separateness was a trauma, it wasn't just something mild and bearable. It might be a series of traumas. Before this, there was no relationship between mother and child. (It's not a relationship when they're just merged and fused together.) The contact with the mother was felt to be broken utterly; it was excruciating for both of them, agonizing.

VH: And this was in some sense, conscious?

FT: In one paper I said that the autistic child has experienced an agony of consciousness. They became distressingly aware of their separateness from the mother in a sudden and traumatic way. Neither of them could repair their sense of traumatic disconnection. Neither of them could do it.

Recently somebody in London sent me an article about an exhibition in Switzerland of Henry Moore's sculptures. The person who sent it to me said, "I think you'll see that this touches on your work." How right she was! Moore's sculptures show that he understood a great deal about what the autistic children have taught me. This is particularly so with his last great work. The photograph of Moore's last great sculpture, "Mother and Child: Block Seat," will be on the cover of my new book, *The Protective Shell in Children and Adults* (1990). The article describes it thus:

> The mother is seated. One of her arms is like the arm of an upholstered chair on which the child balances. The two features which the sculptor possesses are elsewhere, they're not on the sculpture. One is the nipple of her left breast which does not stand out, but is a hole, like a mouth of a bottle. And the other is a protrudence on the child's face which is like an inverted stopper for that hole, a stanch for that wound, a lie for that nourishment. (Berger, 1989, pp. 143–144)

They're both wounded, they're both damaged people, both mother and child. The article continues, "In Henry Moore's last great work the mouth has become the mother's nipple." I'll show you.

The work is expressive of what I've been writing about. There's a black hole, there's a child all swathed, trying to make a connection with that hole. The protrudence that replaces the child's mouth would fit into that hole, but then that's not a proper functional connection. It's an autistic object, as it were. The mouth has become functionless, it's not sucking. It's got this protrudence instead of a mouth. The only way they can connect is by this protrudence. It blocks that empty hole on the mother. It's not a sucking, functional connection, it's a blocking connection, and that's what autism is—it's a blocked state. Joyce McDougall has written about what she calls "The Cork Child" who, she says, is used to fill the hole of the depressed mother's loneliness and emptiness.

VH: It's amazing, isn't it?

FT: It's moving. So confirming to me that I was on the right lines because Moore didn't know anything about what I wrote. He's done it absolutely from his own experience. I think that perhaps he himself had quite a big autistic bit. Many of the autistic children, when they come out of their autism, are artistic or musical. I think they may be the artists of our generation. There's one thing I've left out. In that scenario of the mother and child being over-close, the father is often absent, either geographically, because of his work, or emotionally absent. And so the father's influence is missing, and this is a great loss because, as Margaret Mahler has said, metaphorically, "The father cuts the umbilical cord."

A number of different situations can give rise to autism. But the central situation is that both mother and child feel wounded, vulnerable, and at risk, and they do what they can about it. The child wraps him- or herself around with lovely sensations such as "autistic sensation objects" and "autistic sensation shapes." The mother develops her own form of protection. Some of the mothers I have seen are always on committees and such-like things. These give them a sort of shell. They're trying to keep alive.

VH: Do you mean manic defenses?

FT: Absolutely, the manic defense has a core of autism. They're trying to survive, and they want an almost impossible survival because this traumatic separation of their bodies has felt worse than death. It's made them have a terrible fear of death and dying. For them, death is not a normal, natural process. For them, death is falling into a black hole of nothingness. And so they are very frightened children and very frightened mothers.

VH: Would you assume the mothers themselves had inadequate parenting and lots of missing structures?

FT: Probably it goes back and back to defective parenting, yes, sadly. But in a way we can't do anything much about those past generations, but we can perhaps do something about this generation.

VH: What works with these children?

FT: They're quite a handful, these children. When I worked at the Putnam Center in Boston, Massachusetts, which was then a treatment center for autistic children, I went into their homes and helped to look after the children. And I don't know how the mothers managed it. So they do need somebody else. I found that the cases of mine that went best were where the mother had employed a nanny or a mother's helper or something like that.

VH: When I was at Reiss–Davis, Rudolf Ekstein had a unit for autistic children, and the children were there most of the day.

FT: Autistic children are frightened of groups, they're terrified. Somebody from Italy used to come for supervision to see me, and she had two autistic children and another that wasn't autistic. She suddenly decided she'd have a little group of three. It was dreadful. It was agony for these children. They were frightened; they're very frightened of groups. I think if they have a one-to-one situation in a unit, and each child has his or her own person, then they feel protected. They can go around in the unit and do a few things together, for example, perhaps eat together. But they are with their own person.

If you go out to the little village where I worked, you'll see my therapy room. Of course, I worked in London for many years and had ordinary consulting rooms, but the consulting room I'm most fond of is this one which I had in a little village called Lee Common. It had been a shed for ponies. It made a most inviting children's therapy room. It was like a den. The parents used to sit in the summer house just across the way, which had heating and everything. You'll be horrified at this, but my husband used to walk about in the garden and they would come out and talk to him and tell him all sorts of useful and interesting things.

VH: It was an important human contact for them, I'd think.

FT: Well, he wasn't a professional, but he was a distinguished looking senior man, and they used to tell him most useful things about the child. And then I would also see them every so often. When they wanted to see me, I would see the parents whilst my husband took the children to a field. In one case there was a sister as well—not autistic, and younger. My husband used to take the two children up to the field. This was up the road from our cottage, and there was a swing and a slide. They used to play there whilst I talked to the parents. It was all very unconventional, but I think when you're experienced you can do a few unconventional things. It worked very well. It didn't seem to me to confuse the transference situation. The family used to drive down at the weekend from a town in the north of England. They'd bring the child to me. After his session they would go on to London where they had relatives. They would spend the night with the relatives and then drive back on the Sunday morning, so that the child could have his session and then drive home. Towards the end of the treatment, they bought a caravan which they left in a field in the next village to where I lived. They had a country weekend in the caravan. They had bikes, and they would bicycle up the hill to the village where I lived for the child to have his treatment.

Being in the country meant that the seasons became important. For example, the child, as he began to talk, would say it was "daffodil season." Or it was "trees-coming-out season." In the autumn there were the chestnuts and sycamore trees. He used to bring a bag of these things that he had picked up on the road. The therapy became part of the natural scene, and it was the most natural therapy that I've ever done. It was really enjoyable for both of us and for the parents.

We had a swimming pool that my husband had made. They didn't go in as a rule. However, one very, very hot day, when they arrived absolutely dripping with sweat, they asked if they could use the pool. I said, "Of course," and they all had a swim. They didn't impose. They never had it again. So it was a natural sort of therapy. In a way I think you have to make the most of the possibilities you've got and be willing to be a bit flexible.

VH: I'm interested in the objects you used with autistic children. Each child had a little group of play toys of his own?

FT: Each child had his or her own drawer in which the toys were kept.

VH: What did you put in it?

FT: Very simple things. I put a family, you know, mother, father, children, and baby.

VH: Little plastic toys?

FT: They were made of pipe cleaners. I didn't have too many. A giraffe is very important, an elephant, and a horse, and a cow, and sheep. I always used to have a humming top. I don't know why, but it seemed to be very meaningful to these children because it hummed and it whirled round and round. Also, I think, a jack-in-the-box might be useful.

VH: But wouldn't that frighten them?

FT: Well, after a bit they'd get used to being frightened. You'd be there to talk about it with them. The thing would jump out unexpectedly, and I'd say, "I think when you were a little baby something happened a bit like that to you. You had such a shock. You thought you were all nice and warm and cozy with mummy, and suddenly you went all cold, and you found your body was separate and mummy was separate, and it was horrible." I found that to dramatize things helped a lot.

VH: It's lovely to hear you talk about what you would be saying to a child.

FT: Some of my colleagues are very doctrinaire, and they would say that you mustn't dramatize, because it puts too much of you into the situation. Well, that might be true for other patients, but autistic children are different. I used to stamp my feet and say, "Oh, you felt so angry," and I used to do it for them because they couldn't do it for themselves.

VH: Because they haven't got the words?

FT: They haven't got the emotions. It would help them to feel that it was all right to have feelings and that you could express them dramatically without the whole world falling down. The roof still stayed on. I found it was most helpful to dramatize things.

VH: What do you do when they take soft, fluid, runny things from their bodies and elsewhere and rub them on to you?

FT: That's an "autistic shape," an "autistic sensation shape." I would say, "You know, I think you're wanting to make lovely, smooth things that make you feel quiet and peaceful." They're like tranquilizers, really. "They make you feel all quiet and calm. You were feeling a bit worried and a bit churned up inside. If you feel as if you've got these lovely soft things, it makes you feel all right. But I'd rather you didn't do them on me. You do it because perhaps you want to feel that we're joined together. But we're not really, you know. My body's separate from your body. But you can do it over there, and I understand." I would talk quietly, in a calming sort of way. They would begin to feel settled down. I find that the hypnotherapists have tapes that are used for relaxation. It is the same sort of idea. I think this using of their saliva to make shapes is their attempt at relaxing and tranquilizing themselves. I would let them do it on me for a bit. But then if I found I didn't like it or it was upsetting me, I would say, "You know, I would rather you didn't do it on me." When I first began treating autistic children, I used to say all the stock interpretations. It didn't cut any ice because these children are different from any other children that we see. They are blocked, and the only way you can unblock them is to help them to use things for their proper purpose, for example, to use toys properly and not in a wayward way.

VH: You certainly have to improvise, to try what will work.

FT: If you play it by ear, and say what you sense is going on, not using stereotyped interpretations, you're better off. A psychoanalyst whom I supervised had a little boy who was frightened of having his hair washed and very frightened of the shower. The psychoanalyst brought out interpretations which are very valid for some patients, but which were not valid for this boy; they were all about his mind and that sort of thing. I suggested that he was afraid that his skin was going to be washed away—or afraid that his hair was going to be washed away. He was frightened that he was going to lose his protective covering. The physician came back the next month and said, "It was amazing. The child immediately responded and began to play. He came and sat on my knee and let me stroke his hair." It's just a common sense thing, a simple thing. We've become so clever that we don't think of the natural, normal things. These children have had this terrible experience of separateness. They felt they were shorn of a skin. They felt they were being skinned alive. They're always frightened of being skinned alive. Thus, the shower, the hair washing was terrifying for the little boy. And, of course, going to the loo is frightening also because they're afraid they'll drop down the hold.

VH: Any loss is terrifying. Do you think this is because they felt that the mother and their skin were the same?

FT: Oh yes, they felt joined. That's right, they were one skin and one body. Yes, then they felt wrenched apart and felt wounded. This sense of being hurt was compounded because they felt that the mother couldn't help them because she was so wounded too. It's a terrible incredible situation when you really think about it. If you think of the people who bark at the children and do terrible things to children who have this awful, agonizing situation at the base of their being, it makes you quail. They do it with good intentions and work very hard at it, yet it's all so misguided.

VH: And then the parents are involved too, they're supposed to follow up and reinforce these behaviors.

FT: That's right.

VH: Then, there's an even more toxic thing going on there too.

FT: That's right. Instead of saying to the mother, "Take him on your knee and stroke him and stroke his skin if he feels a little bit upset."

I know that these children don't like you to touch them. However, gradually they'll let you touch them. You don't do it too much. But you can help the mother to do quite lovely things, mothering things.

VH: As the therapist, how do you handle the touching?

FT: Well, I don't know, I just sort of play it by ear. I sort of feel if they'll let me, or if they won't, I don't bother them. Some people tickle them to stimulate them. It's too much for them. They don't want this sort of stimulation. They want to be gradually enabled to have the ordinary sensations. The autistic sensation objects they hold are to make them feel strong and powerful. That's why I think it's quite good for them to be in a small educational unit because they can be helped to be powerful in another way, that is, by acquiring skills. That's the way they can become powerful, and a very gifted teacher can help them with this.

VH: How do you talk to them about the hard things they are carrying? Do you interfere physically or not?

FT: It depends, you know. Again, you play it by ear. Perhaps you don't talk about this at first because they're secrets, these things are secret. When they wiggle their bottoms to feel their feces, that's all very secretive so you don't talk about it because they would feel invaded. You leave them alone, at first, but gradually they begin to feel that you're sensible and that you're all right, and they feel a bit more safe with you. Then you're able to talk to them about it. You say, "I know it makes you feel lovely and strong, doesn't it? It's fine that you should feel very strong. But there are other ways of feeling strong. Perhaps you could bat a ball and that might make you feel strong," or something like that. But you do need to understand the dynamics of the illness to be able to respond properly.

VH: Would you ever say, "You could take my hand and feel strong?"

FT: Ah yes, oh yes. Oh yes.

VH: Because together we're strong?

FT: Yes, together we're strong. When they're playing "Ring-a-Round-the-Rosie" and that sort of thing, there's a point where they all fall down. That brings in the moment of separation—of sudden disconnection and helplessness. It's not, in a way, preparing what you are going to do. It's knowing the dynamics and then out of your intuitions you find yourself responding and doing all sorts of things you never thought of doing. When they feel you're on their wavelength, then they start to open out. Perhaps I liked working with autistic children because I'm a bit autistic myself.

VH: I did want to ask about the contribution of your own personality. You were analyzed by Wilfred Bion, off and on for 13 years?

FT: That's right. Fourteen!

VH: I know you've written that he was kind and that he kept his space. He didn't raise your fee.

FT: No. It was marvelous, looking back. I took it for granted at the time. In later years I found out how very well-known and respected he was. But then, you know, I didn't know he was this distinguished, famous person until right at the end. Then I found that he was so respected everywhere.

VH: What are the memories of the Tavistock Clinic that stand out for you now?

FT: It was like everywhere else, a mixed bag—but it was a wonderful training. Dr. John Bowlby was so scholarly and generous, and Mrs. Esther Bick was a wonderful teacher. She was a very fanatical lady, but a splendid teacher and a very good clinician, and it was really a wonderful experience. After a while I got very friendly with Martha Harris—who later married Don Meltzer. But at the time I'm talking of we were students together. I got very friendly with her. My husband Arnold was a busy professor of electrical engineering in Birmingham University. He was willing that I go up from Birmingham to London for the week, which was very good of him. We'd bought a large house, and we'd made a flat on the top. The lady in the flat on the top said she'd feed Arnold. Her husband was at the University too. So it was all arranged. I came up to London every week. At first I lived with a friend who had two children, and I slept in their nursery. One of them was a bedwetter, and the other one kept white mice so it was a very stinky bedroom. Still, it was kind of them to give me a house-room so that I could get this wonderful training. After a while, Martha Harris said, "Why don't you come and live with us?" So I gave her a pittance every week for staying with them. She was married to Roland Harris then. He was a lecturer in psycholinguistics at Brunel University. He was a remarkably intelligent and good man with Quaker inclinations. He died suddenly, which was a great shock and tragedy for Mattie. She and Roland were very much loved by Arnold and myself. A little later Mattie married Don Meltzer. She died tragically some years ago as a result of a car accident.

VH: You must have had some contact with Donald Meltzer.

FT: I had supervision with Don, and it was an eye opener. It really made all the difference to my work. He is a very gifted supervisor and a superb clinician. I've seen patients who've been going to Don who've improved beyond all recognition.

VH: Let's go back to your training and intellectual development. You trained in child psychotherapy and not in psychoanalysis.

FT: They didn't take anybody over 40 in the Institute of Psycho-Analysis. I was 36 when I started the child psychotherapy training, so that by the time I finished I was 40. Anyway, I didn't want to train to treat adults—I liked children. And I wanted to work with children. I didn't see any point—apart from status—in analyzing adults, and besides, I think a child psychotherapist has, in a way, as much status in the community—not perhaps in the smaller world of psychoanalysis, but in the community. The child psychotherapists are well-established now. They have become very respected, and they do very helpful work.

VH: Let me come to another aspect of your training. How did you choose Bion for your training analysis?

FT: Mrs. Bick said, "You're going to Dr. Bion's for analysis."

VH: She arranged your training analysis?

FT: Yes, I myself didn't know Dr. Bion from Adam. But she said I was going—so I went. He had rooms in Harley Street. I went into his office, and he sat me down to talk to me about analysis. I thought, I've never seen anybody I disliked so much in all my life. I think it was that I really didn't want analysis. I wanted to train as a child psychotherapist and not to have a personal analysis. But one went through analysis to become a therapist. I reacted against that requirement. For myself, I felt very well-balanced. Everybody said I was very well-balanced. I felt very normal. Everybody agreed. I realize now that I had adjusted on a superficial level but that I had a deep depression underneath that I had kept at bay by autistic maneuvers.

VH: It seems like you felt more that it was a task they had sent you to do rather than a privilege.

FT: That's right, it was a thing you had to do. Also, I may have been afraid that this deep depression would become uncovered.

VH: Instead of working with the children, which was what you wanted.

FT: Oh, I could see the relevance. I knew that you had to clean your own windows before you tried to clean anybody else's. But I thought, well, I'm so normal and so well-balanced that I don't really need it. I didn't go to analysis in desperation. I thought I was fine! Only when I finished did I find out that I wasn't so fine after all. But back to the beginning. Dr. Bion said, "Do you know anything about analysis?" I said, "No, not anything really." He said, "Have you read anything?" "No, not really." He said, "The only way to know about analysis is to experience it." And my fantasy is that he picked me up and threw me onto the couch. I'm sure he didn't, but it seemed like it.

VH: How many days a week?

FT: He treated me four times a week because I had to get back to Birmingham.

VH: It seems like you felt, "Oh heavens, there go so many hours of my week."

FT: I did—and money too—I did. But, I agreed. I know the first week—I can remember, it's vivid in my mind, lying there. He said something, and I thought, "I've got something rare here." After that, I stopped disliking him and realized that he was a very unique person. This may sound like being wise after the event, but I really didn't know he was at all well-known. As far as I was concerned he was a rather burly sort of man who had great, big brown eyes that rather frightened me, and I just didn't take to him at first.

VH: Do you remember what he said that made you say, "Well, maybe he does have something special?"

FT: I can't remember. I can remember thinking—well, I felt really quite in awe. I really began to be in awe of him instead of thinking he was a nuisance. I thought, "This is something special."

VH: He made you aware that you had feelings, all kinds of feelings.

FT: Oh yes. He didn't talk about my past ever. I kept thinking, he's never hearing about my childhood. He never talked about it. He talked about the present and I don't know that I went into the past. Perhaps I did—but *he* didn't. I know he never talked about the past. It was all to do with the present and awful silences!

VH: All in the transference?

FT: Oh, yes, absolutely. After a time I began to realize that he was somebody special. When I qualified, I went to work at the West Middlesex Hospital and Sydney Klein was there. He was the psychiatrist in charge. He came to me once and he said, "Your analyst gave a quite unique paper at the Institute," and then, through Sydney, I began to realize that Dr. Bion was something rather special. However, I knew that he was special even if no one had told me that he was. But in a way, it was only when I finished, 14 years later, that I began to appreciate what he'd done. I think, in some ways, the most important things happen *after* the analysis.

VH: Fourteen years seems a long time. How do you keep a reluctant patient, who doesn't want to be there, 14 years?

FT: I did want to go there as well, and I was ever so good, as the autistic children and their mothers are good. I always turned up because this was part of the training, and I had an obligation to be there. I had this English thing—a sense of duty. I always turned up and always on time, absolutely on time. I was a model patient! Also, Dr. Bion had a good sense of humor and that was important to me. On the surface I was this very well-balanced patient who didn't need analysis. I thought that Dr. Bion was very lucky to get such a cooperative patient. But then one day he said I was "impenetrable." I was hurt, cut to the quick. I didn't realize how right he was. I realize now that I had a deep trauma underneath from which I protected myself by being impenetrable.

VH: How did the analysis come to an end, then, if you were "impenetrable?"

FT: Suddenly the feeling welled up. "I've had enough of this, I'm stopping." I know it's not very creditable to me to say all this, but it's true. And also it wasn't 14 years unbroken. I mean there was the time I went to America for a year. I said I hoped I could come back afterwards. Dr. Bion didn't say, "Well a lot of people want to come to me." He said, "I'll see what I can do," and he took me back. He was incredible. He must have had so much pressure on that vacancy, and I was not really a very good analysand—and I wasn't paying very much. He was a very ethical man. Well, then, I lost another baby and I was very ill, and I was away for nearly another year, I can't remember. So I had that as a break, and then he took me back again.

VH: I'd like to ask you about something else. In your paper about Bion you said something to the effect that he could break the rules because of his kindness.

FT: Or because he was so experienced. I think you have to know the rules to break the rules.

VH: When you had lost the baby he wrote your husband. Did you call him up? Did he call you up or did he just hear it through the grapevine in order to write your husband?

FT: I'm sure I wrote to him, when I was in the hospital. . . . Yes, I remember telling him about the drugs I was having there. I think he also wrote to me. You see the Kleinians are terribly strict and to write to the husband of somebody would be a bit off the record, as it were. But it's a natural, normal thing to do, and a very kind thing.

VH: But he wrote to Arnold in condolence—and not to you?

FT: Oh, I'm sure he'd written to me. Oh no, it wasn't that he'd written to Arnold and not to me. Oh no, no, no. It was the fact that he wrote to Arnold, and he also said that he'd had a very unhappy experience himself because his first wife died in childbirth, and he shared with Arnold his similar sad experience, which was, for a Kleinian, a bit not keeping to the strict rules. It was a very kind thing to do. I think it was a great comfort to Arnold actually, at the time.

VH: Do you have the letter that Bion sent your husband?

FT: Oh no, isn't it silly of us? You know, we're not people who keep things. Some people are great hoarders, but we're not, we're always so busy. It was a lovely letter. Even then, I didn't know how famous he was. By that time he was sought after all over the world, and then suddenly, after he had done all this, I said, "Thank you very much, goodbye."

VH: You mean you terminated just like that?

FT: Yes. And he said, "I don't think it's a very good idea." And I said, "Well, I think it is"—and off I went.

VH: Certainly, you must have thought about this later—terminating so suddenly.

FT: Well, yes. I must have continued, actually, until the holidays because I was ever so good. But in leaving suddenly I think I was repeating what happened to me in my childhood. I woke up one morning and my mother said, "You're not going to school, we're leaving your father." And off we went. There was only one bus a week through the little village where we lived. My father was away at a conference, and we went with a big, black trunk of my mother's and stood at the bus stop waiting for this bus to take us to the station. We just walked away suddenly, abruptly like that, and I was very fond of my father. So, I think I was, maybe, repeating this terrible, sudden, abrupt break from somebody I really loved, and I was left with my mother, somebody I really didn't respect very much. I felt terribly sorry for her. She was a very panic-stricken woman and very bewildered. I used to help her sort things out. Her religion had made her more and more fearful.

VH: So Bion was like the father you left. But you had to figure this out after the analysis.

FT: My mother and father were both in the Church of England. My father was what is called a lay reader. He was a professionally trained lay reader. My mother was what they now call a deaconess. She had trained at a very prestigious place in Chelsea. She had a heliotrope uniform with a very long veil. It was very becoming, actually. They were both working in the Church of England. I would see my father in his white surplice, going into the pulpit and giving sermons. Mother talked at "The Band of Hope" and at "Mother's Union" meetings. So I was brought up with people who talked in public.

My father lost his faith as the result of the First World War. He was in a prisoner of war camp, and in the prisoner of war camp he thought a lot. He was a very interesting, original, rather eccentric man, my father. He thought a lot, and he decided that he didn't approve of the church's attitude to war. So he became a pacifist. He decided he wanted to teach because he felt that was a way of affecting the younger generation.

In middle age I suddenly got phobic, and so I'm very sympathetic to people with phobias—I suddenly got terrified of groups of people and of talking to groups of people. I went on doing it, because I had lectures I'd committed myself to give, but I was very stiff and frightened. I was screaming with anxiety before I went, and I was very stilted. I kept on because I felt I shouldn't give in. It made me realize that underneath I'm very frightened of people and of groups of people, much as the autistic child is. I think that, like them, I felt threatened by a nest of predatory rivals such as I've described in my last book. After 2 years the phobia went away, thank goodness. This phobia came after I'd finished analysis with Dr. Bion. I think it might have been related to ending with Dr. Bion. Perhaps I ran away to avoid the predators who were threatening to take the "analytic breast" away from me. It's a very elemental experience that is described on pages 48 and 49 of *The Protective Shell in Children and Adults* (Tustin, 1990).

VH: It was terror?

FT: Yes. It was partly terror of the black hole that my first little autistic patient, John, taught me about. It was at the time when I was treating John, and he was telling me about this black hole. I know I saw this black hole all over the place. I think partly it was that I had to experience it with him in order to understand and help him. There was this black hole that was going to swallow me up. It was a very educative experience, but really quite dreadful at the time. And yet it sounds funny, somehow I was amused at it. I was sitting outside looking at it thinking, "Aren't you being funny. For you know, there's not a black hole, really." It was quite an experience and made me realize that I've got a lot of autism.

VH: Can you tell how it feels—or felt—to you?

FT: A sort of deep depression about separation, because that's what autism is, a protection against a very deep depression about finding that they are separate from the mother's body and have got to experience being dependent on her in a very rival-ridden situation. My mother was a somewhat sentimental lady, and I'm sure very lonely, because my father was most unsuitable as a husband for her. She was a superstitious and narrow-minded person. My father was an interesting man, and he followed A. S. Neill. My mother thought that Neill was a wicked man. Neill was a very progressive educator in England who ran a school called Summerhill. Summerhill was a progressive school where the children went to classes if they wanted to. I remember on one occasion my father took me to stay at Summerhill. The place was untidy, but I loved it. Anyway, he was a very eccentric man, very intelligent, very imaginative. He really *thought* about his religion. It meant a lot to him, but not in the same way as my mother. She was a real conservative—she was high Tory. He was very left wing—a socialist—an anarchist really.

My father was friends with Neill. Neill was analyzed by Wilhelm Reich, so I met psychoanalysis early. My father was influenced by Neill, and he tried to run these village schools, where he was the headmaster, along A. S. Neillian lines. You can imagine! The village people didn't understand him. When the children were in the playground, he went and played with them. It was great fun really. Anyway, my mother was very attached to her religion in a superstitious sort of way. Not really very intelligent, although I think my father examined her and thus made her less intelligent. I mean I love my father but I can see his faults—and there *were* serious faults, as I look back. My poor mother was without any sense of humor at all, and so she found him insufferable.

VH: That contrasts to what you said about Bion.

FT: Yes. But my father had a great sense of humor. My mother must have been lonely, very lonely, and she enveloped me. It was a symbiotic thing in a way, I suspect. Oh no, it was fusion, she tried to make me as if I were a part of her body. She'd say, "This is my daughter," almost as though I were a limb of her body, if you know what I mean. And I used to hate it even as a child, I thought there was something not right. Anyway, she was very fused with me because of her loneliness. She was very, very depressed and unhappy. She didn't like the country. My father loved the country. He loved putting on a cloth cap and walking in the country. From my mother's point of view, that was dreadful. She was very snobbish, and her idea of pleasure was to put on white gloves and go in a box at the theatre. My father sneered and made fun of this. My mother, poor thing, was extremely lonely, and she used me to block up the hole of her loneliness. But I wasn't a very good subject for it in a way. So I think when Dr. Bion left—I mean, when I stopped with Dr. Bion, you heard what I said! I think I must have sensed that he was going abroad or something, and that the ending was coming because I know I suddenly said, "I want to stop—I don't want to come any more." And he sighed and I remember hearing a tiny little voice, "Well, I don't know if that's a very good idea." I was so set on it that I hardly heard him. So I stopped. And he went to America.

VH: You stopped abruptly?

FT: I think so, or perhaps he said to wait until the holidays or something like that. I can't remember. I'm afraid I'm not a very good reporter of these long-ago affairs. Looking back, I think I was picking up that Dr. Bion was going to leave England.

VH: Weren't you afraid of the grief that you would feel losing him?

FT: I've no idea.

VH: But you had been analyzed!

FT: I'm sure I was one of those very impenetrable people. Looking back, how bored he must have been. He must have been bored stiff, but he was always very patient with me.

VH: You know what's so lovely? It's that even if that is so, you apparently learned with him how to penetrate the children who themselves are encapsulated.

FT: Oh yes, I got a lot, you know, that I never realized I was getting. Someone once said, "You know, you took Bion in from the air in the consulting room." It's quite right. I can't really read Bion. I mean I do read it, and I'm very influenced by it because later on, I suddenly find myself doing something new in the therapy, and I realize it's what I've read in Bion, although it didn't seem to make much sense at the time.

VH: You do seem to be saying that Bion, the two of you, failed, in some way, in getting to the deeper levels of your depression.

FT: I have a bit of an idea, that perhaps it's only when you finish that you really feel the depression about separation. The analysis is preparing you and strengthening you, but you can only experience this bodily separateness and the pain of it when you are actually experiencing the separateness at first hand.

VH: So not during termination, but after?

FT: Afterwards. I think it can only happen afterwards, perhaps when you are on your own. After all, we die alone in the final moments.

VH: It would be disabling to someone not as savvy as you.

FT: I coped with it because of the analytic help I'd had. Also, for a short time I sought help from another analyst, Dr. Stanley Leigh. Dr. Bion was in Los Angeles.

VH: Someone else might kill herself—emotionally, even actually!

FT: Oh, I *was* suicidal. I thought of killing myself. But, you see, I think the work that Bion had done had strengthened me to cope. I couldn't have tolerated the thought of suicide otherwise. I remember once, when Bion interpreted suicide, I said, "Stop it, that's dangerous, don't do that." It's something I know I shoved away. You see, I was terribly naive. Which was a great advantage, in a way. Everything was new and fresh. And Bion was good in that way. He was very willing to see what was really going on and not to interpret from the textbook. He wasn't tied to textbooks or to sects or anything like that. I really appreciated him when I finished, though for 14 years I'd found him a bit of a nuisance.

VH: A nuisance?

FT: I didn't want to go to bare my soul to somebody else. It was private to me. I didn't really want to go along and talk about what was happening to me. It was all very private to me, thank you very much.

VH: Sort of like your father?

FT: My father was a very private man. My mother was like a jelly, she oozed all over. You can tell I really do find it difficult to respect my mother. I was very kind to her, and I sort of looked after her through to the bitter end. But we had nothing in common. I had a lot in common with my father.

VH: How old were you when your mother left him?

FT: I should say about 12.

VH: Where did she go?

FT: Well, we wandered around the country to various friends and relatives. For a whole year I was out of school, and I loved school. School was what kept me free of the emotional hot bath that I felt I lived in at home. But then finally she got a job in a North Country town as a deaconess—as a church worker. They didn't pay very much because only well-off ladies went into that as a profession in those days. It was a bit like social work in the early days, and you just got a pittance pay. She also looked after an old lady, with whom we lived, who had been her landlady when she first came to this North Country town as a young deaconess. She was really very resourceful and courageous.

VH: There was sort of a loss of status.

FT: I expect it was, really. I had always thought that my father was something rather special. My mother went to work in a rather rundown church. All the people who were hanging on to this rundown church were religious in a very practical, narrow sort of way.

VH: So a child's feelings of anger or need wouldn't have been allowed?

FT: Oh no. Oh no. I was a very good little girl. I was brought up in this religious atmosphere where they used to sing, "Jesus Wants Me for a Sunbeam." It's only really this last year that I have been able to feel that my mother did a very dreadful thing to me—but the poor thing couldn't help it.

VH: You must have left Bion a bit bewildered.

FT: Yes, I expect I did. I always saw my mother as being bewildered. *I* was looking after *her*. I remember in the War, the First World War, it was very dark in the blackout. I was only a little girl then. My father was in the forces, and my mother couldn't see the curbs because it was dark. I was small so that I was near to the ground and could see the curbs. So I led her safely through the darkened streets. I felt that I had to take care of my mother, I think, from being a baby. She was such a bewildered, panicky woman; I was very efficient and good at doing things. I felt sorry for her most of my life.

VH: So letting someone take care of you would have been a major resistance?

FT: Oh yes, you're quite right. I hadn't thought of that. I think I felt, "Poor Dr. Bion, I've left him so abruptly." I think I did . . . Yes, to let somebody take care of me is quite a bit. . . . When you first came, because I'm just getting better from being ill, I told you a bit about my medical history. The doctors were a bit irresponsible—neglectful and everything. But anybody in their senses would have said, "Look, I must have a second opinion, et cetera." But I didn't do that, I didn't let anybody look after me. I knew that, vaguely, but it's really becoming clearer as we talk, you know. I think it is that I didn't let anybody look after me. Also, as you will realize, I was brought up not to give people trouble.

The autistic children are just the same. Their mothers are often crying out to look after them now, although they had not been able to do so when the child was first born. I remember seeing a mother waiting for her child to come back from therapy. The mother came forward with open arms, but the child ignored her, turned his back and walked away. I can see that mother now, sinking back, looking so disappointed and so hurt. The mothers aren't cold. They give the impression of being, but they're longing to be warm with their child. The children can be little tyrants. They're very cruel to their mothers in a sort of quiet, underhand way, not in an open way. My sympathies were always with the mothers rather than with the children who are so uncaring.

When I was at Tavistock, we had somebody from Argentina who said he's been treating autistic children. He said that autistic children's mothers were cold and unloving and everything. And I can remember standing up and saying, "But look, the mothers of autistic children I've met are like some of my best friends." He looked at me as if I must have some very funny best friends! You will realize that my mother was not like the autistic children's mothers. She was soft, pathetic, and rather sad. The autistic children's mothers are very competent and confident in a brittle sort of way. Also, I was not wholly autistic!

VH: Did you ever see your father again?

FT: Yes, when I was 27. I was married, and I saw a letter from my father in The Times newspaper, so I wrote to him and went to see him. My parents never divorced because of their religious principles. My father was living with a very delightful person, and we immediately became friendly with each other. My husband and I went to see my father and his "common-law wife," Gladys, many times. When she became ill, I nursed her until she died. My father died a little while later.

VH: You've spent so much time with me today, and given me such a splendid interview, that I've risked being cruel too, in extending it beyond the time I meant to occupy. We could spend, I suspect, many more hours. But let me thank you for your kindness, and let's stop here.

After this interview was approved by Mrs. Tustin and accepted by *The Psychoanalytic Review* (Hunter, 1992a) for publication, she and I continued to correspond. She expressed concern that some audiences "might not be knowledgeable enough to understand the intricacies of the human feelings caused by analysis." She wrote to me that "many apparently well-adjusted people, particularly those who have a manic defense, have a deep-seated core of autism which covers a very, elemental depression associated with undigested traumas about bodily separateness. They get by in an ordinary life, and perhaps only encounter this depression when they come to their life's end, and have to face death, that ultimate experience of bodily separateness—perhaps some people even avoid it then. It seems to me that the autism covering this deep, unacknowledged depression is a stumbling block to creative functioning in many people—or, as with Henry Moore, who was aware of it throughout his life, it can be a stimulus to creativity. Freud knew about it when he wrote of 'the background pull to the inanimate.' It was stimulus to him. It's interesting that he mentions this in his most controversial book *Beyond the Pleasure Principle* (1950). It obviously contains much distressing material, as does this interview." She continued, "Dr. Bion helped me to know—knowing can have a healing effect on this deep 'black hole' type of depression, but in the end I had to experience all the elemental terrors associated with it—hence, the phobia I encountered of people (forage of predatory sucking rivals)."

She hoped her interview with me would help introduce some people to this experience. She certainly felt the blocks to creativity and self-confidence caused by deep-seated pockets of autism are important to understand. They are not an underlying psychosis, but automatic protective reactions to trauma that we all possess, which in autistic children are overused to such an extent that it constitutes a pathology.

Mrs. Tustin very much wanted those who read this to be aware that many people, like herself, go through divorce and turbulent distressing childhoods and yet emerge to have useful and interesting lives. Last of all, she wanted to note that "analysis doesn't always come to an end in a tidy way—all neatly parcelled up with a bow on top—but that it goes on after the physical contact has finished, and that perhaps some of the most vital work is done then."

Note. This interview originally appeared in Hunter (1992a). Copyright 1992 by the National Psychological Association for Psychoanalysis. Adapted by permission.

Case Discussion

Not surprisingly, Mrs. Tustin reminds us that Roselyn has autistic bits. Further, she says the patient has no control over her mother and is overwhelmed by her undifferentiated feelings. She, too, points out that Roselyn has no maternal container and no space for the expression of feelings, which results in a consequent fear of feeling.

Frances Tustin opened her comments on Roselyn with, "She has a big autistic bit. You will remember that she said, 'If I think, I feel everything is whirling.' Many writers have written about the whirling sensations that autistic children have. They're a very autistic thing. They spin objects and whirl themselves. I think it's to get the feeling that they exist. It's sort of centrifugal. It makes them feel that they've got a center—that they do exist. Rotation also prevents collapse, and that is one of the things that autistic children fear. Things like tiny pins seem to be attacking and pricking them to cause them to collapse. The 'black hole' (Tustin, 1966, 1989) is a collapsed sensation. I think that's the feeling they get when they first experience bodily separateness after a very tight fusion with their mothers, which was pathological. I wrote about this in my latest paper (Tustin, 1991). When they first become aware that their body is separate from that of the mother, they realize that there is space. And so they whirl and whirl in order to feel attached and held together and all right. Your adult patient has similar feelings. Whirling is to control the feeling of being in space."

I said, "She doesn't feel contained."

Tustin responded, "Absolutely, they don't feel contained at all. As infants, they have this pathological 'adhesive at oneness' with the mother, and then when separateness from her is experienced, it is traumatic, and they feel wrenched apart. They feel as though their skin is being peeled off them. They also feel that they've lost a supporting limb. They feel that the only way they can keep held together is to roll around and around and around."

Tustin went on, "With these patients, you're not really sure that what you're seeing is not something you're putting into the situation yourself, because the transference situation is a fusional one. It is difficult to differentiate oneself from them." Tustin reads from the material of "An Hour." "I'm in space (*holding on to self*)." Tustin went on, "How right you were to give her time. I used to come in too quickly with interpretations, and I think it upset these children. They want a bit of space, to experience the space, but to experience the space with someone who understands—someone who isn't damaged or wounded." She added concerning the use of brief silences: "It was good that you did that, and then you said, 'The pain, and feeling so alone and in danger.' That's what they felt when they found that they were not joined onto the mother's body. They felt so alone and in pain, wounded, skinned alive, a most dreadful feeling. So this interpretation really moved her. She *felt* the sensation of the migraines for she said, 'When I get closer to expressing my real feelings, I get migraines like an implosion, holes in the universe where stars have exploded in a black hole containing all my back-into-myself self. Words seem inadequate.' How right she is! How well she puts it."

I pointed out that in astronomy there is a "black hole." Tustin agreed and said, "But when the little autistic boy patient who taught me about 'the black hole' used this phrase, it was a long time before the astronomers had come up with the notion of the 'black hole.' " Tustin went on, "It's a real deep blackened place. But how well she's describing those migraines. I think these children have been in such a state of 'adhesive at oneness' with the mother, with no space between them, that their feelings also have no space between them. They're all stuck together—rage, terror, grief—all in a bunch."

I asked her, "My adult patient really does not experience the rage. What she experiences is the terror, the wish for life to be over. The mother was suicidal herself and did dramatic things. And I do think she's right about the migraines. I think she is right that she doesn't want to need anything, and she doesn't want to have any anger."

Tustin said she understood this in the light of her own experience. "The patient's rage is mixed up with so many other feelings." She then talked about the protective shell and the "autistic capsule" (S. Klein, 1980) of such patients and about the 14-year analysis with Bion which she terminated suddenly. She said that suddenly, after he had done so much for her, she said, "Thank you very much; goodbye." Bion said, "I don't think it's a very good idea." Then she said, "Well, I think it is," and off she went. She added, "I must have gone on until the holidays because I was a very 'good' conforming patient! I think I sensed that he was going to leave England." She felt that in breaking off so suddenly she was repeating a traumatic situation that had happened in her childhood when her mother suddenly announced that they were leaving her father who was away at a conference. She was very fond of her father. "So I think I was, maybe, repeating this terrible, sudden, abrupt break from somebody I really loved, and I was with my bewildered mother whom I pitied rather than respected. I felt very sorry for her." Tustin felt that she had had to take care of her mother.

I said I thought that letting someone take care of *her* would have been a major resistance. She agreed and said that on one occasion Bion had said that she was "impenetrable." Tustin then spoke of her belief that there may be some feelings that can only be felt after the analysis is terminated, but that the analysis is preparing the patient and strengthening him or her to bear them.

She went on to say that she had a phobic episode after her termination with Bion. She said, "I suddenly got terrified of groups of people and of talking to groups of people. . . . It made me realize that basically, I'm very shy and very frightened of people and of groups much as the autistic child is. I was suicidal." She went on to say that she thought that she was experiencing "the black hole" that her patient, John, had taught her about. She realized that she had "a lot of autism because of my deep depression about separateness." She felt this also applied to my patient Roselyn. She said that Dr. Sydney Klein's paper, "Autistic Phenomena in Neurotic Patients" (1980), was very relevant to such patients and was very meaningful to her after her phobic episode.

I said, "I've worked with Roselyn all these years, and I cannot—maybe she's like you were with Bion—I can't break her out." Tustin agreed.

Then she reassured me, "It'll come when she's ready. I think Bion understood that. I couldn't have these feelings until I was ready, and you can't do it until you're ready. I mean, it's just an intellectual thing in your head. You know? And imploding is about. . . . It's not just pure rage. As I say, it's rage, grief, terror—all stuck together, and in a way it will help her if she differentiates these feelings one from the other. They're so undifferentiated."

Tustin mentioned that if autism is not treated early, "it rolls on and gets thicker and heavier, and so older children are very difficult to treat." By implication, she was saying that the autistic structure in a person may be progressively harder to treat as the person ages. She felt this was because autistic people feel they have "lost control of the things that were supporting them." They then experience an avalanche of feelings; they feel absolutely overwhelmed by great waves of feelings, and it's a torrent of feelings that are undifferentiated. "It's rage, grief, terror—all of these primitive feelings—they're all unsocial feelings. They don't have social emotions such as love and hate," Tustin explained.

I expressed my confusion. In one of Tustin's papers, she had mentioned "shame and grief." Tustin said, "Yes, you're quite right to take me up on that. Grief and shame are too socialized and conceptualized. It's the feeling of being collapsed, of having lost control, of helplessness. They feel that something has happened to their body, to their psyche-soma. They don't feel, 'I'm so sad because I've lost my mother, or because my mother isn't there or because I want my mother.' It's a physical feeling. They feel devastated. What I found helpful with the children was to say to them, 'I know how you're feeling.' It's no good saying, 'I think you're feeling afraid or you're feeling angry.' I would just say you're feeling like this (and I would give a pained exclamation). I would also say, 'You feel as if you're going to be swept away.' (You see they're afraid that they're going to be swept away by this avalanche of feelings.) Talking with you has sort of helped me to get this clearer. You see, the patient feels she's being formed in a centrifuge. I think that when she whirls, she's trying to precipitate herself as a 'being,' as a crystal of being. And these are not feelings to do with emotions, they're feelings to do with a sense of 'being,' with a sense of existence. They're existential feelings."

I said, "And with my patient, of having no connection."

Tustin agreed, "Yes, of having no connection, of being adrift in space, and that is terrifying."

I went on, "That raises another question. It is almost impossible, in my experience with treating children, not to have some physical contact with them. With adult patients, there is a great taboo about having any kind of bodily contact. It always makes me wonder how a person internalizes the feelings just from words."

Tustin agreed and said, "I know. I remember in my first little book, *Autism and Childhood Psychosis* (1972), when John was screaming, I said, 'Against the rules of my Kleinian training, I took him on my lap' " (M. Klein, 1930).

I asked, "Do you understand the reasoning behind those rules?"

Tustin responded, "I think it's thought to be seductive and sort of reassuring. You should do it all through interpretation. But you see, I don't really think it's true when it comes to these autistic children or even with patients with an autistic capsule. With anorexics I would often stroke their hair . . . their head. I was very careful to do it in a fairly cool way, a sort of soothing way, almost like being one of their autistic shapes (Tustin, 1986), but with the implication that there is a *person* other than themselves who can give them shapes that are soothing and comforting and tranquilizing. But I think you have to be careful. I think it's good to have a rule, but that you can break it in certain extreme circumstances.

You have to respect the rules before you can break them." She went on, "Of course, the rules are to protect patients from emotional and physical abuse. There have been some dreadful cases in England where patients have been emotionally or even sexually abused by psychotherapists who did not have the strict psychoanalytical training that we have."

I said, "I felt that my diagnosis of the severity of her illness also influenced my technique."

Tustin agreed, "That's right. Some people would 'go over the top' in their compassion with this patient, and I think they don't want that. I'm sure you'll agree. I'm sure they don't want that, and it wouldn't be helpful to them. But just to make contact with them in a very gentle way; I mean, for example, just to stroke their head. As I've said in one of my books, if they flap with their hands, I hold their hands and say, 'I'm holding the flap. I'm holding the flap. Tustin is holding the terrible feeling that everything is going to pieces—Tustin is holding it,' and they would stop flapping. I did feel something went into me, as though I were absorbing it—you know, taking it into myself."

I agreed, "That makes special sense to me with these people who feel they have no skin or no container, but I also know that you have to contain with words."

Tustin replied, "Yes, but you can do it with a little bit of action. I think you've got to be more active with autistic children and autistic bits. I think you've got to be more active because actions speak louder than words in some states of terror." She went on, "But I think you've got to play it by ear very cautiously. If you touch autistic children, they often flinch away; so you've got to play it by ear. It's a very delicate and even dangerous thing. It needs a lot of self-discipline because we are dealing with extremely powerful feelings, and, as we know, the transference situation can be very involving."

Thinking of my patient I asked, "Don't these children know when they're seeking it?"

Tustin said, "Oh, yes, they do. Absolutely; but again, it's something you have to play by ear and to tune yourself into. And if you're tuned in well, they'll feel that you're with them. On the other hand, you can be too empathic so that they feel that they're fused with you and that they haven't got any separateness."

Tustin then related of her experience of supervising a very gifted psychotherapist who was training at Tavistock. She said, "She's treating this autistic child. This therapist said to me, 'He doesn't speak very well; his words aren't very clear. His mother says that she understands every word.' But the therapist says, I feel I have to say, 'Now, Joseph, I haven't really understood that. It wasn't clear enough for me.' She feels that it is important not to seem to be part of his body."

I asked, "Can too much empathy support the autistic pathology?"

Tustin replied, "That's right; you can be too understanding, can't you? It's a very delicate balance. There are certain principles that you adhere to, but you can't have rigid rules. I felt very wicked when I took John on my knee, but he'd fallen and banged his head or something. And he was shrieking."

Then, Tustin was supportive of my work with Roselyn. She said, "But that's a lovely session. That's a beautiful session. I think you're really in touch with her. You say you're afraid you'll go mad with this feeling of whirling. You enter into her feelings. Such patients feel that this big wave of sensations is going to engulf them, and it is the feeling that they won't exist. What they're busy with are the feelings associated with existing and surviving—not with relationships to people or even to objects. The hard objects they hold in their hand (Tustin, 1980), they're not objects in an objective sense; they're sensations, they're hard sensations. They're not a classified object, and these shapes that they have, they're not classified shapes. Some therapists find it difficult to understand this because they think that if a child starts to talk about shapes or to draw shapes, he is using 'autistic shapes.' (I wrote about these in the *International Review of Psycho-Analysis* [1984] and in *Autistic Barriers in Neurotic Patients* [1986].) Autistic shapes are unconceptualized. They're sensations, they're not anything objective. They're endogenous and subjective in terms of their body. We've struggled so hard to get to the state of living in an objective world. That's why we find this autistic world so troubling. If we experience it with a patient, we think we're going mad. It's worrying, perhaps because it's a state we've known when we were on the verge of madness."

I said, "It seems like you were very aware as you went along that you were creating, that the child was becoming; it wasn't a revisiting something. It was more a new stepping, a new place."

Tustin agreed, "Autism was a state he'd got into as an infant in order to protect himself."

I thought that this related to Roselyn; I said I believed that she needs to be able to accomplish a new state of trust and security.

Tustin referred to her patient, John. "Yes, but the autism was a state he'd got into in order to protect himself against this traumatic sense of disconnection. Not every baby has that. I think this autistic protection is an innate thing that we tend to use in situations of traumatic crisis, but autistic children use it in a massive overall way. And it becomes a static way of life. So that, in a way, it wasn't that it was a state that was normal in early infancy as I had once thought (Tustin, 1991, 1992). They had engendered it by their protective sensations. These had diverted their attention away from this terrible sense of disconnection, the 'black hole,' the feeling of not being contained, of not being 'held,' and all those other awful things we've been talking about, and all the terrible, massive 'stuck together' feelings that threatened them. So they engendered these diversionary sensations, and this helped them to feel safe. The autism is engendered as a desperate effort to feel safe. If we invade their privacy by being seductive, they feel very threatened. We must avoid this at all costs."

I had looked at the Henry Moore sculpture on the cover of her book (Tustin, 1990). I said that nothing in Tustin's writing related to perversion, but that all this reminded me of patients who obsessively rape people or masturbate constantly. "There's the hole, there's the nipple—it seems to have to do with not feeling and yet feeling."

Tustin agreed. "Yes, it is a perversion. Being callous and not feeling. How right you are because I know there's perversion in all this—Chasseguet-Smirgel's paper on perversion means a lot to me (Chasseguet-Smirgel, 1983). It's deviant, and it's perverse. It's not anything to do with ordinary emotions. It's to do mostly with sensations."

I said that when I saw the Henry Moore sculpture on her book this had come to my mind. Tustin agreed enthusiastically, saying, "That's right. It's to act out something that is very perverse, but Moore does it in a creative way. That's fine, but autistic people act it out in a nonsymbolic way."

I said, "The connection with the object has nothing to do with intimacy."

She agreed, "That's right," adding, "Do write a paper about this!"

She concluded, again referring to the Moore sculpture with the breast with its great black hole: "I think that's a very powerful image, isn't it? It means more and more to me as I look at it. I was so interested in your patient." I had told her a story about my patient. Tustin remembered this and asked, "Didn't you say that on one occasion she went and looked at this Henry Moore statue?"

"Yes," I said, and told her the story: "It was in the museum when she was about 8 years old. The family was moving, and she went to the museum with a group of children, and she stood in front of this huge Henry Moore sculpture with the big lap, smooth as could be. She was drawn to it, and she literally had to be removed from it."

Tustin interpreted, "And it was at a time of disconnection and disruption. They were moving." Tustin thought it was important that Roselyn had remembered to tell me this. We concluded with Tustin's saying, "I'm sure Henry Moore must have had a very abrupt disconnection from his mother that was troubling him, but he used it as a stimulus to creativity. He had found himself in space."

John Bowlby

The late John Bowlby made many contributions to psychoanalytic research, especially in his theories relating to attachment, loss, grief, and mourning. He believed that what really happened in a patient's life is as important as unconscious fantasy.

This interview took place in his small, plain office at Tavistock Institute and Clinic in London on February 15, 1990, 11 days before his 83rd birthday.

I left the London subway burdened with the video camera and all its paraphernalia including the tripod, two tape recorders, notes, and camera, only to discover, with dismay, that there were no cabs. Eventually someone pointed, vaguely, indicating that somewhere up the nearby hill and through a residential area there was a large clinic. I saw no signs. I was anxious I would not find the clinic. The streets were deserted. Actually, I was early and had caught my breath by the time Dr. Bowlby greeted me. Nothing in his speech or demeanor betrayed his age.

Dr. Bowlby was not given to theories not verified by research. He was a scientist. I was surprised there was no analytic couch and began the interview in a state of awe. I had *The Atlantic* magazine (February, 1990) in my hand. The cover article, "Becoming Attached—What Children Need" (Karen, 1990), describes Dr. Bowlby's and others' work on attachment. I was surprised he had not seen it yet. He seemed pleased to accept my extra copy as a gift. The next day he expressed his and his wife's pleasure in the article.

Interview

Virginia Hunter: So you hadn't seen *The Atlantic*?

John Bowlby: No, I'm glad you think well of it. It was a good article. I thought it was very well done, comprehensive, accurate, and well written. I hope it will get around. Does it have a big circulation?

VH: I don't think it's small. It's more for intellectuals.

JB: That's my impression. That's fine, after all, it's important to intellectuals. They should be informed. I'm all in favor of that. I thought it was excellent.

VH: In nearly everything of yours I've read, you mention that you wished people understood your research and your findings about attachment better—that therapists understood it better. And I'm wondering, could you talk about the things you wished therapists did understand better?

JB: I think there are two main points in all my work which, on the whole, therapists have not paid very much attention to, although things change a lot. Nowadays more and more people do pay attention to these things. The first one refers to the importance of real-life events. There's been a strong tradition in psychoanalysis to emphasize fantasy and to underplay the importance of real-life events. This, of course, goes right back to Freud because in the 1890s he advanced his ideas that the causation of the troubles from which his hysterical patients suffered was sexual abuse. Then, he said, these events had never occurred, they were the patient's imagination and wishful thinking. The emphasis thereafter became fantasy.

As a psychoanalytic student, I was almost forbidden to give attention to real-life events. (I'm talking about the 1930s now.) I was working as a child psychiatrist in a child guidance clinic. There, of course, we were giving a great deal of attention to real-life events and, consequently, my aim in research from that point onwards was to call attention to real-life events, and their adverse influence on personality development. I deliberately focused on separation and loss because those events can be well documented and unmistakable. In those days we had no means of doing any systematic research on parental behavior and parental attitudes to treatment of children, no videos, no tape recorders, no nothing. I'd recognized this was of enormous importance. I simply focused on separation and loss as something I could get my teeth into.

There's still, I think, excessive emphasis on fantasy. I was at a case conference at a very well-known clinic, in the United States, 4 years ago. A case was presented by a well-known psychoanalyst of a woman with a great many emotional and sexual problems who reported that she had been sexually abused by her older brother. And the analyst was by no means convinced that this wasn't a fantasy. In fact, I think if he had opted whether it was real or not, he would have opted *for* fantasy. Well, I had absolutely no doubt that this woman was telling a true story—the whole thing was absolutely typical of what you might expect from that sort of experience. I said my piece, of course, in no uncertain terms. I asked the analyst whether he'd read the literature on sexual abuse in childhood and its consequences. I was really rather horrified to find that he was totally unfamiliar with any literature on the subject.

I think it's not only untherapeutic, it's antitherapeutic. It has a very adverse effect on the patient if you doubt his story. I believe it is far better to believe a story even if you subsequently find it isn't quite true than the reverse. I think one should always believe what a patient tells you if there's a huge amount of evidence that it's valid.

In my experience the shortcoming of what patients tell you is that they don't tell you important things, partly because they don't remember them. So much of one's work, in fact, is in helping them to discover what did happen to them. Our job is to help the patient explore his own past, his own thoughts, his own feelings, discover who he is or what he is. It is important to help a patient sort out what was real and what is or was fantasy. I would encourage a patient to give me, in the greatest possible detail, all the memories she has of what was done or what she thinks was done or said. And I would encourage a patient to go over it, scrutinize it, look at it, consider it. If a patient says, "Well, did my mother say this or that or didn't she?" I would say, "Well look, I don't know, but you must think that one out." If, for example, she says, "My mother said she wanted me dead," I'd say, "If you go back to where you think your mother said that and think it out, well, did she really say it? And if she really said that she wanted you dead, then it was something so frightening and dreadful that perhaps you didn't want to hear it. Maybe it was quite real but you didn't want it to be real."

VH: Some patients have a hard time reconnecting their feelings.

JB: Well, again, one has to say, "I think these memories were so frightening that you don't want to remember the feeling." The last thing a child wants to believe is that that was horribly true. The more we know about the kinds of things that can happen and do happen, the kinds of experiences children have, the more we're likely to be able to help patients recover these memories and tell us about things that they feel perhaps very shocked about, or ashamed of, or they've talked about or tried not to think about.

The other side of this coin is the extent to which a parent has contradicted, denied, that bad things happened. A parent may say, "I didn't do that, I never said that, you're lying, I didn't say that," when in point of fact he or she had said it. A parent can attempt to deny things the child has already experienced, so that is something to be explored. In some cases, a parent says, "You mustn't talk about this. This is completely forbidden, and if you mention one word of it, I will murder you." So, I think there can be huge pressures on not saying, not remembering: "You mustn't remember this, it didn't happen, and you mustn't say it happened." Patients need help to disentangle what's real, what's fantasy. I think all this emphasis on fantasy is positively damaging. I think it's misleading, it diverts attention from what matters, and it discredits patients, discourages patients, and so on.

Now the other huge area, that I've done my best to draw attention to, is that a person's desire for comfort, protection, reassurance—especially when they're distressed or unhappy—is not at all childish, it is the natural state of man when upset. It's not babyish or childish. It's not weak. It's not dependent and so on. If therapists hold that view, they are going to convey it to their patients in one shape or another in their tone of voice, in some sort of phraseology; they'll imply that this is something the patients should get out of. Many patients' real feelings are a desperate desire for comfort, and whenever as children they felt a desperate desire for comfort and protection, far from getting them, they've been rejected and frightened. They may be terrified that if they were to express a desire for comfort and protection from you, you will behave like their parent. You won't sympathize, you won't respond, you will condemn, you will pour contempt, ridicule. Those are the two things that I've been plugging all my life.

VH: How could psychoanalysts not know that what really happens to you matters?

JB: It all goes back to Freud. Freud was a person who we all know had enormous influence. He drew attention to some very important things. He said some very valuable things, and he said some terribly mistaken things. This whole business about real-life events and fantasies, that's entirely the influence of Freud. There's no doubt about that at all; it's all in the literature. You see, once you call attachment "dependency," you at once put an adverse evaluation on it. In the ordinary course of events, people say you ought not to be dependent, you must be independent. Some anxious person who is desperately looking for comfort and assistance is looked down upon as being a rather poor, weak thing. You see, there are various places where Freud attributes that kind of emotional problem to overindulgence in childhood. But it isn't overindulgence at all, it's exactly the reverse. But again, it's all in the literature. So we have to recognize that Freud had some very adverse influences as well as some very useful ones.

VH: As I understood the literature, you were so offended by Melanie Klein's reaction to your patient's mother being hospitalized that you really, sort of rebelliously said, "This is going to be my life's work—to prove this woman wrong."

JB: That's right, quite right. I was training to be a child psychiatrist, and I was working with two social workers who each had had their own analysis. They were very alive to the importance of real-life events and the way in which parents' problems impinge on children. I've always said I learned more from them than anyone else.

VH: Who was your analyst?

JB: Joan Riviere. She was a Kleinian.

VH: You were supervised by Klein?

JB: I was also supervised by others and by Ella Sharpe.

VH: How did you decide you'd be an analyst, that you wanted to become an analyst?

JB: I went to Cambridge to read medicine, and I became increasingly interested in what we would now call developmental psychology. My third year at Cambridge I read psychology; after that I then gave up medicine for a year. I didn't go straight on to medical school and clinical training. I spent a year in a school for disturbed children, and that was extremely revealing and valuable to me. I worked in a very small school where the orientation was that the present problems of children stemmed from adverse experiences in their families. It was a version of psychoanalysis. It gave emphasis to real-life events. When I was there, there was a very intelligent man, John Alford, who had had some personal analysis. What he said to me, towards the end of this year is, "What you ought to do is complete your medical training, train as a psychoanalyst and become a child psychiatrist. There are two institutions in London which you could go to. One is the Tavistock Clinic and the other is the Institute of Psycho-Analysis." I hadn't heard of either. We discussed it between us, and he said he thought on balance that the Institute of Psychoanalysis offered a rather more systematic and thorough training. So I went to the Psychoanalytic Society. I also completed my medical training and trained as a child psychiatrist. That was extremely good advice, and that's how I came to do the sort of things I have done.

VH: When you were young yourself, you separated from your parents to go off to boarding school?

JB: Yes, I went off to boarding school at the age of 10.

VH: Can you tell me something about your childhood?

JB: My father, Sir Anthony A. Bowlby, was a rather leading London surgeon, and he subsequently became the President of the Royal College of Surgeons, so he was a top surgeon.

VH: A very busy man I would think. Was he very occupied with his profession?

JB: Well, yes and no. He was very busy, but he was a great believer in long holidays. He took 2 months in the summer. We lived in London. I was number four in a family of six—two older sisters, an older brother, then me, then another brother, and then a sister. My elder brother and I were very close together. He was 13 months older. We've always been very much alike. We've always been good companions and good friends, and we've also been very competitive. It was, as I said, a fairly straightforward, fairly close—not all that close—but fairly close, professional-class family living a pretty traditional lifestyle, with nurses, of course.

VH: Caretakers?

JB: We had one head nanny who, in fact, joined the family when my elder sister was a baby and stayed with the family until she died at the age of 97.

VH: Oh my goodness! Are all six still living in your family?

JB: No, two have died. My mother lived to be 90. My elder sister is still living at the age of 90, still hale and hearty. The next sister died some years ago. My elder brother is now 84.

VH: What does he do?

JB: He worked in industry. He was a managing director of one of the big engineering firms in this country.

VH: And your sisters—the two older sisters?

JB: Musicians, fiddle and cello, and they did teaching and so on.

VH: Who's after that?

JB: Then I come and then a younger brother who was never very successful. He had thyroid trouble. And then a sister, who will be 80 in a month's time, who's very hale and hearty, married to an economist and has a family, two boys and a girl.

VH: Are there a lot of children in the family? Those are the first ones you've mentioned. I know you have children.

JB: Yes, my two elder sisters were unmarried. They were the First World War generation. They would have married men who were killed in the war. My brother has two daughters, both of whom are married, both of whom have children. My wife and I have two boys and two girls and seven grandchildren.

VH: Are they following in your footsteps?

JB: No. They're much more technically minded, computers and engineering and all that sort of thing.

VH: How did your ideas influence the way you raised your children?

JB: My wife's family had a tradition of raising children that way, so she naturally practiced it and, of course, I followed suit. And our children carried on in the same way, I'm pleased to say.

VH: What was your mother like?

JB: A very active, straightforward person. She'd been brought up in the country, daughter of a country parson, Rev. Canon Hon. Hugh W. Mostyn. She didn't marry early. My father was, I think, 40 or 43 when he married. My mother was 31. There was never any question of her having a career or advanced education or anything of that sort. But she had a good marriage—a surgeon's household, with six children with several servants, staff, was quite a little empire to manage, especially during the First World War when my father was in France as a consultant surgeon. My mother held the fort, as you might say.

VH: How old would you have been when your father went off to the front?

JB: Seven. 1914. So we didn't see much of him. He was home for a week's leave pretty regularly. When I was born, my mother, Maria Bridget, was 40 and my father was 52.

VH: Very old!

JB: Yes, it wasn't unusual for parents—for people to marry a bit late in those days, but they married later than average.

VH: I didn't want to interfere with your thoughts. I thought maybe you were going to say something more about your childhood. Your speaking of a nanny makes me think of another question that I have. In

America, I guess here, too, we see a lot of mothers who feel entitled to have children even though they're planning to leave them in 2 weeks with a caretaker. I know I've read that you disapprove of this. With the mothers going off to work very soon after the child's born, what kind of preventive measures would be important for that mother to be thinking of?

JB: If a mother doesn't look after her own child, she must make arrangements whereby there is some suitable person who is a full-time caregiver, who is going to stay with the family. Now, in days gone by, this notion that a young woman became a nanny and looked after the children and stayed on in the family was very common. My own nanny stayed on and looked after my mother until my mother was 90, until my mother died.

VH: That's the upper class. It's not the lower class or the middle class.

JB: No. It was the rule. In my childhood, in the sort of social class in which we were living, it was common.

VH: From what you're saying, babies shouldn't have to change people a lot.

JB: Changing can be extremely damaging from the start. Nowadays, it's very unusual for women to stay on in the family. People have their au pair girls who come for 6 or 12 months and then move on. This is all very unsatisfactory and the children aren't happy.

VH: There is one loss after another.

JB: Looking after your own children is jolly hard work, but you get a reward. Looking after others', unless you are going to be a kind of substitute mother to them over a long period of time, it's very unrewarding.

VH: In my private practice I'm seeing more and more borderline children presenting at around age 7. More than, say, 10 years ago, and it seems to have some relation to the number of caretakers.

JB: Oh yes. Some of us have been aware of it for a long time. I think we know what enables children to grow up healthy, happy, self-reliant, and confident. We've got a lot of evidence, which all points in the same direction, and if we ignore it, well that's society's problem.

VH: How would you summarize that? What do children need to grow up to be happy, secure?

JB: They need a mother figure who will care for them. She doesn't have to be on duty day in, day out. If she can get some assistance from her own mother, her husband, or one of her own sisters, the more help she gets, the better. But they should be responsible for their own children.

They should be the principal caregiver. And if they are not the principal caregiver, then they must try and find someone else who will be. Someone who plays that major role through the child's childhood. We know that works extremely well. Fortunately, it still works in a lot of families. As clinicians, we're concerned all the time with the casualties of the system where the children don't have that kind of ongoing, affectionate, encouraging care. In many strata of society, 50% or 70% of children do have it. There are still a large number who do have it, and women who think this is a worthwhile job.

VH: You apparently feel or felt that going away at 10 was a good thing?

JB: No, I don't.

VH: You didn't?

JB: No, I didn't think it was a good thing. It sounds absurd now, but during the war, 1917 to 1918, there were some air raids on London. And that was the only reason that my brother and I went away together to boarding school—he was 11, I was 10.

VH: The war was, of course, quite different for Americans.

JB: The air raids were thought by my parents to be unsettling to us children. I think their idea was mistaken. The raids were very trivial, but anyway, that was, in fact, the reason that we were sent away at that age. My parents didn't really believe in it. The fact that we went to public school at the age of 13 was a different story altogether. There were plenty of children, boys anyway, who enjoyed boarding school in their teens, but that was different. I'm very much against young children going to boarding school.

VH: You believe in attachment as being essential and necessary and rich, as a part of life, from birth to grave, as I understand. Professionals in most psychoanalytic institutes keep their connections with their analysts. They may resolve the transference neurosis through analysis, but they keep the attachment, I believe. And yet the literature seems to indicate that analysts and analysands should totally cut their attachment. Do you have any thoughts about what your research would say about that in terms of relationships?

JB: I think these clean, clear cuts are a very silly idea. I think it's much more sensible to retain links. I've always done so with my patients.

VH: That would not follow along with Kleinians.

JB: No, on the whole Kleinians seem to be rather remote from patients. I'm sure they vary.

VH: Something else in terms of attachment: I don't quite even know how to phrase the question. We see so many adults and children now, or I do, that may be functioning very well and yet they feel like they don't have a container around them. They feel like they don't have skin. And I'm thinking, now, about the concept of "the body near mother." With children that we see in therapy, we usually, somewhere along the line, hug them, or pat them, or make contact with their skin. In psychoanalysis there's a taboo on any physical contact. My own experience with some of these adult patients who have psychotic structures or autistic structures is that there are times when a gentle touch does seem to contain them, to help make some kind of feeling connection to them that they might not be able to make otherwise.

JB: I know just what you're talking about, and it's a hot potato. You see the difficulty is that touch can so easily mean sex. It needn't, of course. But, once you identify touch with sex, which has been done in the theoretical literature, you're in difficulty. There's no doubt touch and sex are connected. They're not inevitably connected, but they are somewhat connected. I think Freud was alarmed that the therapeutic encounter would involve sex, and he was adamant that this was a dangerous line. I think the truth of the matter is that in therapeutic work touch can, in certain circumstances between two people, be very valuable and therapeutic, but it also has to be used with quite a lot of discretion, because between a middle-aged man and an attractive young girl it could so much more easily mean sex than anything else. I think probably on the whole it's easier for female therapists than for male. But again, I'm sure, there must be situations where a female therapist and a male patient—

VH: What do you mean? Why would you say that it would be easier for a female therapist than a male therapist?

JB: You see, most patients are women, and I think female therapists and female patients are unlikely to get involved in a lesbian relationship. They might. On the other hand, a male therapist and a female patient is potentially dangerous.

VH: You're thinking men are less trustworthy than women?

JB: No, I simply mean that a male therapist and a female patient are statistically more likely to land in a sexual relationship if they aren't careful.

VH: I understand what you mean, and yet I have some feeling that you are giving men a bad rap.

JB: I'm a man myself. The truth of the matter is there is more seduction on their part, by men, than there is by women. That again is statistically correct.

VH: I'm certain, statistically, you're right.

JB: As a male therapist, one has to be careful about using touch, but that doesn't mean to say I haven't used touch, because I have.

VH: Can you say more about that?

JB: I helped a widow in a very distressed position, grieving for her husband, and I put my arms around her, and I let her cry on my knee. So, I'm not adverse to it, but you need to stay in control.

VH: It's such an important subject, I think, because people seem almost phobic about discussing it.

JB: Sure, it's something that is both very important and full of pitfalls. It's a difficult subject to do systematic research on for reasons we've discussed, and there is very little systematic research in point of fact, and that's a pity.

VH: You apparently caused quite a stir with Anna Freud and Melanie Klein when you first began to present your papers. What do you remember about that?

JB: It disappointed me, of course, that they didn't agree with me. I always hoped that I would persuade them. Melanie Klein had such very different ideas, and she was totally unable to compromise. You either agreed with her or you didn't agree with her, and if you didn't agree with her, you were out. Anna Freud was a different kind of person, much more modest, and an easier person to get on with. With her, it was rather strange because in all matters practical—home, young, small children—we were in complete agreement, and all the work on separation she valued very highly. But when we came to talking theory, she had no use for my ideas at all. She felt very wedded to her father's ideas, and any ideas that seemed to her to contradict her father's ideas she wouldn't have anything to do with. My personal relation with Anna Freud was very good, which I'm proud of. On practical matters we agreed; on theory we disagreed. I thought her theories simply didn't match her practice. Her ideas were based on her father's theories, which didn't fit.

VH: Winnicott seems to have had great regard for your work, but also some questions.

JB: Yes, I always held the view that Winnicott and I were singing the same tune. We were essentially giving the same message, but again he didn't like my theoretical ideas. He and Fairbairn were always concerned with real-life events. But, insofar as I used ideas derived from ethology, Winnicott didn't go along with that. I downplay these differences. My concern with theory is because of its practical implications. If people go along with the practical implications of my theory, I can put up with disagreement about theory. I do believe a lot of psychoanalysis theory is misleading and mistaken and gives people the wrong ideas and leads to bad practice. That disturbs me. A lot of people, I'm thankful to say, do not practice what they preach. They practice something much better than their theory would dictate. And that's a good job, but I think it's better to have a good theory than a bad theory.

VH: You're talked about abuse a lot.

JB: I've said too little, frankly. I've been appalled at how ignorant we have been—I have been—about physical abuse and sexual abuse. I was totally unaware of physical abuse until 1960. I was really unaware of sexual abuse until about 10 or 15 years ago. Most of my professional career has been lived in ignorance of these things, and I think that's terrible.

VH: How could that be in a clinic?

JB: If you don't look for things and don't ask about them, you don't find!

VH: I started out in child welfare where I was removing children from the home because of abuse. Very early in my career it was in my face.

JB: I've said time and again, that social workers have always known about these things, but psychiatrists have not, psychoanalysts have not. That's been the tradition in which I was brought up, I was taught, I practiced—ignorance, total ignorance.

VH: It would be hard to be with a child and a mother, in the same room, and not become aware if the mother moves her hand and the child flinches.

JB: You are well alerted to these things, and some of us weren't. What you are alerted to you notice, what you aren't alerted to you probably don't, especially if you have been taught not to.

VH: It does seem strange to me because I don't think you could see an adult patient or a child patient without thinking about intimacy, what kind of attachment they make or don't make.

JB: There are a lot of professional people who can see a lot of patients without being aware of any of these things.

VH: I do family and group therapy as well as psychoanalysis. I find your theories on attachment very helpful in doing family therapy in terms of "What just happened in the family that caused this ruckus?" Usually something happened to break off the feeling of security. I find it very helpful in working. It's so commonsensical.

JB: I developed all these theories because I'm a clinician and because I wanted to fit theory to clinical experience. That's what it's all about. I do maintain that my theoretical ideas are much closer to the data. The difficulty is that theories are very, very powerful. The theory that you are taught, the theory that you apply, the theory that you teach becomes such an integral part of you that you cannot get away from it, you cannot think in any other terms.

VH: So it always biases you then, in some way.

JB: There are people who can yank themselves out of their theoretical framework and can adopt a new one, but it's a big job, and it's not something you can expect a lot of people to do. They don't, never have. This is true whether they're physicists or chemists or geologists or—it doesn't matter what they are. What they're embedded in they practice, they teach, and they have great difficulty in changing. It's in the nature of the animal. Insofar as I've been a bit of an innovator, I've come to recognize that people don't change. This is also true of patients. We've all got resistances and defenses and all the rest of it. The truth of the matter is, that when we help a patient reorganize his feelings and thoughts and look at things afresh, it's a whopping great job. It's very slow, and it's all uphill. And the same is true of scientific theory. Theories are very, very powerful. I'm really proud I have drawn into the field some very, very able people, starting, of course, with Mary Ainsworth.

VH: Who else comes to mind?

JB: Colin Parks, who initiated all the work on bereavement. He worked with me for 10 years, from 1960 to 1970, roughly speaking. And in the ethological world Robert Hinde, and in the child development world all the people whom Mary Ainsworth has trained; Mary Main, Inge Bretherton are all influential, and so on. They're all very admirable, able people. So the field is now being explored by first-class scientists doing first-class research of high clinical relevance. That I'm very, very proud of.

VH: And rightly so. Are there clinicians whose work you admire?

JB: Too few, unfortunately. I've been reading, just this last week, an excellent paper by Alicia Lieberman in San Francisco. She worked with Selma Fraiberg before Selma died. Alicia Lieberman took her Ph.D. with Mary Ainsworth, and then she worked with Selma Fraiberg, and she is applying attachment theory in a very systematic way in treating mothers and infants. But they are rather few still.

VH: Did you come by writing naturally?

JB: Well yes, I think I did, to be quite honest. I enjoy writing. The first book I wrote was published in 1938, so I've been writing all my life really.

VH: Do you have some theories about who writes easily and who doesn't?

JB: Well I tell you, I think that one major problem is that when people start writing they think they've got to write something definitive.

They think they've got to write something important. I think that's fatal. The mood to write in is, "This is quite an interesting story I've got to tell. I hope someone will be interested. Anyway, it's the best I can do for the present." If one adopts that line, one gets over it and does it. But people get terribly inhibited because they think they've got to do something much better than they can do. I know various people who don't write, and I think that's the reason.

VH: Did you write as a child?

JB: When I was at public school I wrote a lot of essays, and I suppose I enjoyed it. I wrote home, and some of the letters I wrote home were quite amusing.

VH: Then your parents kept them.

JB: Every now and then I've seen a letter which they thought worth keeping.

VH: Do you think the response of the parent has something to do with encouraging creativity or writing?

JB: Well I suppose it must play some part. I don't think my parents ever particularly praised anything. At school, I was regarded as a reasonably competent essay writer. I think I was above average actually, but I wasn't outstanding in any conceivable way.

VH: When you started your first paper as an analyst, did you have a mentor or were you on your own?

JB: The answer is I did it on my own. My first paper to the British Psychoanalytical Society was called "The Influence of Early Environment on the Development of Neurosis and Neurotic Character" (Bowlby, 1940). It was about my observations of families in a child psychiatric setting.

VH: Was this after you were shocked by Klein?

JB: It was simultaneous.

VH: That event seems to have really affected you very profoundly. It just sounds like you were so mad at her.

JB: Yes, I thought she was just plain wrong, and I thought it was desirable: (a) to say so and (b) to produce evidence that that was the case. I was told in no uncertain terms that it was not an analyst's job to pay attention to real-life events—as explicit as that.

VH: So the belief was that basic trust had nothing to do with whether the child could depend on trustworthy objects or not?

JB: Well, I'm reluctant to say—I'm so utterly out of sympathy with this tremendous emphasis on autonomous fantasy that I just don't know what they did think or didn't think.

VH: I'm laughing because it does seem quite amazing to me that a child's trust has nothing to do with the real world.

JB: If you put it in that form, I suspect that many of them would qualify their opinion. If we go back to the founding fathers, Michael Balint, Fairbairn, and Winnicott believed in real-life events. Melanie Klein has played this very peculiar role in which, on the one hand, she's put emphasis on object relations; on the other hand, she's downplayed real-life events. It's been a very ambiguous role. She put tremendous emphasis on early autonomous fantasies, infantile fantasies. Although, if you had put it to her point blank, "Do you really not think that the child's real-life experiences are very important? she'd say, 'Oh no, of course I don't.' " But when it came down to practice and theory, she'd pay absolutely no attention to these things. I really have seen a lot of patients in my time, one way or another, and I've learned a very great deal from a limited number of patients. I've made appalling mistakes. It appalls me how much I've missed in the past, how inadequate I've been. That does really rather shock me.

VH: Does something particularly come to mind?

JB: I'm thinking of a particular patient who told me a great deal. She was a very disturbed woman, agoraphobic and anxious, a very difficult, aggressive, hostile woman. She told me a lot about how her mother threatened her with this, that, and the other. I gave far too little attention to that. I didn't really take it in at all. I think that was terrible. I'm sure she was telling me a lot of things that were absolutely true and of great importance to her whole life. That's just one example. Although I was plugging real-life events, there were a whole lot of events that I didn't give a lot of attention to—sexual abuse is one. Physical abuse is another. This particular patient talked about threats. I learned from her. I gradually learned that these things are enormously important. I had to learn the uphill way. I had to teach myself because no one else taught me. They taught me all the opposite.

VH: It sounds as though you could have written wonderful things about family therapy using your theories.

JB: Well, yes, but you see it took me a long time to work the theory out. I got onto the right track in 1957, but when I came to write these three volumes on attachment and loss, I was learning all the way. It took me a long time to work all that stuff out. Had I had more time, then I could have given more time to family therapy, but I simply didn't have the time.

VH: You created a wonderful body of work. Thank you so much for the time you've shared so generously with me.

As I waited for my taxi, I saw Dr. Bowlby dash out the front door of Tavistock. He was wearing a very British tweed hat. Like a 20-year-old, he jumped into his car, put it into gear, and drove off—82 years old and still undiminished in vigor!

His body of work shows the same energy and vigor of mind that his manner did. Though he is often quoted and referred to, he has not received the recognition he deserves in psychoanalysis. His work largely came out between the 1950s and 1970s, a period that was marked by stress on the individual rather than on family relations.

Today, at the beginning of the 1990s, we are likely to have a clearer understanding of the importance of family interrelationships and developments in child-rearing practices. Psychoanalysts have been and will increasingly be turning toward child and infant research, which Dr. Bowlby's work so effectively illuminates. And thus, although he has not received the recognition that he might have in psychoanalysis, it seems likely that in the 1990s analysts will turn to Dr. Bowlby's work for inspiration, and it will continue to have vigor in this decade.

Note. This interview originally appeared in Hunter (1991).

Case Discussion

In harmony with his life's work, Dr. Bowlby says the patient is unable to sort out what is real and what is fantasy. He states that Roselyn's childhood abuse has led her to mistrust attachments. He goes on to say she has an internal conflict between her wish to express her feelings and her fear of doing so.

Not surprisingly, John Bowlby's beginning focus was, "She was never quite sure nor is she now, what is real and what is fantasy. In relationship with her mother, she still isn't. I would focus on this not being quite sure what is real and what is fantasy because I think the important thing to do in therapy is to help a patient sort that out." He went on explaining that technically, "I would encourage her to give me, in the greatest possible detail, all the memories she has of what her mother did or what she thinks her mother did or what she thinks her mother said. And I would encourage her to go over that, scrutinize it, look at it, consider it; and if she says, 'Well, did my mother say that or didn't she?' I would say, 'Well look, I don't know, but you must think that one out. Go back to where you think your mother said that and think it out. Did she really say it?' "

His interpretation to the patient would be, "If she really said that she wanted you dead, then it was something so frightening and forgetful and dreadful that perhaps you didn't want to hear it. Maybe it was quite real, but you didn't want it to be real." I pointed out that the patient could "think" it was real but often was disconnected from her feelings. Bowlby said he'd say to the patient, "I think, well, these memories were so frightening that you don't want to remember the feelings."

Bowlby went on to explain the patient's defenses. "There are two reasons, I think, why a patient who's had a horrible time over a period of time won't remember. One is that she has been threatened by her mother and told by her mother this, that, and the other, and of course she's witnessed her mother's attempted suicides and so on—all those things. The last thing a child wants to believe is that that was horribly true. It's much nicer if it wasn't true. If it's so horribly true—there's one aspect of it—she doesn't want to believe it's true. She doesn't want to remember her feelings."

I said to him, "Another part of her wants to insist every memory is true because if I say anything like, 'In your mind,' she's really fast to tell me, 'No, it was not in my mind. It happened.' What she doesn't want to think about or feel is that she needed a good mother." I went on to tell him, "There were episodes where she would be so overcome with fear that she would sit on the floor and hold onto the edge of my Oriental carpet." I referred to these times as psychotic transferences.

Bowlby corrected my terms asking, "Did she feel in danger from you personally? I wouldn't go into transference unless she felt that you were the dangerous person."

I pointed out that she had never missed a session, but there were certainly moments during an hour when her observing ego lost its ability to observe. "While it was not constant by any means, she really did feel, at times, that I was a real danger. Even small events like a change of appointment would be experienced as something I chose to do on purpose to humiliate her or fool her."

Bowlby responded, "When she says you did it on purpose, you did it to humiliate her, I think I would then raise the issue, 'When do you recall your mother having done it on purpose?' I would take it straight back to her mother."

Bowlby was a careful listener and a generous respondent, saying, "My difficulty is I feel it's coals to Newcastle, three-fourths of it, you know, or nine-tenths. All I can do is emphasize the points that I would go for." He pointed out how some of the parents of abused children contradict and disconfirm the child's experiences and observations. Of my patient, he said that the mother may have said, "I didn't do that, I never said that, you're lying." He went on, "A parent can attempt to deny things which the child has already experienced so that is something to be explored, and also, you see, if a child said, 'I wish you would be kind to me,' her mother might say, 'You don't have any wishes of that sort, you aren't that sort of child.' In other words, flat contradictions." He continued, " . . . a parent can disconfirm a child's feelings: 'You aren't angry with me. I know you aren't angry with me.' So all this disconfirmation is very confusing to a child."

Bowlby felt it was important to help Roselyn remember some of the good things about her mother; that her mother did have some reasonable periods. He would say, "Now, were there ever times when your mother was kind to you? Can you recall any occasion when you hoped that she might be kind to you?"

I responded, "You know what happens when I do that? I become the most terrible, on-the-mother's-side person, and I am instantly the enemy, and I'm trying to set her up to be fooled again. And that's her words, 'If I think a good thought about my mother, then it will turn out I'm a fool and she's fooled me.' " I said, "She gave her wonderful gifts and wonderful clothes and then the next minute would whop her."

Bowlby said, "My guess is that her mother had fooled her. When she claims that you're on her mother's side, I think you perhaps need to dispute that and say it isn't true: 'I realize that your mother did behave as though she were kind; you were fooled, and you felt awful.' " He was sympathetic to how hard the work was. "I can see it's the devil's own job."

In thinking about Roselyn's difficulty in distinguishing what is real and what is fantasy, Bowlby wondered if she had had any previous therapy. When I said that she had, he wondered, "Since she is obviously very allergic to any suggestion that what she remembers of all those horrors of her childhood was fantasy, wasn't real, it may be the previous therapist had possibly taken that line."

I responded, "She didn't tell him. From what she's told me, she didn't tell the previous therapist—she kept her mother secret. She still has anxiety when she tells me some of these things. Her mother's dead."

Bowlby said, "She's still afraid her mother will find out."

I agreed, saying, "She was forbidden to tell anybody. She once told the Girl Scout leader about how physically abused she was, and the Girl Scout leader, assuming the child just needed attention and was making it up, called up the mother and reported. The mother knocked the heck out of the child. The one time she broke the silence, she felt that bad things had happened."

Bowlby said, "She was instructed by her mother never to say one single word about this."

I replied, "And her father also. Not directly, but by his always saying, 'Your mother's nervous; forget about it.' "

Bowlby responded, "She's had a lot of input, saying, 'You mustn't talk about this; this is completely forbidden. And if you mention one word of it'—I think almost certainly they would be very crude threats in one shape or another—'I will murder you if you say a word about this.' So I think this huge pressure on not saying, not remembering, and this terror that if she talks to anyone about it, it will leak around to her mother, just like the guide story. You're going to phone up her mother; her friends are going to phone up her mother. Her mother's going to find out about this."

I pointed out that she felt like a bad person; felt if her mother threatened her that way it must be her fault. If her mother said it, it must be so. Bowlby felt strongly that this mismatch between what a child experiences and observes and hears and her mother's disconfirmation of it all is why she can't disentangle what is real from what is fantasy. He felt she was told, "You mustn't remember this, it didn't happen, and you mustn't say it happened." It was never confirmed. It was often disconfirmed. Bowlby had no other suggestion except, "I think all you can do is go over it again and again."

I asked, "Do you have some thoughts about the impact on a child's mind when the environment is that attacking in terms of the migraine? Because the migraine—she's had biofeedback, she's had hypnosis, through the years, she's had Endurol. When I try to get her to look at the possibility of anger, she doesn't experience anger. She only experiences terror, no anger. She'll get angry at me. She can trust me if I'm late or some small infraction. She can sort of trust me with that."

Bowlby thought, "In a sense, anger and anxiety are closely related. In certain circumstances, if a person feels confident, she feels anger. If she doesn't feel confident, she feels frightened. And I can believe that at her age, she felt nothing but fright. I mean she couldn't dare be angry. I think it was totally unimaginable to be angry in her situation where she was so vulnerable."

Somewhere in the description of a piece of an hour I had used the word "contain" with the patient. Bowlby was quick to say, "You know, I hate this word contain. It's so silly, a bit of jargon. What you really mean is there's no one there to comfort you. Holding is comforting. I think the only sensible word to use in that context is 'comfort you—comfort you or protect you'—those are the two words which really have a meaning. This word contain, everyone uses, but it's a silly word."

Bowlby added, "I think it's interesting she says, 'It seems like when I get closer to expressing my real feelings, I get migraines.' I would be tempted there to have said, 'What are these real feelings?' "

I said, "It comes out when there's a choice, for example, between what her husband wants and what she wants because she's very deferential to everybody; and there's a lot of masochistic sort of surrender that she goes through very often in her life. She's terribly accommodating to everybody."

Bowlby understood, "Well, I mean she had to be with her mom. I can understand all that."

We talked about a few times when Roselyn had really been conscious of her angry feelings but had expressed them in letters or poems rather than in person. I mentioned her use of elaboration of short stories or poems to make a point. Bowlby commented technically, "I suspect pursuing that is not really productive. It's a diversion from the real problems. There are patients who are wonderfully good at telling you endless fantasy stories, what have you. I regard that as foolish. It's all a way of not telling you what's important, and so I think that any therapist who what I call, chases these defenses, is simply playing into the patient's problem."

We talked about my patient's attachment. I said, "In terms of attachment, I hear the black hole or her feeling of nothing under her as saying, 'I didn't feel at all securely attached or supported.' How would you hear it?"

Bowlby said, "I would, too. This poor woman has never had or virtually never had the experience of being comforted and protected and supported. In a sense, I had a glimpse of something about her migraines." He went on, "She said, 'When I get close to expressing my real feelings, I get migraines.' At that point she goes off into black holes which I regard as diversion because what she said is, 'I get closer to expressing my real feelings but I don't express them.' And consequently I think my line there would be, 'Well, let's see what your real feelings were. They obviously terrify you; that's why you have to go off into the black hole.' "

He spoke of her transference feelings. "Well now, you see, her real feelings are a desperate desire for comfort. A desperate desire for comfort and protection, and whenever she, in the past, has felt a desperate desire for comfort and protection, so far from getting them, she's been rejected and frightened and what have you. I think there's little doubt she's terrified that if she were to express her desire for comfort and protection from you, you will behave like her mother in that you won't sympathize, you won't respond, you will condemn, you will despise, pour contempt, ridicule. And I think all that needs saying right here and now."

I described the flavor of her resistance. "She does something pretty nasty to me pretty often. She will tell me, 'You don't need to care. I don't need your caring. You're paid; you don't need to care.' And it's really a pushing back into me of my caring feelings. Or an attempt to push them back."

Bowlby responded, "Insofar as there is this conviction in her mind that you will, in fact, express nothing but contempt and scorn for any desire she might have, she is then going to turn the tables on you."

I said, "Interpreting it makes this such a tiny little bit of headway. With some people you interpret it for 2 years and they get it."

Bowlby understood. "Her basic experience in life is that whenever she's wanted comfort and protection, she's been threatened, ignored, ridiculed, or what have you, and consequently she constantly believes that this is the only way that anyone will ever react, and she's mean to you."

He suggested that a paper by Selma Fraiberg (1982) might be helpful. "The paper is about treating these very damaged young mothers who have never experienced any comfort or protection. The technique she was using was simply to say, 'Well, of course you felt absolutely miserable; of course you wanted desire and comfort; of course that's all you wanted, and you never got it.' In other words, make it absolutely plain that you know just how she did feel. I think that's a very valuable paper," he said. He went on, "It's the only place where I've ever found someone who abdicated expressing all the feelings—a therapist expresses all the feelings they know that patient did have. They aren't asking how the patient felt; they're telling them how the patient felt. I think that's important."

I said, "You wouldn't worry about putting words into her mouth—in seducing her. In a way, you are trying to seduce her into feeling her real feelings by giving her the feelings."

Bowlby responded, "Yes, and you see, by expressing it this way, you're indicating that you understand and sympathize with those feelings. You don't say, 'I understand and sympathize,' but you make it plain that that is, in fact, what you do because that's the way you say it."

I said, "She told me such terrible stories sometimes that she would hear me sniff because it made me tearful. I would have tears, and she would eventually hear me sniff, and it would upset her very much in terms of 'You don't need to cry for me.' " I went on, "It really freaks her out, and I would interpret it."

Bowlby wondered, "When you say you interpret it, in what way?"

I said, "You felt as a child you didn't deserve anyone's love and sympathy, and now when you have it, you feel that you have to push it away."

Bowlby responded with excited animation, "Because you expect me to be rejecting and hostile—you see, on the one hand you're showing how distress made it—made her own distress that much nearer the surface. But she still believed that the only reaction from you would be contempt, rejection, et cetera, et cetera." I said I had lost my objectivity in crying for her. Bowlby corrected me, "You responded with sympathy and caring about her—she had to reject it in such a way. She rejects you because she expects you to reject her."

I reported, "It's like you were offering her poison, like it's going to injure her, and she's also expressed concern that she's injured me. That comes up a lot. If she feels I'm visibly moved by something, then she feels my being visibly moved injures me somehow."

Bowlby said, "I wouldn't take that too seriously. I think what she's frightened of on that occasion is that if you're going to be visibly moved, then she might be visibly moved, and that's the one thing she can't afford ever to trust. She doesn't trust you."

I pointed out, "That's when she gets the most defensive. You can just see her anxiety and defenses go up real fast."

Bowlby shared his own experience. "This reminds me of a patient whom I treated over a long period of time. She was an extremely hostile, difficult woman. She's the woman who I mentioned yesterday who used to tell me about the threats her mother meted out to her. I didn't take her seriously. I know now I should have. But every now and then, when things were going reasonably quite well, she became very quietly hostile and needling, finding some sore spot and pushing. And I used to get irritated. Well, now this person was getting under my skin, so I said, 'Why do you have to get under my skin?' Her reply was, 'I can't take kindness'; and what she then went on to say was that when she felt that I'd been a little bit kind, she had to needle me and show that I wasn't kind and that I got irritated with her. What she couldn't afford, you see, was to hope for kindness and not get it, and she didn't expect to get it. She felt it would be better not to hope."

I said I found the paradox of Roselyn coming for therapy four times a week for years, and yet her terror of hope, difficult. Bowlby responded, "It's just something you have to latch on to. You have to latch on to hope because it is difficult. I couldn't agree more. It is all so difficult. She is so convinced that there will be no real kindness, and, of course, she's so convinced that in fact she's been fooled. At an unconscious level. She is all the time expecting you to fool her."

I pointed out, "Often when she starts to report some past terror, she suddenly seems to become psychotic. She'll look around the room curiously and sometimes Roselyn will even say, 'She'll get me, she'll get me.' "

Bowlby said, "She switches into a totally different gear."

I said, "It's as though she suddenly feels her mother's presence. It feels really like she's psychotic. It doesn't feel hysterical."

Bowlby said, "I think the more you can help her realize that those feelings are just exactly what she did feel in the past, the more she'll realize that *that* is a true girl. She did experience that, so to speak, in the past because the important thing to my mind is that she experiences these things and then locates them where they belong. They belong in the past."

I said I agreed but, "That's another thing that's so hard with her in addition to getting her to feel her own feelings. The phrase I've developed is that her mother has 'no past tense.' And she doesn't. And I keep interpreting it, and sometimes I feel as though I need an exorcist. I cannot get this woman to have a past tense."

Again, with humility, Bowlby said, "It's not as though I know about this. I don't. I'm simply saying this is the way I would set about it. You see, I think there's one thing which—she told you this a dozen times, and you've registered it a dozen times. They still don't believe that you believe it to be true, or I think somewhere in her mind, she doesn't think that you really believe it."

I responded, "She will also question if she *should have* believed it."

Bowlby went on, "That's a critical thing, you see, because this difficulty, did it really happen, was it really true? The more her mother has disbelieved it and disconfirmed it, the more doubtful she (Roselyn) is whether it is true herself, and so to some extent she's trying to convince herself that it's true when she's trying to convince you it's true. She doesn't believe some part of it is true. She supposes that you don't think it's true, either."

I reported Roselyn's first dream in the analysis and my feeling of difficulty in helping the patient realize she did deserve good care. "In that first dream, there's a party in her home and there are guests and there's dinner. And in the bathroom window there appears the face of this waif street urchin child who wants to come in. And in the dream, Roselyn pulls the blind, threatens the child, shuts her out—is absolutely humiliated that she would even be there. She doesn't want anyone to know she's even there and feels this child should be punished for having wanted to come in."

Bowlby interprets, "After all, that's exactly what her mother did towards her as a child. She has taken her mother's attitudes aboard. When she thinks, feels, behaves like that, she is simply siding with her mother."

I asked, "What do you say to her? I've said everything I can think of."

Bowlby asked me, "Just give me a little excerpt of what she might have said."

I gave him the example he wanted. "She says, 'It had to be my fault. It had to be my fault that she hit me. It had to be my fault. Anybody who begged and pleaded and humiliated themselves so should have died. They should have chosen death.' "

Animated, Bowlby said, "Well now, I would respond to it and maybe you do too. Anyway, I would respond by saying, 'Yes, you're talking just like your mother, aren't you? It's your mother's voice, not yours.' I think that a child who's been subjected to this type of experience year in, year out—I don't know how many years, but many, many years as a child—this is ingrained, and it's not surprising it takes a hell of a time to get it out. I think you've got to stick to this line and plug it in using different idioms and different lingo and be pretty forthright. 'That's just your mother speaking.' "

I asked if he had ever successfully treated a patient this disturbed. He said he had and that "You just have to keep plugging for a very long time." He reassured me that if I kept going the way I was, she wouldn't commit suicide.

I said, "I was often anxious with her saying, 'I'm only living for you, and I'm only alive because you want me to be alive not because I want to be alive. I want to be alive because I want to be alive.' I have said things like, 'You think I don't know that you want to live.' I've said, 'It's true I want you to live, but I believe you wouldn't be here unless you wanted to live.' I feel very uncomfortable with this, the responsibility she's trying to place, and I don't want to push her away from attachment and feeling we're together, and I want her to live, and yet I also don't want her to load me up with that responsibility. I feel uncomfortable with this."

Bowlby was clear: "I think you've just got to live with it."

I wondered, "How would you handle a patient saying something like that to you?"

He replied, "I just—there's no words. I mean I know what they're doing, but there isn't anything one can usually say, and I mean if they say, 'I know you want me to live,' I'd say, 'Yes, of course, I do.' "

I said, "At times she will say—really argue the right to suicide with me."

Bowlby was adamant, "I wouldn't rise to that at all. 'Okay, if you want to commit suicide, it's your affair, not mine.' I mean, I would be really quite forthright about that because what a patient of that sort is trying to do is, in fact, a form of blackmail; and I think one mustn't rise to it. I think it's better that the affirmation comes from your behavior and your tone of voice. I don't think you can say it. If you show that you are concerned about her and concerned to go on seeing her, and you make notices that you'll be sorry if she committed suicide, I think that's all you can do. I think that in principle I'm against attempting reassurance; I don't think it really works."

I went on, "I have some feeling that she needs to feel the connection and that she's wanting me to reaffirm it. Theoretically, where my mind goes is that if you had parents who never affirmed your value or your worth or your wonderfulness, there seems to be something, sort of sincere, in her seeking someone to say, 'I value your life,' that she didn't get as a child."

Bowlby replied, "I'm entirely with you. If you feel that she is saying she is desiring that, you can say to her, 'Look I think you need someone to reassure you that you are a valuable person.' "

I asked, " 'You need' or 'you want?' "

Bowlby said, " 'You want.' I would also say that you wanted your parents to feel that and to assure you of that in contrast to what they did do and say. But they didn't, and that's a terrible thing to have to recognize. If the patient feels that, I can't do what they didn't do. I think what I'm really saying is, as a therapist, one cannot make good what happened in the past. All you can do is help a patient make the best of her recognizing that the past has been very damaging and appalling."

When we considered the place in "The Hour" where I said, "If you feel your real feelings and trust me with them, you're afraid you will go mad and cease to exist," Bowlby and I felt differently. Bowlby empathized, "No, I don't agree. If you're feeling your real feelings, you will appeal to me for comfort and protection and are terrified I'll reject you and pour contempt on you." I said something more about Roselyn's having all this stuff inside, "boiling up." Bowlby was quick to respond, "I don't like that image of yours as though it's all steaming up inside and wants to come out. I think that's an awfully bad metaphor because, you see, if I'm right, looking for comfort and protection is quite a specific form of behavior, and it is asking for quite a specific type of response; and it is the response she has no hope whatever of ever getting. I believe if you make the claim that that's what she wants, that she has no confidence that you'll understand or sympathize or respond, there's a simple, basic, interpersonal transaction. Quite specific, she wants to behave like this, and she wants you to behave like that. That's where this metaphor 'reservoirs'—it simply misses the bus, and the word 'contain' misses the bus."

I said, "Her fear of madness, I think, is very real though."

Bowlby was firm, "I wouldn't pay any attention to it. Because it's not central to the issue. She's not going to go mad if, in fact, you are dealing with her real interpersonal feelings and she is not going to commit suicide either. You deal with what matters. And as I say, what matters is her hope for care and protection and total disbelief that anyone would ever reciprocate."

I explained my fear. "Maybe the two episodes she's had where she was psychotic served a purpose. In part they hold me in fear because they did scare me. The time when her husband called me and the burglars had come to her house and emptied everything out, she really was not even responding to hand movement or voice or anything. She really was off the deep end, and it really scared me because I had the feeling she actually could have gone off the deep end at that point. And the time when she felt the doctor might kill her really scared me in terms of showing she could lose her mind, I guess."

Bowlby supported, "Yes, I do know just what you're talking about. I think all you've got to do is grin and bear it because I think if you're there and respond to her in a human way, she won't do it. If that isn't enough, then there's nothing you can do. All I can say is, I've had suicidal patients, and they haven't committed suicide; and I just carry on in the way that I'm describing and simply hope for the best."

I asked, "Have they had psychotic episodes?"

Bowlby replied, "No, but I wouldn't be too disturbed by brief psychotic episodes because there is bound to be some decompensation." He went on, "I think the really important thing is to deal with what she is actually feeling, and, I mean, we've plugged this particular one about care and comfort and protection and so on. But I believe this is what it's all about." I asked if perhaps her saying she felt like a crystal was a result of my not having comforted and protected her. I thought he would feel I should just keep saying warmly, "You want me to comfort and protect you." Bowlby agreed, "In one shape or another. I'd try to vary it a bit, but essentially I'd say, 'Of course, you have absolutely no belief that that could ever happen or I could react in that kind of way and that all you expect is contempt and rejection.' You see I'm putting this in absolutely straight interpersonal terms. You won't behave like this; you expect me to behave like that. This is all behavioral. It's feeling behavior. The word 'contain' has no feeling in it at all. It has no action in it."

I conjectured, "I think it's a word we use perhaps to avoid intimacy as therapists."

Bowlby agreed. "Yes, I know. I mean, it's used in this clinic all too horribly often. I'm blowing up at you for using it because there's too much going on here. But you see, I think it's completely silly and misses the bus. When we're talking about human interaction, human behavior, I treat you this way, you treat me this way. I expect this; you expect that. That's what it's all about, and that's what it was all about when she was a child with her mother."

I said, "Comfort and protection are illusions really. She has to internalize the relationship in the end to obtain a feeling of comfort. Is that right? Somehow she has to interject that."

Bowlby replied, "What one's hoping to do is to help her discover that even if her mother never, ever responded with kindness, protection, and comfort, and only with hostility, that is not the way everyone in the world behaves. There are lots and lots of people who would respond with comfort and protection. A person who has had that experience—whatever experience you've had with your mother—you carry as an expectation. That's how people behave. That's how other people in that role—maternal role, let's call it—abound. A patient is generalizing from a sample of one; her mother is a sample of one; and she has had that experience; and so you see, it's rather like you are in an airplane, and the airplane crashes, and you escape. Well now, how do you react to airplanes from that point on? Airplanes crash—that's their nature."

I asked, "Can you elaborate the ability and potential of analysis to protect the patient?"

Bowlby repeated, "Responding with comfort and protection."

I asked, "How do you respond with protection?"

He said, "You indicate that you're on the patient's side. If someone came in with a hatchet, you would stand up. It is indicative of how you feel and would behave in certain circumstances. This is exactly how other people handle her."

I went on, "There's another paradox in that she wants protection from the feelings she feels."

He affirmed, "You can't give her that protection." I agreed that would keep her ill.

Bowlby went on, "Sure, she's got to—what one hopes to enable her to do is to express what she wants and hopes for, which she never expects, and to discover that someone else understands it, respects it, and is prepared to respond. One is trying to help her recognize that generalizing from her experience with her own mother, a sample of one which was absolutely true and just and buried in the past, doesn't necessarily apply to the whole of humanity."

I asked, "What would you predict with the migraine? Would the feeling of comfort and protection eliminate the migraine, or would the freeing of the anger?"

Bowlby replied, "Initially—I'm concerned with her comfort and protection, as you see at the moment, because there is plenty of potential anger but she hasn't had it—and people won't. I think one of the important things here is always the contempt: 'Silly little crybaby, you just bug off.' That type of total rejection is what she expects from you. Help her discover that maybe that isn't the way everyone behaves."

I wondered, "Do you have some thoughts regarding somatic expression of the lack of a secure base?"

Bowlby concluded, "Well, yes, I suppose I do. You see, people develop psychosomatic symptoms. Precisely which psychosomatic symptoms they will exhibit is anyone's guess. It might be asthma, it might be gastric pain, it might be God knows what. I don't care. The issue is what precipitates, what is the basic thing in them that precipitates whatever the symptom is."

Ernest Wolf

Dr. Wolf is a well-known Kohutian who has written a great deal regarding selfobject functions. In this interview he gives a remarkably full account of how he came to be a psychoanalyst, and allows us to see the origins of his special capacity for empathy.

This interview took place on September 14 and 15, 1990, in the book-lined home of the gracious Ernest Wolf and his wife, Ina. Dr. Wolf is on the faculty and a training and supervising analyst of the Chicago Institute for Psychoanalysis. He also holds a faculty position in psychiatry at Northwestern University. The range of his learning, as evidenced by his publications, is remarkable and includes translations from German, essays on Freud's intellectual development, studies of theory and clinical practice relating largely to self psychology, and the application of psychoanalytic formulation to understanding literature and art. His wife shares his interest in literature and has coauthored one paper with him on Virginia Woolf.

After concluding the first interview, Dr. Wolf shared with me special books and photographs and generously offered to show me his videotape of Kohut's last presentation in Berkeley; he commented on it warmly and generously, indeed, with such feeling of friendly memory and loss that tears came to his eyes. The gift of his playing the tape for me and his sharing of his own responsive feeling toward it characterize well the nature of the man. The warmth, generosity, and hospitality, along with the ease of intelligent exchange encouraged by Dr. Wolf and his wife give an insight into the course of Dr. Wolf's career and suggest he has carried into his own life and relationships his belief in responsiveness and empathy.

Interview

Virginia Hunter: How did you first decide you wanted to be an analyst?

Ernest Wolf: In 1951 I was 30. I was doing a psychiatric residence in Cincinnati when I decided to become an analyst, because the important people, the ones that I respected, were all analysts.

VH: Who were those people, and what were the things they taught that impressed you?

EW: The chairman of the department was Maurice Levine who probably had the best department of psychiatry in the country at the time, and he was a very, very impressive person. He used to have case conferences, once a week, that would be attended by all the professionals in the department; we would present cases and discuss them in the group. His ability to grasp quickly what the patient's conflicts or symptoms were all about was impressive. In his department was Milton Rosenbaum, second in the department. He was equally outstanding. He later became the first chairman of psychiatry at Albert Einstein and later the first chairman of psychiatry at the Hebrew University of Jerusalem in Israel. He had a very distinguished career, and we worked together. One of your [Virginia Hunter's] supervisors, Lou Gottschalk, was in the department. He was an excellent teacher and researcher. He had been in the Public Health Service, and they saw to it that he got analytic training, and he was one of my supervisors. And then there was Luis Wise who later went to Seattle, Washington, and there was Phil Piker who stayed in Cincinnati, and Fred Kapp, Donald Ross, and Henry Lederer. All these people were analysts. All of those teachers and students were proud to have commuted from Cincinnati to Chicago.

VH: How far a commute?

EW: It's about 300 miles, and since courses at the Institute are on alternate weekends, all day Friday and a half-day on Saturday, it made it possible for them to come in every other weekend and then go back and have their regular work. It was set up that way by Franz Alexander [who directed training at the Institute] with the conscious idea that it made it easy for people from other cities to have psychoanalytic training. So today there are institutes in Denver, in St. Louis, and in Cincinnati. At one time they were just local groups of people interested in psychoanalysis who would commute to Chicago—they became really Chicago colonies. If they had a minimum of five training analysts, they could start their own institute. We now have the same relationship with Minneapolis and Milwaukee.

VH: What year did you apply to begin your training in psychoanalysis?

EW: I applied I believe in 1954 after an interruption in my training in 1952. I started the residency in July, 1951. In December 1952, when I was a 2nd-year resident, we had our yearly routine chest X-rays. In January, they told me I had a lesion in my lung and that it could be tuberculosis or histoplasmosis or coccidiomycosis, the latter of which are fungus diseases, endemic to the Ohio Valley. They slapped me into bed, and after 3 months in bed, my skin test turned positive for histoplasmosis. But the guinea pigs that they had injected with the sputum that I had coughed up died of tuberculosis. So they had a diagnosis of tuberculosis, and it meant being shipped off to a sanitarium. I went back to Baltimore to my family to be hospitalized in a sanitarium. Also, since I was still a citizen of Maryland, I got free sanitarium hospitalization there. I was one of the first patients to get isoniazid and streptomycin, which is an effective drug against tuberculosis. Anyway, the lesion shrank a little bit and no further sputum was positive. After months, I was discharged. We, Ina and I, were already engaged at that time; so 2 days after I got out of the hospital in October 1953, we got married, in Baltimore; and I returned to Cincinnati by November for the year left in my residency. It was during that year that I applied to the Chicago Institute as a candidate. The dates are very close.

VH: You had come from Germany at what age?

EW: I was 18 in February 1939, and I came to the United States on March 30, 1939.

VH: Could you tell that story?

EW: I grew up in Germany. I was the oldest of three. I have two sisters, one 2 years and one 6 years younger. When I was 12 in 1933, the

Nazis came into power. From then on the handwriting was on the wall that I had no future in Germany. No future for education. Jews were no longer allowed to go to university. No future business-wise. They made it very difficult. So when I was 15, in 1936, I decided that I wanted to leave Germany and emigrate to the United States. I traveled to Stuttgart where the American consulate was and applied for a visa. It took 3 years to get that because at that time, just as now, there was a quota. The quota for Germany in the 1930s was, I think, 27,000 a year from Germany. At the time that I applied in 1936 it was filled. For the next year it was filled, and my number didn't come up until March, 1939.

VH: Where was your home town?

EW: Aachen. The French name is Aix-la-Chapelle. It's on the border of Germany, Holland, and Belgium. If you can imagine the point where the three countries meet, on the German side, that's where the city is. We were close enough to the border that we could go by streetcar or walk across the border.

VH: And what did your father do there?

EW: My father was in a business that sold fabrics for men's suits to tailors and department stores. The family had owned it since the 1890s. In the 1920s, it passed to his older brother, and my father worked for his older brother. In the early 1920s, after the end of the First World War, my father was one of five in his family, three boys and two girls. My father passed his share of the business to his brother-in-law-to-be because in those days, at least in Germany, young girls needed to have a dowry in order to get married. That became her dowry, and she married the bookkeeper of the business. Then he himself started a new business in another city, Gelsenkirchen, which is where I actually was born in 1921.

VH: How did you understand your father's personality? It was a large family, and yet it seems, as you describe it, he sort of gave away his birthright. How do you understand that?

EW: I always understood it as very generous on his part and as having a sort of sense of responsibility to his family. Also, that he was somewhat adventuresome, I thought. Rather than being part of the family business, where he probably would have to do like the others, he wanted to be out on his own. So he founded his own business. Unfortunately, that went under in the Great Depression. So that he had to return back to the home town and become merely one of the employees in the family business.

VH: How did that affect you?

EW: It affected me—it gave me a sense of inferiority, in a way. I didn't feel quite—I couldn't feel as proud of him as I wanted to be because he was only an employee in the firm where my uncle and aunt were the bigwigs. They were the owners, and he was just an employee. It didn't go over very well.

VH: You've talked about deidealization in some of your work. You're really saying that sort of happened to you, as I hear it.

EW: Yes, yes, yes. There was somewhat of a deidealization, a disillusionment in him. He was a nice guy, my father; but I began to wonder about his competence since his own business went bankrupt, even though there was a Great Depression, and that wasn't necessarily a sign of personal failure. And then having to work for his brother. That was less than admirable. I was aware of that as a youngster. It made me feel inferior to my cousins.

VH: How did your mom react? What was she like?

EW: I don't think that she—if she reacted to it, I'm not aware of it. What was she like? A very warm, I almost said loving kind of person. I was the favorite. I was the oldest, and I was the only boy. Clearly I was the favorite. There were two favorites. My youngest sister was the other favorite because she was the baby. She got all kinds of special privileges because she was the baby. I, by that time, was 6 years older, and I didn't really deserve it. I could even baby her myself. My parents had a good marriage from what I could tell. My mother deferred to my father very much. When he was there, he obviously was the boss. She was a very competent housewife. She, in contrast to him, was a high school graduate; he had not been. He had had a kidney illness as a youngster, which forced him to leave school. At the time, in November of 1938, the night of the crystal chandeliers, the *Kristallnacht*, the Nazis sort of had a rehearsal for their later misdeeds. They went into all the Jewish homes and arrested all the men and did a lot of beating up. My father was traveling at the time and was arrested, so she suddenly had to run the family. She certainly turned out to be very energetic and very competent, which I must admit, at the time, astonished me. I hadn't expected it.

VH: What did you expect?

EW: I expected more that she would wring her hands and not know what to do. But I was surprised. I had never had any real occasion to observe her outside the house. As a matter of fact, outside the house she wasn't active, except maybe socially. I had no idea that she could be competent in facing off some bureaucrat. I had no idea that she would have the courage to go down to the police, bang the table, and want to know where my father was. That sort of thing. I had no idea she had that in her. There had never been any occasion for her to do anything like that before.

VH: Did they ever return your dad? What happened to him?

EW: Oh, the local police in Gelsenkirchen. He was visiting some cousins. He got beat up together with some other men and taken to jail. Then the next morning they were all supposed to be taken to a concentration camp. The local police at the jail somehow decided that he was too sick to be transported after the beating. So because of that they kept him in jail for 3, 4, 5 days. Then they let him go.

VH: Then what happened?

EW: He came home.

VH: Then what happened?

EW: Nothing.

VH: But what about the war? What happened in the war to the family, to your sisters?

EW: By that time we were gone. They're both now in Baltimore.

VH: So they came, too, to this country.

EW: They came too. They came later. I came first in March 1939. They went to Sweden about 1 or 2 months before I went to the United States in March. In January or February of that year they went to Sweden on a children's transport. Two or 300 Jewish children were taken by the Swedes.

VH: Without their parents?

EW: Without their parents.

VH: Your parents left too.

EW: I left in March. Because of the children being in Sweden without their parents, there were some people in Sweden who were taking them in as refugees, who then tried to get my parents to come too. They succeeded. In August, 1939, both my parents went to Sweden. In September, the war broke out.

VH: Did all their five brothers and sisters get out too or did they stay?

EW: Do you mean my parents' brothers and sisters?

VH: Your father's, yes, and your mother's.

EW: On each side there were five. Less than half of them got out, half of them did not. One brother of my father's, his oldest brother, got out. The other three siblings did not get out. They were killed. On my mother's side, one brother got out and went to Brazil. Another brother got out and went to Holland. When the Germans occupied Holland, they recaptured him, so to speak. Her two sisters did not get out. So those three were killed. So of the five on each side, two survived. My parents each had one surviving sibling.

VH: What was your mother's maiden name?

EW: Hoffmann.

VH: All of these uncles and aunts, people that you were close to got killed. How did that impact you?

EW: My grandmother, who I was very close to, was killed also.

VH: Your mother's or your father's mother?

EW: My mother's mother. My father's mother had died back in 1931 or something like that. I still knew her, but she died in the 1930s. It has had a very important impact on me. I had a very intense feeling of fear and hatred of the Germans. And it is only now that I am beginning to recover from that. This is over 50 years later. I don't know much more that I could say about that.

VH: Do you ever go to Germany now?

EW: Yes. I'll tell you how intense the feeling was. The first time that Ina and I went to Europe we rented a small car in Amsterdam, in Holland. I wanted to show her where we had lived in Germany. It was right near the border. We drove and when we came to the German border, I could no longer drive. She had to drive. I was so terrified that I would have maybe the slightest traffic mishap and would have to confront a German policeman.

VH: How old were you then?

EW: This was in 1967, about 21 years ago; I was 46.

VH: And that much fear that you would have a rage reaction or fear that you would be hurt?

EW: Consciously that I would not be able to speak, that I would be paralyzed. That's fear of rage, isn't it? I was going to say that reminds me a lot of Gerhart Piers. You know Maria Piers and Gerhart Piers. Gerhart Piers used to be the director of the Institute here in Chicago. When he first went back, as an adult male, in his 40s, for his first return to Germany, he simply could not go in, period. He stayed in Switzerland, and his wife went in and out without him.

VH: I thought of the Kestenberg research. I've treated a number of people whose parents had been in concentration camps. How did your parents react when you first said you wanted to leave and come here?

EW: They were opposed to it. I was only 15. They felt that this man, Hitler, was a madman and that was obvious to everybody. This was the country of Beethoven and Mozart, Kant and Schiller. This was a civilized country, and no civilized country could have a madman at the head of the government for very long. Somehow this just couldn't last. Nobody anticipated what was going to happen.

VH: It was too horrible to anticipate.

EW: Yes. Until this happened, nothing like that had happened in any civilized country before. Uncivilized areas of the world are where we might think of this kind of thing happening. But we never would have thought that would happen in Germany. They were opposed to my going. They said by the time I was grown up things would be back to normal. I was, on the contrary, insistent. I applied for the visa. Not only that, when you apply at the American consulate, you get a number which puts you in line. I urged them to apply too so they could get a number and get in line. They didn't. I finally persuaded my mother, about a year later, to apply; but she got a number that was higher than mine. I wasn't able to persuade my father until much later. So the three of us had different numbers at the American consulate. Mine was 5,960 or something like that. My mother's was 11,000 something, and my father's number was in the high 20,000s. It shows you how people felt. When they got to Sweden later in 1939 and then wanted to go from Sweden to the United States, my father had to go as a dependent upon my mother who had the lower number, or they would not have gotten out of Sweden.

VH: How did that go with the marriage when she said, "I'm going," and he said, "I'm not?"

EW: He was not a tyrant. He probably said, "If that's what you want to do, but I'm not going to do it. I think it's useless, I think it's unnecessary." He might have said that. But he would humor her.

VH: So they eventually ended up here too?

EW: Yes.

VH: Now, how old were you by the time they got here?

EW: Well, they got here a year later than I did.

VH: Only a year. So how, when you left at 18, how were you going to support yourself? Did the family gather funds and say, "We'll support Ernest and send him off?"

EW: No, no, no. First of all, even in Germany, they had foreign exchange controls. You could leave only with 10 marks, which was roughly the equivalent of $4 at the time.

VH: Four dollars!

EW: Four dollars to land in New York. Fortunately, my father had a cousin who was a physician in New York. He was the one who had given an affidavit for me to come over here.

VH: What was his name?

EW: His name was Paul Weil. He is dead now. He was a first cousin. He had a practice in Brooklyn, in general medicine. As a matter of fact, he was a refugee himself. He'd only been in the United States since about 1934 or 1935. He emigrated from Germany to the United States. By that time, by 1939, he had established himself a small practice. He was on the faculty of one of the medical schools as well. I don't know for what reason he left Germany, at the time. It was after the Nazis came to power, but he had to leave. Something happened, and he had to leave. He came through our town, and we smuggled him across the border.

VH: And you still don't know what happened?

EW: Happened to what? Why he had to leave? No, I didn't know. Look, this was when I was 14 years old when he came through. So I was part of the smuggling operation. I used to be the lookout, running ahead. We knew the border very well because every Sunday we used to go on hikes.

VH: Through the woods.

EW: Through the woods into either Holland or Belgium.

VH: But when you finally got to New York, you didn't say, "Hey, cousin, what happened back there?"

EW: No. Because by that time everybody had to leave. I just assumed that he left because he was Jewish, and he knew something terrible was going to happen with the Nazis. But thinking back on it now, back in 1934 when he left, either he was very farsighted in what was going to happen, or something was going on that he had to leave at that time.

VH: He was a doctor in Germany?

EW: Yes. Anyway, he had some obligation to us because we had stuck our necks out to smuggle him across the border. So when my father wrote him that I needed an affidavit to get an American visa, he did it, and that's how I got my visa and came to New York in March 1939. There is something else in order to make this understandable. Sometime early in the 1900s, an aunt of my father's had emigrated to Baltimore. He knew that. That's all we knew, and that her last name was Strauss. I don't know if we knew her first name or not, probably not. After I got the affidavit from my cousin, Paul Weil, we were looking for affidavits for my two sisters so that they could go too. So my father wrote to the Council of Jewish Women, I believe that's what it's called, in Baltimore, saying, "Back in 1900 so and so, an aunt of mine emigrated to Baltimore. Can you help me find her so we can get affidavits for my two little girls?" So they wrote back saying they could not find her. It just so happened that the lady who was President of the Council's name was Strauss. She had a cousin whose name was also Strouse. The two ladies decided that they were going to give the affidavits. So they gave affidavits for my two sisters, and they said they would take them into their homes. My sisters were 12 and 16 or so. They were to be taken into their homes until eventually my parents could come. So when I arrived in New York, I wanted to go down to Baltimore and see what kind of a home my sisters were going to. My parents wanted to know this too.

VH: They must have been worried to death.

EW: Yes. They were going to send their little girls to strangers. So, after I had been in New York for a week, I went to Baltimore on a Greyhound bus to look over these two families. They were very nice and very gracious and very generous, and I stayed in Baltimore. I stayed with them for my sisters until they came a year later. So they kind of took me in.

VH: So you liked them better than the cousin?

EW: Yes.

VH: Why? What's the difference?

EW: My cousin was a struggling bachelor and New York was a—the Depression wasn't over yet, in 1939. Jobs were extremely hard to find. When I came to Baltimore they said, "We will find you a job; you will live with us."

VH: They were more enfolding, or more gracious, or more welcoming?

EW: Yes, they were Americans. My cousin was a struggling refugee. They were established Americans, upper-middle class, fairly well-to-do. I stayed in their home, and one day after I had been downtown for something or another and came back to my room, there was a bed full of clothes—underwear, shirts, socks.

VH: They really adopted you.

EW: They adopted me, right. That was hard to resist, and they found me a job.

VH: Doing what?

EW: The job that they found me was filling furniture polish into bottles, loading them into cartons, then moving the cartons onto trucks, which was not the sort of work where I flourished, but it was a job. I made $11 a week, about 22½ cents an hour, I think. It was still a 44-hour week then. That was the job they found me—at first. Then, after I had been there about 2 or 3 months, one of the family's friends, who was a surgeon at Johns Hopkins University, heard of an opening as a technician in one of the laboratories at Hopkins.

VH: So you knew you wanted to be a doctor by then.

EW: No, but I had been trained as a laboratory technician in Germany.

VH: At 18?

EW: Yes, because I had left school at 15, roughly. Things were so unpleasant at school.

VH: You were a dropout?

EW: I was a dropout in a way. I got beat up too often.

VH: Because you were Jewish?

EW: Yes, yes. There were two Jewish boys in my class, and we got beat up regularly. I finally didn't want to put up with that any more so I left school. There was a local laboratory that did all of the water analysis and testing for the city water department. And they did assays of ore and metals for various industries. And the man, Dr. Heinrich Justen, the chemist who owned and ran this laboratory and school, risked his livelihood by daring to let a Jew, me, become his student. The Nazis could easily have closed him down, maybe even sent him to a concentration camp. Though he probably was not fully aware of all the risks he incurred by accepting me, he also consciously felt an obligation to take me in because 20 years earlier, during World War I, his life and limbs had been saved by a Jewish doctor after having been severely wounded by Allied shelling on the Western Front.

Dr. Justen was a tall, friendly, wise, and courageous man whom I much admired. It developed into a warm relationship. On my first return to Germany after the war, in 1966, 27 years after leaving Germany, I visited him in Aachen. He was an old man by then. We reminisced over a bottle of Mosel. He also ran a school, a kind of a training program, to train technicians to do that sort of work. I took the course. So I had some background in chemistry as a chemical laboratory technician, when I came to the United States. That was enough to get me a job at Hopkins in one of their laboratories where I ran chemistry tests for this particular surgical team that was doing research on shock. They tested the blood of the dogs that they were working on. That was the second job I got. That is what sold me on going into medicine. Because, and this sounds silly now, you will know when I tell you. But to see those interns walking in those white coats, with stethoscopes hanging out of their pockets or around their necks was the height of glamour to me. "That's for me," I thought. That's how I decided to go to medical school.

VH: But you must have had to make up a lot scholastically in order to go to medical school, wouldn't you, having stopped at 15?

EW: Well, yes, in the fall of 1939, after I had been in Baltimore 6 months roughly, I started taking courses at Hopkins at night. They also had a night college. I had brought my report cards from school in Germany. I submitted them to Hopkins so they could tell me what courses I would have to take in order to be admitted to Hopkins as a college student. I was missing 3 or 4 years of high school.

VH: That's quite a bit.

EW: Yes, but when they looked at those report cards, they either mistranslated them, or I don't know what happened. They admitted me with advance standing just on the basis of those report cards. I wasn't going to say no.

VH: You must have felt a little bit like an imposter though.

EW: I felt like an imposter until I graduated from medical school. I felt like a total imposter, you're right. I started at Hopkins at night with chemistry, math, algebra, calculus, trigonometry, those courses. After 3 years of that, I was getting very good grades so the missing years of education didn't particularly bother me. But one day the chemistry professor called me into his office. I had gotten straight A's in those chemistry courses. He called me into his office and asked me what I wanted to do. I had matriculated as a chemical engineer. I was going to look for work as a chemical engineer. He called me and said that of the last 10 Jewish graduates from this chemical engineering program at Hopkins, only one had a job as a chemical engineer. The nine others were doing other things. One was an insurance salesman, one was doing this, one doing that. Was I aware that it was very difficult for a Jew to get a job as a chemical engineer? Which really shocked me. I wasn't aware of that at all. It made me decide that I was in the wrong training program. I was training myself for something that I couldn't get a job in. Besides, I was shocked that there would be anti-semitism in America also.

So by that time I was infused with this idea of becoming a doctor; yet I could see no way of getting premed or of financing medical school. Remember, the only money I had was what I was making as a technician. It was $18 a week. I think by that time it was up from $11. I decided to go to pharmacy school with the idea that I would get close to medicine and close to the field that I liked and also wear a white coat. Now I think about how silly that is, but that's what I wanted. I recall that Dr. Justen always wore a white coat when I saw him in the lab. So I left Hopkins, where I was going to night school and applied for a scholarship from a Jewish charitable organization and went to the University of Maryland Pharmacy School. Because of the courses I had taken at Hopkins, they put me directly into the 2nd year, as a sophomore, in a 4-year program. I was there for 2 years in pharmacy school. I enjoyed it. During the 4th year, I was one semester short of graduation, I got drafted into the U.S. Army! So, talk about feeling like an imposter! I had all this education, but I had never finished anything—no high school diploma, no graduation from college. I was in the army for 2 years, and when I came out, of course, I had the G.I. Bill. I decided that now I had the means to go to medical school.

VH: What did you do in the service?

EW: Because of my coming from pharmacy school, they first put me into a pharmacy in a general hospital. There were only two pharmacists in the hospital.

VH: First they put you in boot camp!

EW: First I had basic training, which I tell you I did not love. It was in the desert in Texas. I know just what those people in the Kuwait desert [Operation Desert Storm] feel like.

VH: Where in Texas?

EW: Camp Barkley, Abilene.

VH: Ah, yes.

EW: You know that place?

VH: I know the area. It's forsaken by God, I think.

EW: That's right. We used to crawl on our bellies with the rattlesnakes.

VH: Yes. In fact, they even have rodeos down there for rattlesnake hunting.

EW: Yes. Actually, some of the recruits got killed by rattlesnakes. So I didn't love basic training. They put me into Glenna General Hospital, Okmulgee, Oklahoma. It is about 40 miles outside of Tulsa, an Indian community, Okmulgee. I was one of the two pharmacists in the hospital. Since there were only two pharmacists, that meant one of us had to be on call every other night. I didn't like that idea. I couldn't leave the base. I had to be at the hospital every other night. In the clinical laboratory at the hospital there were eight or ten technicians. So they were only on call every eighth or tenth night. The same medical officer was in charge both of the pharmacy and of the laboratory. I had had the laboratory experience in Germany. I learned how to test and analyze blood, so I was able to persuade him to put me into the laboratory instead of the pharmacy.

VH: So after you got out of the service, then you went into medical school?

EW: After I got out of the service—I came home on May 5.

VH: You remember a lot of dates.

EW: Certain dates are biblical dates. I called one of my classmates from pharmacy school on the phone. He said, "What are you doing?" I said, "Well, I'd like to go to medical school I think. I've got enough credits, but I guess it's too late in the year to apply." By that time they've got their class picked. He said, "Oh no, today Dr. Wiley [who was the dean and the professor of biochemistry] said somebody in the class for this fall had dropped out and there was one opening." So I went down there, and they didn't want to give me an application at first. They told me it was filled. I said I wanted to fill out an application even if the class was filled. I insisted; they gave me an application, and I filled it out. They accepted me.

VH: How do you understand what happened to you, that you got the TB? That was before you were analyzed. The man I know today, you wouldn't think would ever get TB.

EW: Well, first of all, I had had a ghon lesion, which is a primary TB infection, when I was a boy, 8 or 9. But that apparently had all cleared up.

VH: Unpasteurized milk?

EW: Unpasteurized milk. So this was a second TB, a flare-up of this early ghon lesion. Why did it flare up? After all, I had come through a lot before that. I think it had to do with an assignment I had to do my first year as a resident psychiatrist. During that first year, we had to rotate through to the child guidance home, which meant that in the evening after we had finished everything, our work, we had to go over to the child guidance home and help them put those kids to bed. You know how kids in a child guidance home are? This is like what Bettelheim had here in Chicago. These were inpatients, older children. There must have been about a dozen in this child guidance home. They were there for 6 months, 1 year, 2 years. They were very disturbed children.

VH: What's the primary diagnosis?

EW: I don't know. They were acting-out children. Two of the residents from the department of psychiatry were always assigned to the child guidance home to spend the evening and to put the kids to bed to learn something about children. It was thought to be educational. Clearly they needed help in the evening. These kids would have the greatest fun provoking the staff, particularly those guys, these residents who were greenhorns and who were not allowed to do anything. The worst we could do was to hold one of the kids. We couldn't hit back. There were some nasty kids. I don't know what I did; I did something that earned me the reprimand and rebuke of the director of the child guidance home. I was called in, given a lecture, and told this was improper behavior. I must have talked too roughly to one of the kids. I must have gotten a bit provoked. That shook me up, and I think it was in the wake of that that the TB flared.

VH: Sort of a humiliation?

EW: Very humiliating and sort of threatening to my career. I was a resident starting out in psychiatry. I had only been there a few months, and I get this severe rebuke about my behavior. I became very dubious about myself.

VH: And scared, I would think.

EW: And scared, yes. In today's language I fragmented, and I gave the TB bug a chance to act up.

VH: Do you have something you'd like to say about fragmentation, somatization?

EW: I think there is a balance in the body between whatever constant invasion there is of bacteria, viruses—infectious and degenerative diseases versus the immune system of the body fighting it off. Sometimes the invading organism even gets the upper hand, and the immune system has to mobilize, and you get a fever; you get more white cells in the blood, an inflammatory reaction that fights it off. That's the healthy reaction. Well, this inflammatory reaction, this immune system reaction that fights off the invaders, I think, can be damaged or, at least temporarily, put out of action by psychological stress. If the immune system is really damaged, then you get a condition like AIDS.

VH: What was your support system like at that point?

EW: My support?

VH: Primary objects?

EW: I was in a strange town, Cincinnati, away from my family who were in Baltimore. I knew one person on the faculty at the University. I was surrounded by other residents I had just gotten to know. I didn't have much of a support group. I was in a new situation, around mostly strangers.

VH: You haven't, to my knowledge, written papers on somatization.

EW: No, I haven't.

VH: And yet, you'd think from this experience that it would be a point of special interest to you.

EW: It was. I became very interested in traumatization. When I came back from my own stint of tuberculosis and went back to the residency, I took a year's psychosomatic fellowship, a fellowship in psychosomatic medicine. At that time they were very much influenced by Franz Alexander, his views on psychosomatic medicine. I was very interested in that. But since then, I've been so caught up in psychoanalysis per se, and at the same time Franz Alexander's theories have lost their scientific standings. I have not gotten back into what used to be quite an important interest of mine. If I had the time, I would probably become interested again. But in order to really be interested in that, one has to be in a hospital setting where there are psychosomatic patients. If you have a ward like that, you can do research, you can study people like that. Patients that come into my office are not prone to be research minded. Rarely do they have psychosomatic diseases as an important symptom. So, opportunity hasn't presented itself.

VH: Why is that in your practice? Because a lot of the patients in my practice have psychosomatic illnesses. How is it that your patients don't?

EW: I don't know. People come to me because they are depressed or because they're anxious or because they feel they can't get along with other people. They don't come to me because they have migraines or—

VH: Or stomach pains.

EW: No, the main—

VH: Or cancer.

EW: No. Why that is I don't know. I really don't know.

VH: Do you have a theory regarding cancer?

EW: I think there are genetic factors, and I think that the carcinogenic factors are there, in the body, being held at bay by anticarcinogenic factors in the body. And it may very well be emotional factors or psychological factors that weaken the body's ability to fight off the cancers and then allow the cancer to spread. I think there are important psychological triggers involved. But I think the main battle is between something that is either a virus or a gene or something. That's just a general approach. I'm not a specialist.

VH: How did your psychiatric supervisors react to the tuberculosis? Because I know when I was in the VA hospital I worked on a psychosomatic ward. In fact, I think I had the first groups on a TB ward. In those days, at least 30 years ago, they had sort of a profile, there were a lot of profiles written on the personalities of people who had gotten TB. I'm sure you've read some of them. Did they treat you any differently? Were they more caring, was there any change in their attitudes toward you?

EW: I don't know whether they treated me any differently, certainly not because I was a psychiatrist. They treated me like most other TB patients, except because I was a doctor, they probably treated me a little differently. But I have no way of really comparing. I was on a ward. I had my own little room on this ward. I had lots of visitors, my fellow residents, faculty, people would come to see me. I will never forget, one of my fellow residents came in, and he said he was an Air Force colonel who was being sent to our residency training program to learn about psychiatry. He was a nice fellow. He was the only one who was really honest. He said, "Wolf, I'm glad it's you and not me." He was honest. I know the others felt that way too. But it was an unnecessary thing to say. They treated me very well.

VH: When you later got into a psychiatric residence—I know when I was at Reiss–Davis there was a lot of talk about all this stuff going on about our personal dynamics and our teachers' personal dynamics. Did you get a lot of that because of the TB?

EW: No, it was too serious an illness to do that. Remember, this was before the drugs were proven to be effective. When I got to the sanitarium, there were people there who had been there 25, 30 years. No, they had me read *The Magic Mountain*, the Thomas Mann novel, which takes place in a TB sanitarium. It was a serious illness. Not like it is today where you have a good antibiotic. In those days it was just bed rest. As a matter of fact, the question was, should I go back to Baltimore to that sanitarium or to Saranac, New York, where, as a doctor, one could go and be treated for free, in the mountains. But if one got cured, one had to put time in as a doctor at that sanitarium. Day for day. If you had been there for 3 years as a patient, you had to stay for 3 years as a doctor. Ina and I talked it over, and we decided we would go to Baltimore.

VH: But in those days, even 30 years ago, there was almost a paranoia about the disease. People were very worried about anybody who had had TB. Not as worried as they are about AIDS now, but close.

EW: Yes, yes.

VH: And particularly in the medical field, I would think they would have been very monitoring and worried.

EW: Yes, but I must say that when I got out of the sanitarium, back in 1953, they. . . . I didn't run into any of that. At first I went back to work half time. They were pretty cooperative with that. I would work a couple of hours in the morning then go home and take a nap. I would work a couple of hours in the afternoon. After 3 or 4 months of that, I got the okay to work a little more. It took about a year before I went full speed ahead and finished the residency.

VH: Thank you, Dr. Wolf, for letting me and our readers know so much about your history. It is an inspiring story seldom seen in the analytic literature. What did you do after you finished medical school?

EW: I had a general internship in Cincinnati at the Jewish Hospital. During that time, I applied—I hadn't made up my mind yet that I was going to be a psychiatrist—I applied for psychiatric residency and for residency in just general medicine. I took one of the psychiatric residencies. I did it after being interviewed by Maurice Levine who was the chairman. I was so impressed that this was the place I wanted to be trained. I also was accepted at Topeka by the Menniger Clinic, but I preferred Cincinnati.

VH: Why?

EW: I thought it was a better residence. I thought—when I went to Topeka for my interview—Topeka is a cow town! It's a small town, with not much going on. Cincinnati is a big city which has opera, which has a symphony. I decided to stay in Cincinnati where I had made some friends. I haven't regretted it. It was a good residency. It pointed me directly to Chicago, like these other faculty people, to get my analysis in Chicago. Since I had had tuberculosis, I couldn't do what they did and commute on the weekends.

VH: Because you had to rest.

EW: Because I needed too much rest. So I had to move to Chicago to get my analytic training.

VH: So who was your analyst?

EW: The first one was Maxwell Gitelson. He was a very, very well-known analyst. He was president of the American Psychoanalytic Association at the time that I was in analysis with him. I was in analysis with him for 2 years.

VH: Only 2 years? Was that your training analysis?

EW: He was the first training analyst.

VH: Ah, there's a story here.

EW: Yes. He was a classical analyst. He was the kind of analyst who wouldn't say a word for maybe two or three sessions in a row. He used to complain about my wife. He said, "You leave here after the end of a session, and I think I've got you finally in analysis. Then you go home, and your wife puts you back together. I have to start all over again the next day." Do you see what he's saying? He was trying to fragment me with his interpretations. And then she would put me back together. Either there was hostile silence or hostile interpretations. I have never spent 2 worse years in my life than those 2 years of analysis.

VH: How many days a week?

EW: Four days a week. It made me a self psychologist without my knowing that at the time. It taught me how not to be as an analyst.

VH: Can you elaborate?

EW: It taught me that prolonged silence is a hostile thing that doesn't help the analysis. It taught me that attacking the patient, telling him all kinds of bad things about himself, does not help the patient, does not help the analysis. To break down somebody's defenses by abusing them with this or that does not help. He was a classical ego-type psychologist.

VH: "Evil" or "ego?"

EW: Both.

VH: But how had he become a training analyst?

EW: I don't know that much about the history of the Chicago.

VH: You said that he was also president of the American.

EW: He was highly respected. When I complained to people about my terrible analysis, they used to look at me as though there was something wrong with me. "You have one of the best analysts in the world!" they would say. "Everybody would like to be in analysis with him! What are you complaining about?" I believed it. I thought there was something wrong. I really did. I thought there was something terribly wrong. I became more and more depressed and more and more fragmented. I felt terrible all the time.

VH: Your wife must have been scared to death that you would have another episode of TB.

EW: I don't know whether she thought of that or not.

VH: I would have been worried about it if I had been your wife.

EW: So that was a very, very unpleasant experience: when I finally quit.

VH: You just said, "I quit," even though you were in training?

EW: I didn't quit the training.

VH: But it had to be really scary. How do institutes handle it when a student says, "I quit" on a famous analyst? Did he write any reports saying you were unsuitable for training?

EW: No, no. There's a rule at the Chicago Institute that the analyst cannot report an analysand. Of course, they break that rule occasionally.

VH: Behind your back?

EW: Yes, but I don't think Gitelson did.

VH: He was trustworthy in that respect.

EW: He was a trustworthy person, very respected. He wouldn't jeopardize the respect he had by breaking a confidence.

VH: I gather he's dead now.

EW: Yeah, he'd had one coronary before I saw him. I once heard him make some noise in the back of his throat, and I thought, "Oh my God, he's going to drop dead." I looked around. He knew exactly what I was thinking. He said, "I'm not dropping dead yet," or something like that.

VH: Did he interpret that as hostility, something you brought to the transference? That can be very powerful if someone is trying to tell you it's transference.

EW: Yes. No, he had hung it on the transference. He kept on saying that I really didn't want to be analyzed. He said, "You want to become an analyst, you don't want to be analyzed."

VH: Was that true?

EW: It was and it wasn't. Certainly I consciously wanted to be analyzed. That was clear. I also consciously wanted to become an analyst. But I also wanted to have a relationship. I wanted to feel that I was working with somebody, and with him I never did. He used to tell me that I didn't like him; that that was more important than my wanting to be analyzed.

VH: But would he associate it to your father, that you really didn't like your father or would he relate that to himself?

EW: With him. We never got to the point of his making a genetic interpretation. We struggled for 2 years, and the analysis never got off the ground. Never during those whole 2 years. Most of those 2 years was my waiting for him to drop dead.

VH: Awful.

EW: Awful. So when it finally came to an end—and it finally came to an end by mutual agreement—we agreed—

VH: . . . that the two of you were going nowhere.

EW: That we were going nowhere. And that 2 years was giving it a good try. He agreed. Then I accused him, that it was his fault. I had expected someone warm, someone responsive and so forth. And he admitted that maybe that was a contributing factor. I then went to the dean of the Institute.

VH: Who was that?

EW: That was Joan Fleming, a very tough, tough lady; and I was scared to death that I would be thrown out of the Institute. As you can well imagine. And she said—and it was the best thing anybody could have said to me—she listened and then she said, "Well, you didn't understand him, and he didn't understand you." And that was that. Then I went looking for another analyst.

VH: Back to ground zero on a training analysis.

EW: There was no training. I wanted to get another analysis.

VH: That's a lot of money to—

EW: Since his most frequent interpretation to me had been, "You don't want to be analyzed, you just want to become an analyst. That's why you are here. That's why the analysis doesn't work," I went to somebody who wasn't a training analyst for that second analysis. I figure if he's not a training analyst, we'll go moving this resistance that he says is what's keeping me from being analyzed, which was the logical thing to do.

VH: So they counted the first analysis as the training analysis?

EW: No.

VH: You were going to have that analysis, now you were going to go have one that's not a training analyst. So that means you're still going to have to have a training analysis down the road?

EW: Right. That was my plan.

VH: That means three analyses?

EW: That's right. But if the man, your analyst, who you respect because everybody respects him, everybody thinks he is great—

VH: . . . says you should—

EW: . . . they say, "It's all your fault. It's because you have this particular resistance." What am I going to do except believe that even though it doesn't feel like it, he's probably right?

VH: So you're going to go clean it up before you go get your training analysis. Very good, okay. Makes sense to me.

EW: I'm a persistent cuss, which shows I really wanted to become an analyst, doesn't it?

VH: Yes, yes.

EW: So I went into analysis with Charles Kligerman. He was on the faculty of the Institute, but he was not a training analyst.

VH: Why did you pick him?

EW: Well, there's a story to that too if you want to hear it.

VH: Go ahead.

EW: At first, after I left Gitelson, I went to another training analyst whose name was Sam Lipton. The reasons I went to see Sam Lipton were because a good friend of mine was in analysis with him and was doing very well; but the more important reason was Sam Lipton had had a residency or part of a residency in Cincinnati. Cincinnati had become my second home. I loved that department of psychiatry. Maurice had been like my father, so here I was going to an older brother so to speak. So Lipton saw me about five or six times, like a good soldier. And then he agreed with me, that I should go back into analysis. He gave me three names.

VH: But he too thought you shouldn't have your training analysis then.

EW: He agreed. He said I should not. He took Gitelson's words very seriously, that my resistance was from wanting to become an analyst. So he agreed that I should be with somebody who was not a training analyst.

VH: Did you have any symptoms at that point besides the depression that were—

EW: No, and before I went into analysis, I didn't have any symptoms at all. So they—I was what Gitelson once wrote a paper on, the "normal candidate." Into this picture I fit very, very well. He said they were really very sick and almost unanalyzable.

VH: They say that about social workers a lot.

EW: So I was the "normal candidate." I was so sick I didn't even know I had symptoms. What I didn't know when I went to see Sam Lipton was, at that time, he was back in analysis himself.

VH: With whom?

EW: Gitelson.

VH: Oh! How incestuous!

EW: If I had known that, I certainly would not have gone to see him. Anyway, he listened, and he agreed I should go back into analysis, but not with a training analyst. He gave me three names of people who were not training analysts.

VH: Politically, you had not made a good move.

EW: No, no, I haven't made any good political moves.

VH: Apparently you haven't needed to.

EW: No, just a comment on that. Politically, I have never been elected to any office in Chicago, either faculty or at the society. Politically, my name is mud.

VH: Why?

EW: I don't know. I think I'm a nonpolitical person. I don't have the kind of things that make people politically popular. Two or three times, I've run for the Education Council, which is by election. I've never been elected. So politically I'm untalented. My career has gone very well but not politically. I'm nobody as far as the American Psychoanalytic Association is concerned. It hasn't bothered me. I don't want to be president of the society or treasurer or this or that. So maybe there's sense in it. Anyhow, he gave me a list of three names. I picked one, almost blindly, because I didn't know any of them. And my fairy godmother or whoever, guardian angel, I have protected me—and I'm sure I must have one because of all the narrow escapes I've had. Of the other two, one quit being an analyst about a year later, and the other had a coronary and died. So I picked the one who was a survivor. I picked Kligerman, and I was in analysis with him for 6 years.

VH: Four times a week or five?

EW: Four times a week and for a while five times a week. It so happened that they made him a training analyst during that time. So he became a training analyst, and then the analysis counted, even though the analysis started before he became a training analyst.

VH: So, clearly, he was not Kohutian.

EW: He was not a Kohutian, no.

VH: What was he?

EW: He was a classical analyst like they all were in those days, you know, back in the 1950s, early 1960s. They were all alike. The difference between him and Gitelson was that when Gitelson made an interpretation, I felt like I was being criticized and chided. When Kligerman made the same interpretation, I could accept it. I could look at it and, you know, it was the way he did it.

VH: A better fit.

EW: A much better fit.

VH: Who were your supervisors? Who did your training here?

EW: The first one was Therese Benedek.

VH: Now she was very insightful, a wizard I'm told.

EW: Yes, she was a wizard if you understand Hungarian. I am being funny.

VH: What do you mean?

EW: She was—by the time I became her supervisee—she was an old lady. She was half deaf, and she spoke with a very, very heavy Hungarian accent. What I'm saying is that, very often, I didn't understand what she said. Even more often, she didn't understand what I said. But we got through that first case. It was a terminated analysis, and it was good enough for me to graduate. That was the first case. The second case was supervised by Fred Robbins. I saw him this morning in a coffee shop. Fred Robbins was a very, very good supervisor for me. He had very clear ideas about what an analysis was and about how to do an analysis. He could explain it. I liked him, and he liked me. We still like each other. That was a very fine, good experience. The third supervisor was Helen McLean. Helen McLean was an old lady by the time I got under her supervision. I think she was one of those early, one of the founders of the Institute.

VH: An MD?

EW: An MD, yes. As a young woman, she had been one of those people who had gone to the medical school in Peking, China to get it started. She had taught there for awhile. From, I think, a prominent Chicago family, sort of aristocratic in the American sense.

VH: Her husband went to China also?

EW: With the husband. I don't remember his first name. Yes. I think they were both on the faculty of the medical school there.

VH: Now was Benedek married?

EW: Benedek was married, oh yes. She had children. I don't know what her husband did. She had a mind of her own. She wrote various papers, particularly about women. She had a research project where she interviewed women every day of their menstrual cycle and listened to their dreams. It was a large research project. She got to where she could tell just by listening to their dreams what part of the cycle they were in. So there is a direct relationship.

VH: Nobody's picked up on it, obviously.

EW: No, nobody, as far as I know, has picked up on it. She worked on parenthood. She was not the narrow, rigid ego psychologist. She had a much broader view.

VH: Like you do.

EW: Yes, and I learned from her, in spite of my saying I didn't understand Hungarian. I can remember one comment she made when I must have been particularly stupid. She said, "You have no empathy." I think she was wrong. But at the time I didn't know she was. Helen McLean had a supervisory ambiance that was very anxiety-relieving. She sort of approved of and liked the way I was running this particular analysis. She pointed out some things about separation anxiety in this patient, I remember. I don't think I learned a hell of a lot from her, but I felt very comfortable with her. The fourth supervisor was Heinz Kohut.

VH: What do you remember about your first meeting with him? Did you choose him?

EW: Yes, at that time I knew what I wanted. Yes, I chose him. The first meeting with him was long before I picked him as a supervisor. The Institute was still at its old building on Michigan Avenue, 664 North Michigan. The Institute had two floors. The upper two floors I believe it was. Anyway, I was coming from an analytic session with Kligerman, who had his office up there. I was standing at the elevator. There were about three or four or five of us standing at the elevator. This was the top floor of the two floors that the institute occupied. Kohut came along and said, "If you are going down to the first floor, to the ground floor of the building, it's all right to use the elevator. But if you are just going to the floor below where the rest of the institute and restrooms are," he said, "you really should walk."

VH: Because—

EW: Because it is good for the character. Do you know what I mean?

VH: Yes.

EW: You shouldn't indulge yourself so much as to take the elevator just for one floor. You should walk the stairs. I reacted very negatively to this. I knew it was Heinz Kohut. I'd never met him before. It was, to me, a very disciplinary Germanic way to talk—the lieutenant cracking the whip. That was my first encounter with Heinz Kohut. It was negative. I then got to know him a little better when he taught a course when I was a candidate, which was about 10 years later. He taught a course, a theory course, at the Institute. It was my 2nd-year class. It was the best course in the whole curriculum. Everybody knew it. He did teach a beautiful theory course. He knew classical analysis backwards and forwards. During that time he was president of the American Psychoanalytic and had to be away frequently. Phillip Seitz was a substitute teacher who also was a very clear thinker. That's when I got to know Kohut well. I began to appreciate and admire his talent. He was not, certainly not in the classroom situation, a very warm kind of person. But he was the teacher. He was there to teach. You listened. He would put forth, and you listened. Those were the early contacts with Heinz Kohut. Then when I was ready for my fourth supervised case, which must have been—I graduated in 1968, it may have been 1967, I knew that I wanted Kohut for the supervision.

VH: Was he hard to get?

EW: He was hard to get. Lots of people wanted him, but I got him.

I don't know if I was lucky. Probably the way I got him was to ask for him way, way before I needed my fourth supervisor, so I got on the list.

VH: What kind of case did you take to him?

EW: It was a girl, early 20s, whose chief complaint was shyness, timidity, some depression. It was interesting because I thought this was going to be a narcissistic personality disorder. I took it to Kohut, and he listened for a while. Then he said, "No, this was an oedipal kind of problem."

VH: Surprising! Did you agree with him?

EW: At the time I agreed with him because it was he who said it. I was just a candidate who—

VH: Yes, but this was your fourth case. You were a psychiatrist.

EW: Yes, but I went along with it. Let's put it that way. Since then I know that I was right and he was wrong. At the time I followed him. And I'll tell you a little bit about how I got into the self psychology group, okay?

VH: Yes.

EW: In the late 1960s, he began to write the first book called *The Analysis of the Self* (Kohut, 1971). By that time he'd already published two or three papers on narcissism, and some of the new ideas were in that. His good friends, his own generation of analysts, were beginning to react badly.

VH: Who was that?

EW: Well, there was a fellow named Martin Stein of New York, a well-known analyst there, who was a personal friend. There was Kurt Eissler, who had been a good personal friend of his, as a matter of fact. Even later on they would still remain good personal friends. The Eisslers—his wife is Ruth Eissler—they are both still alive. Ruth Eissler had been Kohut's third analyst. They were in Chicago. They later moved to New York.

VH: Who had been his first two?

EW: The first analyst was August Aichhorn who wrote *Wayward Youth* (1925). Upstairs, I could show you a picture of him and Eissler together. The second analyst was someone by the name of Marseille. I don't know his first name, the second name was like the city in France. I don't know much about that analysis. He never talked very much about that one. The first one, with August Aichhorn, probably was a very good analysis. Aichhorn, you know, treated a lot of delinquents. He was the first one to be interested in delinquent youth. And the way he treated them was by sort of fostering their idealization of him. He sort of did everything to make them idealize him and to make himself an important person by manipulating the transference. Once he got them to that, then using his position of influence, he would then direct them to stop the delinquent behavior.

VH: Would he have had them in analysis or would he have had them in psychotherapy?

EW: Psychotherapy. That was psychotherapy because he did not interpret this transference, this idealizing transference. But he used the transference as a way of influencing them. This was in the 1920s, you know, when analysis and psychotherapy were still pretty much mixed up with each other. Anyway, this is a pretty important historical fact because obviously Heinz Kohut must have been 18 or 19 when he went into analysis with Aichhorn. But he must have known or learned about Aichhorn's ability to be idealized and manipulate the idealizing transference. Because the idealizing transferences are also an important aspect of Kohutian self psychology. The difference being that Kohut did not use the transference to manipulate, but as something to be analyzed with the patient.

VH: Was Kohut a delinquent youth?

EW: No, oh no. The very, very opposite. He told a little anecdote about his analysis with Aichhorn. Kohut apparently was the very opposite of the delinquent. He was a very good boy, well-behaved, upper-middle class. He was so well-behaved that it became an irritant to Aichhorn until one day Aichhorn came out and said, "I wish I could inject some of that delinquent serum into you."

VH: Why did he go into analysis at the age of 18?

EW: That I don't know. But I imagine that Kohut was what we would call a pretty neurotic kid. He was an only child. He was born in 1913. The war broke out in 1914. His father was drafted into the Austrian army. So his father was away during most of those early years. That alone accounts for some disturbance. And I don't know much about his mother, but he was pretty close to her. Later on she followed him to Chicago. She went on to live in an old folk's home and died in Chicago. I never met her so I don't know what it was. But he was an only child. His father had been a concert-type pianist until his career was interrupted by the war, when he was drafted into the service. When he came back, he could not continue his career. I don't know what he did after that. When Kohut was an adolescent, they hired a tutor for him. He never went to public school as a youngster.

VH: Was this because his mother couldn't separate from him?

EW: He was sort of a bit aristocratic. I don't know the real reason. Heinz Kohut was a private person, and he did not talk very much about his childhood, hardly at all. We know very little about his background. What I'm telling you is about little bits here and there. And they did not let him go to public school, and he never got to learn how to be with other children, being an only child at home and not being allowed to mix with other kids at school. They had this tutor who came in every day from whom he learned. So he felt about himself that, because of that, he never really learned well how to deal with people his own age. Socially, he felt himself to be a little bit awkward.

VH: Well, apparently he was.

EW: Yes, to some extent. But he did become part of the inner circle in psychoanalysis around Anna Freud. Anna Freud was a close friend; and whenever she came to Chicago, which was occasionally, she would stay with Kohut, as a guest, at their house. One of the anecdotes that he told about Anna Freud was that she wore a beautiful amber necklace. And Betty, who was Heinz's wife, admired it. One day she admired this necklace very much. So when time came around for Anna Freud to leave, as she was saying goodbye, she took off the necklace and hung it around Betty's neck as a gesture of appreciation for the hospitality. So they were good friends. And they corresponded, and they would exchange birthday cards and other holiday greetings. The same thing with Eissler when they were in Chicago and when they moved to New York. There was a friendly correspondence going back and forth. He was close friends with Heinz Hartmann. In fact, he once showed me a letter that he got from Heinz Hartmann, the last letter he ever got from Heinz Hartmann. Hartmann died shortly thereafter. The essence of this letter, as I remember, was that Hartmann was complaining about the disabilities of old age. But there was one thing about old age that was good, the wines get better and better. The wines that we can afford to drink, you know. Kohut was a connoisseur of wines. This gives you a little insight into who his peers were, who he was close to. And after he had been president of the American Psychoanalytic Association, he was the vice president of the International Psychoanalytic Association. And he was sort of the heir apparent to this circle. He was younger than Anna Freud, Heinz Hartmann, Kris, and those people; and he was to be the next president of the International. That's when he started writing his ideas. And before he knew it, he was no longer vice president of the International. He never got elected president; and when he went to meetings, people who had been his colleagues, who knew him and would greet him and do whatever colleagues do—have a cup of coffee, a glass of beer—they would no longer do that. He would walk down the hall, he said, in the hotel, and so and so was coming the other way and would no longer look at him—you know look away—pretend they did not know him. Psychoanalytic power!

VH: And pressure to conform.

EW: Heinz was a person who needed to be in a relationship with people. He was not able to be solitary. For all his privacy, he could not stand being really alone.

VH: He needed a lot of mirroring, from what I understand.

EW: Okay. That's right.

VH: Is that fair?

EW: I think that's fair. We all need it to some extent. So he had to begin to collect a new circle of colleagues around him which then turned out to be younger people.

VH: Who was in that inner circle of his?

EW: The inner circle. There was John Gedo, Paul Tolpin, David Marcus, Arnold Goldberg, and Paul Ornstein. Later, either around the time I got into it, or maybe even later, Marian Tolpin and Anna Ornstein became part of the group. Because John Gedo dropped out, which left the "sacred seven," as I recall.

VH: The what?

EW: My wife Ina called them (us) the "sacred seven." Well, when he started writing the book, he needed someone to discuss the book with.

VH: Why?

EW: He needed to read it to somebody and get their reaction. And their reaction had to be good—he needed a positive reaction, not too sharp a criticism. That's the kind of person he was. So he formed a circle of people to whom he started reading the book, chapter by chapter, as he was writing it.

VH: And you?

EW: No, not in the beginning. If there were others, I don't know. There may have been others. There may have been George Klumpner, I don't know. Sometime later, towards the very end of his writing the book, I was asked to join him in the circle for specific reasons. I had become very good friends with John Gedo. You've read some of Gedo's material.

VH: Yes, and I want to ask you about him.

EW: John and I had had a great time investigating and writing some papers on early Freud history, which, in a way, Kohut was responsible for to some extent—namely, Freud's adolescent correspondence with Fluss. Harry Trosman had found them some place among the Ernest Jones' papers, and then they were published in *Psyche*, the German journal. And then they asked Heinz Kohut to write a commentary on this correspondence to accompany this publication. Heinz Kohut, at that time, was deep, deep into his new ideas and did not want to bother. His closest of all the younger colleagues, at that time, was John Gedo. But John Gedo didn't read or write in German.

VH: So he needed you!

EW: So he needed me. So John Gedo and I got the correspondence and wrote a nice little paper on this correspondence called "The Ich Letters." It was a nice little paper. So because of that, Gedo and I got to collaborate on other things, too. Then Kohut was invited to Berlin to give a lecture on the anniversary of the opening of the Berlin Institute. I don't know the exact location. But he was the honored guest to give a lecture. Gedo thought it would be a nice gesture if we, together, translated this lecture he gave in German into English and presented it to him upon his return from Europe. That's what we did. I translated it into English. Gedo polished some of the phraseology, and we gave it to Heinz. Now, of course, Heinz Kohut didn't need us to translate it into English. He could have easily done that himself. But it was nice that he already had a translation to work from, to polish himself for publication. He was very taken.

VH: It was an acceptable gift.

EW: It was an acceptable gift, and I think Gedo probably urged him to take me into the group. I was a nice, bright, young man, and so forth.

VH: Is Gedo older than you then?

EW: No. As a matter of fact, he's younger.

VH: That's what I thought.

EW: Yes. Gedo must be about 4 or 5 years younger. I'm not sure exactly how old Gedo is. But he was the closest to Kohut in this particular group at that time.

VH: What made him leave, then?

EW: We'll come to that. So that's how I got into the group. That's how I got asked to participate in those meetings at Kohut's house, which were sort of at regular intervals, where he would discuss his current work and so forth and so on. Occasionally, the whole group was invited for dinner. Kohut's wife, Betty, was a gourmet cook. It was very nice. He was born in 1913, so 1973 would have been his 60th birthday. His book appeared in 1971, *The Analysis of the Self.* A little bit after the book appeared, and by this time, he was totally isolated from his colleagues because of his writings.

VH: Not locally, but—

EW: . . . nationally. On the national scene. There was no occasion for him to be in public, to give a lecture or anything. So John and I, John Gedo and I, were talking about what we could do to provide a forum for him so he could talk about his ideas. And I think it was my idea, but I don't clearly remember, to have a 60th birthday party to honor Heinz Kohut. To me it seemed a perfectly logical thing to do. Here was this genius, I thought, in psychoanalysis. He was the only one who had really new ideas, who had obviously good ideas. He was the best known of the analysts in Chicago. He had been president of the American. He was going to be president of the International. He deserved to be honored by the Psychoanalytic Society, I thought. I also happened to be on the committee of the Analytic Society that had something to do with programs.

VH: So they did let you be on one committee.

EW: Yes, but that's my point. I don't remember what committee it was. So I got up at a meeting of the Chicago Psychoanalytic Society and made a little speech about the great man we had in our midst. His 60th birthday was coming. The Society should sponsor a psychoanalytic conference in honor of Heinz Kohut. Fools rush in where angels fear to tread. They turned it down cold. It was just awful. There was a group of analysts who got up, who were just outraged at this proposal. In a way, they had a point. The Society had never, never, ever honored anyone for a birthday, 60th, 70th, 90th or whatever, for any reason. Why was this guy any different? That was ridiculous.

VH: Heaven forbid we should break tradition!

EW: Right. Right. A fellow analyst of whom we are already jealous and envious, we should honor him? They didn't say that. But I was stubborn. I went around to about twenty colleagues. I said, "If they don't want to sponsor this meeting, we'll do it ourselves." We needed some money to get started, some seed money. So I went to about twenty colleagues and persuaded each one to give, I think it was $150 apiece. That gave us enough money to get started. Paul Tolpin, George Pollock, and I formed a committee to do it. We got Pollock to be on the committee because he was the director of the Institute. Unless we had at least his passive blessing, it couldn't have been done. He was very nice. He said to go ahead. He would give us all the Institute cooperation we needed. Go ahead. Well, you know who did all the work.

VH: Ina?

EW: Exactly. She did all the work, and we got busy writing people, inviting them to be on the program. Of course, it was Kohut who selected the people to write. He knew who he wanted. We got a very high-level response from people like Carl Schorske, who was a professor of history who had written on Freud in Vienna. We got him to talk about that. We got Lawrence Friedman from New York to talk about theory. Alexander Mitscherlich who had really resurrected psychoanalysis in Germany after the war, came over with his wife. He was a well-known analyst. Paul Parin came from Switzerland. We did all right.

VH: You did a thing that people would have had a hard time declining.

EW: No, they all could have declined.

VH: But I mean, once you got it together it was such a prestigious program.

EW: That's right. We had a very prestigious program. Over 600 people came. It was a success beyond my dreams and beyond Heinz's dream. Rene Spitz came from Denver. We got a very nice letter from Anna Freud. She could not come but was encouraging, congratulatory. So we had a very successful scientific reunion, a great turnout. And Heinz appreciated my efforts. I really thought this man was a genius. That he was the greatest since Freud. I still think so.

VH: You said that. I read that, and then Giovacchini took great exception and wrote a whole paper countering that.

EW: I know. Giovacchini and I are friends, but he disagrees with me on that. I really think so. I certainly thought so at the time. That's why I did it, not for political purposes. Heinz knew that I felt that way. He appreciated that. That was the first great self psychology conference, in 1973. After that, Kohut said, "We need a casebook." At that time he was beginning to think of himself, a little bit, as a great man. Since Freud had written all those case histories, he thought that he needed case histories. And so our little group was reorganized into a casebook group. John Gedo was the leader, and we met once a month over at the Institute. The group met with Kohut and everyone in the group brought a case, one of his own cases that he had been analyzing along self psychology lines. We would all discuss this case in great detail: history, diagnosis. Only one case at a session. Maybe sometimes two sessions of the group. Out of that casebook came the book called *The Psychology of the Self: A Casebook* (Goldberg, 1978). But you notice that it isn't John Gedo but Arnold Goldberg who's the editor.

VH: Yes, I noticed that.

EW: All right. But in this group everybody brought their own case.

VH: Who wrote them up? Was there a secretary for the group? There had to be.

EW: No, we wrote up our own cases.

VH: Oh.

EW: Then we presented them to each other. And after we heard comments from the others, sometimes critical, sometimes not so critical, we would go back, reword them until they were acceptable to the group.

VH: That's nice.

EW: It was a lot of work. But you can also imagine that presenting one's cases to one's siblings causes a certain amount of tension, right? Who likes to have his own cases looked at this closely and criticized?

VH: I think it's great to learn.

EW: Yes. No matter how careful one is, some people's feelings will get hurt, right? John Gedo's feelings got hurt, so he withdrew from the group.

VH: Did you stay friends?

EW: Not for very long after that.

VH: How do you feel about that?

EW: How do I feel? I very, very much regret losing John's friendship. The collaboration that we had was a beautiful collaboration. And I think he was very important in drawing me into the group, getting me accepted into the group as one of the members when the group was in its early stages. It had started before me.

VH: But why would he have split with you too?

EW: Because my loyalty was to Kohut. Our own personal relationship lasted a month or two after this where we talked, but eventually—

VH: Did he leave the Institute?

EW: No, but he has by now, yes. He didn't then, but he did leave the group. He's an extremely talented person. He was a very valuable member of the group. His loss was felt by all of us.

VH: A lot of narcissistic injuries?

EW: Oh, yes. Around the same time, John and I were coeditors of a book we were going to publish. We had collected various papers from people, and they were going to be published by Johns Hopkins University Press. He had two papers in it. I had two papers in it. Other people had papers in it. And things were going on in the Hopkins Press, political things, on the basis of which they suddenly decided they didn't want to publish the book, and this was around the same time. John blamed me for the debacle, and even before they turned it down he wanted to be the senior author of these two editors, he and me. I said I wanted equality. Even though he had a longer standing, I wanted equal billing. He thought that was outrageous on my part. So that's when our personal friendship came to an end. But that narcissism, it was my narcissism wanting to be equal with him. It was his narcissism of wanting to lord it over me. Add this to the other things that happened, and I don't think I've talked ten words to John Gedo since then. This happened almost 15 years ago.

VH: And it's clear you were very fond of him.

EW: Yes, yes, yes.

VH: What do you think of his work now?

EW: I think that, in essence, it is self psychology. I don't think he has clearly strayed from the work he did together with Kohut. He's given a new emphasis to certain aspects, but that really doesn't make it different. To call it "self-system" instead of self and certain things like that doesn't really make it essentially any different. He has maintained, since he became isolated from the self psychology group here, he had a need to have some relationship with others. And so he sought, after that, to be more involved on the national scene with the American Psychoanalytic, with friends there, which meant he had to tone down some of the differences.

VH: What do you think has been your primary contribution? Which ones are you most fond of?

EW: I am most fond of my contribution to the theory of treatment, to technical things, my emphasis on the psychoanalytic ambiance, the treatment ambiance. I wrote a paper early in 1976 on "Ambiance and Abstinence." I think that's a paper that I am very fond of, that Kohut was very fond of. It grew out of the negative experience of my first analysis. It stresses the importance of the responsiveness of the analyst, the importance of having a friendly, nonjudgmental ambiance in the analytic situation. Unless you have such a positive ambiance, it doesn't matter how correct or incorrect your interpretations are, the patient can't hear them. You have to have a certain ambiance in order for the treatment to work. If you don't, the patient may be well analyzed but gets not one bit better. He doesn't improve. The next thing that I'm fondest of among the things I wrote about is that I've added to the list of the three selfobject transferences. Kohut talked about the mirror transference, the idealizing transference, and the alter-ego transient transference. I've added the ally–antagonist transference, adversarial transference, which I think is an essential aspect of an important selfobject experience. I've added the efficacy experience—the fact that the experience of being able to make an impression, a dent on the world is a necessary experience for the cohesion of the self, to enhance the self.

VH: What about the adversarial transference?

EW: I think that the ability to be in opposition to someone who will be an antagonist, but a benevolent antagonist, is a necessary growth experience. The 2-year-old who says "No" is going through the stage of negativism. He needs to do this about the time the sense of self first emerges but has to test that I am a person. The only way to really test it is to be able to say "No" to somebody else. He has to do this to find out that he's not just an extension of the other person, but that he's a separate person.

VH: But wasn't that already talked about by Freud in terms of autonomy and the ability to express negative feelings?

EW: You might say that, yes. But Freud didn't talk about this as a necessary transference experience. Freud didn't talk about the self anyway.

VH: Elaborate, please.

EW: The selfobject experience is an experience which evokes the sense of self. An example of what one needs is the experience of being mirrored, being confirmed as the self. There's the experience of being part of something great, some other, the idealizing experience. There's the experience of seeing somebody else who's like one. It's all right to be like *that* so it's all right to be like me. Then there's the ally–antagonist experience. The experience I can assert myself against someone and know it's all right. It doesn't mean the world is coming to an end. Then there is the efficacy experience. It's the experience of telling something to one's analyst that will make him change his mind and say, "Yes, I was wrong." Still, the world doesn't come to an end. I have an effect on the world; I really must be existing, right?

VH: I have agency.

EW: I have agency? Yes, have agency. That's another way of putting it. That's what I mean. Now these last two, the ally–antagonist and efficacy–agency experience are transference experiences. I've added to the list of selfobject experiences, and I think they will be generally recognized, sooner or later. We have added another, but that's still—

VH: What's that?

EW: The vitalization–attunement experience. You have to have read Stern's book to really appreciate what that is. It's not totally original with me. Lichtenberg came out with it around the same time. Between infants and mothers, there are certain things that go on. Stern talks about two kinds of affects. He talks about categorical affects. What he means by that is different categories of affects. Different categories mean anger, excitement, sadness, disgust; those are categories of affect. But in addition to that, he talks about not categorical affects but vitality affects.

VH: Like, "Oh, you wonderful child!"

EW: No, you're not too far. Vitality affects are the formal qualities of an affect. It's the going up excited and coming down. The formal aspect. It goes across all the categories. In each category, if an affect comes up, it rises, goes up and then comes down again. It has the formal quality of crescendo and decrescendo.

VH: That's what I was going to say. It sounds like it would go in musical terms better than anything.

EW: So, when the mother is attuned to the crescendo–decrescendo, then as the infant's affect goes up, she may rise physically. Do you see what I mean?

VH: Yes.

EW: In a totally different area of experience, but the attunement is to the crescendo and decrescendo.

VH: So it gives it life.

EW: Right. That's why it's called "vitalization."

VH: So it counteracts schizoid defenses.

EW: Right. So these vitalization affects, I believe, and Lichtenberg believes, are also a necessary experience in the analytic situation.

VH: Not seen as seduction.

EW: No, no. It is when the patient experiences some affect and the analyst's responses to it empathetically mirror it, if you wish. He doesn't just say "Yes" to the patient.

VH: Not flat.

EW: It's going in tune with the patient's crescendo–decrescendo. That makes it a vitalizing, living experience for the patient. That's important and necessary.

VH: I'm thinking about Winnicott's statement—it's been debated in terms of his interpretation—something like "I'm neither as upset as you are, nor as excited as you are." But what you're saying would seem to sort of say the opposite. That one should go along as excited but not—

EW: Not necessarily. Not to be as excited, but the patient feels that the other person really is in tune.

VH: Like if you went in and you said, "Oh, my paper got published."

EW: Right.

VH: He would say, "Really!"

EW: That's it. That's it. Okay. So now we've got three selfobject experiences. Three things that one experiences; and if one does experience them, strengthens oneself.

VH: But isn't that attunement?

EW: It's an attunement, yes.

VH: But you've given it a new word. Why?

EW: I don't care. I don't oppose your calling it attunement. What I am pointing out is that this particular kind of attunement strengthens the sense of self.

VH: Your account counteracts your first analyst who said, "Be flat."

EW: Right, right. But I'm much wider. I'm talking about what brings about a healthy, strong self. A healthy, strong self is created by certain experiences that organize one. These organizing experiences are called "selfobject experiences." This particular kind of attunement is a selfobject experience, like mirroring is a selfobject experience. There are many other experiences that are not selfobject experiences.

VH: Boy, there are going to be a lot of patients trying to heal analysts, aren't there?

EW: Yes, maybe. But I also believe that a good therapeutic situation is back and forth. That it's reciprocal and that the patient has to learn to become empathic with the analyst, just as the analyst is empathic with the patient. It's only by both of them achieving some mutual empathy that you really get analytic progress. It's not a one-way street.

VH: Have you ever thought of writing a paper about the kinship or the genealogy, perhaps, of flat-affect analysts? How many people did your analyst impact with that same deadpanness? Who are the heirs? Can you spot the heirs at your Institute? Do you know what I'm saying? You hear all the rumors about the New Yorkers being so rigid and so forth. I mean, could you write a paper showing how those connected?

EW: I don't think so.

VH: No? But it has to impact on patients.

EW: I don't think so because I don't know who all his analysands were. I don't know who his patients were. All I know is three or four who didn't make it through the Institute.

VH: That's interesting. So little is known, though, about the lineage of analysts.

EW: Very little, yes.

VH: In terms of who was your analyst? In terms of what was passed on from one generation to the next that impacts us all in a lot of different ways. That's part of what interests me about some of this, is that it has been an area very little studied. So, who is the young self psychologist that you most admire? What's been coming out in the literature lately?

EW: These young self psychologists are all over 60 now.

VH: Are there none of the younger ones you admire then?

EW: No, no, we're talking about this group. They were all young men at the time they first collected around Kohut, but they're all over 60. I'm 69 now. I'm the oldest of the bunch. I forget. Michael Basch, I forgot to mention. He was one of the early ones. He was analyzed by Kohut, as a matter of fact.

VH: I've heard Kohut treated people rather badly, actually. Is that not true? Or is it true?

EW: It's not true, no. When he died, several of his patients came to me and became my patients. They, none of them, had been badly treated. They all were very much in admiration. They respected him. Never have I heard anything from them about his not having been a good therapist. I know the rumors that you mentioned. There are some people who think they're great theorists but not great therapists. I cannot say that from the experiences that I've had with his patients.

VH: You would know.

EW: I think I would.

VH: Where do you think, besides these three transferences—are there other ways that you feel your work has gone on from his or differs from his?

EW: I've added to it with these three transferences. I don't think I differ from him. Yes, I differ in one respect. He talked about transmuting internalization. He felt in the process something of the analyst will be added—internalized by the patient.

VH: Some function.

EW: Some function added to his repertory, his structure, and that would get him better. I don't believe that takes place. I don't believe anything is taken in from the analyst.

VH: Nothing is interjection, not even function?

EW: No. Interjection is the wrong word for it. Internalization is the wrong word for it. What I think takes place is that during those intense moments of the analysis, when the patient regresses, the internal structures during the regression become very loose.

VH: Fragmented.

EW: Fragmented. And during that looseness, they can be rearranged like a jigsaw puzzle. When you shake it up, you can rearrange it. You can rearrange it in a better arrangement than it was before. I don't think you add in any new pieces.

VH: That's very interesting, but "rearrange" seems like a minimal statement to me compared to the power of the process.

EW: Well, I would also say that the changes brought by analysis are minimal.

VH: You think so?

EW: Yes. But it's very important when you see a patient before analysis and after, the changes are not great changes. There's nobody who would say, "I don't recognize this person." You immediately know it's the same person. So the changes are minimal, but the changes that have occurred are of the greatest importance. The changes that are occurring are what helps this person, who is very little changed otherwise, to suddenly have dropped defenses. We rearranged some things, and now he can fit into life. He can have creative relationships. He has human empathy and less fear. I think those are very important changes.

VH: And could be more organized, certainly.

EW: And could be more organized. But if you think about the total personality, it's a minor change. What I mean by character structure is when in classical analysis you talk about oral characters, anal characters, obsessive compulsive characters, but that doesn't change very often. If he was a hysterical person before, he is going to be a hysterical person after.

VH: Ethics change. Don't you think ethics change, quite a bit, sometimes for people, even though the character structure is similar?

EW: Yes. Ethics change because the person, after analysis, may be much more empathic with others than before, and that forces a change in ethics, yes. So you see this person, after the analysis, he's the same person. He looks the same. His main behavior remains the same. If he was an obsessive kind of person, he will be obsessive still. If he was a hysterical person, he will still be hysterical.

VH: If he was a borderline person or a psychotic person, he will still be a borderline person or a psychotic person?

EW: He's much less likely to break down. But when he breaks down, he will go into the old pattern.

VH: Do you think that fragmentation is conducive to rearrangement?

EW: If it's controlled in the analytic situation.

VH: Is that different than regression?

EW: Yes. You see, my theory of what happens in the therapeutic process—I think there are two therapeutic processes in psychotherapy, in psychological treatment. One process is what I call the "ambient process."

It will happen just because you put this person into a nonjudgmental, warm, accepting, responsive ambiance. What happens here is that if that person comes out of an environment that is cold and rejecting, certain potentialities that person had are frozen. They no longer develop. Like a plant that is denied water or sunlight or fertilizer, it stops growing. But it's not dead. If you put it into this positive ambiance, then the old potentials can revive and start growing again. That's one process. All you do is put them into a good "facilitating" ambiance and off they go. You don't have to make any interpretations, this or that.

But that's actually only a small proportion of the patients that we see fall into this category. Most of them have had more trauma than just deprivation. Most of them have been injured. And they have—all of this is metaphorical—they have been injured, and they have scar formations. There is distortion of growth. Now for those patients, you need more than just a therapeutic ambiance. What you need is—once they get into the therapeutic ambiance, their injuries and their frustrated needs begin to be revived in this ambiance. They then begin to surface. They, the frustrated needs, become revived and encouraged by this positive ambiance, and then begin to focus on the therapist, the analyst. That's transference. They begin to transfer the demand onto the analyst. And the analyst, if he's analytic, will not gratify those demands but will respond to them in a friendly, accepting way without gratifying. Even if he were not analytically trained and tried to gratify, even if he rocked the patient and soothed him by physical touch, sooner or later, no matter what the person does, the patient is going to be frustrated and disappointed. Right? Then you have a certain disruption in what was a good therapeutic alliance, what was a good therapeutic harmonious relationship. That disruption is the opportunity for therapeutic change. That disruption is associated with, you call it "regression," I call it "fragmentation." During that fragmented state, you can help rearrange the patient's inner experience by exposing that patient to certain corrective emotional experiences, if you wish. Even though—

VH: You're talking about Franz Alexander's "corrective emotional experience." That's regarded with great suspicion, even now.

EW: It is, it is. I'm being a heretic by saying this.

VH: I thought so.

EW: I'm being provocative by saying this. I can get you to listen by saying this. I make a distinction here, namely, that you have to expose the patient to certain experiences, not necessarily verbal interpretations.

VH: And not ones you've manipulated.

EW: And not through manipulation, right. The verbal interpretation that you make to the patient who is in one of those regressive fragmentations because of some frustration, the verbal interpretation that you make is important not because of the information you give to the patient, not because of the content of that interpretation, but because it leads the patient into a new experience. The patient experiences you in a way that for the patient is a new experience. That causes the rearrangement. Then the patient comes out of the regression, reestablishes himself, only now it's a little bit rearranged because of the experience with the therapist. The empathy is restored. The mutual empathy is restored at a little bit higher level.

VH: Do you have some thoughts about a normal life, average life experiences that cause fragmentation and reorganization in a positive way or experiences that cause fragmentation and reorganization in a negative way? I guess rape would be, for example, a fragmentation that would cause reorganization in a negative way, increased fear, increased anxiety, for example. Are there some things that come to your mind that are good experiences for everybody, that are normal fragmentations that have good outcomes?

EW: Well, the minimum fragmentations. Let me give you an example. You know young people often search out death-defying experiences. They get themselves in situations they know are dangerous. I think because at the height of the danger is a certain kind of fragmentation which allows some rearrangement. This is a little bit pathological, isn't it?

VH: It sounds like sort of accident prone, or daredevilness.

EW: It's daredevilness, and it's pathological because—

VH: Counterphobic.

EW: No, I don't think it's counterphobic so much. Only counterphobic in the sense that they are avoiding the death of the self by getting a certain feeling of aliveness from the experience. But it's also the partial fragmentation in the intensity of the experience that allows some rearrangement. They come out of it a little stronger each time. But it's pathological because it's associated with a certain amount of death and actual injury. A perfectly healthy, normal adult goes and jumps from the high-diving board, or goes skiing, or certain activities of the kind. It is, in a minimal way, the same sort of thing. You create moments where you fall apart and moments where you are scared to death and rearrange something. Yet it's a perfectly healthy moment.

VH: Your own experiences of loss and challenge—though not sought for—have been a help to you. I guess I'd say that part of you is a wonderful rearrangement. Thank you.

Note. This interview originally appeared in Hunter (1992b, 1993b).

Case Discussion

Consistent with the self psychological view, Dr. Wolf points out that Roselyn has a faulty selfobject relationship. He goes on to say that the patient had a terrible relationship with her mother, which left her in a psychologically crippled state that led her to think she could not have a good relationship with others. He argues that Roselyn still feels that a dyadic relationship cannot be lasting and secure.

This case discussion took place in Wolf's Winnetka, Illinois home on September 15, 1990. He began, "Your patient has obviously identified herself with Rappaccini's daughter who has been poisoned. Poison in this case means she feels she has been so altered by this poisonous, poisoning mother that her own personality is like poison to everybody else. That's really the essence of it, you know. The rest is elaboration and decoration. Some people like to interpret everything, like to pick up on every little detail and get the associations to it and sort of flesh it out—get the full story. But I really don't think that is always necessary. In this case, the essence is her feeling that because of the poor relationship with her mother—in my language because there was a faulty selfobject relationship with her mother—her own personality has become distorted. She cannot have good relationships with others. She cannot be a good selfobject. She cannot give others good selfobject experiences, only faulty ones, poisoned ones, if you wish. That's what I see." Wolf, of course, was deriving his metaphor from the dream, and his insight was supported by evidence that he had: Roselyn had written a paper in graduate school with reference to this story. She also brought me a copy of Nathaniel Hawthorne's story, "Rappaccini's Daughter," and she had often referred to it.

Wolf went on: "She seems to have a good relationship with you.

And I would be interested, if I had her in treatment and she brought in a dream like this, where the meaning of the dream itself is quite clear, the important thing to me would be why is this dream being dreamt now? Why not last month? Why not a month from now? What is going on in her life right now?"

I said, "It was at a time when she felt trapped."

He said, "Then I would look into the relationship with me into the transference; does she feel trapped with me? Whether something there had gone awry recently that stimulated the dream. When I say awry, I don't mean bad. I mean this is an opportunity to work with disruption."

We talked about how long this treatment could last. (It was over 10 years in duration at the time of the interview.) Wolf shared: "I've had several patients for longer than that. I would imagine you may have her for an indefinite time, and I don't think it's bad at all. If you have a patient with diabetes, then you give him insulin for the rest of his life. This patient has had a chronic insufficiency in that relationship to her mother, and she may need what she gets from you for the rest of her life. And again she may rearrange things."

Wolf suggested technically, "Try next time she goes into a 'blue funk'—a regression—to think, 'What can I do now to help her rearrange what's going on?' 'What kind of an atmosphere can I provide for her, and maybe make a comment, a comment now and then to point her in the right direction?' "

I asked, "Do you have some thoughts about what might help?" He replied, "I would make the interpretation, if you haven't done so already, that she feels, because of whatever went on between her and her mother, she has been left in a kind of psychologically crippled state that makes her think she cannot have relationships with people. Even though she has now had a relationship with you for 10 years, she is still not convinced that even the relationship with you is a lasting one." I told him that she says, in these blue funks, that I am ethical and that I am not going to abandon her because she pays me. Wolf said, "She feels if she didn't pay you, you could say, 'Goodbye. I don't give a damn any longer.' You've made that interpretation to her, I'm sure," he said. "Of course," Wolf understood, "she does not trust that anybody could have a commitment to her. Isn't there a fairy tale about a mother who combs the girl's hair with a poisoned comb?"

Wolf went on to a discussion of countertransference issues. "Your countertransference is that you think you have treated her too long. That 10 years is too long and that somehow you need to bring it to an end. She needs to get better than she is, sooner or later. Otherwise you feel guilty or ashamed that you haven't accomplished it. I think that's a common countertransference because it's an impossible demand on yourself. She's doing, in fact, very well, considering."

I agreed saying, "I think she is, but then I do worry. Because of the cost to her, and yet I don't have any conscious plan to end it."

He said, "I know. But you *feel* guilty about not ending it."

I agreed, "I guess I do. I do feel that maybe if I were a better analyst, it would go faster. Yet I don't think that's true. It's her defenses that keep her from going faster."

Wolf was firm. "She's going fast enough. She may not get very much further. You may have her as a patient 10 years from now. So what! You say it's costing a lot of money. It would cost her a hell of a lot more if she were not in treatment."

Wolf continued his discussion of my countertransference to Roselyn, "You need to not think of her as somebody who is going to finish treatment in the foreseeable future. You need to think of her as somebody who needs an indefinite length of treatment. You don't know how long, who has made tremendous progress, and who will probably make some more when it may be not very dramatic. And that she has a perfect right to take as long and to go as slowly as she wants. And that you're not going to hurry her on. You're willing to see her 10 years from now if it takes it. Then once she gets that idea and she has that assurance of you, things will go better. I think the countertransference that you have, which has to do with your feeling guilty or ashamed about seeing her for so many years, taking all that money from her, not getting her 'well' causes difficulty in you. That makes you feel guilty; therefore, that guilt interferes with your effectiveness."

I agreed, "Yes, I think there's a lot of truth to that. I think about why I am taking her for my research when I've certainly got cases that I could show off and that would look great. But I think I take her because I keep hoping that I've missed some interpretation of her defenses that would allow it to go better. Yet, in truth, I don't think so. I think you're exactly right."

Wolf reminded me to "Say it to yourself not to her." He was reassuring, "Once you say it to yourself, well, you know, it will come across to her by osmosis that you are there for her."

I countered: "I worry, too, about her possibly killing herself. She refers frequently to three poets who all killed themselves. You know who I'm talking about?"

Wolf said, "Yes. It is possible that she will kill herself, but I don't believe she will."

I said, "That is the other question I wanted you to talk about. She doesn't idealize me. Now don't get me wrong. She would say I'm her primary person in this world. But there is no twining, there is no idealizing. One time she noticed she had put on the same color fingernail polish I had, and she wanted to sit on her fingernails. She was embarrassed that she had unconsciously chosen the same color that I had been wearing for weeks."

Wolf stated, "So she has a need to profess some kind of autonomy."

I objected, "I think she needs autonomy."

He asserted, "I think it's a false autonomy. It's a false autonomy. It's just like she feels humiliated by asking for help, as if that is a terrible thing to do. I think that somehow you must help her to accept that none of us are really autonomous. None of us. You're not; I'm not. We like to put on a front and pretend that we are."

Concerning the issues of attachment and true and false autonomy, Wolf strongly advised: "It would help if you start thinking about her as somebody who will be your patient 10 years from now, so that any urgency of thought of her getting out of treatment, of her getting better, is all postponed, giving her time and time and time to gradually do what she wants to do with herself. I think she will begin to be better. Because what I think she's picking up from you, unconsciously from you, is you're looking towards the end of her treatment, and that threatens her with an as yet unbearable disconnection, aloneness."

I agreed. "She says that, and what I really mean, and I do say is that we made the commitment to work until we've got it done."

Wolf agreed, "I think you have to." He added, "I think when she stops picking that up and when she starts picking up that you're going to be there for who knows how long, you are in no hurry, the death stuff will disappear."

I went on, "She never says, 'I think I should quit.' You were mentioning last night that you didn't know if borderlines ever really got well." Wolf corrected, "I think that the borderline schizophrenics don't get well, but they can improve and get better." He went on, "I won't say that of all borderlines. Some can get well. I don't have any schizophrenics in treatment. To me, schizophrenia is partially a biological illness. So you can help some of the symptoms. You can help the patient cope with it, but you cannot get at the biological substrate. Now borderline, to me, is a wastebasket as a diagnosis. To say somebody is borderline means, to me, I have not gone far enough in my own growth and perception to fully understand this person. Therefore, I have difficulties in treating him. That doesn't mean there's something wrong with me. There were a hell of a lot more borderline patients 10 or 20 years ago than there are now in the sense that we understand patients we would have called borderline then. Some of these we understand now. We no longer call them borderline. We call them narcissistic personality disorders, right?"

Wolf continued, "I'm sure that many of the patients we now call borderline 20 years from now or 50 years from now, we won't call borderline. We will understand them. As a profession, we are growing, we are getting better in our understanding. So I think it's a wastebasket diagnosis that time will shrink. But those who are borderline, it means that, at the present time, I don't understand that person well enough. I can't help that person as well as somebody who can understand that person better. There may not be that person in the whole world, a person who can, but eventually there will be."

Wolf made reference to the previous evening when we watched Kohut's last presentation in Berkeley on his VCR: "You understand her fragmentation intellectually, but you don't understand it in the sense, as Kohut was saying last night on that tape, as the fear of all these levels at the same time. You don't feel it fully—what she must have felt when these terrible things happened. You know they happened, intellectually. You know you can describe it. But you weren't there to feel it, and you can't feel it yourself. I think you only understand it intellectually. *I* only understand it intellectually. She needs someone to tell her he or she understands the total experience."

I wondered how I could do it. Wolf helped me. "I don't think you can. I don't think you can really know what she experienced as an infant. I think there will come a day, however, when she will recognize that you can't. You want to, but you can't—that you're understanding as much as you can. Then that will be enough to her to know that you want to really understand. She hasn't reached that point yet. Don't push her. Be there for her, as you are. You cannot change who you are. You cannot change yourself into the mother that she needed. But you *can* understand, albeit imperfectly. That's what she needed. When she can learn that you try to really understand that, I think that will be enough."

I wondered if my anxiety, early in treatment, about whether or not to hospitalize her kept her from regressing to the degree she needed to. "Perhaps," Wolf said warmly, "she felt you were too frantic."

I also brought up one of the times when I had altered the frame, ". . . two times, when the house was broken into. The first time, she didn't flip out. The second time, when they broke in, the whole house was wiped out. Her husband called and said she was on the closet floor, facing the corner of her closet. She would not respond to her name or to movement. He could make no contact with her. He tried to make physical contact with her, and she became hysterical. So he called me and asked me to come."

Wolf was pleased, "Of course you went."

I was relieved. "You would have gone too?"

Wolf agreed, "Oh, sure. It's all right to attempt doing analysis when you're in your office and you're dealing with a patient who is capable of doing analysis. It's all right to tell a child, 'Don't do this' and 'Do that' or to tell an adult, or to make the interpretation to an adult. But when you see a child crossing the street against traffic, you're not going to give an analytic interpretation. You'll grab for the child's hand and pull her back, right? In an emergency when you cannot communicate with words, you must then communicate with actions."

Wolf was adamant that he would not necessarily tell her husband, "Take her to the hospital."

I said, "I think of taking people to the hospital as a disruption in their analysis, to be avoided if it can. I'm not saying at the cost of threatening their lives." Wolf said that in 34 years, he had never hospitalized a patient. But he added that he did not get patients as sick as mine.

Wolf shared his own experiences: "And as far as seeing people for a long time . . . I have one patient who started with me in 1967. He was four times a week, analysis, who now comes in if he needs to. He's no longer regular, but I'm around. I have one patient who started with me four times a week in 1975. It's been 17 years. He comes in once a week. They are both mental health professionals. So you've got a long way to go."

Wolf was curious, "Have you ever fallen asleep on a patient?"

"No." I asked, "Did you go to sleep?"

He admitted, "I have gone to sleep four, five, or six times. I once fell asleep with a patient in the very first interview face to face."

I questioned, "Were they just turning you off that badly? Was it something you wanted to avoid?"

Wolf went on, "It's a countertransference that has to do with the patient being so off in their own world that they're not addressing you any longer. You've become part of the furniture in the room. If they're off in their own world and not talking to you at all any longer, your own self needs the input of being addressed; and if it doesn't get that input, it begins to fragment a little bit. In order to not fragment, you withdraw from the situation. It's the most common countertransference there is. It manifests as boredom or getting tired."

He went on, "Yesterday I told you about Maurice Levin, the professor in Cincinnati. He used to tell a story to us residents about this patient who came to see him, who had seen Dr. So and So, Dr. So and So, Dr. So and So, all these famous psychiatrists and analysts. None of them had helped him. Now he was coming to Levin. Levin looks to him and says, 'So you've got seven or eight scalps on your belt, now you're coming to get mine.' Then he added, 'And that cured the patient.' I must say I'm doubtful that just one interpretation will do it. But you get the idea, I think, that's what this guy was doing. You're next."

I took up another topic: "Yesterday you said the fragmentation produces growth. Yet I seemed to get the feeling that with very fragile people, you feel you shouldn't facilitate regression."

"No," he said. "Fragmentation gives you an opportunity for rearrangement. But it needs to be controlled, it is not an all-or-nothing situation. It shouldn't be unlimited regression because unlimited regression can move to psychosis. I think you have to create an ambiance that allows the patient to relax and regress a little bit. The couch helps. You're doing that. Not only does the patient regress, you need to regress. The therapist needs to regress. Because as you regress a little bit, your own boundaries drop a little. You become a little more porous, more receptive, especially unconsciously. You become more empathic. You hear more things than you would have otherwise. So there has to be some regression of the therapist, and there has to be even more regression on the part of the patient. It has to be monitored. You don't want too much. Too much, then the disorganization is so great that the patient cannot organize himself again. You have ways of stopping regression, of slowing it down. By talking to the patient, by becoming somewhat directive, by calling his attention to this or that; there are many things you can do to slow down regression. If the patient is on the couch, one way to stop the regression immediately is to say, 'Sit up.' "

I asked him, "Would you make everybody stay on the couch? That really seems strange to me."

Wolf agreed, "No, no. Now, for instance, some patients who've been lying on the couch will sit up. They're not sitting in the chair where the therapy patient sits. They are across from you, but they are sitting on the couch. They can swing around and lie down again when they want to, and they do that."

I responded, "You don't seem bothered very much by that."

Wolf agreed, "Not at all." I asked if he would analyze the behavior. Wolf answered, "I might comment or say, 'You must have been feeling you were regressing too much.' I wouldn't say 'regression.' That's too technical. I might say, 'You felt you were losing touch with me when you weren't looking at me, and you need to keep in touch. Maybe you didn't hear my voice clearly enough, so you had to look.' "

Wolf shared thoughts about one of his patients: "This particular patient—I leaned forward, for some reason or another, and she stopped talking. I said, 'Why did you stop?' And she said, 'I'm afraid. I'm afraid you're going to hit me.' I was totally astonished. This was one of these physically abused patients who felt that I was coming close, I was going to hit her." Wolf cautioned, "When something like that comes up and the patient says, 'You were leaning forward; I thought you were going to hit me,' I don't have to say anything. She's already made the whole interpretation right there. I don't have to say, 'I'm not going to hit you.' "

Wolf added: "It shows how one's own analytic experience gets into it. When I was in analysis and the analyst was sitting there and his feet would come up here next to where my hand was, somehow I reacted to those legs there. I haven't thought about it in 30 years. He became aware of it, and he finally switched it around. He took another chair on the side of the couch where I couldn't see him." Wolf went on, "So now the way I sit, they can't see my feet. I thought it had all to do with my not hearing well on the left side. My patients know I'm not far away, but they are aware whether I sit like this or whether I go like that." He moved to various positions in his chair. I asked, "Do you have any more thoughts about the analyst and the feet in terms of how he handled it?"

Wolf replied, "He handled it badly because he made me feel different, ashamed. He made me feel there was something wrong with me. That for me, of all patients, he couldn't stay in the chair near his couch, in his ordinary way. He had to turn things around. He made me feel there was something not right with me. He had to use a different method. It didn't make me feel he was flexible. It made me feel there was something wrong with me. That never was analyzed."

Wolf warmed to this subject saying, "When Freud said not to gratify, he meant to not gratify sexually. You can gratify in other ways. He fed the wolf man; he fed the rat man. He lent them money. He took H. D., the poet, took her by the hand and dragged her into his bedroom to show her one of his statues, his artwork that he was proud of. So apparently that was gratifying for her."

I said, "He seduced patients, I think, into giving him presents too."

Wolf answered, "No, it was not a seduction. He wanted to be a professor at the University of Vienna for years, and they wouldn't let him because he was a Jew. He had a patient who was a friend of the Minister of Education. His patient was well connected with the government; knew the person who made those decisions. He prevailed somehow upon his patient, to take a valuable painting which she owned and donate it to the Minister whereupon he got his appointment as a professor."

I wondered, "What do you think about it?"

Wolf replied, "I don't think it's a legitimate or appropriate thing to do in our present state of ethics. It's not the legitimate thing to do nowadays, but that's why I say it's Viennese ethics. In those days, at that time, in those particular circumstances, I think it was all right. I think it was a perfectly honest and ethical endeavor."

I asked Wolf, "Do you ever give presents to patients—papers, books?"

He answered, "Certainly, no presents. I don't think I've given anyone any books. I have given papers of mine to patients when I thought the topic was something they were particularly interested in or they asked me for a copy of the paper. Otherwise, no. I used to be much more rigid than I am now. You know how we train, and then when I was a resident, a patient came in and brought me a sandwich. I must have looked hungry. Who knows what the woman's fantasy could have been. She brought me a sandwich, and I didn't accept it. Foolish." I wondered if it might not need to depend on the transference. He said, "Well, I don't know." Then—"It would depend on the transference, wouldn't it?" Soon Wolf exclaimed, "Transference, smanference! She was not trying to bribe me."

I answered, "Or poison you."

He agreed, "Or poison me. She really felt that I needed something. It was motherly of her."

I asked, "Did she happen to have a noon appointment with you and know that you were missing lunch or something? Or was she competing with your wife, maybe? Saying your wife didn't take good care of you?"

He said, "It was before I was married."

I asked, "Do you have patients now that bring you Christmas cookies or drawings or things that you would accept?"

"Yes," Wolf said, "there is one patient who occasionally brings me a picture, a photograph, or a book. It's a patient whom I've been seeing for 17 years. I accept it." With this, we concluded our time together.

Peter Giovacchini

Dr. Giovacchini is well known throughout the analytic world for his many important contributions. He has been especially interested in adolescents, psychosis, primitive mental states, the holding environment, and psychosomatic illnesses.

This interview took place in Dr. Giovacchini's home in Winnetka, Illinois, on September 15 and 16, 1990. His home office is paneled in beautiful wood; the room, like Dr. Giovacchini himself, is solid and classical. He announced almost immediately upon my arrival that a patient of his had an emergency, and she was on her way. We would have to stop when she arrived and continue the following day. His clear, unhesitant choice of the patient's best interest seemed to characterize the man.

Born April 12, 1922, he speaks French, German, Italian, and Spanish. He has written an immense body of work related to adolescent psychology, affective disorders; anxiety, panic, and phobias; borderline personality; creativity; and treatment of primitive mental states. His writings are down-to-earth, intense, and profound; they reveal a deep human understanding of the mind and heart of man. His books on technique are considered classics.

He is candid, warm, and relaxed. He speaks easily and unhesitatingly, with a remarkable ability to elaborate ideas in relation to the knowledge and capacity of the listener. At one and the same time he is playful and yet serious. He gives the impression of being both authoritative and one's colleague. He speaks profoundly but listens just as carefully. His knowledge is as broad as it is deep. The overall impression he gives is one of relaxed intimacy and a passion for sharing ideas. My video camera did not seem to concern him.

Interview

VIRGINIA HUNTER: I'd really like to know how you came to be an analyst.

PETER GIOVACCHINI: I think that my entry into analysis was a little different than most of my contemporaries. I began, when I was a young student, in mathematics. I went to the University of Chicago originally because I wanted to study under one particular chemist.

VH: Who was that?

PG: Schlesinger. He's a boron chemist, and I read his book, and I thought it was the height of argumentation and excitement and believed it would be exciting to become his student. But it wasn't at all. Still, I went through the physical sciences and got my degree, a physical science Bachelor's degree. Somewhere around the junior or senior year I began to feel the isolation of the laboratory was a pretty lonely experience. I was only 19 when I graduated; I preferred something more exciting, more in contact with people, but at the same time preserving the researcher's scientific outlook.

So I thought medicine would be an ideal compromise. Of course, going to medical school wasn't easy. The additive quality of the premedical curriculum was really a very strangling one. But I was lucky, I didn't have to go through that competition. It turned out I had all the prerequisite courses in the general science program I had been following. I tossed my hat in the ring, and they accepted me. It surprised me because I wasn't particularly high on the grade point average since I wasn't going to do anything with it except get a Ph.D. Then the war started—World War II. It was a very hectic experience. We finished in 3 years. There was a shortage of staff, so we students were assigned duties that we would not have been assigned if they had had a full house. I became acquainted with the head of the department of psychiatry, David Slight, a contemporary of Clifford Scott. You mentioned Clifford Scott. Slight and Scott were the first two people to have a training analysis with Melanie Klein.

VH: I hope Scott will talk about his analysis with Klein.

PG: Slight would have—but he's dead now. Well, I had idealized him. He was a charismatic, Scottish man, and he liked me. So every time there was a subinternship opening in the department of psychiatry, I got it. I think in my 3 years in medical school I must have served 10 subinternships. He also persuaded me to get a job on weekends at Manteno State Hospital where we admitted all the incoming cases that came from Cook County Psychopathic Hospital. So we saw a lot of psychopathology, a lot of neurological cases, a lot of pathology in general. The thoughts I was having when I graduated from medical school were that I might be a neurologist or a neuropsychiatrist or a neurosurgeon. To me, I saw these as closely knit together, which, of course, they are not. I was in my internship in New York City and looking for a residency. During the war, in 1944, residencies were very hard to get. While I was pondering this, I got a telegram from Slight saying send in your forms, because we have to send them to the government to get your residency approved. I had not even applied, but he thought of this as a fait accompli. So that's how I got into psychiatry.

VH: You were adopted, sort of.

PG: Well, in a way. There was a strange push. At that time there were only two senior staff people in the Department of Psychiatry at the University of Chicago. One was David Slight. He was the Chairperson. The other was Jules Masserman. Others—not senior people—were there, such as Heinz Kohut, who, at the time, had a joint appointment in psychiatry and neurology. He was a neurologist, a very excellent neurologist, by the way; and Sam Lipton was also there. But I was the only resident. The government did not keep its promise. They said they would let me finish my residency before pulling me into the army, but they did not keep their promise. They pulled me in after my first year of residency. As I was leaving I had a conversation with Jules Masserman, and I said, "What do you think about my applying for analytic training when I come back?" Everybody was doing that. In 1945 the war was over; I was going in when most of the people were returning, and they were all going to the Institute. The prestige of our residency depended on whether the resident automatically was accepted by the Institute. The three prestigious residencies were Michael Reese, the University of Chicago, and the University of Illinois because their residents were unquestionably accepted by the Institute. Today such acceptance does not have much meaning. Jules Masserman said, "You might as well go to the Institute because the G.I. Bill of Rights will pay for it." That was his attitude. Slight's attitude was, "Yes, I think you should go to the Institute because when you're at a meeting and you say something antianalytic they can't accuse you of not being an analyst." I did not think those were great reasons. But it was enough, and when I came back from my army duty, which was 2 years later, we had about 11 residents; and they were all in the Institute. Otherwise, you just did not count. I mentioned Kohut and Sam Lipton were there. Charlie Kligerman and Tom Szasz were also there as residents.

VH: Who's Who, literally, in psychoanalysis.

PG: Right, and it was a very competitive program. If someone had read a book and you had not read it, you had to find it and read it. Henry Brosin was our boss, and he was not very interested in clinical work, but he had read everything. He was a real scholar. He made us attend two journal clubs in the evenings twice a week. We had to discuss books and present books. It was very intense and very exciting. I went through the Institute, and for the most part I enjoyed it thoroughly, which again is not what you hear today. People don't look upon their Institute experiences very fondly, at least our Institute.

VH: Why?

PG: There is considerable arrogance, snobbishness, and a condescending attitude toward the candidates. Whereas when we were there, it was different. There was Franz Alexander, a colorful Hungarian. And Therese Benedek.

VH: Who was a wizard, I'm told.

PG: Yes. And Adelaide Johnson. They were very exciting and bright people.

VH: Who was your analyst?

PG: My analyst was Harry B. Lee. His forte was creativity. He had been analyzed by Karen Horney who had been at the Institute just shortly before I got there. Karl Menninger was also there. It was obviously a very exciting experience.

VH: How do you feel about your own analysis? Compared to what you know now.

PG: I've always felt rather negative about it. Whether that's negative transference that has never been resolved or whether that's based upon certain objective elements of the analytic interaction—I suspect it's a little bit of both. Personally I liked my analyst, but he had a combination of rigid analytic formality and neutrality that was marred by an overt friendliness. I took him out to dinner after we finished the analysis. Later, I was at his house for parties. That wasn't all that unusual because the faculty would give parties and invite the candidates. But he had a formal neutrality, combined with sentimentality. For example, one day he took out a handkerchief, "You've got a smudge on your face." He wiped it off. He was maternal. One day I said, "Oh my God, I don't have any money and I've got to buy my wife a birthday present." He said, "Well, I don't have any money either, but why don't you ask John? He always has a lot of cash on him." Still he might sit there month after month and say nothing, never answer questions, and so forth. I think I can best exemplify my feelings about my analysis by the answer to a question that I was asked after my analysis: "What is psychoanalysis?" I said, "That's easy. That's easy to define. You just do two things. You discover the symptoms and then you forbid them." I believe that was characteristic of most analyses in those days. I thought analysis was mechanized. It followed a formula.

VH: It did not help to regress.

PG: Regression was not acceptable. You were supposed to be mature. This was what was so paradoxical about it. Symptomatology and defenses were treated in a judgmental fashion.

VH: You've written about it.

PG: Absolutely. I can remember the first interpretation that he gave me. I said, "I went out with the boys last night." And he said, "Does your unconscious consider you to be a boy?" In other words, here's a childish part of me coming out. And he's dealing with it in a critical way. So what do you do then? You feel ashamed. But it's iatrogenically induced. Some of it might have been there anyway. And yet I could see what he was saying. He was right when he was referring to a childish, pregenital part of myself. So the rest of the 3½ years—I was in analysis for 4 years—were spent criticizing me for having oral dependent impulses. Because I'm defending myself against the oedipus. And then we get into the oedipus. Everything was fine, but it was so mechanistic. Most analyses were that way. Either your anal or your oral impulses had to be worked through by screaming at them.

VH: So you experienced textbook interpretations?

PG: That's the way analysis was structured in those days.

VH: Except maybe Winnicott.

PG: Well, that's another story. But you see we'd never heard of Winnicott. We'd never heard of Melanie Klein. They just didn't exist in the early 1950s at the Institute.

VH: You only heard of Freud.

PG: Freud, Abraham, Ferenczi, Jones, the classic analysts. I remember in journal club at the Institute, saying, "What do we know about Melanie Klein? Nothing. We ought to learn something about her." So we assigned Heinz Kohut the challenge of presenting Melanie Klein to us. He did a 3-hour presentation. He was very good. We didn't do much with it. But it was nice to know something about her.

VH: Who were your supervisors?

PG: I had four of them. It is required at the Institute. Tom French, Kathryn Bacon, George Mohr, and Irene Josselyn. All were very decent people. I can't say I got that much out of them. I enjoyed being with them. Tom French was rather ill at the time—a fatal illness. So Tom talked a lot more about his own experiences with patients. He was worried about the environment, whatever struck his fancy. Since he was ill, many times he just fell asleep. He could not stay awake. That's hard presenting to a person who is asleep. You don't know whether to talk more loudly or more quietly. Irene Josselyn was very sensitive, but she had very few boundaries. She literally brought chicken soup to one patient. To show you how much involved she was with the external world of the patients, we were having a session there one day and she gets a phone call—an interruption. It was a gynecologist who had her patient on the table; her patient had a lot of somatic problems. He perforated the uterus so he is asking Irene what to do. She looks at me. I said, "Well, tell him to sew it up!" I am telling the gynecologist what to do! They were all so closely involved with each other.

VH: It does not sound like the gynecologist was very competent.

PG: Well, actually he was very competent. He had been analyzed by Lou Shapiro, but that has nothing to do with his competence. The analytic community in those days was like a small town in itself, and he did not want to do anything that would be harmful to treatment. I grant you it did not make sense.

VH: Quite incestuous.

PG: Yes, very much so. Actually this gynecologist turned out to deliver our third child. The very first thing he said to my wife was, "I want to meet your husband." My wife said, "That can be arranged." I walked into his office; he knew that I was an analyst. The first thing he said was, "I was analyzed by Lou Shapiro." I said nothing, absolutely nothing. He was embarrassed at my analytic silence. We became very good friends later on.

VH: This was before you became famous. He was still nervous about you.

PG: Well, I don't know about being famous. I think he was nervous about my acting as an analyst at that time. He was using his analytic experience as a leverage to build himself up, and instead he tripped and fell into an analytic situation where he was put into the position of the, let's say, the lower part of the hierarchy rather than in control. He was not in control.

VH: It sounds like there was an anticipation that if you were in analysis you knew how to criticize people and find their flaws and point them out so now they should not have them.

PG: That's very well put.

VH: So he was very defensive. "I already know my flaws. Don't look at them. I've already been told what they are."

PG: Yes.

VH: You grew up here in Chicago?

PG: No, I was born in New York City. It's hard to say where I grew up because my father was an itinerant sculptor. During my youth, he went from commission to commission. He worked, for example, at the Louvre for a short time. He taught there, and he restored damaged statues.

VH: In Paris?

PG: Yes, he restored pieces they would bring in that they needed to be repaired. He was also deeply involved in some fountains. I remember one in Magdeburg, Germany, another in Rome. So, as I say, between the ages of birth and 11 we were perhaps two-thirds of the time in Europe, France, Italy, Germany, England.

VH: What was that like, for you?

PG: It was very interesting. I've just finished reading a book by León and Rebecca Grinberg, *Migration and Exile* (1989). And I've written a paper, several papers, about second generation immigrants. I'm a second generation immigrant. I thought it was a very interesting experience, a unique one. Because this periodic change in environment and uprooting made you flexible. As soon as you got secure in one, you had to start all over with another one. But it became an interesting challenge. I have lived in this house since 1952. I believe that is somewhat of a reaction formation against the first 11 years of my life. I cannot really count the number of schools or the number of places we lived.

VH: And your mom, what was she like?

PG: She was not a professional woman. She was a housewife. She was born in Lucca, in Italy. Have you ever been to Lucca?

VH: No. Where is Lucca?

PG: Lucca is maybe 30 or 40 miles west of Florence, in Tuscany. It's a medieval town. Puccini was born there. Every street is a Puccini Street. It's a charming place. The reason why I asked the question is because the women there are so maternal. I once had to call a colleague there because I was giving a paper in a mountain resort, which is in that area. I remember the operators who answered the phone sounded just like my mother. It's hard to describe if you've never heard it. It's a tone, a matter of speaking; every little child is called *povero bambino*, which means poor little one who needs looking after. That's what she was like. A very maternal person.

VH: Really available?

PG: Yes. She had a lot of friends who would play card games and read—a good deal of reading, but, basically, she was a housewife.

VH: It sounds like your father was successful, but that involved moving around a lot.

PG: He always had a knack for finding work. He was much sought after. When I was 11, he went back to New York and found work. They set him up in a studio, and he did very well there. After that, he decided to come to Chicago because of the World's Fair. He would do something like that. He would leave a secure position and start all over again. But when he started all over again, it worked. He came here in 1934 without a job. In the first few days he found a job that paid $100 a week. Do you know how much money $100 a week was in 1934? That was a lot of money.

VH: How did your mom react to these frequent changes?

PG: Oh, I don't think she ever questioned it. There's another factor. When the big migration came, my uncle, my mother's brother, lived with us. Actually my father and my uncle worked together; my uncle worked for him or with him. My father was the sculptor; my uncle wasn't qualified, but he could paint. It was through him that my father met my mother. The three of them were together when I was born. I was an only child. When we were in Florence, my uncle met his future wife. He came back to the United States with us. Then his fiancée and her family moved to the United States. So we had a rather large extended family. My aunt, her mother and father and four sisters joined us; it was a real caravan. My father was the head of this particular clan although he didn't get too involved with them. He was reserved, but he hired all of them. I remember in New York he was always hiring people. We had a neighbor who was Czechoslovakian, made wonderful dumplings and who spoke hardly any English at all. He hired her as a bookkeeper. His patron was paying all the salaries.

VH: It doesn't sound as though there was enough pain in that background to cause you to have all this awareness of the deeper structures. Yet from your writing, you clearly do—have a deep awareness.

PG: You raise an interesting question. You said that there's not enough pain in my background. Is that required?

VH: I've always thought so. I thought the people who were most empathic, the most able to go into deeper levels did so after having had to traverse them over and over again in their own experiences.

PG: I have a patient who is a therapist, and his saying is, "Well, misery isn't a ticket for admission." What about Winnicott? He certainly, from what we can read, did not seem to have had a traumatic past. When I mentioned at the beginning that my entry into psychoanalysis was somewhat different, this was the point. I do not think I had a traumatic childhood.

VH: You had a lot of moves, obviously, but consistency in your parents.

PG: I had very devoted parents. I could say they lived their lives mainly for me, and they were very proud of me because I was precocious. I was very adult in manner. In fact, that was probably one of the reasons I went into analysis. Because my parents were very dependent on me. I know that I was brought into many decisions about family matters, business matters, that never should have been presented to me. They would even talk about some of the breaches that they had with each other and want me to settle quarrels. I became the mediator. After puberty I stopped doing that. I told them they were on their own.

VH: So they used you as the battleground.

PG: Sometimes. Well, to justify themselves, to justify their position. On the whole I wouldn't say that my father was the kind of man who played with me very much because he didn't know how. I guess his life was fairly hard work from the day he was born. He got an education, then he apprenticed himself at a famous studio in Florence. My mother only went to grade school. As I said, she was a housewife. But you're right; I don't consider that I had a painful background. But I do consider that I had ability to get in touch with the unconscious. I learned hypnosis in college.

VH: Yes, I read your book, where you said that.

PG: I was always fascinated with that part of the personality. If you work in a state hospital, it is absolutely fascinating. I think I tended to dramatize things. Regarding my mental state, it is sometimes questioned by patients. They ask, "How do you know how miserable and depressed we feel if you've never had such feelings?" Well, I can empathize with them. I can absorb their feelings very easily. As I said, maybe that has something to do with being forced prematurely to deal with other people's feelings.

VH: That raises a question. What do you think is necessary in order for people to get a full deck, so to speak, of emotions, and the ability to tolerate, deal with, handle a full deck of emotions?

PG: That's a very channeled question. I suppose the better integrated their personality, the greater their ability to handle a full deck of emotions.

VH: But the integration would come from having had the opportunity before hand, wouldn't it?

PG: Yes.

VH: To experience the different emotions without guilt.

PG: Well, that's the point, to experience your own feelings without guilt, fear, trepidation, shame, or whatever.

VH: Or not in a traumatic environment, I gather.

PG: Yes. I guess Winnicott wrote as much about that as anyone, in terms of the secure, supportive holding environment. I had quite a secure environment.

VH: You don't seem, as far as I could find out, to have been involved in the Chicago Institute.

PG: That's quite true. It's a long story. I'll make it very brief. It's not a very interesting story. They passed me over, at the beginning. Everybody expected me to be made a training analyst. I never was.

VH: That's outrageous.

PG: Finally they, oh 8 or 10 years ago, sat down with me to discuss my philosophy about training analysts. It would not have fit with theirs at that time. How can you be analyzed when your analyst has something to say about your future and your career progress. Your analyst had to report back to the training committee so that they could decide.

VH: But they changed that in Chicago years ago.

PG: Is that changed now?

VH: I understand from Dr. Wolf that they no longer report back. That the training analyst has nothing to do with anybody's becoming a graduate.

PG: Well, Wolf ought to know because he's a training analyst. It was not that way when I was involved. As I say, they kept passing me over and passing me over. I was teaching a course here and there. Then I decided if they don't want me, I do not want them. It finally reached a point where I thought who needs them. I'm not bitter about the people. Many of them are still my best friends. I don't think I'd like to be there now, in view of everything that's happened there.

VH: What are you thinking of?

PG: The scandal with George Pollock. Getting back to your question, I did not leave them. They just never took me. To speculate on the reasons for that may be bordering a little bit on the paranoid.

VH: But surely it must have been envy.

PG: That's what I think. For one thing, I was one of the very few gentiles there. I think that was a factor. I may sound a little persecutory.

VH: But you also are one of the greatest psychoanalytic writers that we've had in my lifetime. It's clear and courageous.

PG: Well, thank you. But they don't read my writings. Well, some of them do. Let me tell you an incident, and you can judge for yourself what this might mean. I was 32 years old, the youngest graduate ever, and I was presenting a paper to the Chicago Psychoanalytic Society. I got caught in the internecine warfare that was going on. There was the Institute group proper, that was the Alexander group; and then there was the Gitelson group who believed less in the oedipal and more in the pregenital phases of development. I was considered the favorite of the Alexander group.

VH: The dreaded "corrective emotional experience?"

PG: Well, I did not go that far. We had given that up. Alex was gone at this point. I'm being interviewed for admission at the Chicago Psychoanalytic Society. I'm feeling rather good. I'm a trifle euphoric. My youngest son was born just a couple of months before that. I'm beginning an assistant professorship at the University of Illinois. I've been out of academics for 4 years and eager to go back. Lou Shapiro was the first one to interview me. He said, "Well, Pete, are you happy?" I said, "Yes, I am." "Well, fine," he said. I figured I could be honest and talk to these people. I considered them colleagues. So the second analyst who interviewed me was a member of the Gitelson group. He was a well-known analyst. I've blocked his name. He died some time ago. He said, "What don't you feel too good about?" I said, "Well, I've been working very hard, morning 'til night, seeing patients, seeing patients, seeing patients. I am a little tired. I'm looking forward to getting back, at least in a part-time way, to academic life." He recommended that I not be admitted to the Society because I found psychoanalysis to be tiresome. They could not keep me out. They couldn't go that far. Francis Hammett was my next interviewer. She was Gitelson's wife. She said they would let me into the Society, but I had to present a paper. I was furious about that. But it so happened that

I had a paper I wanted to present. It's one of the best papers I've ever written, I believe.

VH: Which one was it?

PG: The first one on mutual adaptation and various object relationships. It deals with symbiosis and postulates that two symbiotic partners have the same psychopathology. Something that's become the subject of a Ph.D. thesis where the equivalence of psychopathology had been measured in psychological testing, and it worked out perfectly. But that's another topic. I was not going to fight City Hall. I presented the paper. It was the first paper that had been presented, as far as I can remember, by a young person that was not torn to pieces. In fact, I got a standing ovation. It was a huge success. There was *some* criticism. One was: "Well that's not really analysis," because I got my data from talking to other analysts as well as my own patients. But I was able to meet all of the objections. I remember my rebuttal was about 30 minutes long. People liked the rebuttal even better than they did the paper. The next morning I'm parking my car in the underground garage, near the building where most of our offices are. A few colleagues came up and said in tones as though we had come back from a funeral or as if I had been in the hospital diagnosed as having cancer. They said, "How are you, Peter? Have you heard anything?" As if I were really in deep trouble. I did not think anything about it because I got dozens of phone calls the other way around congratulating me and saying it was a very important paper. But I remember these two or three colleagues in the underground. Now, I believe that was my downfall, politically speaking. Since then I have presented at least 20 papers or discussions to the Society. I have been asked to present to the Institute, but I have never been let in the club.

VH: It really is amazing, depressing.

PG: As I said, it got to a point where it did not matter anymore, the bitterness and the disappointment. But it depressed me too for years. Now I am quite over it. Look at it this way. I've had ample opportunity to teach. I've had a lot of people in supervision, more than any training analyst has. Most of my practice are mental health professionals, social workers, psychologists, psychiatrists and psychoanalysts and their families.

VH: But it does seem that those who have power in all the societies, from New York on, may not be the most brilliant clinicians or the ones who have contributed the most. How do you understand the power structures of psychoanalytic institutes?

PG: That is a very complex issue. It is not much different from universities and other professional settings. There are certain people who are not very good at their profession, but they are politically astute. They capitalize on that. Then they try to surround themselves with mediocrity, because that's the only way they can maintain their security. This is true, I think, in many, many different fields and in many, many different institutions.

VH: So you completed your training, then you're a graduate psychoanalyst. But they still could possibly not let you into the society?

PG: That would be very difficult for them to do. They would have to have some real objections.

VH: But ordinarily they didn't make people present papers.

PG: No. I was being punished for something—well my popularity. The Gitelson group was making me a sacrificial lamb. I was one of the most popular students of the so-called Alexander group.

VH: So there weren't any clear rules here where you have to meet these requirements in order to graduate and to join the Society?

PG: Yes, but they made me present a paper. What's so bad about that? In other instances they insisted on more supervision or more analysis. If I had refused, I would have been accused of being arrogant and narcissistic. These are interpretations that can be used as weapons against you. I know what my Institute supervisors thought of me. They held me in very high esteem. The Gitelson group had an ax to grind. It was ironic that I became Gitelson's protegé. It all turned out well in the end. The institute set up little workshops of four or five people with senior people. They paid us $15 for attending the workshop. I'll never forget what the secretary told me: "Don't tell Gitelson because we're not paying him anything." We met at his house. We had these clinical workshops and became very good friends, exceptionally good friends. I would write papers, and he'd go over them. We might discuss them while having dinner at his home. In fact, people were very soft and tender with me when Gitelson died. They thought his death effected me tremendously, and it did.

VH: Psychoanalytic politics can be really depressing.

PG: Yes. The history of any particular institute is fascinating. A book by Anne Marie Silver reports the history of the Washington Institute. The last chapter of the book was devoted to the history of its politics. It's horrible. It's scandalous. If you look at the British, the Melanie Klein–Anna Freud feud is shameful. But the Washington Institute was just as shameful. The people involved were not as prominent as Melanie Klein and Anna Freud, but there are many similarities. Today many candidates feel resentful of their Institute, whereas when I was a candidate, I tended to idealize my teachers.

VH: I idealized Reiss–Davis when I was there.

PG: The difference is that we were dealing with charismatic people.

They may not have been the greatest contributors to the field, but some of them made their mark, like Alexander and French, Karen Horney, Benedek, and so on. A lot of people are disillusioned. Let me bring up one question that perhaps I should amplify on, and that's the question of what brought me into psychoanalysis. As I reviewed it, it seemed to be an accidental circumstance. Slight and I got together. We liked each other, and I idealized him. He somehow treated me as one of his own children. All of that's true; but, obviously, it went beyond that. I think, basically, it was a fascination with the unconscious, which I became aware of when I was in college. I started by hypnotizing people. There was something romantic about hypnosis.

VH: Yes.

PG: It gave me an opportunity to be exhibitionistic. Little did I know that a psychoanalyst just sits in the background and has very little capacity to express himself. With hypnosis, I was a hit at parties, fraternities, and so on. When I first started practice, I was lucky to get a group of patients who were very gifted. They were scientists; most of them were physicists. It was a gratifying experience. They took to psychoanalysis like a fish takes to water. These physicists accepted psychoanalysis as a science without question. I obtained data about the human mind, both in its most primitive and in its most integrated states. The similarities between a primitive mental state and a creative mental state are fascinating. The creative scientist is in touch with the unconscious. The primitive state is disorganized. The creative state achieves organization, but it goes through a stage of disorganization or a state of primary process. Primary process, however, is not disorganization. It is a primitive operation, but it still has an organization of its own. The fabric of our data in psychoanalysis is clinical, but it can be dealt with in a scientific fashion. Some analysts, Melanie Klein for example, felt that creativity was a healing activity to counteract depression. I do not believe that's true. I think it's an activity in its own right. It's not that a person is creative because he is depressed. I see it as an autonomous kind of pursuit.

VH: Betty Edwards, a Long Beach artist, wrote *Drawing on the Right Side of the Brain* (1989). I read it when I took up painting last year. She says if you are in a state of extreme creativity, at that moment at least, your mind would be focused. You would be in a different mental state. What do you think?

PG: I think that's true. Creativity, since I had these patients, became one of my earliest focuses. Among the first papers I ever wrote were several on creativity. It's a topic that always attracts an audience.

VH: Would you summarize your thoughts and findings regarding creativity?

PG: That's very difficult to do because it's such a vast topic.

VH: I know. But it's such a vastly interesting one too.

PG: I know. Perhaps a creative person's chief characteristic is that he has the capacity to get in touch with his unconscious and can do it in a very comfortable way and not be overwhelmed by it. I remember one of my physicist patients saying that when he's creating he feels like he's on a roller coaster. He's surrounded by fireworks, and it's an exhilarating experience. He feels that there are objects inside of him that are exploding. They have various shapes, cubes and squares, all moving rapidly inside of him. It's a euphoric, hypomanic experience. The solution to the problem appears to him under these circumstances. This man was a very famous physicist. Poincaré described something. He saw objects with different shapes and colors flying around. He discovered Fuchsian functions, a branch of mathematics, with this type of visual imagery. Kekulé dreamed about a snake coiled around itself, the mouth around its tail, rolling down a hill. When he woke up, he discovered the benzine ring, a formula that had been puzzling and eluding chemists for many years. The creative person has a tremendous amount of energy. He's in touch with his unconscious, but he is also disciplined. He has to apply secondary process to refine crude primary process material.

VH: When you were talking about creativity and your patient who had all the shapes, were you thinking of shapes as structures that don't have a home of their own yet or as shapes that are fragments of the self. I'm thinking about children who have learning disabilities and who don't get the shapes right. How does all of that fit together with creativity?

PG: Well, I believe the two things you said are both correct. They don't have a home of their own, and they are parts of the self. With the creative person, they do have a home; but they are dislodged for the moment. They are parts of the self whirling around, so to speak, in a state of unorganization, not disorganization, a distinction Winnicott made. They can tolerate this particular state of unorganization as long as they need to. It may only last a fraction of a second or it may last an hour or two in other instances. But eventually, secondary processes take over. I met Feynman, briefly, when I was a resident at the University of Chicago. Do you know Feynman? He's dead now. He was at Cal Tech after he left the University of Chicago. He exemplifies the creative personality almost in a stereotypic fashion. He was a Peck's Bad Boy when he was at the University of Chicago, but they tolerated him because he was a genius. For example, he had a lot of fun breaking into safes at Argonne National Lab and stealing confidential data. The Secret Service would come up to him the next day and say, "Okay, Richard, give it back to us." They never did anything to him. He also played the bongo drums. He was apparently quite good. If they gave him a problem, he often came up with the answer immediately.

VH: You mean a problem in physics or in mathematics?

PG: Yes. How he did it he didn't know. It just popped into his mind. I'm sure that things were whirling around. At that time, it was maybe just a microsecond. I believe Freud was right—the unconscious is timeless. A long dream that seems to go on for days and days may actually last only a minute. This can be proven in some instances. Feynman had a childish, impish quality. He was also curious about everything. He had a wonderful way of looking at things. He wrote a book about himself that came out just recently (Feynman, 1988).

VH: He's dead now.

PG: Yes, he died of cancer. He became well known to the public at the time the space capsule exploded.

VH: How?

PG: He was the one who took the "O" ring and put it in a glass of water. A very simple thing to do. But no one else had thought of it. As I said, he wrote an autobiographical book. And you could see what a wonderful human being he was. Once, he was in a Caribbean Island. What he liked to do was see the slums. He wanted to see how most of the people lived. This island was filled with Hindus and blacks. His chauffeur, or taxi driver actually, was a black man. At the end of the voyage they chatted a good deal. Feynman had a way of making friends. This black man asked, "Why is it that we blacks here just don't progress, we don't move? I got as far as being a taxi driver whereas these Hindus, they are as poor as we are, yet some of them manage to send their children to school. Sometimes they go to college. Sometimes they become professionals." Feynman said, "I really don't know, but maybe it's that you don't have a history. You don't have generations of tradition. You just came out of Africa, and you haven't had time to build up traditions." It was a wonderful quick answer. I'm sure he's absolutely right. His attitude was, "I don't know, but basically this is what occurs to me." He had a way of looking at things. I'll never forget when I was at college in graduate school many years ago. I was with Arnold B. Luckhardt, Anton J. Carlson—men who were titans in physiology. Luckhardt said, "All redheads are sexually passionate." So Carlson said, "That's an interesting hypothesis. Is that an ex-cathedra statement or have you done research on the subject?" You see how they think?

VH: But you've been a very creative person. How do you describe your own creative process? What happens to you when you get an idea or you begin to think, "Ah, I've got something here?"

PG: It's interesting how that happens. I don't really get ideas. If you ask me—and my publisher does all the time—why don't you write a book on, say, countertransference? All right, I'll write a book on countertransference. I'll sit down, usually in this chair, with one of these little stenographic notebooks, and I say, "Write." I start writing. I don't particularly know what I'm going to write before I start. Still, the ideas get put down on paper. I'm sure what has happened is that I have had these ideas all along. They have been in my head for years and were derived from my clinical experiences. As you know, most of my writings are very clinical and personal.

VH: Yes.

PG: So really what I'm doing is I'm plagiarizing.

VH: But in the best of ways—learning from the experiences of others.

PG: Well, I'm plagiarizing from the patient.

VH: Yes, I know that, and probably your student's patients too.

PG: Yes. Absolutely. Patients are very glad to give me the material. I remember I was talking to a patient over the telephone. He was in another city at that time. He was describing some regressive episode that he had, where he was splitting, a very primitive episode. He was crying, moaning, and screeching like an animal in extreme pain. Afterwards, I asked, "Now tell me, what was happening to you at that time?" He replied, "There are many parts of myself that I've lost. We know my past history. I was trying to regain them. I was trying to put them back inside of me. I couldn't quite smoothly integrate them. So this was very painful physically." I said, "Wait a minute while I write this down." (*Laughs*) It was a direct translation of how regression leads to integration and what one has to go through. He was also telling me what the therapist has to do under those circumstances. I've seen him in those states, and he values our contact. He has taught me not to make interpretations. If I had said, "You're trying to integrate lost parts of yourself," that would stop the process. True, that is what he is trying to do, but I am discussing the phenomenon at a higher verbal level than what he is experiencing. This is a preverbal experience. I have to be there and allow him to have this experience and then later put it together. My comments have to be restricted to what he is feeling at the moment. I might say, "You're in terrible pain," reflecting back what he's experiencing. Going beyond the experience, that is bringing it to a higher level, is going to take him right out of it. Of course, most of us instinctively want to give him relief. We do not want a patient to be in pain—we do not want to see another person suffering. We want to say something that's reassuring and give him relief. It is a terrible mistake. This patient and many others have taught me that. I think one of the reasons I write is to find out what I have learned. I have to put it on paper to be aware of what I have learned. When I start writing, it pours out. I do not have any writing schedule.

VH: Have you read Christopher Bollas's work?

PG: I had an interchange with him about the last book I edited, *Tactics and Techniques, Volume 2* (1975) with a special emphasis on Winnicott's work. Naturally, I asked Chris if he would write a chapter for the book, since he's the secretary of the Winnicott group. He wouldn't do it, because he doesn't want to be identified as a Winnicottian. He doesn't want a cult to develop around Winnicott. He is, of course, very much involved in his ideas, but he thinks deification is wrong, and I agree with him. In my preface, I point that out. Often in psychoanalysis, we tend to idealize the person and forget about the ideas themselves. This can be tyrannical. When I was at the Chicago Institute, no one could say anything negative about Freud.

VH: Nothing at all?

PG: No, one could not say anything. Kardiner wrote a classic paper attacking the psychoeconomic hypothesis. Today, hardly any of us accept the psychoeconomic hypothesis. Kardiner could not get it published in an analytic journal. It had to be published in a psychiatric journal. He said, "Ten years from now people will be talking the same way I am and not giving me credit for it," which is exactly what happened.

VH: This idea we are talking about, of not deifying the work of a few giants—it's important to me. I consider myself an "American Independent," because I don't want to exclude anybody who is useful from any "school." You are very independent too—and not tied to fashions.

PG: I have been very much at odds with Kohut's work. Kohut writes about narcissism. Kohut has this irritating habit of saying a lot of things and not giving credit to the person who really said them the first time. Kohut believed he invented the term "selfobject" in 1971, when he published *The Analysis of the Self*. I did not think much about it. Boyer and I were doing a second edition of our 1967 book. On page 269 in italics, I had used selfobject. It was hyphenated, but it was in italics. I did not think too much about it because it does not mean anything. It's the same concept that Freud had in 1914, of secondary narcissism. But I thought it was a curiosity. So I told Kernberg about it, and Kernberg went around the country and around the world saying, "Giovacchini invented the word *selfobject*." Later, I was reading a book by Modell (1984), and he says "Kohut's 'selfobject.' " The irony of it was, though, that about 2 months before reading that book I was going through the literature, for some reason or other, and I had come across a 1963 article, 4 years before my book's second edition; in a footnote it has the word "selfobject." Who was the man that wrote the article? Modell.*

VH: Let's go back to what you were saying about "shapes." I'm thinking now of Frances Tustin's discussion of the elaboration of the whirling of autistic children, which I guess would say that there again we have shapes; but they're sort of unformed and have no home. Or they had a home, and they lost it. But it seems that there is something very, very primitive about that state. Do you agree with her work?

PG: Oh, yes! I like Tustin. I think her work has been very significant. I do not have any personal contact with autistic children, but I have done some supervision in this area. One of my best friends, Alfred Flarsheim, used to be a consultant at the Orthogenic School. He would tell me of his experiences there. Then I got to supervise some of the counselors. I found Tustin's work very valuable. I think it is very good.

VH: I admire her work so much. I went to England to get it on tape. Some Chicago analysts had not even heard of her. I just was flabbergasted.

PG: Well, I hate to say this, but many analysts in Chicago are not very well educated. You were wondering about my works being read by them. I would imagine that most of the people here have never read my work.

VH: How could they not read a Giovacchini?

PG: I have no idea. I remember one of my residents going to one of the senior analysts not too many years ago. Most of our faculty are graduates of the Institute. This man said to this resident, "Well, Giovacchini's work was pretty good. But, you know, the last 10 years he hasn't written anything." Which was stupid. I've written a book a year in those particular 10 years that he was talking about.

VH: And they're big books.

PG: Yes, they're big books.

VH: You only have to do the research to realize how tall they get.

PG: Most analysts do not really read outside of their own area. They do not even read Freud. I remember being astonished when one analyst said something that showed he had not even read Freud's dream book. He said that Freud wrote *The Interpretation of Dreams* (1900) in 1920! How could a priest not know his Bible? I remember presenting in one of our little groups. Up until recently we have had little seminar groups. In my group I discussed Freud's 1914 paper on narcissism. I remember a very

*Actually, Modell (1963) gives credit to a personal communication from Zetzel, and quotes "lack of selfobject discrimination."

senior analyst from Europe said, "Oh my, that's the first time I have understood it!" Here was a classic paper. This was a very good person. I wanted to tell you about the seminar group because of something you asked about the Institute.

VH: Yes.

PG: For many years, and to this day, some quarters, some people think I have started a second institute. That's not so. However, about 10 years ago, a psychologist came to see me and asked me to start a second institute. He had studied the curricula of maybe 10 or 15 different institutes. Then he did a factor analysis on them and came out with a program. I contacted two colleagues, actually three. Bert Kohler was one of them from the Orthogenic School, the Bettelheim School. We did not want to start an institute. We knew that this would create a furor. We were not going to get accreditation because none of us was a training analyst. We did not want to recreate the same kinds of struggles and political infighting. We felt that's what would happen. We didn't want a hierarchy. My feeling, at the time, was very democratic. The people we would be dealing with were very experienced. They were well-educated, college graduates, postgraduates, private practioners, some on faculties of institutions. What we should do, I felt, is put up a bulletin board. Let a person say, "I feel like I would like to have a course on ego psychology, or Freud, or Winnicott." Write that down. Others that agree could sign, and we'd start a seminar. That is precisely what happened. We started out with three seminars. One was on classic Freud. I taught it. My book came out as a result of that seminar. One was on child development. The other was just clinical, a case presentation. At the end of the first year, we kept getting people who wanted to join the group. We had about 40 people in it. So we had to get other people to teach. We had to rent rooms. We rented conference rooms downtown at the Sheraton Hotel. It went on and on and on. So when people talk about Giovacchini's Institute, this was not an institute. We did not graduate anyone. We did not confer certificates. But it went on for 10 years. Then I got tired of it. What happened was some of the, I wouldn't even call them students, but participants in the seminars, decided that they did want a diploma, some kind of recognition. So they started what they called the Center for Psychoanalytic Studies. I was the director of that, but I had made a very strict stipulation that we were not setting ourselves up as an institute. Well, they finally disagreed with me. I had to resign because I would not support them.

VH: Was this primarily a nonmedical group?

PG: Well, there are M.D.s in it. What has happened with the Center is that it's become more hierarchical than the Institute. I knew that was going to happen. They've become more despotic in their requirements. The students write a paper. They have to do research.

VH: You created a remarkable body of work. I very much appreciate your generosity in sharing this time with me. I'm sure I speak for many in saying, thank you.

Case Discussion

Dr. Giovacchini, known for his work with primitive mental states, believes that Roselyn is terribly vulnerable and experiences frequent posits of disintegration because her mother was so unpredictable, psychotic, and assaultive; and her father gave her no protective barrier. He goes on to say that the patient had no continuity in herself and hardly any holding environment outside herself. He notices that in the early years of our work Roselyn could not hold a mental representation without the symbol being present.

This consultation took place September 16, 1990, in Giovacchini's office at his home in Winnetka, Illinois. Giovacchini began, "This case might be considered to be a classic. I don't think 'classic' applies to everybody we see because everybody is different in some ways. But the material here, I think, is very clear. Basically, you're dealing with a woman who is, and feels, very vulnerable. The states that you're describing I would call states of disintegration. The ego is falling apart in little fragments that are whirling all over, falling apart. They are not contained within boundaries. Of course, it's a state of panic; that's very clearly what you are describing here. . . . The pain of the migraine, and the psychoses that she occasionally experiences—they have paranoid qualities and are attempts to reorganize herself and to achieve stability and homeostasis, once again." Several times he referred to Winnicott for confirmations of his ideas.

Giovacchini continued, taking up the issue of her severe migraines; he saw them as pain that would destroy her if it came from the outside. "She sees it as: 'It would explode my mind, my self. I'd be like little molecules going around any and everywhere.' This is a pain that represents, indeed, manifests the infantile environment which was so painful for her. Her mother was unpredictable, assaultive, which brought her the pain—again, assaultive pain. Her father did not supply her with a protective barrier. The only thing that she could identify with were vulnerable parents. There was no holding environment or hardly any. There had to be some, otherwise she wouldn't be alive. She reminds me of a patient of mine whose mother would beat him up when he was asleep, who would caress him, fondle him sexually then get up and take a shotgun and shoot the cat, cut it in half—totally unpredictable. When a sleeping child is attacked, it means the child can't feel secure when she withdraws into the world of her unconscious. The external world must be a tremendously threatening place for your patient."

VH: Do you know Roselyn heard me, when she told this story the first time, weeping. She heard me sniff, which was disruptive, of course. I couldn't help it. To think of this little child was unbearable. She was very upset that I cried for her because she doesn't cry for herself.

PG: I think she was very touched by it, too.

VH: She was touched too, but also she told me not to do that, because, I think, it brought her closer to her own feelings that are locked up.

PG: Yes, I would agree with that. But anyway, I see this general atmosphere of pain and think of the migraine as a capsule. It's protective. It has an outer wall to it. That's what she's inside of, somehow or other. The pain, in other words, is a container as well as a binding force, which holds her together.

Giovacchini was reminded of Esther Bick and her work concerning the skin ego.

He said that Roselyn's experience was not masochistic. "It is a much more primitive experience. I think at a higher level, the migraine also represents multidetermined rage. Rage is unpredictable in the infantile environment. And again it serves a structuralizing purpose." I told him that she doesn't usually experience the rage. He said, "She might not have developed beyond the level when she was not able to structure affects. But now, she has migraines. I think they localize her pain. The migraine is also a capsule that contains rage as well as protects the vulnerable self."

Then he shifted his focus and took up a major point: "I think the greatest interest in this case is her relationship with you," he said. "You're not seen as the attacking, persecutory mother. You are the mother that she wished she had. She uses you as a holding environment." He explained his ideas concerning mothering needs: "I see the maternal function as having two components to it, background and foreground.

You're talking about the foreground in terms of nurture. I'm talking about the background. You can soothe her. You were there when she had psychotic episodes. A patient of mine, just 2 days ago, came in with a dream. It was a very interesting experience. He dreamt of a woman who had no arms; they had been amputated; and no breasts. In investigating this dream, I said, 'This woman is mutilated. What does that bring to mind?' He has diabetes, and sometimes he feels mutilated. He related feeling mutilated by his mother. Without thinking I said, 'I can understand how angry you might be. Because here's a woman who can't feed you and who can't hold you.' He started crying. Your patient sees you as having arms that could hold her.

"Your patient has been recapitulating the negative parts of her experience. But she's doing it in a way that you can contain it within your office. There's enough of a holding environment that allows her to experience the falling into empty space and to be afraid and to be angry at you. But she comes back. Obviously you have a fairly good relationship. You'll probably see her the rest of your life."

I asked him about the potential that Roselyn had of developing new structures. Again, he referred to one of his own clinical experiences: "I have a patient I've been seeing for 40 years. Ironically, he was referred to me by Franz Alexander for brief therapy. I see him three times a week still. Is he a success story? I don't know. You keep diabetics alive by giving them insulin. They need insulin forever, but they function. He came in suicidally depressed. No object relations, he had a good job, a very bright man, an advertising executive. But he was totally isolated, totally miserable, on the brink of putting a bullet through his skull. Forty years later, he's very successful in the stock market. He's married, he has six or seven children. He's depressed but not suicidally, obviously. He still talks about his Mommy and his Daddy, and how he wants to eat them up. All this primitive material. He says that therapy isn't doing him any good. He's been saying that for four decades. But he never misses an hour. He gave me a wonderful image. Several years ago a magazine came out with an article on an electronic bug. It's about this big (*Giovacchini made boundaries with his hands*), and it roams around. It's charged with electricity. Every so often, it will go to the wall socket, plug itself in, get a charge, and then go roaming around again. I'm the wall socket. He comes in three times a week for his charge and just keeps going. I think that's what you're going to have with your patient."

Did he feel that this was an acceptable outcome? He answered: "I had a fascinating experience many years ago, which will answer your question. It happened to a colleague, and I learned from my colleague. This colleague had a patient who was dying of tuberculosis. She had been in sanitariums. This was before drug treatment; her lungs had collapsed. Finally, someone asked her why she didn't go see a psychoanalyst. It was a last resort. It couldn't hurt. So she went to see this colleague of mine. Seven years later he was still treating her. I remember we were talking about how long an analysis should last. So we asked a senior analyst, Hugh Carmichael. He said, 'Well after 5 years, I discontinue the treatment.' My colleague got very upset abut this. He started talking to his patient about termination. She said nothing. When she came in the next session, she had a handkerchief over her mouth. She showed it to him. It was full of blood. Since he brought that subject up, she started coughing blood. Then she said, 'Look, this is my analysis. I expect to have it as long as I need it. If I'm going to die, I expect you to help me through that. If you have any problems with this, then you'd better go back and get some analysis yourself.' So he went to England and went to see Winnicott. Every year he spent about 3 months there. But I learned so much from that case without having to go through my colleague's pain. I'm treating the patient's husband now. I am not fixed to the idea that an analysis has a beginning, a middle, and an end."

I asked him about his ideas concerning the frame. Would he, for instance, go to a performance given by a patient? He said he would. "When I was treating children, a patient was in a play I went to see. It was a natural thing to do. If an adult patient asked me to attend a play, I would have said, 'Well, let's think about what we can do that's going to be most useful to the treatment. It may be that there is some drawback; it might create some complication. Let's find out. If this can be helpful to you, I'll come. But I doubt that it will be. I think it might be better if we talk about it.' We want to maintain the holding environment, but there is no set predetermined behavior. I might decide to attend."

Giovacchini continued to speak about the "rules" in psychoanalysis: "The reason I am working as I am is because it seemed so ridiculous that the patient had to fit the treatment rather than the treatment fit the patient. Here are our rules. You've got to cooperate with them, or else. That didn't make any sense.

"I remember one particular patient who was like your patient in many ways. Somehow she'd heard of me, throughout her experiences as a patient, from her doctors and psychiatrists. She started reading some of my books. She liked them. She came from another city. When I first saw her, she was clutching one of my books. It apparently had become a transitional object, a part of the holding environment. In about the fourth hour of treatment, she gave me this statuette. It had no facial features, totally amorphous. The arms were cut off. It was about a foot or so, tall and thin. It flared out at the hips a little bit. It looked like a Giacometti sculpture, and I put it right here. There was no question in my mind about accepting it. I knew that if I didn't accept it, that would be the last time I would see her. If I wanted to treat her, and for some reason I did, I had better accept this statuette. This proved to be a very dramatic moment.

The statuette, of course, was herself. She couldn't be held. Whenever she got mad at me, she would pick the statuette up and break it. But I would put it back together with Elmer's Glue-All. To make a long story short, she could not hold a mental representation of me without my actual presence. She felt I couldn't hold a mental representation of her. That literally came true. I needed that statuette; when she broke it, I became very upset. I needed to keep it intact. After about 7 or 8 years of therapy, she came in for one session and grabbed the statuette, but I just sat here and didn't move. I didn't show any signs of consternation, and she asked, 'Don't you care? You always got really upset.' I said, 'I don't need it any more.' She said, 'Oh.' She took it with her. That was the last time I saw the statuette, but her ego defect healed. My countertransference didn't have to reflect it back any more. She could now hold a mental representation of me without my actual presence."

He mentioned the frequency with which he dealt with concrete objects that were used for symbolic enactments. "There was a time that I had many little mementos here, little clay objects: there was a bear; there was a balloon with a basket. A patient made them. They were different parts of herself. She's finished her therapy. Right now, I don't have anyone who does that. At one time another patient brought a picture to a colleague. He wanted the analyst to take his own down and put his up. That's too much of an intrusion. But little things are acceptable. Secahaye would have called it 'symbolic realization.' You're helping them build symbols. I see nothing wrong with that. You're making a symbolic relationship in which the patient gives a part of herself to you and so will know that you care for her. But it's all symbolic. She's not asking you to put out your breast and feed her."

Arnold Goldberg

Dr. Goldberg, a preeminent self psychologist, edited Kohut's Casebook *(1978). He himself has written several books regarding the idealizing transference and narcissistic personality disorders. He makes sharp criticisms of gurus and regimented thinking in psychoanalysis.*

This interview took place August 30 and 31, 1990, in Dr. Goldberg's office in the building occupied by the Institute for Psychoanalysis in Chicago, where he was director at the time. Like his office, which is modern and uncluttered, Dr. Goldberg's mind is sharp, and his concentration on matters at hand is total: He and his office come directly to the point, without small talk, without evasion. He holds to the highest standards in psychoanalysis, and this makes him a candid and sometimes unsparing judge of his own work and that of others. His range of knowledge is as remarkable as is his ability to bring it to bear on a great variety of subjects.

He set high standards for analytic thinking and research. Behavior of the analyst toward the analytic patient must be impeccable. Most people fail, by his understanding, to live up to this standard. He seems to want to be seen as an intellectual, an aristocrat of the mind, but he is also extremely humble about his own accomplishments and limitations.

Only he, probably, would be humble about his extraordinary accomplishments. Dr. Goldberg has written or edited over 50 published works on such subjects as adolescent psychotherapy, narcissism, empathy, and self psychology. His books include *The Psychology of the Self* (1978), which he edited, *A Fresh Look at Psychoanalysis: The View from Self Psychology* (1988), and *The Prison House of Psychoanalysis* (1990). He encourages psychoanalysts to give up gurus and rigid thinking and to keep an open mind. He is the prime hermeneutician of psychoanalysis in the present day.

Interview

Virginia Hunter: You were born and raised here in Chicago. How did you happen to become an analyst?

Arnold Goldberg: I think I've told this story before to people, but I'm always surprised the way it comes out when I tell it again. I think I always knew I was going to be a psychoanalyst and went to school with that in mind. I learned about it when I was 10 or 12 years old when my sister went into analysis. I was always very interested in the whole idea of learning about people. When I went through college, I thought maybe I would become a psychologist, but it became clear to me that you had to go to medical school to amount to anything in psychoanalysis in America. So I went to medical school, and that's where I thought I would not become a psychoanalyst. I loved medicine. I loved going to medical school, loved being a doctor, loved it. But I went into psychiatry. Actually, Mort Shane and I were interns together. He went one way, and I went the other. I came back to Chicago for my residency, went in the Army for a couple of years, came back, went into a different residency, and then took personal analysis.

VH: With whom?

AG: Three analysts.

VH: Who was your main one?

AG: My first analyst was a man named Vander Veer, Adrian Vander Veer. He was a child analyst, who smoked incessantly, coughed a great deal, and died of a heart attack about a year or so into my analysis. I, thereupon, gave up cigarettes and went to see someone else. He saw me in a once-a-week supportive way. I went back into analysis when he had enough time. That was Fritz Moellenhoff, a wonderful man. He was a tall, thin, aristocratic German with a dueling scar and a marvelous accent. He was someone I was very fond of and who, I felt, was very fond of me. That, I've always felt, was my analysis. Fritz was from Berlin and had been analyzed by Hans Sachs. He came over with his wife during the Hitler regime because his wife was Jewish. Fritz, himself, was not Jewish. He was at the Menninger Clinic for a while, and then Alexander brought him here. That was the heyday of analysis in America and in Chicago, in the 1940s and 1950s.

I went into analytic training and finished my analysis here. Some time after that when I had mental problems, I went back to see Fritz, and he said I should see Therese Benedek. So my third analyst was Therese Benedek, who I didn't think was very well suited for me. She helped me with my problems. I finished—finished both my marriage and my treatment with her, and I have no regrets about that, but she was a much different kind of analyst. She was given to a kind of a mystical analysis. You would walk into the room, and she would say something like, just for an example, "Oh, you got the job," or some off-the-wall statement, which would be right. It turned out that she was usually 99% percent accurate. But, for me, it had a kind of eerie feeling to it. There was something magical about her all the time. And people swore by her because she had this uncanniness of perception. I didn't take well to it. It was an okay analysis, but I never felt it was all that good. We always had good relationships afterward. We had good rapport, but Benedek had this reputation of being a wizard. People swore by her. I suspect one of the reasons I never liked that analysis so much is that I didn't take to that quality. She wanted to be a "wow." She wanted me to say, "Oh, Dr. Benedek!" I never bought into that. I had enough problems of my own. She had people who just fell all over her. She was very good, but I never took to it. But I'm very unusual in that regard. Everyone liked Therese. I'll bet you couldn't find one out of a thousand who had anything negative to say about her. She was sweet. She was clever. She was funny; but boy she wanted you to think she was "it." I never liked her pronouncements. Fritz was much different. A wonderful guy who adored Therese. They were the best of friends. I'm sure that's why he sent me to her.

VH: Before I turned on the tape, you spoke to me about the importance of your sister in your psychoanalytic history.

AG: Oh, yes, my sister was very important in my growing up; very much of a mother figure for us, my brother and me. She is 7 years older than I am. She's a psychiatric social worker and is retired in Florida. She raised us after my mother died when I was 13, but she was already raising us long before my mother died. She went to the Chicago Institute when she was about 19 years old, got into treatment here.

VH: On her own.

AG: On her own, yes. She was in treatment with a woman named Doris Fishback who moved to San Francisco. I never knew anything about that woman. I had these idealized feelings about the Institute for Psychoanalysis. I thought, "That's the place to go when you're unhappy—and I wasn't happy—that's the place that helped my sister; and my sister was everything to me." No, I did not stumble upon *The Interpretation of Dreams* (Freud, 1900) when I was 16 and fall in love with any of that stuff. I didn't read any Freud until I went into training. I am not, forgive me, a person particularly interested in "Freudiana." I don't care if he joined the B'nai Brith, or if he had an affair with his sister-in-law, or any of that other history. My early interest was quite different, and it has affected the way I understand psychoanalysis today, as a therapeutic enterprise. Once at a meeting, Ray Schafer, Bob Michaels, and I were all talking. And I asked them, "How did you get interested?" They all had one of those great stories. You know those intellectual stories of, "I read *The Interpretation of Dreams*, and from that moment on, I knew my destiny." I never had any of that. I find it very difficult to read *The Interpretation of Dreams*. So no, I'm not one of those. I'm sorry, I wish I had one of those stories.

VH: Your story is a very human one.

AG: Well, after all, it was me. I'll grant you that. I'm convinced that my sister is overjoyed that I became a psychoanalyst. And my brother, I have an older brother as well who is a lawyer, who probably wanted to be a doctor, but something happened, and he didn't go to medical school. So I was the baby of the three, and I was the one who was probably the most successful.

VH: And your father?

AG: My father was a laundry man, and my mother was a housewife who spent a lot of time working with him in the laundry, and that's why my sister took care of us. He was a very smart man. My mother was a very smart man, though she had no real education beyond high school.

VH: You referred to your mother as a male!

AG: My mentor, Heinz Kohut, used to say, "When you make a slip of the tongue, it's a momentary disambulation of one's self." It's just that. I don't make much of such slips.

VH: To run a successful laundry business for two emigrees who didn't speak English initially required a lot of talent.

AG: Yes, my father was real "spiffy." It was unfortunate that he came over from Russia when he was 17; he should have had more education. My mother was brilliant in mathematics, even though she was not well educated. I've often said to people it was very clear that the children were never to take after their parents. I would never be a laundry man. I remember I went through residence with Dick Grinker, whose father was Roy Grinker, whose father was Julius Grinker. I had never known any tradition like that of doctoring. I was trained to believe, "Whatever you become, don't become what I am"—be better than your parents.

VH: Your mother died early. Your first analyst died early. You didn't have a family or a tradition to fall back upon. Clearly, you had a lot of losses to deal with.

AG: Well, yes. I used to think it was the worst fate possible. When Vander Veer died, I was mortified, beside myself. When I went to be trained, one of my first supervisors was Joan Fleming, who did parent-loss studies here. I kind of presented myself as a "parent-loss" patient. I always thought of myself as a "parent loss." I always thought that everything you talk of as "parent loss" I embodied, and this is what I needed to help in others when I treated them. The first case I got to present to her, that I wanted to analyze, was a case of parent loss. Since then I changed a lot of my ideas about parent loss.

VH: What have you changed?

AG: Well, there's been a lot of research in Chicago, and I think that my feeling, now, is that one-parent loss is much less significant than the kind of help that the surviving parent gives to the child. When my mother died, my father got very depressed. My father became ill, and I think that was much more of a blow than the gradual acceptance of her death.

VH: What was his illness?

AG: He had hepatitis. He recovered, but he was very depressed and out of it. I am convinced that my personal psychology, my personal kind of psychopathology, predates the loss of my mother. I don't know if it made that much of a difference. You want to know what it was? Well, she was a depressed woman, and I think I have much more of the characteristics of a depressed person, as a lot of analysts do. You know, they have a depressed parent, they try to become the cure of that depressed person. They try to make that person better. They handle all their rage by their rescue fantasy, and so forth. I think that all my feelings toward her are the nucleus of my profession. I think her death probably put a stamp on it.

VH: You seem to have a love of language, a love of not just the science, but also writing, editing. How do you account for that?

AG: Writing is perhaps one way that depression helps, because to read a lot requires a lot of time alone. What's more, long before writing there is reading—another very solitary activity. There's only one way to learn to write and to learn to love language, and that is to read. I am an addicted reader. I read all the time, everything. I always have upset a lot of people because I read so much and in so many areas. I have, all of my life, read everything I could. I am a very fast reader. I am a very wide reader, and I'm convinced that's the only way one learns to write and to speak. That's the advice I give anyone who says, "How do I learn to write?" You have to read a lot. Most of the people whom I read to edit, and most of the books I read, are just terrible writers. Most of them are terrible. There are a few good writers, but not very many. I read a lot of fiction. I don't read, interestingly enough, at all, history or biography, such as you are doing right now.

VH: What kinds of things, in terms of leisure, do you read?

AG: I read a lot of mysteries. I like detective stories, spy novels. When we were on vacation, I must have read a dozen books. There was only one good one that I read. It was by this Japanese author. Estelle Shane suggested I read it, *Remains of the Day* (Ishiguro, 1990), a very good book. And I read a lot of philosophy.

VH: That certainly shows in your writing. You've made reference to Chomsky in several of your writings.

AG: I've read a lot of his political writings. He's a fascinating, far out, leftist. He writes well. I respect him. I think that over the years, as I learn more about his concepts, I believe them less and less. I don't think he is very much a Cartesian. He feels these structures are innate and inborn. I think I've drifted away from that kind of a feeling. I think Freudian psychology is very Chomsky-like in that it is, in effect, too philosophical. It's all neo-Kantian. It says there are inborn things, given, innate hard wiring, and there's the Freudian and the Kleinian fantasies, like Piaget has his cognitive stages. Chomsky is of that same ilk. At certain times in the developmental scheme, the program clicks on and you are ready for language, reading, whatever, oedipal fantasies, sensory motor skills—all those things. And we've all become very wedded to them. They are so neat to feel that it's all fixed, it's innate, inborn, and so forth. I think there is a certain appeal to that, but I wonder if it's the seduction and isn't quite accurate. Many people feel you can explain language accurately without the imposition of these deep structures.

VH: Your parents did not speak or read English as their first language. How did your childhood family handle language? Was there a lot of conversation?

AG: I don't think we were particularly communicative. Although I must say, in my present marriage, my wife's family, whom I'm very fond of, they are people who talk a great deal, but don't talk about many things. In my early childhood we'd talk about everything. We didn't, probably, talk to the degree and extent and the absolute breath and depth about a few things, as my in-laws do, but with my parents there was nothing that was not talked about. My in-laws are such proper, decent, and respectful people that they know what to avoid. That obviously comes from my background. In terms of the use of language and the infatuation with language, no. I have a very dear friend who is a linguist, and I've learned a lot from her.

VH: Who is that?

AG: Her name is Bonnie Letowitz. She's very good, and she has taught me a lot. I've learned a lot about Lacan, but I will never be a Lacanian because you can only have one God in this business. Although I have a friend, Paul Ornstein, who's had a whole bunch of them. Otto Kernberg once said to me, "You know, I don't trust Paul Ornstein because he keeps getting involved with these gurus." He was involved with Michael Balint. Then he was involved with Maury Levine, and now he's involved with Heinz Kohut. I think it's just the real need to latch on to somebody, but with Paul it stopped with Kohut.

VH: You said in one of your case discussions, that concerning Lacan, change comes out of conflict, that change comes from disruption in harmony. So Lacan's abrupt ending of hours was an attempt to do something dramatic that might evoke change.

AG: I have a new book coming out next week, and there's a chapter in there that deals with Lacan's short hours. The guy was a nut. But he has attracted very intelligent followers, for instance this very, very good writer, Stuart Schneiderman from New York, who obviously over-idealized Lacan's ability.

VH: He's an interesting talker.

AG: Schneiderman?

VH: I think so.

AG: I think his book is, but I've never heard him speak. He is one of those; and I don't mean to depreciate him when I say he's a great apologist who writes brilliantly about the droppings of Lacan which he's picked up. I think great men need apologists like that. In his book—I think it's hilarious; but he doesn't mean it to be hilarious, he explains the terrible behavior of Lacan in all kinds of ridiculous ways. But the truth was Lacan was a jerk. He misbehaved all the time. He may have been mad from child abuse. Like Meltzer, he was brilliant and grandiose and megalomanic. Yes, he saw things that other people didn't, but he didn't behave well. There's a story of how he was in a restaurant, Roman Polanski comes in with this beautiful girl. Do you know that story of Lacan?

VH: No, I don't.

AG: He makes a big fuss over her in order to put down Polanski. Schneiderman says this is wonderful, that Lacan could do this. Really, it's so embarrassing that Schneiderman would have to justify this kind of behavior. I don't think that Lacan was interested in helping people. I think what Lacan is interested in, is fascination with language. I think that Lacan's short hours only served his own narcissistic needs. Then he made up some rationalization like you've come to know. Psychoanalysis is filled with misbehavior that becomes rationalized.

VH: That sounds like an interesting subject.

AG: They yell at patients, and they say they needed it. We fill our sessions all the time with trying to excuse what we did when we fall short. It happens all the time, and I'm sure you've seen it.

VH: Yes, but I think you have an example of your own in mind.

AG: Yes, well, I would be a little more cautious now. Some people I know will write these long tomes on countertransference and how they use their countertransference to treat patients and the value of one's countertransference. Many of these skirt with the problem of how can I cover the fact that I didn't behave well? I'll write an article on countertransference and make it into the "Look how I managed to use the bad and make it good." I review a lot of books. I reviewed one for the American Psychiatric Association. It is a book about all the greats of psychotherapy who appeared at a particular conference—the first Milton Erickson conference, in Arizona. Seven thousand people came, and all the geniuses were there—Szasz, Victor Frankel, and just a whole body of them. Each was more impossible than the next. One of them, Carl Whitaker, said that he would only treat people for his own good. He only treats people to help himself. He's someone who supposedly does family therapy. These are all very disturbed, narcissistic, megalomanic characters who act out and then say, "I think I'll form a cult or a theory or a school or something like that."

VH: But Whitaker does have interesting ideas about adolescence.

AG: Yes. And Lacan says some fascinating things about language. Szasz says some critically interesting things about control. I did not mean in any way to diminish this collection. I'm sure Meltzer is great on whatever he writes about. There is still the fact that they misbehave. And their behaviors contaminate their theories. There is no way, and I say this recognizing that I'll get an argument, to condone Lacan's 5-minute hour other than he didn't know to behave himself. There are many hours where I think nothing more will be accomplished after 5 minutes, but that doesn't give me license to say, "Okay, we're finished now." That's what I mean. These guys get away with all kinds of things, then build it into a theory. There's no way you can condone saying, "I'll only treat people for myself."

VH: In an interview I did with André Green he talked about his split from Lacan. He felt that Lacan was brilliant, but he allowed no possibility of disagreement.

AG: That's Lacan. He's a tremendously idealizable figure for these people. He meant a great deal to them. They really cling onto him. This kind of charismatic or messianic person can draw people to them. But that's not to excuse the fact that he was a terrible person, a terrible person. You must read that book. Chapter after chapter of these gurus, who say only: "I'm wonderful, I'm marvelous, I'm terrific." Just terrible. Lacan and those people are utterly insistent on being mystifying to read because they have such gaps.

VH: I have a question. It has to do with my own despair, perhaps outrage. In my own practice I see families with children, where, say, three preschoolers in the same family have ended up hospitalized. It seems to be becoming a regular—

AG: Business! Yes, we see the same thing here in Chicago. It's just a business.

VH: I know it's business. Then you have the problems where the insurance company wants everybody put on drugs. It's as though we didn't know how to treat them. Where do you think all this is going? Is it a disease of the society? Or a disease of the mental health business?

AG: You should look at it from the society's point of view. We are a society of "druggies." We criticize and penalize and hospitalize some people who take drugs. We condone and respect and support other people who take drugs. If your doctor gives you Prozac and you take it, then you're a good patient. If your local cocaine dealer gives you crack, then you're a thief and a bad influence. It varies with society. I think there's also a point of view that has some historical merit to it, and that's that interest in psychology oscillates sporadically. And you are living through a period now where there is this diminishing interest in the unconscious, in psychoanalysis and metapsychology. Now, you're involved in short-term treatment, quick fixes, superficial ways of doing things, and so forth. But I think that there is a historical process and that we'll come out of this. More and more, but not enough, we've seen the people who have been interested in psychopharmacology, all the quick fixes, and so forth, becoming reinvested in depth psychology. So I think there's a chance.

VH: How does the present cycle affect your teaching?

AG: Well, you become kind of fatalistic about it. I've taught for 10 or more years now at the leading psychopharmacological training center in Chicago. And I teach the residents in psychiatry, all of whom have gone through this kind of center to learn psychopharmacology. I teach them only psychoanalytic psychotherapy, but I still win awards. In fact, I just won one a month ago for the best teacher.

VH: This is your second award for best teacher, I think.

AG: Yes. The head of the department said that if he had it to do all over again, he would become a psychoanalyst now that he's learned and listened to what we have to say. Wait, there's a sad ending. The resident now, who's running the program, said the only thing of value in the whole program is the class I'm running in the afternoon on obsessive compulsive disorders. The only thing that is valuable in all of his training comes from my class. But none of them do any psychotherapy. They do Prozac and all this other stuff.

And so I decided there are salvageable people, and there are unsalvageable people. Salvageable in terms of what we are talking about. Are these people trainable to be introspective and to care about feelings, have connections, and so forth? There are some that are and some that aren't. And the ones that aren't you may as well not worry about, and not fight it and recognize that they, right now, are in ascendancy. There is nothing you can do about it, at least in medicine. Not true, however, in other fields. Social workers and some psychologists and a great number of people, especially in history and literature, are very sensitive people who could benefit from the kind of training we have to offer. The people who go to medical school who go into psychiatry these days are not—they're just not that kind of people. They didn't have whatever you and I had when we were 3 or 5, whatever that made us want to be what we were, what we are. The residents who come through training now, they're very nice people, they'll never be psychoanalysts. Do I despair over that? I don't mind. They get interested. They hurt their patients less. They understand what giving the drugs means to the patient. So I have some kind of a good effect on all of them. But I don't think the future of psychoanalysis lies in medicine.

VH: Where do you think it lies?

AG: Oh, in the nonmedical field.

VH: I'm delighted to hear you say that. I myself, for a long time, couldn't be considered a psychoanalyst in the United States because I couldn't belong to the American Psychoanalytic; my training was not in an American psychoanalytic institute.

AG: You've come from a generation of social workers between the ages of 30 and 70 who were mistreated. They were kept out of analytic training.

VH: We went to places like Reiss–Davis and had analytic training, but it was called "psychotherapy" then, even if you saw the patient four times a week and were supervised by a member of the International.

AG: This happened all over the country. It happened in all of America. My goodness, I know some outstanding social workers who were just never given the opportunity. A lot of it was sexist.

VH: I know psychologists, who were males, also who were told, "Yes, you can come to our institute, but you have to sign something saying you will not practice clinically."

AG: I myself love to be a doctor. But I really am amused by all the doctors who terribly resent the M.S.W.s and Ph.D.s and all those others, who are going to be psychoanalysts. They just hate it. I know why they are feeling that way.

VH: You know it?

AG: Oh, yes. Part of it's money. Part of it's all those things that have to do with, "I did it. I went to medical school. I'm someone special. How can *you* be a psychoanalyst?" That's it. Part of it's bad. Part of it is the whole masculine ego of America. But, nonmedical analysts are the wave of the future.

VH: Do you see the old controls as masculine power?

AG: Well, but that's part and parcel of the sexist orientation, isn't it? I see it more as a narcissistic issue, pride and insistence on being special. To hear some doctors talk, it's not. Now there's some truth to what they say. You do learn, in medical school, a kind of caring for patients that you sometimes do not see in people who haven't had the training. Therefore, it's a trainable quality. I believe in that. I think empathy is trainable. But I think that many of the residents in psychiatry now simply are not interested enough to ever be analysts. That's what I meant by that previous distinction. Should we, could we, must we train nonmedical people to be analysts? Absolutely, and to be also attentive in terms of patient care.

VH: I want to turn more specifically to your work. How did you happen to get involved with Kohut, or become a follower of Kohut? And then I want to ask where you feel your work has differed from his.

AG: I was supervised by Kohut. He was my supervisor with my first control.

VH: I thought Joan Fleming had been your first supervisor.

AG: She was supervising when I was a resident. Then she supervised me with my second control here. In Chicago, the first and second controls are kind of close to each other. He was my very first control supervisor. And some time after the supervision he asked me to put together something for a presentation at a regional conference in Chicago. He was going to present something on narcissism, and he wanted me to review some early material on narcissism, which I did. I read it at the conference. Kohut could just take off and talk about almost anything and have the audience absolutely spellbound. He didn't particularly use anything I said, but he talked brilliantly. Then he asked me to be an assistant teacher in a class that he was giving. Later he invited a group of us to go over his first book. It was very clear that he made it easy for me to do some things, to become involved with him. At that time, I was joined with John Gedo who's my coauthor of a book. John and I and others used to go over to Kohut's house and go over the chapters of his book. I used to assistant-teach his class here. Lo and behold, we became a group of disciples, followers.

VH: Was Wolf in that group also?

AG: I think he came aboard somewhat later. I think that group was Gedo, Basch, myself, the Ornsteins, and Dave Marcus; I think that was all. Some of this is written up as history and it's available. I may have the names all wrong. Marcus left; then we decided to put together the casebook that I edited. Heinz very much wanted a casebook called *The Psychology of the Self* (1978). That was very difficult. Because on the one hand, Heinz didn't want to get directly involved in it. I don't know whether I was picked to be the editor, or I became the editor by default. I don't remember how that came about. That was the business where Gedo got himself in a snit and left our group.

VH: Could you elaborate on that?

AG: Gedo got very angry, beyond reason, at something that happened. He directed a lot of his anger toward me because I was the editor of the book. He left in an angry fashion and has remained outside of self psychology and outside of our group up until and including today. He has tried very hard to become something in his own right. I don't think I can judge his success. In the circle I move in, he is not important. But he struggled mightily to either put down self psychology or to do something with it. I don't know. Most people that I talk to don't really think about him very much. Although I really wouldn't be surprised if, somewhere, he has a following. I just don't know. He's a very difficult person, very difficult.

VH: But we've interrupted the story of your history with Kohut.

AG: After Gedo's departure, we continued to meet with Kohut rather frequently. Finally, he asked me then to take over his class that he was teaching. We got that book out, and held the conferences, and it just went on from there. I think he felt very strongly that I would have to carry on his work afterward. When he died, his wife and son asked me to edit *How Does Analysis Cure?* (Goldberg, 1984). I said, "Sure." There are a lot of people nowadays who would claim to be the carrier of Kohut's ideas, thoughts, and so forth. And it happens in every group that there are differences, dissenters and splinters. I think I learned more from Heinz than from anyone else that I ever knew. He was an absolutely brilliant psychoanalyst. He could be a very difficult person.

VH: In what way?

AG: Well, he was what he wrote about—a very self-centered, narcissistic person. But he was not anything like those crazy gurus. He always behaved himself, always handled himself well. He was always polite, dignified, proper. But he was very sensitive, touchy, self-involved, and I'm sure that's how he learned so much about what he wrote about. There are many such people, but they are not as smart as Heinz. You pay a price for every relationship in some way or another. Some of them pay off, and some of them don't. It was worth whatever it took to be with him, because you could never leave him without learning something.

VH: You sound as if you have some injuries, too, though.

AG: From Heinz? Personally, he was a difficult guy to get along with. He understandably needed this group and used all of us in some way. If I sound injured now, it was probably more the problems I had with his family in terms of editing the book *How Does Analysis Cure?* I had a lot of difficulty with his widow. But on the whole, I got much, much more out of my relationship with Heinz than I ever gave, and I still get more out of it. There's no doubt about the ledger balance in that.

VH: From what you are saying, it seems that he had some difficulty in recognizing or having gratitude toward his followers.

AG: He needed to be sure he was idealized. Yes. It was hard for him to do it for others. People complained about Heinz, that he never recognized the people whom he got his ideas from. He never quotes other people or credits other people with ideas, and they're absolutely right. He wasn't going to do that. That's the way it is. He was a self-centered man who told me that when he started writing, he stopped reading. He used to read everything, and then one day he stopped, and he just wrote. And so necessarily his bibliographies are not filled with references to other people. There are wounded people all over the country, very, very mad at Heinz because he didn't recognize them or he misquoted them, and all this stuff.

VH: But his "inner circle" weren't wounded.

AG: No. That bunch still meets and talks. We've been enlarged, and we still have good relationships. The only real falling out in that bunch was Gedo. Since then, we've had a lot of other people come and leave. We have difficulty. There is a lot of argument now with Stolorow, Brandchaft and that group. A lot of us feel that they are going off on a path that is not self psychology.

VH: In what way?

AG: I think that there are a lot of theoretical difficulties. A lot of feeling that Stolorow's ideas of intersubjectivity really are not self psychology. There are theoretical differences and clinical differences. I think that's part of the struggle that's going on within self psychology now. I want to differentiate between theories and how people actually conduct clinical practice. Bob Stolorow, for instance, is very smart and has a lot to say. Clinically, I think he is a self psychologist. Bernie Brandchaft is probably a wonderful clinician. Every case I've heard Bernie talk about is remarkable. But I think their ideas about intersubjectivity really are at odds with self psychology. Intersubjectivity sounds to me like a two-party relationship with a great deal of emphasis placed on the particular set of feelings, ideas, and fantasies brought to the meeting by the analyst. They give equal credence to the analyst's participation in the encounter with the patient. That's why they say, "*inter*subjectives"—*between* subjects. When I heard cases in that debate, they put great stress on what you the analyst should do, lend to, participate in, add to, or create in this particular event. I think that is not self psychology. I think self psychology is founded on the older ideas of transference—to wit—the patient is the fundamental center of the treatment, and the analyst is a selfobject, used or not used, assigned functions, not assigned functions. But to make too much of the analyst's input is to equate the participation of the two persons, and I don't think it should be. I think it should be a tilted one. The patient is the center. It is an interpsychic, not an intersubjective milieu, and the analyst becomes part of the patient's psyche. The analyst's subjectivity is not part of the encounter. Like my friend Anna Ornstein said, when one of these people presented a case, "Who's in analysis?" They make it sound as if you spend all the time thinking: "What did you do now with the patient?" "How did you influence?" Or, "What's your countertransference?" That's the essence of intersubjectivity, that it tends toward an egalitarian posture of patient and analyst. Is that clear?

VH: Yes, it sort of makes me think of what some clinicians do with parents of children in therapy. They sort of insinuate to the parent, "What did you do to your child that failed the child, that didn't mirror the child?

AG: Yes, self psychology, for a long time, got into this trap of blaming the parents. "How did you run it?" Analysts got into supervision, and it was a reverse in breast-beating. "Not that you're to blame, but—"

VH: You've written about the mistrust of patients with psychotic structures and the difficulty of maintaining empathic linkage when some patients are in severe regression.

AG: Why is that? One patient comes to mind. I cannot, will not, get in whatever kind of empathic linkage she needs. It's beyond me. Maybe someone from somewhere can, but I can't. We both know it. She's accomplished a great deal, but severe regressive states for the two of us are more than I can manage. That's true of many of these cases. We're just not up to it. She once said, "You are no good to me when I am in very, very regressed states. You don't get in touch with me. You don't help me." And she said, "A lot of times, I come here when I am like that, and you hurt me more than you help me. I'm going to stay away during those periods." And she does. Often more subtle, but it seems more blatant and striking than the histories we used to hear. Now we're seeing patients who could never before get into psychoanalytic therapy. You yourself are probably willing to go further and longer with very, very disturbed patients who never had those kinds of opportunities except for those rare Frieda Fromm-Reichmann or John Rosen experiences. But the vast majority of severely disturbed patients were not seen by psychotherapists until it was too late.

The sickest patients routinely these days are seen by the nonmedical analysts, especially the social workers, who always get the sickest patients. The people who are in the front line of mental health are not the psychoanalysts. But more and more of them are drifting to analysts, and the analysts are taking on sicker and sicker patients, much more than they used to. I used to read Frieda Fromm-Reichmann. I would think, "Boy, there's someone who's up to it." I immediately associated to a patient she was treating—she was a schizophrenic woman. She sits down and realizes that the patient has urinated in the chair that she, Frieda Fromm-Reichmann, was sitting in. Should she proceed to sit in this damp environment throughout the hour? Some can do that, but not me. Probably when I first read it I thought, well, you're either going to have to go into neurosurgery, or learn to do that. Now I feel that I couldn't do it. I never will do it.

VH: But is that mirroring or is that mutual regression?

AG: Well, whatever reasons are, whatever it ultimately comes to, you have to get to it to be able to make that discrimination. You have to get in touch with it enough to say, "Now I understand what you mean, and I can respond to it, or you shouldn't be here." Then you have to make a technical decision, such as: "I don't think you should be so regressed"; or "let's wallow in it for a while." I think that's a different argument. But I do think you have to get in touch with some of this head-on. We should not assume that everyone's capacity is ours, nor that everyone's limitations should be ours.

VH: You talk a lot about fragmentation. I don't do psychoanalysis solely. I do a lot of work with children, parents, and also do some group therapy. I'm seeing, or hearing, more and more, what I consider borderline children, presenting at around age 7. Some parents seem to feel "entitled"—it's the only word I can use—to have children. Yet they don't seem to have much concept of anything except dropping them off 8 weeks after they are born with the caretaker, with more and more frequent changes in caretakers. Are you seeing this as a general rule?

AG: I don't see kids. They report a lot of cases to me at the medical school and hospital, and I supervise cases. There's no doubt that the kind of histories these days are different than what we used to hear and that the open demonstration of childhood trauma is sometimes astonishing. Something like you've described and sometimes even more brutal, sometimes physical. To give you a theoretical answer, the cause, Kohut would say, a lot of these people have never really achieved cohesive, consolidated selves; therefore, they are always oscillating in the borderline between psychosis and gradually, barely holding themselves together. The steps toward further consolidation never really take place within this balance. Another answer is the ability of a therapist to stay in an empathic contact with those very, very archaic states for long periods of time is almost impossible. Very few therapists can even do it. It's upsetting, terrifying, demanding.

VH: I've seen a lot of professional families. They want to send their child to the child psychiatrist. I see the parents. I usually spend the first 2 or 3 years just dealing with their feeling that they don't need to be there. The surgeon doesn't need to be there, the psychologist doesn't need to be there. It's as though they've brought the kid in and said, "We had this structure we were trying to force this kid into, and it didn't work. Now we want the doctor or you to force this kid into this structure. And we want to try to catch you in the waiting room and tell you what the structure is we want you to force him into." That's a lot of my work. They seem to assume that you can force people into this mold somehow.

AG: You see more narcissistic disorders.

VH: Mentioning narcissism makes me think about narcissistic gratifications. How do you handle the wish for these? For instance, do you ever give gifts to patients?

AG: I might, I might not. "It all depends"—that's the answer. I don't see anything wrong with it. But do I? I don't remember doing it, but I would do it. I suppose I'd given them articles, books. Yes, just the other day I gave a patient a book off the shelf to read. I think that's such nonsense, to have those kinds of rules. I've always thought, "What in the world difference could it make?"

I was visiting in Australia and was sitting at a friend's house, and he invited this analyst, who he told me was a very, very strict—I think he said—Kleinian. He was a nice guy. He was there with his wife and was telling me that his daughter had a show that week at an art gallery. He had stayed away from the opening because he knew one of his patients was there, attending the opening. The analyst's wife said to me, "Well, wouldn't you have stayed away?" I thought this a nutty idea. The way she asked me was as if it were really a moral issue. My thought was, "Isn't it just as damaging to a patient to think that she is strong enough to keep you away from your daughter's opening as to see you at that event?" What kind of justification can you make to balance that I will do it or I won't do it? Besides that, we have people who call up ahead for the party list. I think anything that comes up like that when you start to make a rule or regulation about it, you don't understand it. Of course, if you sleep with a patient, you're unable to treat him because you don't understand what's going on any more than if you yell at the patient, or any of those other things. If it becomes understandable, great. But to make rules about it is just nuts, I think. "Don't give them gifts." "Don't let them take pictures." "Do this, don't that." I think the limitations are wrong. I know many people who say that they're just uncomfortable at a party when their patients are there. You can't argue with that, but there are people in Australia who say, "Well, you can't go to that art gallery if your patient is going to be there." I thought it was a little bizarre.

VH: You've written about what you call "shared ownership." Knowing that they were interested in art and that you were interested in art would be one more shared thing, would it not? Perhaps it would be positive knowledge.

AG: That's why you should help people who share a lot of your background, a lot of your culture, a lot of your language, and whom you like. If you can identify with them, they with you, you know, some patients are just a breeze. You hit it off at the beginning, and you continue to hit it off, and it works very well. Some patients you'll see for years and years and years and always miss it a little bit; you never really grab them. That's the other issue of the limitations that we all have. We all know, you know it now I'm sure, that there are some patients that you'll never be able to treat. You can get supervision, and you'll never be able to help them. I think we all, over the years, get the patients we deserve.

VH: What do you mean?

AG: Well, I mean we get referred patients we can work with. We sift out the patients we can't work with. We end up with what we can live with. A lot of this is done beyond consciousness. It's done by referral sources; they know what to refer to you. It's done by all kinds of hidden selective processes.

VH: Do you have more to say about shared ownership and the implications of that in psychoanalysis? Because it seemed to me so important the way you were using it. What do you consider analysis that is shared?

AG: What I was thinking of was that the concept: The constituents of the self are the selfobjects, the others of the world who respond to you the way you do when you idealize. And so there is no clear boundary between you and the outside. There is not the subject–object dichotomy as is so common in the way we speak. But we consist of other people, and the way we make these linkages and connections has to do developmentally with very different kinds of tasks. The thing that you can do in a psychoanalytic process is to share, connect, come together by mutual understanding. You understand something together. When you understand something together, you connect with the other. We speak of ownership, and we feel that when we say something is "mine," it is a way of extending and expanding the self. If you listen to me and you say, "Yes, I think I understand what he is talking about," you're starting to get it. Then you're going to make it yours. You're going to put your "Virginia stamp" on it. It's going to become a Virginia-owned thing, but it's also going to be Arnold's because it's mine. For that moment that we're together, that we're linked, that we're mutually together, we really encompass one another. I think that is the basis of understanding what the self is, in the sense that we are composed of, consist of, constituted by other people. So we're never a self-enclosed entity. Rather, we are networks of relationships. That's what I meant by shared ownership. It's nice in an analytic pursuit—that we can see how our self expands to include someone else.

VH: You've been a tremendously creative person, tremendously. Do you attribute that to shared ownership?

AG: Oh, yes. I think I become creative by puzzling out what in the world someone else would be interested in. That's my own way; it's nice that you say it's creative. I think I'm more innovative than creative. I think of new configurations. I don't think I've come up with anything that's that inventive or original.

VH: Even one paper is a creation. You're really talking about originality now, aren't you?

AG: Yes. I think that the way I do it is to wonder all the time about intriguing and interesting other people. That's why I'm a good teacher. That's why the students like me because I never lose sight of the audience.

When I write, where I think, it's always that way. Now, it may well be that that's my individual style of creativity, and other people can really work in splendid isolation and come up with the great ideas and never care if anyone sees them or reads about them, and so forth. But I believe in a transfer of creativity, and the transfer I have is a varied one. Is that going to interest you? Are you going to like this one? Are you going to respond?

VH: You're really saying that creativity—"Can I interest someone? Would I interest someone?" Maybe mother?

AG: How do you get a smile out of her, do you lift up that sad face?

VH: What do you think goes into making a good analyst?

AG: I don't know. I've never been asked that question before. Usually I think, when I teach, or when I go to conferences or classes I've heard almost every question; but I don't know that I've heard that one. What goes into making a good analyst? The first thought that came to me when you said that was curiosity. I suspect that there are certain kinds of personality configurations in early-childhood rearing that makes for certain kinds of analysts.

VH: What do you mean?

AG: Well, there's the kind of analyst, let's say who works with one kind of patient very well but not with others. The kind of analyst who might be a good teacher but not that good a clinician. There's the kind of analyst who can be a good administrator. There's the kind of analyst who can work with a wide variety of patients. There's the analyst's analyst. You know, that's the one that someone goes to as the last resort, who sees the special patient. So I think there is a variety, a grab bag of possibilities, as to what makes a good analyst. How many good analysts have I known? I'm always surprised at how good some of these people are. And I wouldn't have thought they were good. But when you see them practice the profession, sometimes the best in them comes out.

VH: Who would you say is the analyst's analyst?

AG: In Chicago? It's known that it's Lou Shapiro. Everyone, for many, many years, has known that. If worse comes to worse, if no one else can help you, and everyone—you go to Lou Shapiro. I have never gone to Lou Shapiro, but he's known as that. Kohut was not. I'm sure he was a very good clinician, and people swear by him, but no, he was not that special person. Ernest Kris was, in Boston.

VH: I think we have a lot of people in California who maybe need a second analysis and don't have it because we don't have such people. I don't feel you've said enough about how your work differs from Kohut's or what you feel your special contributions have been.

AG: I feel that when a new set of ideas are developed, in any science, it's important to use them and exhaust them before you start to change or modify. And I think that we have a period of using the ideas of self psychology as extensively and intensively as we can before we start a bunch of changes and modifications. I think that Kohut was constrained by his allegiance to classical psychoanalysis, and so he had a lot of ideas about structure and a whole bunch of theoretical ideas concerning structure and representation. He didn't understand the early years in child development. He was not that equipped to talk about semiotics or language. I think there's a lot of extension of his ideas in those arenas. I don't find myself really at odds with him because I think his theories, like all theories, are limited. I think we've pushed his to its limitations. So I don't feel that I am, as some of the people who were followers of Kohut, that I'm going off and extending or expanding or changing his ideas that much. I would say I more filled them out than anything else with the understanding that he had certain limitations to his own training and allegiances.

VH: You feel your major contributions have been filling out and extending.

AG: Yes.

VH: Making them solid.

AG: Yes, I would hope so. My personal interests are really a little apart from psychoanalysis. It's the philosophical ideas about psychoanalysis, its status as a science, its relationship to other sciences, its way of looking at data and utilizing data that really interest me. I don't really think I've made any real contributions clinically. I think that I've made out a few different kinds of characterologies that I think belong to self psychology. I've made these fleshed out from the theory, but I don't think that's a major contribution. I think I'm a good teacher, more than anything else.

VH: I thought, "If I had to characterize you, I think I would call you 'the guy who tried to relax psychoanalysis.' " Do you disagree?

AG: No, although I think I probably have a reputation of being much more critical and argumentative, and that I suffer fools very poorly and that I am much more of a careful thinker and delineator; and I can't stand fuzzy thinking or loose thinking, and so forth. Heinz did a little of that, but Heinz had a genius that I haven't come across in other analysts. And that's one of the things that one can hold against me, since I'm so critical of so many of my colleagues and contemporaries and teachers. Heinz was just a very unusual person. I mean, he was really a genius. I find very few others. There are a lot of very smart people in the field, and as I said yesterday, a lot of them are very talented, very good analysts. But I don't think they are really giving a contribution, that I know of. I probably would be really called to task. I don't know of any real contributions other than Kohut.

VH: Well, how about Stern?

AG: Well, he is not really making contributions to psychoanalysis. He's doing kind of necessary empirical studies. It's good. It's important. Whether it has applicability to psychoanalysis is still questionable. We try to make connections. I think that Heinz was interested in it, but I don't think he would give much credibility to it as analytic data. And, no, I don't think he's, in that field, competitive.

VH: How about Christopher Bollas? For example, the "unthought known."

AG: I've only heard him speak once. I've only read a few of his things. I find he is in the same group as Winnicott. That is, they write in a kind of an exclusive way—let's say that it is a precious, secret, special way that might make them good therapists. Their work is intriguing in a single case, but I find it has very little generalizable, theoretical substance. I read Winnicott, and I've talked to people about Winnicott, and there always comes a point in the discussion—though there's no doubt that he's a wonderful man—where you kind of shrug, and you don't really know what the theory means. With Winnicott, you could go over a couple of passages, and it would be intriguing and interesting and fuzz up after a while.

VH: Perhaps you have not given enough serious consideration to Winnicott and such followers as Bollas.

AG: Yes. Well, I'm perfectly willing to take that criticism. I've not done the reading. I gathered that he's very critical of self psychology. I think that part of the difficulty psychoanalysis now has, we do not treat creativity very well. We are so concerned with allegiance and correctness that we kind of discouraged creativity. Now, you could say, "Well, aren't you one of the people because you don't read people like Bollas and others?" I don't think so. I think I try to read as much as possible. I've never been taken by what he wrote, but I'm willing to say I'm wrong there. I try to read Lacan and Meltzer and Bion. I think I spend an awful lot of time reading Bion and getting next to nothing out of it. Laplanche too. I think I've tried all of these people. And given my personal failings, I've gotten very little out of any of them. I got an awful lot, maybe because I knew him personally, out of Kohut. I see no comparable figure in analysis to Heinz. I know and respect Charles Brenner. He's a brilliant man, but he's not as creative. Jake Arlow is one of the smartest people you'll ever meet; but they're smart people, that's all. They're not innovative in any kind of way.

VH: What did you think about Margaret Little, for example?

AG: When I read the stuff of hers, I thought, "This is an interesting, fascinating clinician." I think a lot of these people are very interesting and fascinating clinicians. I don't know that they have raised the science to kind of a new level or given a new conceptualization base.

VH: If I had to say "profiles in courage," she would be tops on the list. If *you* had to say, who were the courageous?

AG: The most courageous analyst, I think, was Ferenczi who had great ideas, innovative ideas, startling different ideas and had to struggle to get out from the umbrella of Freud. When Freud dominated analysis for so many years, there were very few people who could match him. There were a lot of very smart people, but either they went the road of Wilhelm Reich or Tausk, or they were like Abraham and the others. They were beholden to the great man. Since Freud . . . I know the same names that you know, and I'm not impressed by any of them. Not that I'm disdainful of them, but I don't think that they reached a new, different level. I really don't see any important forward steps in psychoanalysis after Freud. There were people who investigated borderline psychotics. There were people who wrote about depression. I used to read Edith Jacobson endlessly, and I never understood her. I met her; I talked to her. She's a very nice lady. I think she's a wonderful therapist. I think that book of hers, *The Self and the Object World* (1964), is not worth much. Many fine people have all made contributions. I don't think there's very much good to read in psychoanalysis anyway. People just don't read period, either novels, fiction, nonfiction, or much about anything. Do you think people read a lot?

VH: No. And I don't think people talk a lot about intellectual matters either.

AG: That's true.

VH: They don't tell stories and share philosophies.

AG: They certainly don't write letters.

VH: I think there's a general erosion on depth and looking at insight, the caring end of it. But Chicago is a special place concerning intellectual tolerance. I've not heard about the Chicago Institute, that there was a great deal of political debate going on between the Kleinians and the Kohutians and the Freudians and the object relations people, that somehow they didn't seem to have the hostile splitting, at least it's not known. How have you avoided that?

AG: The Chicago Institute is notoriously not given to splitting.

VH: That seems so.

AG: I don't know that we want it. Possibly because they're just too lazy to go out and start a new institute. I don't know. Many people have said, "Why don't we go form a new institute?" You hear it every now and then, but I don't think anyone would do much more than order the stationery. So there has never been a strong movement to break away. So we all live happily or unhappily under one house. There was never any ideological difficulty until Kohut and his self psychology came about. There certainly is no doubt that there is a clear "pro" and "anti" self psychology movement in the Chicago Institute. I think there could still be cordial, thin moments of friction and animosity and sometimes outright hostility; but it's settled down. And the interesting thing is that our most vehement anti self psychologist, once transported to Kansas or Denver or New York or anywhere else, starts to become pro self psychology. I don't think they realize how much it's snuck into their circulatory system. They are recognized as, "Well, you come from Chicago, so you must be a self psychologist." The best example is this friend of mine who was, if anything, in Chicago, totally neutral. He moved to Israel and is now the staunchest self psychologist in all of Tel Aviv. But, no, we haven't had that. The Chicago has sort of had all kind of difficulties for other reasons. I was on the committee for a while that studied those incidences. I felt that ideological issues are excuses for what are just narcissistic problems of very ambivalent people, and other people very easily hurt. That's what these splits form about and around. I don't think people leave just because of these basic ideas. They only cover it with that. The only bad part is, it's so much easier to say, "I could not work with him because of his feelings about infantile fantasies," than because he never invites me to his parties. That's bad.

VH: But you must have had some part in maintaining harmony. This has to be built into a structure of analysts and their training somehow. Maybe by intellectualization or identifying the potentials for splits or something.

AG: In order to what? I don't know.

VH: To keep it from happening.

AG: I agree with you. I don't think anyone has really studied this here. It certainly has never happened here. It peaks up every now and then, but it's just never been that way. We had a leader, for a while, in Chicago, by the name of Lionel Blitzstein. He had a group around him. Then Alexander, who was the dominant figure in psychoanalysis in Chicago, had a very strong group around him, had a powerful influence. Many people, including Kohut, were very much against Alexander. After

Alexander left, Piers took over. Piers was this wonderful gentleman who would allow anyone and anyone's ideas to flourish. When Kohut developed his ideas, he already had a group around him. There was just a lot of animosity, but there was never any idea that they would split off from the Institute. Beyond that I don't know the answers. I know many, many people that have approached me and said, "Are you going to form a new institute? Why don't you form a new institute?" You may have had someone come up to you some time and say, "Why don't you give a party for a hundred people? Why don't you give me these assignments?" They'd like that to happen, would like you to do it. I don't want to form a new institute. That's the last thing in the world I'd do. It's so much work, with so little result.

VH: And loss of energy.

AG: I have never seriously entertained the idea. There are splinter groups, you know, people who work. Peter Giovacchini is a good example. Someone, who for reasons that are almost lost to obscurity, left the Chicago Institute. There are different stories, and I don't know what the truth is. He has, over time, had little groups around that. But I don't think anyone ever felt that there would be a Giovacchini Institute or Giovacchini group to build a new ideology. It was pure and simple a case of personality. It is always that.

VH: Every time?

AG: I think so. Everyone I've studied. And the American had a big study on it. They came out with the conclusion that it was ideological, and I studied the same stuff they did, and I got that conclusion also. I think it's always narcissistic.

VH: Then there's been a great deal of it in the field.

AG: Oh, yes! Kohut said he learned everything he learned about narcissism when he was president of the American.

VH: You were also, in that book, questioning what would have happened if Bowlby and Freud had seen the same patients, in terms of how they would have observed them differently, since they both claimed to be observing the same phenomenon?

AG: You've got to believe in Buddha. You've got to know that there are many realities. If, in our Western orientation, the scientific facts, we like to think that there are fixed facts that we perceive and observe. We would all agree on the Kleenex box on the table; and if you didn't agree, there was something wrong with you. I think we've learned through the years now that all perception and all reality is that of a constructive enterprise, and that the participation, the input of the observer, is a codeterminant of what is to be seen. I cannot believe that Bowlby, Freud, or anyone else would ever see the thing the same way. That's why I think Kohut made a very powerful contribution when he said, "Diagnosis of the patient cannot be made without consideration of who is the diagnostician." If you take the patient and you fly him quickly in a sealed plane to Otto Kernberg and have him see that patient and say this is a borderline, then whisk him on a plane out to Los Angeles and let Brandchaft see him, Brandchaft won't see the same patient. It's a different patient because the patient has been perceived differently. It's different contacts, and what happens between the patient and analyst determines who the patient is. I can't imagine any other conclusion. Why would we want it? Why would we insist on there being some kind of fixity about a patient?

VH: What do you think are the primary issues facing analysts right now? What direction do we need to go in?

AG: The title of the book I wrote is called *The Prison House of Psychoanalysis* (1990). It addresses that question. It says that much of analysis has been locked into the strait jacket in terms of their training programs, their literature, their allegiances to great figures, and their practice and that we have, over the years, become rigidified in terms of this is the way you do things, and this is the way we train people. These are the people who most look up to. This is what's accepted. It happens in any science. After a while it becomes somewhat fossilized and somewhat smug, and psychoanalysis has suffered because, as it becomes more and more and more sure of itself, it becomes ignored by a lot of the rest of the world. Something that's kind of moral, self-centered, and unimportant. And yet they cling to the business of standards of correctness and certainty. I think that's unfortunate. I think that's something psychoanalysis has to get away from. We have to get away from knowing things for certain. We have to get away from the heroes that we have had. We have to get away from the knowing how to train people and knowing who to train and knowing what's right. I think that, from the book, I have some theoretical explanations for it. In reality, I think we are living through it now. We're having to train people we didn't use to train. We're having to consider alternate ways of treating people. We've got to loosen up all around, or else it will be the death of us. You know it's a dying field as it is.

VH: You're really now saying that we have to do more psychotherapy as well as psychoanalysis.

AG: Well, you just told me that there is a difference. I don't know it myself. You must know the difference. There are two guys I know who know the difference.

VH: Elaborate.

AG: Well, look in the field today.

VH: Regression, I think, is the difference if I had to say.

AG: You're lucky you don't have to say because this is an endless argument. Either they're different, or there is a continuum, or they are the same. Merton Gill says as long as you deal with transference they're the same. Other people say as long as you sit up, four times a week, you're in analysis. Other people say as long as you're analyzed by a member of the American, you're in analysis, otherwise you're in therapy—all this garbage. They had a conference recently at the American in which they presented cases in therapy versus cases in analysis. How could you tell the difference? Were they different? The usual lies.

VH: I thought Gill said if you were an analyst whatever you did was psychoanalysis.

AG: Because you pay attention to transference, yes. That was his point. But if he ate a corned beef sandwich, it's probably not analysis.

VH: That's funny.

AG: Analysis is always supposed to be deeper, profounder, and better and more expensive. Therapy is supposed to be the lesser, the bad child, the kid who didn't quite make it. When you said should you do more of one or the other, I think we have to study them to try to determine what, if any, are the differences. And then change them accordingly. I think most people teach therapy, teach a kind of diluted psychoanalysis. It's a long involved argument. I don't know that we'll settle it. We have a lot of problems in analysis, in the field, that we have to attend to. We are best served by being less certain of ourselves and more open to innovative and creative ideas about the field; and we have become too involved with the certain foundations of psychoanalysis. There is a book, I think Adolf Grünbaum's book, called *The Foundations of Psychoanalysis* (1984).

VH: You mentioned that in your paper on rules I think.

AG: Yes. And, of course, my feeling is that it is our undoing, to have foundations. We don't need certainty of foundations or absolutes or anything like that. We've got to beware of the rules, the regulations, the certainties, the structures that are so twisted upon us in our field. We have to always be questioning and inquisitive to safely understand more. I think the only healthy way to be really effective is to never know for sure what to do.

VH: Thank you very much for this interesting interview.

Case Discussion

Dr. Goldberg points to Roselyn's need to develop an idealizing transference. He goes on to say that she was unable to idealize her malevolent mother and consequently developed a psychotic system of thinking. He states that Roselyn is longing for protection and for an omnipotent merger.

This interview was held in Dr. Goldberg's office at the Institute for Psychoanalysis, where he was director, on August 31, 1990. He began by saying he was going to disappoint me because he wanted to hear a lot more about the case before he could review it. He had no specific direction, topic, or question. I am very comfortable talking about this case and proceeded to do so.

Early on, I made a Freudian slip, calling my patient's former therapist "patient." Dr. Goldberg stopped me here. I was quick to say I did not feel her former therapist, whom Roselyn had seen for a number of years, had really understood her. I probably did feel that this therapist needed to become a patient, I admitted.

I continued to talk about the case. After some time, Dr. Goldberg intervened again to suggest I should not use two pronouns when I said of Roselyn's mother, "She took knives and sliced her wrists." Clearly, I had made it ambiguous who was to be killed, and Dr. Goldberg places heavy emphasis upon pronouns and clarity.

Later I clarified: "There were other times when she literally sat on my Oriental rug and tried to explain to me about negative and positive space and how you can fall through negative space. If you look at your rug, there are many spaces. These are what she's calling the negative spaces." Dr. Goldberg said, "Yes." I waited briefly for him to say more, then resumed the story. After a while I described one of Roselyn's psychotic episodes that occurred when her house, for a second time, had been vandalized and burglarized. Dr. Goldberg said, "They just broke into it." I elaborated the story with the information given in the case summary. The patient's husband asked me to come to the patient's home. Dr. Goldberg asked, "And you did?" "Yes," I said and elaborated that I had sat outside her closet talking to her for about an hour. Dr. Goldberg asked, "Did it work?" I explained I had eventually been allowed in the closet with Roselyn and had put my arms around her and rocked her for another hour—and that had "worked."

I had mentioned the day before that one of the interviewers had been very upset with me for having "broken the frame" in this way. Dr. Goldberg was indignant, "And someone jumped on you for that?" I responded by saying, for example, André Green had praised it but that Hanna Segal had "minced meat with me about it." She felt I should have told her husband to take her to a hospital.

I went on to say that the interesting thing to me is that after these occasions, "Later she had no memory about any of it, of my being there. So even though she was able to use me to reconstitute herself, later either there is an amnesia or a denial or a disavowal; and I'm at a loss to understand that it doesn't. . . . "Dr. Goldberg said, "Retrospect."

I am adding the verbatim transcription at this point because paraphrasing it would cause it to lose some of its quality.

VH: I'm not idealized. I'm not internalized.

AG: It doesn't register.

VH: I don't get idealized. Why?

AG: What happens between the two of you? What's the nature of it?

VH: What do you mean?

AG: You can't tell from the little bit that you wrote there. In that hour it sounds like she was very scared, and you were very supportive and reassuring. Is that usually the case?

VH: There are times when the fear that she is going to go crazy or that she is going to kill herself or that her mother is alive, that psychotic structures keep reappearing.

AG: If someone were to ask you, "Why are you presenting this case to the people you're presenting it to?," what kind of an answer would you give me?

VH: I want to know if I'm doing something not helpful.

AG: As opposed to I think this is an interesting case.

VH: Because I don't understand what, and if, I'm doing something wrong.

AG: So you're kind of in the nature of wanting supervision. You have some qualms about whether you're either treating her right, or competent to treat her right, or whether someone else would do better? Or do you have a feeling of there's no doubt in my mind that you're the best therapist for her.

VH: There's no doubt in my mind that I'm the best therapist for her and that to change therapists would be detrimental for her. I find that she has much trouble internalizing—but I think she *has* internalized me at times. But there are other times when I think she is so terrified of taking in a new object for fear that the new object will destroy her. Or that the new object will fool her.

AG: Fool her?

VH: Fool her.

AG: Trick her?

VH: Trick her. She'll believe that I care about her, or she'll believe that I'm a good person, or she'll believe I'm a safe person.

AG: She doesn't trust you.

VH: Yes. It will fool her and—

AG: You've never been able to deabuse her of that misperception. Is that right? You've never been able to convince her that you're an honest, trustworthy person of integrity.

VH: She knows that.

AG: But she doesn't act that.

VH: It doesn't make her feel safe. But if you said to her, "Virginia is a dishonest person, or she's not trustworthy, or she's going to attack you," Roselyn would dispute these.

AG: She doesn't accept that.

VH: She would fight and say, "Don't be ridiculous."

AG: What's the puzzle then?

VH: Why—

AG: Because you said something before about the structure. You've obviously gotten different ideas from different people.

VH: Why can't she keep a new object, me, and the belief that she's safe?

Dr. Goldberg shared his theory, "Well, here's the way a self psychologist would conceptualize it. It's kind of shooting from the hip, and it's kind of unfair; and, therefore, it runs the chance of being completely wrong. But for what it's worth, I think you correctly said, 'Why doesn't she idealize me?' I think this patient very clearly falls on the spectrum. I will talk about self psychology, of the developmental processes of idealization. The developmental line of idealization begins with the child merging with a figure of strength, omnipotence, and so forth. Indeed, she had a very powerful mother. A mother who, in her mind, although scary, was also all powerful. Who else can smoke when there's oxygen in the room except someone who is extremely powerful, God-like and loaded with powerful feelings, affects, situations, and so forth? So, the idealization that begins in every child must begin and take the form of 'I can merge with you, you great omnipotent other person, if you're safe and secure.' The idealization fails when you get into the Tausk (1919) influencing machine, where the person is malevolent. If you read the early Viktor Tausk, he talks about the influencing machine as being a narcissistic aspect of the genitals, usually of the psychotic that he was talking about, that the other person tortures, mistreats, abuses, is mean to, and so forth. You've now moved away from the normal development into the kind of psychotic, paranoid, delusional, quasidelusional system that we see. This patient is oscillating all the time in this never-never land or this borderline land between near paranoid psychosis. 'You are out to hurt me but also yearning to please and protect me. Look after me. Let me become you, be together with you.' "

Dr. Goldberg went on, "When she is psychotic, the therapeutic task is a very clear one. That is to allow her to develop and maintain an idealizing transference. Then you say, 'Well, gee thanks, Goldberg. I knew all that. Why doesn't it take place? What are the impediments?' The impediments, of course, are always twofold. One, the patient is not able to do so because her pathology is so severe that she must protect herself from you. That is equivalent to real annihilation. So that she stays on the borderland all the time of oscillating between merging and stepping back from it because this would destroy her. The quasidelusional system is something akin to a restitutive of phenomena. 'I know you're out there. I know you're going to hurt me; but as long as I know that, I'm okay. If I relax my vigilance, then I'm lost forever.' That's where you always find her."

I added that she was terrified she'd give me power. Dr. Goldberg went on, "Then you say, 'Well, damn it, why don't you come into my hands and merge with me and idealize me?' Then you come to the second part of the dual problem. One is the difficulty that lies in the patient. The second is the difficulty that lies in the therapist and the analyst. That, of course, is where the supervision and the teaching take on a different path. Because then we say, 'Is there something about Virginia—may I?—that prevents the patient from idealizing her?' Those aspects are something you in your own analytic work are best able to appreciate—to wit: How much can I allow her to see me as all powerful? How much can I feel I do know all the answers? I do know what's going on. I do understand her. I have no misgivings. I am the fountainhead of truth. Now, Goldberg's worry about that comes in the form of Virginia going around to gurus and saying, 'Where is the answer?' Whenever you go to a guru, that shows that your own idealization problems are not solved and completely worked out. So you go and say: 'Hanna, tell me what to do.' And she says: 'Do this. Don't do that.' My feeling is that's the problem. You need to know, just like she needs to know, that you and the patient are searching for an omnipotent person who has 'the answers.' 'Thank goodness! I finally found someone in Tibet or Nepal who can tell me, here is the answer. Here's what you do, et cetera.' So all of this—excuse me—irrelevant stuff about should you hold her hand, should you cuddle her, should you take her, is ridiculous. Honestly, it doesn't matter. What matters is that the relationship is always frothed with, how much can she turn herself over to you? Your worry is 'How much can I really most assuredly take her over?' That's the basis of idealization. If you could take that step, then she could start to move along the path of idealization. I could talk about that if you want, but you had a question."

My question was how he would technically handle a patient saying, "You're the only thing keeping me alive." Dr. Goldberg understood that this was a difficult burden no therapist can long live with. He wondered how I do handle this. I replied, "Basically I say, 'It's true that I care that you're well, but your life rests in your own hands.' " Dr. Goldberg responded, "But that to me, and to her, means ah shit! You're not going to take it all over. I want someone who has everything. You see, that's the yearning. The childish wish for idealization is without qualification. And all of the things that you say, 'Yes,' but which you can't help but say, 'don't get me wrong, do not allow the idealization to develop and take place.' " I countered, "Because as soon as I say something in that neighborhood, she would say, 'I have to live for myself, I know that.' "

Dr. Goldberg said, "Yes, but you've thrown her away; and she has to fall back on her own grandiosity." I felt even if I didn't throw her, she throws herself back. Dr. Goldberg elaborated, "Of course, because the moment you accept the limitations, you are deidealized. In the true flowering and nurturing of an idealizing transfer, this cannot take place. I'm not saying it should take place, but that's the nature of this therapeutic problem. The nature of the treatment of the supervision would be to study in detail the failures of idealization, the minor touchy disappointments, and the rage that ensues therefrom. But to get involved in such absolutely trivial questions as should you hold her hand? Should you cuddle her?—that's outrageous. And to think that you know anything about the patient other than what he tells you and how the two of you connect is as equally outrageous. I think it's very clear that, I think you're right, she is a person yearning for idealization but unable to idealize. That's her problem. The solution is not a hard one, but I'm not saying it's a possible one. It has to do with, is she able to do that, short of annihilation. If so, can she do it with Virginia, whose countertransference difficulties will be severe because Virginia is always beset with her own limitations. And so Virginia says, 'Well, I will find someone who has no limitations. I will travel all over the world and I'll find someone who knows for sure.' Sure, you can do that, you can meet with them. As I was telling you yesterday, we've got gurus up the gazoo in psychiatry and psychoanalysis. You'll find all kinds of people who'll say, 'You've come to the right place. I know the answers.' And, of course, they will all have dealt with something exactly this. You said something about the patient's anger and aggression and hostility? I think it is a great mistake to look upon this patient as filled with rage or hostility or any of those things. She is yearning for an omnipotent merger. She is enraged and bitter and hurt and resentful because they continually fail. That's the reenactment of the mother. She had this powerful mother who periodically, erratically, but resolutely, let her down."

I mention that Roselyn had once noticed she had chosen fingernail polish the same color as mine and it upset her. Dr. Goldberg said, "It's a beautiful example. It's a beautiful illustration of how she's so afraid she will lose herself in a merger, a very archaic merger, with an idealized other. And there are all sorts of qualities in you that both encourage the merger and push her away." I asked him to explain "push her away." He said, "When you said something like, 'I can only do so much, then you have to decide for yourself. I want you to live, but . . .'—whenever you introduce a 'but,' a limitation, a failing, the idealization falls apart." I replied, "Let's go back to this thing, 'I only live because I'm in your hands.' "

I will now resume the verbatim transcript as it accurately conveys the enormity of the struggle.

AG: When you say, correctly, "Hey, you're the one who has to live for oneself," when you deliver that kind of reality statement to the patient, which you should, and must, and ought to do, you also necessarily prevent her from further idealizing you. Therefore, you would say to me, "What am I supposed to tell her? That I can do everything? I am able to solve all her problems? I can rescue her?" That would be crazy. You can't do that.

VH: But why pretend to be God?

AG: Yes, but that's what she wants.

VH: But she's not a stupid patient, on the other hand.

AG: Right, but we have to be—

VH: Her primitive part may want that, but her intelligent part would quickly attack me for having made that assertion.

AG: But that's the dilemma, how to be a God without being a God. How to be the powerful person that this person needs, and yet continue to confront reality at every turn. That is the dilemma that you live with, right? The self psychologist will always tell you, "Please, please, don't try to be more than you are. Never promise more than you can do. But recognize over and over and over again how you must disappoint her, and help her to see the inevitable daily disappointments that she's living with, with you." They say that's where the treatment lies. To the degree that you can help her recognize the inevitable disappointments, to that degree she can idealize you. There you are idealizable. Not because you can stop her from killing herself or because you're God-like, et cetera, but because *you* can understand her like no one else can understand her. That is what is idealized.

I felt Roselyn and I were getting there. Dr. Goldberg responded, "Yes, that's why I can idealize Kohut. And you say, 'Well, gee, he had all kinds of flaws.' Of course, he had all kinds of flaws. I don't idealize him because he was a Boy Scout. I idealize him because he saw something that allowed me to see something. That's when you open the gates of idealization. That's the way she'll idealize you. When you come to all of us and say, 'Help me with this patient,' you are saying, 'I have failings.' The patient says, 'Oh my God, my analyst has failings.' That's okay, but she has to go back and review in a constructive fashion how she feels about the fact that you don't have all the answers. That is what is then idealized. That kind of living through difficulty. Is that all clear?"

Dr. Goldberg was emphatic, "Therefore, don't worry about aggression. Don't worry about hostility. Don't give a hoot about holding, cuddling or any of that stuff. It is so much a—what's the word I'm looking for? It will get you away from the mainstream of things. You will soon see whether the patient is able to start the road toward idealization." I thought Roselyn had started down the road but said, "But if I, in trying to articulate what I think she's feeling, use the word mother, 'There must have been times when you longed for a safe, caretaking mother,' all hell breaks loose." I stated that sometimes Roselyn would try to stop the sessions the week before I am scheduled to leave on a trip.

Dr. Goldberg explained further, "That's because she's trying to control the inevitable, the disruptions. The tendrils of idealization are always forming; and then if you can break them, then she's terribly disappointed that if she can break it, she can master her past experiences and act upon them. But selfobjects are notoriously not identifiable. It's a function, not a person. This is not an object relationship; it's not taking in a new object. This is no interjection or internalization. This is a connection of a linkage that fills her out and completes her. So that you would not have a separate configuration of identities to the degree that your successful ideals don't mean much, because you're a part of her. What you would like to do, would like to be, has made it one of the countertransference problems. That you want some kind of recognition in your own right is always a hazard with these kind of narcissistic patients who need you for self-esteem functions, and not to recognize you as a person."

Dr. Goldberg went on, "The hour is moving. But I think the technical aspects of this treatment have to devote themselves to the day-by-day, tiny disappointments and the day-by-day empathic breaks that you and she can talk about, that will allow her, once she feels, 'Hey, this person knows what she is talking about.' Then she'll idealize you. She will idealize you in a way you can handle. That's the way idealization has to work. So forget everything anyone told you." I replied, "But she does think I know what I'm talking about. What she says is, 'Why can't I remember and believe and trust and keep the feeling of being safe?' " Dr. Goldberg felt the answer might be, "Either she's afraid she'll lose her identity, or you are making other kinds of disappointing empathic breaks that you and she haven't talked about. I'd have to go through the protocol to see. But it's one or the other. I must say, though, that long-standing cases like this that are so borderline, often fall in the category of what Kohut talked about: patients who are telling you over and over again, 'Let's leave well enough alone. Because I will lose whatever I have if I do form closer transference-like relationships.' They're begging you not to have the zeal and the enthusiasm to deepen up the relationship."

I asked Dr. Goldberg to elaborate. He said, "Yes. Kohut said there is a group of patients who are basically 'schizoid.' He used the word differently from Gunthrip and Fairbairn and all those others who laid claim to that word. He said these are people who are so aware of the fundamentally fragmentable and fragile selves that they always defend themselves against any meaningful selfobject relationship, because they know that it will lead to further fragmentation, disintegration when there is a disruption. And so, what they're always saying, in one way or another is, 'Let's keep this at arm's length. Let's not get too involved. Let's not get too connected. Let's recognize how vulnerable and fragile I am.' And he said the treatment of those people is different from the analytic treatment that allows the regression. The treatment with those people is to shore up their defenses. To help them to use the mechanisms of isolation, denial, disavowal, and so forth, so that they build a protective wall against their fragility. He was very strongly of a mind that these people were not to be analyzed because they're basically psychotic. And I think that, yes, she may fall into that category. The warnings that she's always sending out might be 'that's enough.' The way she gets your nail polish and then she changes it, she may be saying, 'Oh my God, I almost merged with you, and then I would be destroyed.' "

Dr. Goldberg wondered why I was so ambitious for her. I responded, "She's chosen it. She came saying, 'I have already had 6 years of twice a week, and I need to make myself feel like a whole person who is not in danger of constant fragmentation.' She's very, very bright; she's smarter than I am. She reads some of the psychoanalytic stuff. 'Unless I can figure out how to deal with it, I don't want to live.' " Dr. Goldberg replied, "The diagnostics are a challenge. There's no doubt a lot happens. Well, a lot of that is physiological. You do the fingernail thing. Let's say you made the interpretation, 'I think you changed your fingernail polish because you're afraid of becoming like me, next to me, or having a oneness with me'—whatever vocabulary you use. If that allows her to go back and use the fingernail polish, then you'd say, 'Oh, I think diagnostically this understanding is letting her continue.' If the fingernail polish is talked about, and she says, 'Well, sure I changed it. I got the feeling that you looked kind of funny at my hands.' Then you'd say to yourself, 'Oh, well, maybe this is when we interpret that,' so that there are always laboratory tests in the consulting books that allow you to make these diagnostic distinctions that will allow you to say: If she's really afraid of losing herself, then I could be as empathic as anyone, and the worst thing in the world could happen to her. Or, are there emphatic failures that are not allowing this to happen?"

I continued, "As I finally hear her, as I believe what we are doing, her fear was I would say, like her mother—her fantasized mother—'Huh, you thought mommy and me. Now I can hit you and destroy you. You're my child and I'll attack you. I don't want you to wear my fingernail polish or look like me, not you.' So it was a fear, as I heard it, a narcissistic injury at wanting to be connected. But she also believes that an attack will follow her wish." Dr. Goldberg corrected, "Her fear was that once she connected, you'd merge, then you'd slip back to being a paranoid, influencing machine. You'd manipulate her. Then she falls into the category of 'leave it be.' If we had enough of the clinical material, I'm sure we could make that kind of distinction." I went on, "Well, with the nail polish, she ended up wearing it, saying she liked it, and even if I did like it, it was okay."

Dr. Goldberg said, "When I give you the Kohutian attitude, you must realize there is a counterattitude. I think a lot of people in California would say that if you hang in there and persevere, that she will coalesce." I said I believe that. Dr. Goldberg considered Roselyn to be a difficult patient to treat. "Well, if you believe it," he said, "then it may happen.

But that's where you are in agreement with her. I don't agree. I have no doubt that if we went over—and we're going to have to stop because I have to go home—if we went over the case day by day, we would easily see where, and if there were an empathic disruption, where they could be repaired, and where idealization could take place. It's not a difficult case to comprehend. It's a difficult case to treat because she is so brutalized by life. I think, I would suspect, though I don't have evidence for this suspicion, that you're more afraid to be idealized than you let on because she's a handful." I agreed that being responsible for her life was frightening. He replied, "That's what being idealized means. When you have a little baby, and he looks up to you and says, 'You're everything.' " I said, "Yes, but the baby may not leave my office, or she may let go of the steering wheel of her car and have a car wreck. I can keep hold of the baby."

Dr. Goldberg said, "I understand, but they say, 'You are responsible for my life.' That's the dilemma you have, right? That's why it's hard to treat these people. That's why Heinz used to say, 'Being idealized is one of the most painful things in the world for us.' Because it gets us so hyperstimulated, we keep saying, 'Hey, I'm not that smart. Come on now, I'm just one person.' That's what the case is." I responded, "I say, 'Together we will get it fixed.' " He felt she would like that because I was trying to share the blame. I said, "Or the credit." He concluded, "Of course, we can get the credit, but she will give you no credit, she'll give you all the blame. That's what kids do to parents nowadays."

Rudolf Ekstein

Dr. Ekstein is well known for his many publications regarding autism, childhood psychosis, child therapy, fairy tales, and supervision. He was one of that distinguished group of analysts who immigrated to the United States during the rise of Nazism in the 1930s.

Dr. Ekstein came from Vienna where he had received his Ph.D. in Philosophy and studied at the Psychoanalytic Institute while Freud and his daughter Anna were there. He fled from Vienna to London in 1938 when the Nazis invaded Austria. From London, he came to the United States and soon secured a master's degree in social service and met his wife in Boston. He went from Boston to Brooklyn, later to the Menninger Clinic in Kansas in 1947. There he became a training analyst, director of the Southard School, and wrote his first book. Later he came to Los

Angeles and the Reiss–Davis Child Study Center where he became director of the Childhood Psychosis Project. He has written some 10 books and over 500 published papers. He has a Ph.D. in Psychoanalysis from the Southern California Psychoanalytic Institute. Dr. Ekstein has been a teacher and training analyst for several psychoanalytic institutes in Los Angeles. In addition to analyzing patients, he has been a dedicated teacher and generous seminar leader and lecturer. He has always made time for students, and his home is a rich museum of the history of psychoanalysis. Rudi, at age 81, is prompt in responding to correspondence or phone calls. He continues to give a great deal to the psychoanalytic movement and to those who seek to know his mind and to share their own ideas.

Interview

VIRGINIA HUNTER: I interviewed Rudolf Ekstein on March 2 and 3, 1991, in the living room of his home, where he has conducted seminars for many years. I asked if it had been 50 years.

RUDOLF EKSTEIN: No, not quite that long. Since about 1958. It's interesting that a house, when people live in it, has a history like the people who live in that house; and if one could look around this room itself, one could most likely make a good guess on the pieces of art, the posters, the replica as they all would give away a great deal about the history of a person. This is not only our living room for parties, but I have used it for many, many years, also, as a seminar room. Whenever people come here and sit around in a circle, they get not only the atmosphere of the teacher but something about the history of psychoanalysis, the history of man's involvement with psychoanalysis. I have always been interested that so many people in schools and in universities, in colleges—even in institutes—have empty rooms with an empty wall, a white wall; and I always wonder how one could sit in a seminar that way. And I remember back to the days in Vienna before 1938 in the Viennese Psychoanalytic Institute there. I never saw empty walls. I saw bookshelves, I saw pictures, I could somehow get an impression from the environment itself; and I would know something about the culture, and I think I want you to understand this room. It's actually easier for me to talk that way because, of course, I know what's in most of these books, and I only need to look and remember and to make psychoanalysis and its history alive for me and my seminar group.

VH: In the *L.A. Psychoanalytic Bulletin's* honor issue for you (1990, Spring), Rocco Motto mentioned something about the house and that it had increased in value by 25%, and I was wondering if that had been a joke between the two of you. I would imagine it has increased over 300% since you bought it.

RE: There's no question. At the time that we bought the house, it was very difficult for us because I had just come from the Menninger Foundation, and in the Menninger Foundation, if one was employed there, one didn't stay there to make money. The interest there was to think, to analyze, to supervise, to write . . . to lecture, to write books. My first full book came out there even though I had published a great deal before. When we came here and bought that house, I was also, at that time, employed at the Reiss–Davis Child Study Center; I found it very hard—to buy it. Of course, Motto was right. It was a fantastic investment, but at that time I knew nothing about investments. I knew nothing about real estate; for me it was a place where you live, where you bring up your children, where you have something that documents your life that you want in your rooms in order to feel truly at home. In other words, it was a home. And I was almost surprised when people sometimes told me, "Did you know what a wonderful investment that was?" I did not think in terms of investment, and I still don't.

VH: Was that because your father, as a military man, didn't think of investments either?

RE: My father was not really a military man; he had to serve in the First World War. My father was a very simple bookkeeper. He worked . . . there was hardly any possibility to save a great deal and to have much insurance. When I came to America, I came with $24. When he came a year later, I could say he came with $10 that he had left over because everything was taken from him by the Nazi government that had invaded our country. That was the Kuwait of the time. No difference. Unfortunately, at that time, the Americans and the French and the English and the coalition did not come to save us. They did not come, and the only thing that indeed they did . . . they would permit many of us to become immigrants and to live in America.

But what I meant to say is that the conception of how to spend money or how to make investments was different. The word "investment" was something new. Maybe I learned it from my wife because she's an American-born person. She worked in a bank as an accounting clerk, and, therefore, she had some kind of an idea about investments. I was as naive about it as they come, and I am now almost as naive as I was then. But you invested . . . I thought . . . you invested in children; you invest in the patients you treat—you invest your energy because you want to help them. I think of emotional investments and not of financial ones and maybe that is not the best quality to acquire in America—but it's what I brought from Europe. In Austria you thought very differently. You lived in an apartment. We had a small apartment in Vienna where my father brought up his child, he cared for the next of kin. He had, as it were, a life. It was completely different than the kind of life that most men would have here in the States. It was, as it were, for all of us a fantastic change to go from the Austrian culture between the wars, I mean before Fascism came, to grow into the American culture which was a culture of steady growth. We had new buildings in Vienna that the Socialist city government, at the time, built for people so there would not be homeless people. That still existed there. The expression "homeless" I never knew. I learned it here.

VH: Rudi, nothing I have read about you says anything except that your mother died. When and how did she die?

RE: I lost my mother very, very early. I was a little boy. My father then employed a woman who ran the house and became like a mother figure.

VH: But how little were you?

RE: I was between 3 and 4.

VH: So your mother died when you were—

RE: I lost a mother that early. . . . It was an early loss and my father was . . . there was still the war going on . . . he could not even be at home, and he had to turn me over to a stranger; but the stranger did not turn out to be a stranger. She was a wonderful, faithful, Catholic lady who took me sometimes to church to pray with me and taught me prayers for Papa. She taught me he would come back from the war, and I was utterly convinced he would. The war ended and school started, and I began to become a little student.

VH: What was your mother's name?

RE: Charlotte.

VH: How old was she when she died?

RE: I would have to think now . . . I lost her as a very, very young person.

VH: But how old was she?

RE: No, no, I was just saying I think she was a very young person at the time. I would imagine she would be in her very early 30s. I have it somewhere, of course, written down. This is so long ago. I grew up a person who has no strong living concept about her. The concept I have, that is alive, is the lady who brought me up then. You know, I have a picture here that would give you a pretty good idea. There's a little picture, showing me as a little boy here, over there, with mother and father, and not long after that, never again.

VH: How did she die?

RE: The way people die. Of that I have almost no knowledge.

VH: And so your father didn't talk about it later, when you were older?

RE: My father talked about many things, but from then on, as a man, he sort of went his own way. He did whatever he could to remain faithful to the obligation to bring up the child; that is, to bring me up. I can best explain the most remarkable thing about his way of educating me through an anecdote. When I was about to go to the university, after I had graduated from high school, he thought at first I should become an engineer. He thought that would be a great profession. Then he thought maybe I should be a lawyer, because one of the relatives—he said the most successful man in our family was a lawyer in the city, and was very well-known. He was, for the total family, for all the people who were involved there, the most successful man.

VH: On your father's side of the family or your mother's side?

RE: That was on my father's side. I believe the man was his mother's brother. But anyway, what happened then, he thought I should study one or the other. When high school was about over, the question was will you go to university and study law, or will you go to the technical university and become an engineer? I began to rebel. I didn't want either. I said, "I want to study psychology." He went to a counselor and asked what I should be. To this day I remember the face of that man. It was the first time that I got to know a helper beyond the teachers. We sat there. I brought up my case, and my father brought his version of what should become of me. The man made the following remark. He said to my father, "Herr Ekstein, look here, Rudi wants to study. He will be through with his studies." This was about 1930. "He will be unemployed whether he is a psychologist, an engineer, or a lawyer. So why don't you let him study whatever he wants?" What he tried to say to my father, "You want, of course, for him a profession, an occupation, that gives him safety. None will give this. We live in times of which we have no idea what will come. You might as well let him, since you can pay for the studies, you have a job, let him study whatever he wants." And my father decided to allow me to do what I wanted. And I entered the University of Vienna.

VH: Do you think his thoughts, that maybe you should go to a trade school, came from his school conference earlier, some years back, around age 12 or 13, when you weren't doing so well in school?

RE: You must have read that somewhere . . . that was 5 or 6 years earlier. When professors had told him, after I had been in a hospital a few months because of an ear condition, that I would never make it in high school. I should, therefore, go to a trade school.

VH: Amazing.

RE: I remember to the day when my father told me the story. He said, "I would so much love that you could have a university education and become a doctor." He meant not a medical doctor, but simply a doctor's degree. "What shall we do?" And I said, "I would like to become a doctor." He said, "Okay, I leave you in school, and you repeat the year." And I repeated the second grade in high school. I was 10, 11 or 12 years old. When I repeated, I ran into a teacher who taught German and French. He was an Adlerian, which of course I found out only much, much later after I had finished high school and maintained a contact with him. And like a good Adlerian, he helped me to give up the feeling that I was worthless—for the first time, I got in touch with the idea of what an inferiority complex is. He helped me to get over it, I remember to the day how he did it—

VH: What did he do?

RE: He had a marvelous way. Let me tell you. I wrote an essay. I still have the essay among my possessions.

VH: Is that the one about heroes and the warriors?

RE: Yes, my father brought the essay to America. He kept all my school essays. And it was about *Hagen from Tronje* and a *Nibelung*, who was heroic and risked his life to save the king, if you like, to save the father, to do whatever he could and in fighting, he lost an eye, as he fought the evil hero.

VH: Not an ear?

RE: Not an ear. Later, when I studied as an adult, I realized that I described myself. I would protect the father, a new version of an oedipus complex. You know it was not the father who was killed, but the mother who had died. I will in spite of that ear, in spite of the defect, I will go on winning. The professor told me, "This is a beautiful essay, read it to the whole class." From then on I knew I could read in front of the class. I have still a little bit of excitement when I have to give an address somewhere, address a few hundred people. I feel a little bit like I felt at that time, when I wondered, what will the children say. The children accepted it, and many of the audiences accepted, it and sometimes they don't. One learns after a while to know not all that one conveys to the people is fully, is equally accepted. But from then on I was a different person. The same boy who flunked a grade, became, within half a year with that one teacher, one of the best students in the classroom.

VH: I'm sensing that the years between 2 and 12 or 13 were painful years for you. You've never written about them that I'm aware of.

RE: Well, they were. . . . I don't know how much I would write about it, but I could sort of explain it through one anecdote. I was about 4 or 5. I lived with this lady who took care of me alone.

VH: Your father was gone?

RE: Because the father was gone. He was at that time, I believe, somewhere in Slovakia, with the armed forces of the Austrian Emperor. One day as we were standing in the house, and the lady who brought me up spoke with the concierge, I had gone to the door and come back full of excitement. I'm scared, I'm scared. What happened? A soldier is coming into the house, and I was afraid of the soldier. Soldier, police, at that time, were not encouraging to me. They looked around the corner and said, "But Rudi, it's your Papa, it's your Daddy." The father in uniform had come back from the war. It was over. The uniform was dirty, the winter coat was dirty. Later, the father took the winter coat to a tailor, and the soldier suit that he had and turned it around so that only the inside was visible; and the dirt was now inside, and I got my first school suit and began to go to school. That's how the war ended. My father was home again. He was not a dangerous soldier, but he was a kind daddy, and from then on life became organized.

I was allowed to go to school before I was 6 because my birthday is in February. Instead of letting me wait half a year, I was permitted to go to school provided I would manage, and so on. Then school started, an organized life started; I had a safe home again and grew up in that same house where all that took place, until I had to leave it in 1938. Whenever I go back to Vienna, I go there . . . the woman who was the wife of the concierge, she's still alive there, and we visit. Of course, all the other people changed. It's the same house, nothing has changed.

VH: What's its address?

RE: It's in the Ninth District. And it is Hunzpasse 12, Ture 16. Hubway, Huss Street, because there were—in the old days, a grove of nut trees.

VH: Do you think you'll ever have a plaque on it?

RE: No, I don't need a plaque there.

VH: The rest of us might want to see it. Was your father a soldier already when your mother died? Was he gone when she died?

RE: No, I think he entered the war rather late, when actually anybody would have known and suspect the empire would fall.

VH: How long did the Catholic lady stay with you?

RE: Forever, you know. And I remember to the day—and I can again give it to you through an example—when this dreadful war now started with the conquest of Kuwait, the robbery of Kuwait, I dreamt that I heard her voice, if you like, the mother substitute's voice, "Rudi, I'm"—(in German, of course, in Viennese dialect)—"I'm snow-white, I have white hair, I am helpless, come to Kuwait and save me." And, of course, I woke up and realized, I tried to save her, to help her to leave Europe, and not to die in the war, in poverty and illness, but I was too late. I had a feeling that many of us who were successful refugees, that we cannot quite get rid of the guilt feeling for the people who were murdered by the Nazis in the concentration camps in the Holocaust. We were not strong enough to save them. Sort of a little bit like events in Freud's life, who had sisters and relatives whom he could not save.

VH: But the Nazis wouldn't have been after a Catholic, would they?

RE: They would not have been after her except to take things away from her—you know, we gave her the apartment, we gave her all the furniture. Robbery was going on. After all, we know in this country that it's not all that ideal. We have drive-by shootings. So she was then impoverished, lost all that we had left for her, because after the war when she was still alive we could send her gift parcels and some money and help her out, but in the last pictures that I have of her, she's helpless, ill, and in poverty.

VH: When were the last contacts with her?

RE: After the war, I would imagine 1946, 1947. I have somewhere, you know, the exact knowledge of when she died; but I don't have it in mind right now.

VH: That's a lot of losses, isn't it?

RE: I had once a party here when I was 50 years in America. The people invited were all either from here or Vienna, all former refugees. You wonder what it will be like for the next 50 years with the people from Kuwait or from Iraq or from Iran. They lost in the war and will try to survive and to overcome. I feel sometimes, you know, when I hear that beautiful song, *We Shall Overcome*, the black song. We had it all before them. Can one overcome? One can. But not completely. And the best of analysis cannot wipe out what one must remember and should never forget.

VH: What was the Catholic lady's name?

RE: Emilie Neudorfer. And I used to call her—because I couldn't say when I was little, Neudorfer, it was too complex—so I would call her Neffa. I put together the words.

VH: Did she have family?

RE: She had some family that I got to know, of course. They lived sort of in neighboring districts, and she would go sometimes visiting, and I had sort of a distant relationship with them. You know, as if you imagined, you had someone employed in your home and maybe some occasion occurs where you visit the home of her sister, mother, or whatever. And some of the members of that family, the men, interestingly enough, were very successful and important people. In those days, like then in America, the girls in a family did not have much schooling. It was usually the men that made the career. It was only the beginning of the liberation of women. Universities were usually full with males. For example, I cannot remember for the life of me that I ever knew about a female lawyer in Vienna. But there must have been some.

VH: Were there aunts, or . . . I know there was an uncle who gave you your first copy of Freud.

RE: That's right. There was an uncle who gave me the first copy of Freud. He was my father's brother. And there was his wife, who happened to be also a Catholic. It was very interesting that many of us in Republican Austria had to overcome what then was reintroduced anti-Semitism that led to the Holocaust. There was always anti-Semitism in Vienna, but there were many exceptional situations where people fused just like here. There are still a lot of antagonistic feelings toward blacks, and nevertheless you can see over and over again that black man is white and white man is black. One can overcome. We are all the same.

VH: You have so many things, and yet all the things of your mother's family or your father's family had to be left behind.

RE: All was lost except a few things came with me.

VH: What came with you?

RE: The books came with me.

VH: Which ones?

RE: I can show you, lots of important novels came. The first Freud books came along with me. But there came other things, for example, that my father brought. He brought a cup, sort of a metal cup, that soldiers in the war had in their uniforms so that they had some water to drink. And the usual thing where you put in water or where you could cook a meal if you were at the front. They're still upstairs. Nobody would use it or drink from it, but it is sort of like a piece of antiquity. He had that in his hand. He would drink water out of it. And it lies there and reminds us of old days. He was even able to save a number of photographs of the old days so I have photographs of the relatives, but the rest is gone. Strangely enough what we have, what he brought along, just to give you an idea of where value is for people in those days, he brought along all my report cards, beginning with elementary school, from first grade up to the last. I escaped for my life; I had no time to pack even. He brought them along a year later. He brought along his own report cards, from his school; you know, in other words, from his school time. And I still have them somewhere in the room. So interesting, what one thinks is important.

VH: I wonder what those first four report cards of yours showed, because you clearly entered high school with low self-esteem and trouble, some trouble. And then it changed, and the gift and the genius emerged and just kept developing. But it sounds like they would be so-so, those early report cards.

RE: There is a report card that has, at the beginning of the term, a lot of what we call F's here. You would then see the breakthrough; and only if you look at the report cards, you see that one can get out of a stupid hospital and recover, because the hospital was not only lost time, the hospital was trauma after trauma. I mean if I would give you an idea of how one was treated there, you would not believe it—

VH: I would like to know. I am working on a paper about medical trauma.

RE: I said, innocent sadism. It goes like this. I am in one room. And I vow to help . . . the nurses thought I should help . . . there was a little boy of 4 at my left. I should carry the candles and the holy cross to the bed of a person who, in another room, was dying, so when the priest would come he would give her the last confession and the last benediction so she should go to paradise. And I have never forgotten as I went to carry those things, which was meant to be a kind gesture—right?

VH: Scary.

RE: I was to slowly go to the bed and I tried; I turned my head to the right so I would not have to look at the dying person and put the things there . . . 11 years old! Or, a similar situation; there was a boy who had, since he couldn't swallow, they had to make a hole in his throat and put in—what was it called? Tracheotomy. You know, a little pipe. He was being fed. But, of course, this was just to let the air through. The other one was all right, and what happened to that boy when he would eat . . . he couldn't manage, and he would vomit the food. And the hospital nurses of that time made him eat the vomit so he would become disciplined. And I saw it in front of me. I could tell you 10 other such things.

VH: Go ahead.

RE: Some hospitals haven't changed here in America or in Europe; that is, psychologically. Understanding for the sick child was simply unknown—one didn't know. Rather I'm trying to say how long it took before we began to train nurses in ordinary medical hospitals or surgical hospitals to get insight. You think it's any different here?

VH: No, Rudi . . . in fact, I contacted a hospital to say I'm seeing little children who I think were traumatized almost as frighteningly. They were strapped to boards, taken on gurneys, taken away from their mothers and terrible things—even those MRIs are terrifying stuff for little children. They won't let you research it.

RE: You, of course, ask me all these questions with the idea in mind, how does such a little boy, semiorphaned . . . going through an illness . . . going through a war . . . going through the starvation of the beginning of the Republic become a psychoanalyst? How does one overcome trauma? One turns it around and will now help traumatized persons. The next thing came, when I went to school with that teacher who said, "Read to the whole class about *Hagen from Tronje*." He would come to me and say, "We happen to have a couple of boys who cannot learn, and they will flunk. I have recommended to the parents that they hire you as a tutor." Yeah? I was now 12 or 13 and began to tutor children. And what the teachers in the classroom couldn't do, I did. The children passed. And, actually, my hopes . . . all my studies at the University I could maintain, (since my father didn't have that much money), by earning some money as a tutor. And it was because of that experience that I got more involved with the question of what does one learn, and how does one learn? And I knew how to help a child learn. I became more and more interested and said, therefore, I will study psychology.

But then came the next obstacle, since there is no life without obstacle. The obstacle for us was that the psychology that was taught at the time was like here—academic psychology—not to understand the mind of a person and the feeling of a person, but rather to have the development of how does thinking start, how does smelling start, how does touching start, and so forth, and so forth. Those are the kinds of observations that somebody does who observes babies, but it is not psychoanalytic. The interest, at the time, was to divide the person into touching and smelling and seeing and hearing, and so forth. Nobody could get his act together. This is the way it went. When I worked with whoever the child was, I asked, do I understand the way this boy feels? Do I understand what it means? When I tutored for someone, if they didn't want to study, I tried to understand what they were feeling.

I speak about the enormity of the task of understanding children. I'll describe one scene I never forgot. I see this boy—who lived sort of between the house where I lived and the school. And I would go there . . . in a rather poor part of the Ninth District, and I would teach, tutoring him in his own home. They had a small apartment. I would work with him in the bedroom. Now these people had the usual double bed. The parents were in the dining room, next to it. The boy, opposed to learning, would crawl under the bed. The lady of the house—just to describe the kind of house, was an unbelievably clean lady—but as is very often the case with such very clean ladies, under the bed was enormous dust. It was only clean where it could be seen. I crawled under the bed where the child was. He said, "What are you doing here?" Ludwig was his name—he says, "I'm going to stay here." I say, "I will also stay here. If you're under the bed, I'm under the bed." "But remember that you were employed by my parents in order to teach me something." I say, "Well, I can teach you also under the bed, if you want to learn something. But as long as you're under the bed, I'll stay under the bed." He would come out, and he would say, "You have to teach me French, then I would come out, with all the dust." "Okay." He said, "There's no good air. Open the window." So we open the window. He would say, "Now I'm going to jump out the window." I would say, "Well, if you don't want to learn French and would rather jump out the window, jump out the window." He would say, "You let me die?" "If you want to. I couldn't help it." "All right, let's start." He came out from under the bed, he closed the window, he didn't jump out the window, and so on. Hour after hour the same provocations. And, of course, I realized—I didn't need to read psychiatric books, that was where the relationship with the parents was involved. The father was there. He would come into the room and almost trample the child to death, because all he knew was to beat him up, mercilessly with his feet—to stamp on him. I would say, "Look, let me do it, I'm gonna get this child through school; but I am the tutor, leave us alone." The parent let go. The mother tried to protect the child from the father. The child did whatever he could to irritate the father and to fight with the father and to show that the father didn't know what to do. . . .

It was a risky business to help children who are on the verge of opposing and at the same time deal with the father, who could not tolerate it, and a mother who tried to protect the child from the father and could not. I also tutored the sister, the older sister, and strangely enough, I still have contact with that sister who now is a middle-aged lady. She became a nurse and lives somewhere in Australia. Her brother lives in England. He was saved, too, when Fascists finally arrived. I had, at that time, to deal with children who gave me sort of an idea of what symptomatology could be. And it was beginning with this kind of child that I began to also have contact with the Psychoanalytic Institute. One of my first supervision cases of tutoring of psychopathology with Willi Hoffer was around that child.

VH: This very child you just talked about?

RE: Yes.

VH: That was your first training case?

RE: That was one of the first training cases, but you must always remember I was then trained to be a psychoanalytic pedagogue because I wanted to be a teacher who understands the soul of children and not just the subject to be taught . . . who does not just know German grammar, but how can one help a child to relate to such things as German grammar, which is more complex than English grammar.

VH: I'm fascinated. You were getting in the child's space . . . you were saying two things to that very first child that you used to teach us. One, that you must get in the child's space; two, that you must allow the child to be in his space as he wants to be.

RE: The whole secret of what I did later, many years later, when I treated psychotic children! Unless the child knows you can be like him, you can have that kind of mind, you can understand it, will you never get the child to want to also figure out your mind. All psychoanalysis is this way; all psychotherapy is just this. All the work at the Orthogenic School that Bruno Bettelheim did was always the same. I don't have to reeducate the children, let's say the way behavior modifiers would do. But rather, I understand what he brings to me, it means something. If he goes under the marital bed, I could have said, "What you really want, that's why you don't want to study; you want to know what your parents do in bed, and you want to be under the bed and listen." Instead of that, I said, "I also love to be under the bed," rather as if to indirectly say, "I also want to know what goes on between Poppa and Momma. So we both want to know what goes on with Poppa and Momma." And then he would say, "But then we'll be studying." And a new struggle comes. "I don't want to know what Poppa and Momma do because that's what you want, I want to study." I say, "But I don't want to study, I want to be under the bed. I want to find out about Poppa and Momma," if you can follow me. So he says, "All right. Let's go and study. Open the window. I find it unbearable in the world that I live in. I could imagine jumping out the window." "If you think you would rather jump out the window than study French, or whatever else we did at the time, we'll see what happens after a while." The rebellion is then born. He says, "You want to join me in the rebellion? I won't let you rebel. I won't let you betray my parents who pay for tutoring, when really you do nothing. You must teach me something." All of a sudden, little Ludwig became a learner. But that didn't happen overnight. It took weeks. Endless time. And from there, I went on to get an interest more and more in children. I moved away from tutoring to the therapeutic path. Of course, what I did with that boy was already therapy, you know, but it was not yet therapy in the way we would do it if we had an office, and so forth.

When I work with children now, I know I do sometimes more for a child when I get him away from the meaning of his dreams to the meaning why he wants to crawl under the bed. In other words, he was a child who was acting out. The thought, if only I knew what my parents do in bed when I hear it, does my father beat up my mother? I hear her . . . sighing. I hear noises from there. He does not know that it is the noise of people who have immense pleasure. But, rather, he does something to her. He must. Because that's the way it goes with oedipal fantasies. The teachers at the Institute, who observed this with me, said, "You know, maybe you want to choose between being a teacher and being a child analyst." A child analyst? And I again had the same experience . . . could I ever do this? Yes, I could. And all of a sudden, I found myself more and more fixated to a new idea. I want to be like those who teach me. I want to be like Anna Freud, I want to be like Willi Hoffer, I want to be like Bertha Borenstein, and Edith Buxbaum, to just name a few names of that time. And . . . but it's impossible. For example, I'm not a medical doctor; I will have to be a refugee, and I will come to America; and they will not accept somebody who is only a Ph.D. And Freud always thought that the best who surrounded him, at that time, were none of these. Because, for him, psychoanalysis was a psychology and not a part of medicine.

VH: It sounds as though you were a learning-problem child yourself.

RE: Right.

VH: How do you analyze that child?

RE: That I was?

VH: That you were before you had that very special teacher who helped you feel valuable and worthwhile. It sounds like he changed your life around.

RE: I would do exactly the same that that teacher did. If I were a teacher.

VH: Well, how would you analyze that child if you had been his analyst?

RE: If I had been his therapist?

VH: Yes, that little boy.

RE: I would do the same. I would take every production of his body, even his shit, and admire it. Because a little boy who still defecates in his pants when he's 4 years old, or whatever—

VH: Was that you?

RE: That was not me. Such a child gives a present to his mother. I will never forget, you know, there was a famous German analyst, Frieda Fromm-Reichmann, who was then quite a quasi-Sullivanian, and I heard her lecture. She described a patient who for months and months or years did not permit her to enter her room in the mental hospital. But one day, she says, "Come in." And she said it so nicely. Fromm-Reichmann said, "You let me come in because I want to help you." And the patient said, "You're wonderful. It's so nice . . . can I touch your cheek?" "Of course, my child." The patient was a young woman, and she calls her "my child." The woman comes to her and touches her cheek and smears it with feces that she had in her hands. That's why she let her come in. Frieda Fromm-Reichmann said to her, "Such a nice gift you give me. I know that you wanted to show me and your mommy that you did your duty." The feces, for her, was the valuable gift of a tiny girl, regressed as the patient had, to the level of a small child, to experience herself always as somebody whose mother had never loved her and who felt no one would ever come . . . but she must try! So one more try, because the lady was persistent and knocked at her door day after day but did not insist on getting in. "Come in." And then she touches her, and as she touches her with the feces, Frieda Fromm-Reichmann says, "What a beautiful gift. You're a lovely, lovely little baby that wants to show mommy that you can do it." It never happened again. The more official, and more, how shall I put it, the more orthodox treatment started.

But sometimes the opening gambit is not orthodox, like me crawling under the bed with all the dust. I would do it now, too, no difficulty. I did in America you know, with children who play on the floor and did not want to talk to me . . . so I would also sit on the floor, and I would do the same that they do with their toys and play. We learned it out of a Viennese atmosphere in which free associations are made. Sometimes free associations are like free actions—free acting out, free play, and I join in a game; I can do what you can, I do it too. And when that happens, something very strange happens. If I can identify with the patient, and transfer that way. After a while, the patient comes to the point where he says, "And how will you do it? Or, how will you say it?" I sometimes work with people who speak another language. And I think of a patient who comes from Mexico, a Spanish patient. So I try my best to speak at least a few Spanish words. I have a patient now from Germany. I try to speak the language. Even if it's a special fantasy they have. That's, after all, Freud, that's all he did. Not because he demanded dreams, but that's what people brought him. So he said, "I think your dream is important." You know, rather than saying, as old-fashioned doctors would do, "Now tell me, what are your complaints?" The person may come in and start out, "I had a dream." You know such as I remember to the day my first dream in analysis.

VH: Can you talk some about that early Institute and who was there and what kind of cases you had? How many times a week did you see them? It sounds like they were more tutoring sessions than they were the kind of thing you were teaching, as I remember, at Reiss–Davis.

RE: I think the time at the Institute has to be considered in two phases: One is that you took seminars and you took courses. We had some brilliant teachers there. There was Anna Freud, there was August Aichhorn, with whom one worked on delinquent cases. There were a variety of famous people who belonged to the Institute and taught young teachers, and so forth. But then there was a second condition that is not quite known here. It was highly recommended and made almost into a moral condition that you go into analysis. That you cannot understand other people if you don't fully understand yourself, and there came then the decision to go into analysis. This was a psychological decision to make because it could get you far away from most academic of the life of the Institute. It was also a financial decision. But, fortunately, it was done by an Institute that was not guided by analysts who had nothing in mind but money; you know, the mighty dollar or the mighty whatever. I began with a kind of scholarship. I mean, to give you an example, I happen to remember what I paid for a month of analysis five times a week. Not like you do in America.

VH: With Hitschman?

RE: No. I paid what Freud would get for an hour, approximately for the whole month.

VH: Who was the analyst?

RE: In this case the first analyst that I had, that Anna Freud suggested for me, was a man by the name of Kronold. His name is shortened; he was originally a Dr. Kronengold. And this man would charge me for 1 month, approximately what Freud got for 1 hour.

VH: Had he been a student of Freud's?

RE: He was a Polish analyst who participated in the program for psychiatric pedagogues and helped others whenever he could in order to make an opportunity for us to be analyzed.

VH: Do you know who his analyst was?

RE: I think I knew once, but I have at the moment forgotten. It could be, you know, that he was analyzed by Anna Freud; whoever it was, I have forgotten it. We have met in the meantime.

VH: Is he still alive?

RE: He is still alive. He is an old man. And a few years ago, I saw him—

VH: In Austria?

RE: No, no, no, no, he's in New York. He escaped too.

VH: Is he a member of the New York—

RE: He's a member of the New York Society.

VH: How fascinating! And you saw him five times a week for how long?

RE: I saw him . . . you know, I wished again I would have held calendars back. I started that training in 1935. I think I came to him in 1937. At that time one of the conditions was that you took 2 years of courses before they would recommend you; you also ought to have an analysis. And then I had him a number of months, and the time came after the Nazi invasion, the last hour we both escaped.

VH: So less than a year.

RE: It's very, very short.

VH: And how many training cases had you seen?

RE: I saw all children, and what we did with the children would be considered here child psychotherapy; and I was considered a psychoanalytic pedagogue.

VH: So how many cases did you see with weekly supervision?

RE: What we would do is, I would have a variety of these cases I would bring up with the one or two people that I had then as supervisors. I report in the group another case with Aichhorn, I remember; then I reported a case to Hoffer and Hartmann, who had a seminar; and I reported again another to Willi Hoffer alone. That's approximately the way it was.

VH: I had the impression in reading something that your individual conferences with Willi Hoffer were held sort of walking down the street. Is that true?

RE: Not always. I would visit him. But some, literally, occasionally were that way. For example, Hitschman, my analyst, told me that he had some of his hours really walking down the street with Freud himself. Freud sometimes saw people this way. In other words, all the orthodoxy that one fantasizes allegedly existed under Freud, is untrue. It was a liberal Institute. It was an Institute that made all efforts, for example, financial efforts, to give people like me a chance to be trained there.

VH: And it sounds like a lot of the supervision was what we would now call group supervision.

RE: Some was group supervision—

VH: Seminars and group supervision.

RE: But then what is also important to be said is that, at that time psychoanalysis was not a money-making undertaking; but it was a *movement*. When you look up there, in my library, you find volumes up there; they are all called *Die psychoanalytische Beweghrup* . . . that was the name of the journal. It moves. You know, they must have had that from Galileo, when he stood before the Inquisition and insisted, "But the sun, regardless of what you say and what you will do to me, is moving. It is not the fixed point that Christianity, at the time assumes, in order to make people faithful." It was considered a movement. In many ways, it was almost like a political movement, and most of that movement, politically speaking, was sort of on the left. Even if a man like Freud wants to go together with Adler, and they all vote together, decide they will vote for a Socialist finance minister in Vienna—because if he gets reelected, then there will be money for schools; there will be money for kids again; there will be houses built for the people. In other words, they were true liberals . . . many people think of them, you know, even those that did not belong to a party, they would belong to the left part of the Democratic party here.

VH: Some of what you've written made it sound as though Freud himself was rather aloof, or even unavailable, to the students like you. Is that accurate?

RE: No, he was not aloof. I think this man was then an old man, and he was beyond giving ordinary courses. What he did then, he had, as it were, a special group that would meet on Wednesday nights with him. Many people have written about it like Sterbo or Hitschman or Hartmann or Kris . . . these people were around him, and they met Wednesday after Wednesday. But the official work of teaching, you know, by that time was over. Anna still did that. Of course, she was a younger person. At the time she was in her 40s. Freud, by that time, was not well; and he had then a small group, I believe, that went on for a short time, of course, also in England. He escaped to England in 1938. Of course, he died. Cancer finally won out.

VH: Whose seminars do you remember and why?

RE: The most powerful experiences—they're number one, Anna Freud.

VH: Tell me about her and your relationship.

RE: With Anna Freud, the relationship, I suppose, can be explained best if I describe what she did. In Los Angeles I presented, for the first time, something that I never learned in Vienna, that was not done in Vienna officially. I don't know who did it; but I did, namely, I worked with psychotic children.

VH: That's the autistic children you were working with?

RE: Yes. I would bring such a child, whom I had treated, together with another friend of mine. We worked together on a case. We had written a paper together. Seymour Friedman, here in Los Angeles, is an extraordinary creative analyst. Anna Freud was to discuss the presentation. She would get up, and she did the same as once in Hampstead when I had a similar case. She would say, "Well, you know, I never treated such a case. And, therefore, what I say, comes not out of experience, but just comes out of listening to you. Let me discuss it the way I see it." Then she would start to discuss this really psychotic child. And she would get the diagnostic ways of looking, in America, because we call a lot of things psychotic and borderline that one would have never called that in Vienna.

VH: What would you have called them in Vienna?

RE: In Vienna you would have spoken about a severe neurotic, and you would not have called it a psychotic person. Psychotic persons there are of a different variety.

VH: Are you meaning to say "psychotic" and "autistic" in the same category?

RE: No. I think that autism and childhood psychosis—I mean I would put it this way, an autistic child is a psychotic child. But I think there are a variety of ways that one can be psychotic; the same way that there are a variety of ways that one can be neurotic. You notice I don't call a hysteric an obsessive compulsive. I don't call an obsessive compulsive a character difficulty, but they are neurotic. And then we have developed more and more in America, an extension of this; namely, the borderline child. I wrote once in one of my papers about the borderline child. Many papers that have contributed to the literature in books or in articles deal with the way we diagnose in this country, and the way we diagnosed at the time in Vienna. It was a different way.

VH: Can you go back to your early experiences with Anna Freud? What kind of person was she? From the vantage point of a young man, single, 22 . . . where was this lady? What do you remember?

RE: I can only describe the way it was. When Anna Freud talked, when I heard her talking for the first time; ah, I remember saying to Dr. Hoffer, I had never seen her. She came in, and she talked. And I said, "You know, this was such a strange experience. Such a strange experience. I've never heard anything like that. I think I'm going to give up the study of pure philosophy." But in the end, you get a Ph.D.

VH: Because of all those mechanisms of defense she listed? What made you think now I have to go do something else?

RE: The defenses she read in a course. I deeply remember what she spoke about. She spoke then to that particular group about the place of psychoanalysis in the educational processes. The "defenses" we studied in another seminar. That, by the way, we studied at the time that her book appeared. The book appeared in 1935, and a few months later, we began to read this book. This book was something completely new, and it seemed, at the time, like an enormous revolution. I mean, I could jokingly say, it wasn't really Freudian. Because even though in Freud, of course, you find many of these thoughts, but not put together the way Anna Freud did it. I think that her contribution, at the time, was, for us, as if we entered a new world in psychoanalysis. But more than that was the appearance of the woman.

VH: What did she look like? As a man, how did this woman strike you?

RE: She was sort of the woman that you wanted—if only I would be older, I would fall in love with her. You know, and I don't know who ever fell in love with her—

VH: No one, apparently, male—

RE: I know better. It wasn't quite that way. She was loved a little by many people, sort of a fantasy; but you never know whether they fall in love with her because she was the daughter of Freud or because she was inviting. Because at that time she was dedicated to psychoanalysis, and you responded to her as a teacher. You could, as it were, literally, hang on her lips. And, of course, I didn't hear her too long; but then when I escaped to England, I heard her again. She brought to England, education and psychoanalysis; and, of course, she brought the immense movement that was created there. Whenever I met her later, a relationship developed. I had various correspondence of letters from her, letters to her, work that I sent her. I want to tell you, whenever she was critical, she was objective; and you always learned something. Such as when I gave the first paper on childhood psychosis for her . . . I believe it was the paper on the space-child.

VH: That's what you've said in some of your writings.

RE: I would then, afterwards, sort of rewrite the paper, and I would see better, in my own terms, without feeling that she imposed her view. She was an absolutely tolerant person. By the way, unlike the Kleinians then, who believe there is only one way to go. She never had that. With her, I felt I had utter freedom to think what I wanted. And in the meantime, you know, as long as she was alive, whatever I had, I sent to her. You may have seen the different eulogies that I wrote about Anna Freud. The experience with her—one left her a free man. I could go where I wanted to. Such as, for example, what I write in these different papers on the psychotic children. By no means was Anna Freud in it, but it was only through Anna Freud that I could learn to think. The same was true for my philosophy teachers in Vienna, Schlick and Wittgenstein. I learned from them how to think. And I learned from her and similar teachers how to think analytically. I never felt that I had to be dogmatic. I saw once, in Salzburg . . . a poster. I was teaching in Salzburg, and in that room where the patients sit was a big poster. I have it now here in my collection because they gave it to me, and it says in German, "Sagemir, in Welcher Sprache Soll ich zu dir Sprechen"—"Tell me in which language shall I speak to you." And I thought, how come they knew it? I thought only I knew this. It is my invention. That I listen to a patient; I don't force on the patient the lingo of analysis or whatever else it is. Somebody comes in . . . and she speaks Prussian German. I try to speak German; and I don't tell her it's a resistance, to speak German, and she should speak English. If she has a Viennese dialect, I go for the Viennese dialect. If she comes in and she speaks English with a Mexican dialect, I try whatever I can, a little bit to adjust myself. I rather try to listen just like Frieda Fromm-Reichmann did with the patient who "talks" with her feces. You talk the language—or at least understand—the language of the other.

I remember I had a patient once who was a Viennese with a strange history. He was a Viennese, and then he came to England, and then he came to America. When he talked about his early childhood, he talked Viennese. When he talked about the time he was to become an engineer, a student, he talked German. When he spoke about England, where he was a refugee, his English sounded a little British; and when he came to America, it became Americanized. Of course, you could always hear these different accents. And I learned automatically to always speak like him. And long after his analysis when I met him again, I asked him once, "Tell me, what helped you?" I helped him to go back to Vienna, to dissolve a terribly bad marriage that he had here, to find another woman in Vienna, to become again an engineer there, to work there, and to end his life as a happy man. He's dead now. And I asked him, "What helped you?" And he said, "You know, I want to tell you, I forgot all; but one thing that I remember. You always spoke like I spoke." He felt that I go for the feeling that was expressed in his language, that I never tried to be above the language or below the language or whatever it would be. And you know, we have different schools in Los Angeles of the different groups that exist. They insist you must speak their language, whether the Freudian student or the Sullivanian student or the Kohutian student or the Reichian student . . . students do that, and I think one has to be an older, a maturer analyst in order to give that up.

VH: Rudi, how do you understand that? It's one of the things I wanted to do these interviews for. There are so many different theories and schools, as you point out. And some people, who are in truth, bright people—you don't think of them as sheep—seem to get so hooked in to having to think in one way.

RE: I think it has to do with the fact that we all have not quite given up the early conflict in us. We must speak like a father, and then we rebel against the father; and we find a new orientation and we find a new god, but we're constantly looking for a god. And sometimes the god is the theory. Allow yourself to speak like a poet, like someone who's not afraid of a metaphor. Many people in the beginning of learning must do exactly as they are taught before they become themselves. And I think the greatest thing that analysis can do is to let a patient that one has, rather for example a student, to grow away from us and not become a follower. I am a Freudian; it's all right, but I am not a follower of Freud. Because if you read what I write, you will see that much of it did not occupy him; other things occupied him. And much of the language that I use didn't occupy him. It all goes back, not only to my education in philosophy, but to that very early, helpful teacher. When you write, write so that it's *your* story.

You know, I remember I learned the following from my first teacher: he would say, "You know what you do, you go home, and you look at this picture that you have there. And you imagine for a moment that this still picture has movement, but a camera took just one shot. You know, like you want to have a shot of my face, rather than the movement of how the face looks before and after and after. And now imagine when you look at this picture there, what happened there before, and what will happen afterwards, and imagine a story. And the story is just an illustration in a book." That's what one does in analysis.

For example, somebody tells me a still picture, the manifest part of a dream. What happened before? If you remember when Freud said, "What day residue is left in a dream? A, B, C, D." And now we will first hear about this part and that part and that part, and suddenly you see that the manifest content of the dream moves from yesterday to tomorrow. If it's only yesterday, you know, if only the past is important, you have forgotten adaptation. If it is only adaptation, you have forgotten the trauma of the past. Then, to look at pictures this way, so that when somebody comes and tells me in 5 minutes what's up, why he comes to me, already I have a story. Because I can imagine what could have been there before, and what could there be afterwards. I simply say to myself, "Every still picture is meant to be a story." You know such as when you look at this picture here by Picasso, up there with the mother and the baby. What happened now? What will happen 10 minutes later, and what happened before? And I could well imagine. There was a crying baby. And the mother woke up. And she was scared. And she took the baby. And she took it to the breast. And then afterwards, she will sing a song, and the baby will go to sleep; and she will go to sleep. She will say, "It's wonderful to have a child."

When you imagine why the artist drew this very quickly, he had a story in mind. I have a man in analysis who's an artist, even though what he puts on the wall, what he puts on the portrait, is a still picture. If it's a good picture, it tells a story. You know, such as I show you the photographs of the German lady who came to interview a few of us who were driven out and yet had done something with themselves in the world and maybe been invited to come back. The face tells the story. The manifest dream content tells the story. What was afterwards, you put afterwards. Now, of course, sometimes, I can guess, I have enough empathy to read the face. You know, such as I had somebody coming in the other day—I looked at her face, and I knew something happened. And I said to her, just like this, "What happened?" And she started to cry. "I called my father," she said, "I called my father. He has cancer." One look. Then I have to fill out. What was the relationship to that father before? Divorce? Rather complex situation. She holds on to him. He remarries. The mother is there, the father is here, and she tries to get her family together in her head. And then she telephones because she wants to maintain contact with him. And he says to her, "I have cancer." So as I look at her face, I already have in my mind what happened. Then she substantiates it. And I think that's what they do, let's say, with the manifest content of a dream.

VH: I've always thought of you as the bridgemaker in analysis. You were talking about the bridge between her father and her mother for her—

RE: Of course.

VH: As I have looked at your life and your choices of theory, you've always said, "Well, okay, Kohutians, okay, Kleinians, let me see if I can build a bridge between the two of you that we can all walk on."

RE: Yes. Can we have a bridge? Such as, for example, how nice it would be if only I would know more Spanish. I went off into Mexico to teach there. And I had to teach in English. But then I learned a few Spanish words. Or I read English translations of Spanish writings of psychoanalysts, and I found myself a little nearer to them, even though it is not just my way of talking or looking. And when you can make a bridge, but what else does an analyst do? Let's say that Freud has the theory of superego, ego, and id. What else does he do but to say, "What is the connection between the desire, the lust, the drive, the gratification, the sexual drive, the aggressive drive, and the threatening superego? And who's between?" The ego.

VH: So, Rudi, if you have this group saying, "We are the Kohutians—this is the only theory." You have the Kleinians over here saying, "We're the only ones . . . ." I've always thought of them as sort of primal herds that say, "We get to be the most powerful so we can kill the rivals."

RE: What then will happen? Either the primal herd completely isolates itself—we want to be an island, don't touch us; or the primal herd will try to invade the other country and persuade them they should also be Iraqis, for example, nothing but a primal herd. Perhaps they will become curious. And I think, how shall I put this, shall I say, Freud, a god, gave me curiosity.

VH: I don't think Freud should get credit for that.

RE: All analysts are bridgemakers. They make not only a bridge in the mind of the person, the sick person, let's say between superego and id; but they try to make a better bridge which allows the ego to make a bridge. And so if you have a weak ego apropos ego psychology, and so forth, what kind of ego do I need so I can talk with you? And can talk to myself and with myself? And I think that all analysts are bridgemakers; but the problem with bridges sometimes, you know, like with engineers, some people believe in only one kind of bridge, and there are many kinds of bridges. For example, I can cross the Danube on a bridge. But when I was 17, I liked much more to swim across the Danube.

VH: If you had to compare Anna Freud as a bridge to Willi Hoffer, to Klein, could you play with that—to Freud? Could you play within this metaphor? What kind of bridges were they as people?

RE: I think so, you know. I think with Anna Freud, she came to an early decision; it will be better, they are there, and I am here. We will be polite to each other, we'll talk to each other. But I have my own Hampstead Institute. I do my own work because I cannot use my time in an eternal struggle.

VH: So more in isolation.

RE: Isn't it? In response to Melanie Klein and her school, it has changed a great deal now. We can now talk to each other and sometimes understand each other. I'll give you a sort of a more personal example. I always wished, when I met my dear wife, she would learn German because if she learns German, I can tell her, *Ich liebe Dich.* I love you. I could not put this into English at that time. I can now, but at that time I couldn't. It sort of seemed like an old Viennese trick, you know, talk to a girl in a foreign language; it isn't really meant. I felt if only she would learn German, then, she would believe me more.

VH: Where did you meet Ruth?

RE: I met her in Boston.

VH: When you first came and went to Social Work School there?

RE: When I went to Social Work School there I met her; and I thought, if she talked German, she will quickly say "yes" to me. And she said, "When you are in Rome, you do as the Romans do." And she's right—when I'm in Rome, I would try to do as the Romans do.

VH: What was she doing when you met her?

RE: She was working in a bank as an accountant there. . . . And then in Vienna, she can talk enough German to understand all the German. You know, Vienna is an educated city. She walks into a food store, you know, like a vegetable store, and starts to talk; and the little salesgirls, high school students, talk English better. They hear. You know, and sometimes she's even annoyed. She wants to learn German, you know. So . . . a bridgemaker between languages. A bridgemaker between America and Europe. A bridgemaker between my identification with this wonderful country and my identification with old Vienna. So I have to make bridges. A bridge between me and her, between me and my children, between me and the baby.

VH: You seem to have felt most welcomed into the psychoanalytic movement by Willi Hoffer. As I read what you've written, he seems to be the one who said, "We'd like to have you. Come on in."

RE: I have to use another example. When we had to escape, Freud had left, I came to the institute and Hoffer said, "This is the last evening we meet."

VH: How much older than you was he?

RE: Oh, quite a bit. He must have been at that time 45 or 50—

VH: Oh, a lot older.

RE: I went to him for individual supervision. The group was over because the Institute was locked up. You know? I went to his place. Willi Hoffer calls me and says, "Ekstein, I want to see you; but it can only be 5 minutes. I want you to come," and then he named the place. It was sort of a long stretch where streetcars stopped. I should meet him on one corner. And I meet him, and he said, "Ekstein, listen. I will go"—I forgot now whether tonight or the next day—"to England, and I will do all I can to get you a visa to come to America or to England. I will write to you as soon as I have an address for your curriculum, for this, for that, et cetera, et cetera." We walked and he said, "We will just walk to one end; we don't want to have the police notice us here as if we were illegal workers." He knew I was still in the underground movement. Then we said goodbye. Of course, I had secretly hoped we would both talk for an hour or whatever. In this 5 minutes he said, "You will hear from me." All the anxiety was gone. I knew—and I did—those were relationships in Vienna between me and my friends, between a man like him and us. I heard, and that was, I don't know when that was, how early, shortly after the Freuds left, let's say April, in August I was in London. So what did I do? I called him up. He says, "Ekstein, come tomorrow to the seminar, the seminars continue." He had done a seminar for just refugees, from that old group of psychoanalytic pedagogues. The seminar topic, since all of us would go to America later, was how to adjust to America. He knew nothing special about America! But it was a preparation you cannot imagine, you know. If only I would remember the content of it.

VH: Was Willi Hoffer sort of an idealized father?

RE: No, no, he was different, you know. He was an absolutely reliable, older friend . . . I didn't think of him as a father figure. I even remember that he had a difficulty. He lisped a little bit. You know, he could not talk freely.

VH: Rudi, I don't know how to even get into this subject. As I was preparing to come today, I got very sad.

RE: Why?

VH: I tried to think what it was about. And as I see your tears, thinking about Hoffer, my thoughts were, as I thought about it last night, I can't bear the feeling of losing you and Grotjohn and all my wonderful teachers—

RE: But you get older.

VH: There's a great sadness—and a great love—but a great gratitude for how much I've been given. I assumed your tears were gratitude for how much he's given you or meant to your life somehow.

RE: You know, it's, of course, with all the people, it's also the following, you know. I mean what you have here; well, there are modern books in it obviously, psychiatric books filled with it. But it is a fantastic historic past; and as we get older, the question obviously is, how can that remain in the mind of new people?

VH: Yes.

RE: Students that we have. And you know that regardless of what you give them, they have to make a little bit something different out of it. They cannot help it. There is a famous work by Goethe, "What thou hast inherited from your fathers, acquire it, and make it thine and thee." But when it becomes "thine and thee," it changes. It changes. You know? The books have a completely different meaning. You maintain the inheritance, but then you sort it out. Particularly when you deal with people who are constantly on the move.

I don't know whether I mentioned the last time I met with Fritz Redlich and Bruno Bettelheim. . . . What we did with that hour or two that we were sitting together, each was telling the others how often and how and when and why he moved. And I thought we should have had the life of three people, analysts who accomplished something in their life, and see what brought them together—we came all from the same city. What pulled us apart, when we have to go to all kinds of different places, what brought us together again, and what will again pull us apart.

Fritz Redlich is a professor and also an analyst in one of the societies. He's still living. Each of us never thought he would move. Vienna forever. It would have never occurred to me to go to any other place, unlike in Germany, where many German students always were brought up that they would study elsewhere. I am at the Viennese University—I don't have to go to Berlin or to Harvard, or whatever it was; that was enough. And there, in the same district, I would remain; and my fantasy was, if I get organized and I will earn more money, I will see to it that the two-room apartment will be enlarged. I will buy the neighbor's apartment, and I will have four rooms. I will not move out of the house in which I could work. And with Freud, you know, the same. That was not the first home that he had in Vienna. He had another home, a very famous place, a building that was restored after the Ring Theatre burnt down, and then they built new housing there; and Freud lived in that place. It was even known that when he had a child born, since this was the first birth of a child in the new-built house where once there was a theatre, the Emperor sent him congratulations.

VH: Did you have any relationship with him at all?

RE: With Freud? From a distance and through the books.

VH: But nothing personal? Weren't there parties, or Institute parties, where he would have been, and Anna Freud would have been, and you would have been?

RE: No, that is a different life in Vienna. In the analytical group, isn't it? What you had was the seminar.

VH: That was it.

RE: Not a party.

VH: Not ever?

RE: We had a seminar. What you would do sometimes in Vienna, you know, let's say, I would go with Willi Hoffer, or with any of the others who were part of that seminar to a coffee house.

VH: Who were the others that were in that seminar?

RE: I do remember a few. There's one man, Heutwich, who's still in Vienna who's alive; but the man's a little older than I. There was Huschi Plank, for example, who died in the meantime. She went back to Vienna. Famous kindergarten teacher—very creative person. There was Edith

Buxbaum who sometimes came to that group and taught there. Her husband came to that group. There is a man by the name of Wyatt, who is back in Germany now; Fritz Wyatt, a very creative person, an analyst, and he went back to Germany. And we still have contact. We write to each other. We send things that we wrote to each other. It's sort of like veterans, fortunately not from a war, or of foreign wars, but of the psychoanalytic movement. A group of people who want better education, who want better therapy, who want a more humane society. They continue. I have friends, even—I still have contact with a lady whose brother died a number of years ago, Arthur Weiss, in Israel. We studied philosophy together, and we studied psychoanalysis together. We went to the same places where you could find knowledge.

VH: Let me tell you some more of what I remember of your seminars. I was thinking about that yesterday, and it also made me tearful. Before I came to Reiss–Davis Child Study Center, I had already, as a social worker, risen to be the nonmedical director of a major psychiatric outpatient clinic. When I got to Reiss–Davis though, I hadn't the foggiest idea how to use a chess game to interpret—I mean, I'm amazed that I could have gone as far as I had and known as little as I knew. I could remember the experience of feeling as if every day were like a Wonderland. Well, you can use chess this way. This fairy tale you can use this way. This snake the child has brought to the office you can use this way. It was the most amazing gift daily to me, all these symbolic interpretations.

RE: You know, I, of course, don't know for sure that it's all the psychiatric institutes that teach that to you. When I was a little boy, I simply learned chess, isn't it?

VH: But you didn't learn about the powerful queen and the impotent father and the little pawn child—

RE: No, no. But I did, for example, the following. I got once for Christmas marionettes. I had a marionette theater. And I would be thinking myself into the marionette theater and in that place, out of my mind. I let the marionettes come on the stage; I gave each of them a language, long before I ever heard the word psychoanalysis. I had always a rich and open fantasy life. Whether this idea is to look at a picture and to imagine what came before and what came afterwards. For that I didn't need the Freudians. You know, each of us brings something, if he's lucky, artistic into it. It's given to him.

VH: Something else you gave me that was wonderful, which was like a new thought to me at that time. It seems amazing now that I could have been that old, and it was still a *new* thought. But I remember I had a child who brought a snake to the session, and I could remember in the seminar your saying, "But, of course, he wants you to know how scared he feels, and what it feels like not to know what something's going to do. It's a totally new thing to you that makes you uneasy." That he was trying to let me know how he felt, by doing it to me. It was almost a new idea to me.

RE: Very early, I allowed myself something that very few people allow themselves; namely, to ask myself as what does this behavior mean? I had a kind of inquisitive curiosity.

VH: That was a gift to me. Because I was struggling with should I let him do it, or should I not let him do it? My primary preoccupation was, should I let him bring the snake, or, should I not? You changed it like magic for me. "It doesn't matter, Virginia. It matters what you think it means this child brings this for you." Thank you for the interview and all you have taught me.

Case Discussion

Dr. Ekstein is very interested in the patient's opening gambit of wishing to die if she cannot be helped and her constant fear of being killed or dropped. He agrees with Roselyn that she must liberate herself from her poisonous mother. He states that Roselyn was traumatized by her mother's attempt at suicide. He noted that Roselyn wishes her analyst to give her a reason to live and to help her to feel safe.

This case discussion was held March 3, 1992, in Los Angeles. Ekstein began by describing Roselyn's contradictory motives for treatment as found in my opening words: "She comes for treatment because of her wish to die." He went on, "She says at the same time, 'I don't come to you to help me die. Because I realize there's something wrong with my wish. I want to fight that wish. I want you to be opposed to it.' She couldn't think of a reason to continue her life and so she says to you, 'Give me a reason to live.' Now, we know from then on what we have here is a fascinating beginning where somebody comes to get rid of a symptom and must now fight with you forever, as long as the treatment lasts, to do everything to defeat your attempt to help her to live. She will do whatever she can—isn't it so?—in order to win the battle. It's a strange mixture. She opens up to say, 'I want to fight you on uncommon ground. I want our relationship to be the basis of this struggle.' I know she would say, 'But I don't want to lose. I must win, and the way I win, I die. Try to prevent it.' If you just take those first three lines as an *opening gambit*, you could make a fairly good prediction of what would come. And of course it came. I couldn't keep reading the rest because then I would know what happened. The gambit is set up. You know, it's sort of like a chess game.

"I remember a patient that I once discussed, if you recall, who wants to play chess with me. With Roselyn, the way she plays, the goal is to die, to lose at the game. Normally your goal is to defeat the other's king, to make the king die, to win the battle. But she says, 'Now I want to play chess with you so that I force you to win the chess game. I must lose and you will live.' It is almost as if she turned it around. What can one do with a patient who announces that the goal of treatment is to die? In the transference she says, 'I trust you to understand that my suffering is incurable. There's no reason to continue my life.' So she says, 'Give me a reason.' And you have instantly a fascinating situation, a situation that is—can I give her a reason? If I can, I also know she must fight the reason because in some way all patients do that."

Ekstein continued, "We have learned that our job is to restore the psyche. This patient opens in a way that we could compare to a chess game. The first move is such an uncanny move. It's right away, before the process starts: Checkmate!—'help me die.' I want to play chess with you; kill the king right away. Instead of wanting to play, this patient says, 'No, I want to lose right away before we even bring the board over, before we bring the couch right in,' and what fascinated me so much is the opening gambit. You see, the opening gambit, the beginning of all therapy, tells us what must come. One could almost predict from the very beginning what it will be, what transference will be developed, and how she will bring you from one emergency into another."

I wondered if most patients with this kind of early, "black hole depression" always used the threat of death as their opening gambit. Ekstein said, "The question is whether or not such a patient can come to be involved in the treatment." He felt she would come day after day trying always to turn me into a frustrating mother, making the treatment a desperate family situation. He felt very few patients he had seen in his life were this desperate. He felt I must have wondered whether I wanted to treat such a patient. He speculated that in the beginning my feeling was likely to be, "I don't need her. But what can I do so she needs me? What can I do? She says she needs me."

I mentioned I had wondered at times if hospitalization was indicated. Ekstein spoke of the serious danger of interfering in the possibility of help. "Roselyn might decide you can't be trusted because you stuck her into the hospital. She wants freedom—freedom from pain. Psychodynamically, she is trying to show her mother how she wants to die," he said, "and would see hospitalization as pushing her away. She says, 'You can go to my funeral, my memorial.' " He mentioned that he had once written a paper that compared the way people end their therapy with the way they begin. Some may begin holding on desperately, some with hero worship, some go on forever because they can't let go. Some cases fail, and you wonder about the beginning. Did you fail, was it chance, or characteristic of the process?

He went on, "Some material is developed in the first hour and then over and over in subsequent hours. So sometimes people think, 'How boring.' You know, over and over and over. You know you can't predict what will come, and nevertheless something changes. Roselyn's memory is that when she was 2, instead of being the greatest treasure to her mother, her mother tries to kill herself to get rid of her, and from then on she, over and over, she says to mother, 'I will kill myself to get rid of *you.*' It is such a beautiful act of revenge. 'Look at what my mother wanted to do to me when I was 2. And now I am 45 and am still working on it. Now I'm going to get rid of the therapist by telling the therapist if she continues to be a mother figure who thinks she can cure me, I will only allow her to come to my funeral or come to see me as an untreatable case.' You, the therapist, will never get rid of the guilt that mother should have felt. You will wonder, 'What did I do, as her mother, that made my own baby want to kill herself.' "

Ekstein went on, "Now I found another very interesting thing; she creates, as psychotic people often do and as also most of us do, a private world—you know, such as instead of the mother, the teddy bear. Instead of the teddy bear, she creates little people that appear in her dream or in her fantasy that work something out with her. She pushes the world away, and she has sort of an autistic streak but strangely enough, an autistic streak that has people in it. This was normal enough." Ekstein pointed to the many figures and statues in the room we occupied. He reminded me that he, too, had created a private world, and I would not know whether his mind was here or at the Viennese Parliament or with Mozart at the Viennese Opera. In a way, we all have little people in our minds whom we talk to—our conversation with memories.

He continued, "But the psychotherapy with a psychotic involves the attempt to take her style of life away from her, because the schizophrenic or the autistic creates an exile for herself. She wants to stay in exile, and we want to chase her out of it. How long shall one permit a person to stay in there? I do not try to coax them out. Rather, I do it the other way around. I say, 'Don't come into my world; let me come into your world.' And obviously she does this to you. She presses you to suddenly come to the hospital or else, suddenly surrender her to the doctors who are scared and feel that she has to be hospitalized. Whatever the reason for the hospitalization [he pointed out], the therapeutic focus should be the way she used it. She felt they were going to kill her. Of course, that was her wish. She did the same to you saying, 'Kill me'—isn't it so?—even though she also says, 'I want to kill myself. Can you help me?' So she is saying, 'I'm ill, can you cure me? The best cure for me is: Kill me. You bastard, you want to kill me. I want to die, and I want to live.' "

I pointed out that she was terrified to sleep and of her nightmares. She is afraid she will die if she loses alertness and becomes unconscious.

He replied, "She cannot go and fall asleep because she may not wake up, or she will be killed. Constantly she has a fantasy of a danger that will destroy her, and at the same time, she wishes to end it all. So, you want to say to her, 'Before we end it all, let's begin.' But then if somebody puts the end of life in the beginning and says at the beginning, 'I do not want to be born,' you are in for a struggle. A famous philosopher thought this way: 'The best is not to be born into this world, and the next best is to die as quickly as possible.' If you want the philosophy of pessimists, this is it. 'Why should I be born to this mother? I don't want to give her this joy, and if I have to be born, let me die as quickly as possible.' She arouses in you the wish to prove to her that you are a valuable mother. You are supposed to say that, unlike her mother who could not live with her, you cannot live *without* her. She wants you to tell her, 'Don't do this to me. If you run away, if you die, I will kill myself.' That is the overture to the opera. So what does one do with that?"

Ekstein pointed out that Roselyn and I both often speak about containing, being contained. "What does it mean to her to be contained?" he asked.

I responded, "I really mean holding and caring and protecting. I want to help her feel she can trust, feel that she can be protected, feel that we can create a world that's safe where she's free to grow and can feel that whatever she needs to feel or think is allowed without being attacked and that it's safe for her."

Ekstein said, "I understand, you see, because you speak about your holding action—isn't it? 'I am held, I am safe,' but with that kind of a mother she had, she wonders if you will hold her or drop her. If I go to a doctor, she will say, 'Will he do surgery on me, or will he kill me?' In other words, for her, holding is danger. I remember in Vienna there were beds, like you do with a baby, you have sides on it, you know, so the person cannot get out, or you tie the person to the bed or to the bedposts. It is a way of saying, 'I want you to be safe,' but it also means 'I won't let you go.' " Ekstein went on, "She sees you, in containing her, as saying, 'I don't trust you.' So then she says, 'But I will go; I want to go away because when you hold me I cannot trust *you*.' Then she sees you as saying, 'If I let you go, you will commit suicide. We will put you into the hospital, we will put you into the room, we will put you into a strait jacket, so that you will be safe.' So she maintains an eternal struggle with the hospital personnel and with her psychotherapist."

Ekstein summarized: "Her inner world says, 'I want safe holding, but the moment I am held, it will be exactly the same as with Mother. A suiciding mother would hold me in her dying arms and take me with her; a living mother, a joyful mother, takes me with her to go to the store to buy toys for me.' So in the transference, regardless of what you do for her, your embrace is like choking."

I said, "Or cutting or dropping."

He agreed, "Sure, either she will fall, or she will be cut, or she will choke." Ekstein went on, "It is as if she said, 'Come in now to give me an embrace, and I know I will die in the embrace.' Very often, even in more normal people, we have responses like that. I want to be in her arms, protected, never let go. I also need to be independent. I want to be held as long as I want to be held. But she wants to hold me as long as she wants to hold me and you have here, now, the internal struggle between her and her mother. A suiciding mother says to a young child, 'I love you, you will come with me to heaven.' We all often think this way. When we lose someone in death, we say, 'Maybe some day in Heaven I will meet you again. I will go with you; I cannot be without you.' From the very beginning now we have a strange kind of holding action. It is the holding action or the yearning for death and the fear of death. Now all this is transferred to you, and she, an educated woman says, 'I want to die.' "

I said, "You've just given me another interpretation for something that went on with us. It doesn't go on any more, but for many years when I would go away, she would bring me this little bear, and the little bear was no bigger than this. The tiniest little bear you ever saw. Later, whenever I was going to China or Africa, the bear would be appropriately dressed for the trip and in a tiny little bag like a jeweler would put a ring in, and she would ask if I would take this bear. There was always the worry that I might get killed. I think your interpretation would be, 'The baby will go with me, symbolically, to death.' I thought I was keeping the bear safe. I thought I was promising to come back and keeping her safe."

I mentioned Roselyn's use of symbolic enactments, such as the bear that we passed between us during separations. Ekstein responded, "The baby is hers and at the same time it is the baby she wants, her expressed wish for motherhood." He shared a similar experience: "I remember a schizophrenic woman I treated. I was about to go for a week's winter vacation. At the end when she had to leave, she said, 'I don't know who I am. I don't know who I am.' And I realized the interruption for her was a threat of losing herself. She cannot be without me. She cannot be contained without the therapeutic situation. And the way I recall, I suddenly had an impulse. At that time, I had all kinds of figures standing around as I have here, and there was one, a little figure that I had. I forget now what it was, a boy or whatever, and I took it off the table and said to her, 'You know, his name is "Little Rudi." While I'm away, will you take him home and feed him and be good to him so that until I come back I won't have to worry about him? He'll be all right.' " He went on, "She took the Little Rudi, put him in her pocketbook. A week later when she came back, she said, 'Every night I held him to my breast and I fed him. Can I keep him?' 'Yes, you can keep him. I, also, don't want to die.' " He went on, "I turned it around: 'Instead of me holding you, you hold *me* now, and you think,' and the relationship became now an active holding action where she did not need to believe that I would drop her. She held me now, the little boy in her hands, her arms, and she told me without embarrassment that she kept Little Rudi at her breast. It was an embarrassment to me because I thought I was beyond breast feeding."

Ekstein returned to Roselyn: "She wants to have a piece of you. All of us have pieces of other people. To internalize you, she really needs a piece of you, a little bitsy piece of you, whatever it is. We all do that; we keep pictures, we keep things from people who died, in order to maintain relationships. In other words, to try to restore equilibrium that we have in our own mind we say, 'You give me your teddy bear, and I'll give you my teddy bear, so that whenever we're separated, each of us will have a piece of the other.' "

Ekstein went on to say that many of us want visual connection with the past—pictures, and so forth. I asked what he did if a patient brought a camera and asked to take a picture. He replied, "I have occasionally had that happen. I don't encourage it. I just let it happen. I knew, for example, that one of Freud's patients took a picture of him at the end of his analysis. I have a copy of that picture, so obviously it has happened. Those sort of things don't go into textbooks, and they don't need to be in textbooks because they're beyond the ordinary 'legislative' program that you have, how you analyze, how you receive, how you do this or that, how your office should be furnished, and so forth." He went on to say, "Some patients get coffee from the secretary; some don't. Some drink it in the waiting room, some bring the cup to the couch." He felt many people would take exception to allowing this, but we have to live with it.

Ekstein continued, "What is so interesting about the case is the enormity of the picture of traumatization, past and present. It isn't just one particular repressed trauma from the past because she has never quite moved away from the parents, so to speak, psychologically." He talked about her dream. "She brings a dream of a maze, a garden, beautiful and strange. She thinks of Hawthorne's garden. She now begins associating to the dream as she sees it—this way: The daughter moved into the house, and she and the medical student fell in love, and there is an attempt now to get away from the mother figure and to fall in love. The daughter, however, is being poisoned. She is afraid to be poisoned, but wishes to be poisoned—because the beginning of the case was 'Poison me; make me die.' And she cries and cries. And she says now, 'They poisoned me so that I cannot make the last step of liberation. I could now live and liberate myself. I could go to the student who falls in love with me, and it would be the happy outcome of a fairy tale.' Sleeping Beauty was pricked with a poisoned needle; then the prince comes, and he will kiss her, awaken her. Then she says, 'But I will alienate everybody; they let me alienate them.' That was her thought of her mother—poison, and the poison was 'I must die. I will die, and so I make everybody else die,' and she wants to disappear. 'When I hurt myself, I hurt my mother,' and the suicide idea is meant not only to end life but to hurt the mother—revenge. It's almost as if this dream is a summary of the analysis."

He continued onto her association about the selling of puppies for food. "The Americans cannot end the fate of the puppies because they will continue to eat puppies, to make more puppies, and so on. And again we come to Mother because Roselyn felt like a puppy who was meant just to be eaten up by the devouring mother. It's sort of interesting that the whole hour is literally one dream but doesn't even get around to analyzing it because she, in her own way, goes through the whole thing, to sum it up. At the door, she will disappear, and then she thinks of Solomon. Should the one baby be killed, or will the baby be cut in half? And does the baby belong to one woman or to another woman?—and so she sees herself with her parents. Then she thinks of little people, maybe those little people in her mind, that she has created. But they help her to go to the other little world. If she keeps them, she remains psychotic. So she says, 'I am here with a conflict: whether I want to improve and get well, or whether I want to remain ill forever. Shall I keep myself contained in the door, or should I try to get out of it and permit those little people a way out?' And that's where she ends."

Ekstein indicated what he would have said about such an hour. "What you say then, directly, is, 'I'm willing to take in all that you tell me.' Your task is to know what to do with the contents in the container. Her mind is like a marvelous museum. You cannot really digest it. She must permit you to be guided by her through the museum and explain piece by piece what it's all about. What does that mean to you? And I think, if you come to that point, then she is ready, not only to pour out free associations but to permit the other person to reflect them. Before this, she looked at her thoughts much more sort of like garbage, and one wants to get rid of the garbage. Now she can look at them as terribly valuable."

He went on, "She has no order yet. If she can order it and bring it into a new kind of order, then she can do something with that museum. She may say, 'Let's see, I have collected too much of that. Why did I put so much emphasis on that part and I completely forgot . . . ?' You have to become a container and the time has come to look into the container and to sort it. You know, it's sort of a little bit like you put things in a drawer that you just don't know what to do with yet, and after a while, it gets fuller and fuller. She has to bring it into order."

I said, "She's beginning to do that more and more. There's more and more separation. It's not separate, but there is more and more separation between herself and her mother. There's less feeling that she deserves to die."

Ekstein responded, "Eventually we all die anyway some day, you know. When I lost my father, I could not look at photographs of him because they got me upset; I started to cry and to cry. And a few years later, I put the pictures there, tearfully. And now I look at them and become sentimental. But it's a big loss, so for some things we need time before we can unpack them again and get them out there. So she has now a drawer full of tales. And some day she'll allow herself to be opening the container, you being the container, and slowly take out one piece after the other. Occasionally the turmoil will come back; she knows it and she will say, 'I don't want to look at it; I cannot look at it.' What she brings to you now is an autobiography—primary process. What she may bring to you some other time is the biography from the secondary process."

I said, "What has been so hard for me to understand or maybe to believe is that she functions so well in the real world."

Ekstein continued, "The secondary process functions. It's true for all of us. She's not that different. I fell asleep here, and I had a dream on the day when Kuwait was invaded; and I dreamed that I hear a Viennese voice, the woman who brought me up. She says, 'Rudi, Rudi, help me. I cannot help myself. I'm in Kuwait; get me out of here.' That one dream summarized all of life. Namely, I had to run out of Kuwait, in my time, except it was Vienna. And I saved whom I could. She was a Catholic woman. She stayed there. She thought she had family there. She would not leave, but she wanted to leave; and I failed to bring her to America. It never came to pass, and so what it sums up is that when you are happy enough to save yourself, no you don't drown in the flood, in the ocean, you come then to a point; there may be the one you can save, and the others drown; and you live forever, then, with the idea that you could not help. And from time to time, something like this happens in the world, you see, just like it was 50 years ago. That, of course, will happen over and over again to this woman as it happens to every one of us. You fall into this helpless feeling: I couldn't, I didn't, why didn't I? I was not strong enough. And so from time to time the chaos will come back. 'How come I couldn't cure my mother?' she could ask. 'Am I responsible that she wanted to commit suicide? Am I responsible for what happened between Father and Mother?' Already there is strong improvement, and yet some of the improvement is so strong that it doesn't touch the ordinary external function so that many people will not have the slightest idea what goes on on that couch."

I asked, "Is there something I'm missing, some interpretation? Is there anything I'm doing to impede her getting well faster? Is there anything I could do to encourage—I don't know."

He replied, "I think that the first remark I want to make is, why should it go faster? It is almost as if you feel a little guilty if it doesn't go faster."

I responded, "Well, 10 years is a long time. You see people present cases where they say that in 9 months they cured this borderline person perfectly. I've never been able to."

Ekstein agreed, "I think that in the therapeutic world that exists today, there are psychiatrists or psychologists or psychoanalysts who believe that they have to market it this way because patients also demand this. They are too fast. I will put it this way: You cannot cure a borderline in 9 months, even if you are Freud. You cannot. But you can bring about vast improvement, maybe enough for this person."

Robert Wallerstein

Dr. Wallerstein is celebrated for the energy he has dedicated to the psychoanalytic movement. He has written a great deal regarding research in psychoanalysis. He is a master synthesizer.

This interview took place September 6, 1991, in Dr. Wallerstein's waterfront office and September 7, 1991, in his lovely, art-filled home on a cliff overlooking San Francisco Bay. When I interviewed him, Dr. Wallerstein, at the age of 70, was a vigorous and spirited man. His home, his office, and his conversation tastefully reflect the world travels he has made on behalf of the International Psycho-Analytical Association

(IPA), his contributions to psychoanalytic research, his efforts on behalf of nonmedical analysts in America, and his commitment to maintenance of a common ground in world psychoanalysis. His skill at achieving political harmony was evident even during our interview. He deftly took charge whenever he felt my direction might take us into less diplomatic waters.

Dr. Wallerstein has published many papers and made presentations to psychoanalysts all over the world. Popular among his books are *Hospital Treatment of Alcoholism: A Comparative, Experimental Study* (1957), *Psychotherapy and Psychoanalysis: Theory—Practice—Research* (1975), and *Forty-Two Lives in Treatment: A Study of Psychoanalysis and Psychotherapy* (1986a).

Interview

VIRGINIA HUNTER: When did you first become interested in the mind?

ROBERT WALLERSTEIN: I guess it goes back to pre-World War II days. I was born in Germany in 1921, but I came to the United States as a 2-year-old in 1923. This was 10 years before Hitler came to power. My father was a physician in Berlin; and like a lot of other people, he was wiped out by the inflation after World War I. When I was 1, my father, having responded to an ad, took a job in New York City. He sent for my mother and me when I was 2. By the time I got to Columbia College in 1937, I was pretty clear that I was a premedical student and was going to be a physician, maybe an internist like my father or maybe something of a more glamorous kind, like becoming an expert in tropical medicine. I was going to wipe out malaria in India or a place like that. Books like Paul De Kruif's *Microbe Hunters* or Sinclair Lewis's *Arrowsmith* gave me the idea.

VH: A romantic sort of notion.

RW: It was a very romantic notion. I was a freshman in Columbia Medical School when Pearl Harbor was bombed. They were afraid that medical students would drop out of school and enlist, and a couple did the first few days after Pearl Harbor. That frightened the government because they wanted to maintain their supply of doctors. So they put us all into uniform and assigned us to complete our work in medical school.

VH: Right where you were?

RW: Right where we were, and there was a certain amount of military things that went with it. You wore your uniform and drilled and things like that, but basically you were attending school. The commitment began when you graduated. After your 9-month internship, then you would go into the Army Medical Corps where they needed you. They speeded up medical school because it had been four 9-month years traditionally. They strung the four 9-month years together so you got out in 3 years.

When I got out of medical school, I had my internship and actually a 9-month residency and then got picked up by the Army. I was assigned to a general hospital in Ft. Lewis up in the Seattle/Tacoma area. It had 100,000 troops and was a major staging area for the Pacific. I was really an internist. I had an infectious disease ward, and I ran an electrocardiography lab. In the midst of that, while there, I got married in New York. I had a 2-week leave and brought my wife back there.

VH: How long had you known her?

RW: Five or 6 years, but that's another story. When I got out of the Army, I headed back to New York to complete my medical training. At that time, I had vague ideas about the glories of research and did not want, especially, to go into practice, so I applied for a fellowship through the newly established National Institutes of Health, in physical chemistry. I was going to be in a very famous place, the blood fractionation laboratory at Harvard Medical School. This was the laboratory run by Cohen. During the war, he had done the major work on breaking blood products down into the various fractions to be used in battlefield circumstances. They were doing a lot of fundamental research about blood and blood constituents. The National Institutes of Health fellowships had just been created right after the War in 1946, or 1947. I successfully applied in 1948. I was all set to go to Boston and to Harvard and to work as a fellow in this laboratory, and I decided I didn't like that. I decided to go into psychiatry. My wife was a social worker and was working in a treatment center for teenage delinquents and promiscuous girls. It was called Dosoris. The psychoanalytic consultant was a lovely lady, Viola Bernard, who was one of the best-known analysts in the country at the time. Aileen Burton was Director. Those were my wife's interests. They hadn't been mine.

Internal medicine, the way I saw it at Columbia College of Physicians and Surgeons and at Mount Sinai Hospital, you really were at the cutting edge of all the important things that were medical advances. Then when you went into practice, afterwards, you'd be treating people for all kinds of often trivial illnesses, and you very rapidly were out of the academic mainstream. I felt it was hard to combine these; but if you went into psychiatry, then it was easier to combine the clinical career and the research career. I believed Freud's dictum that the road to cure and the road to understanding are the same.

My father couldn't understand psychiatry. Anyway, I had one friend,

David Rubinfine, who had been with me in internship several years earlier, who was at the Menninger Foundation. He's dead now, but he was a gifted, brilliant man. I wrote to Dave and I said, "Help, I'm thinking about going into psychiatry. How is it out there?" He said, "It's great. Topeka's the best place in the country." I said, "That's fine," and I applied. By the time I got to Menninger's, which was July, 1949, David had already left. He was back in New York. But Ekstein was certainly there and was one of the key figures and, in fact, was my wife's chief teacher. They wrote a whole bunch of articles together. I became a resident, and Ekstein was one of the people I got to know quickly. In fact, it was right after my residency when I got on the staff there, which was in 1951 that we started the supervision seminar out of which our joint book came. He and I collaborated on our supervision project; in those days he and I worked closely together. So, anyway, I went to Topeka; but before we went, I had finished my medical residency at the end of December, 1948, and they accepted me in Topeka for July, 1949. There was a 6 month gap, so I went down to the psychiatric service that Mt. Sinai had and said, "Can you take me for a 6-month period as an extra resident?" and they did. So I had 6 months there.

We planned to be in Topeka for 1 inpatient year and then to return to New York and go into an analytic career. We went for 1 year; we stayed for 17, from 1949 to 1966. We never went back to New York except to visit. I did my whole residency in Topeka and was offered a very good job, applied for analytic training in 1951. I finished that in 1958. My first job was at the Veterans Administration Hospital there. While there, I was assigned to the alcohol ward. A bunch of us created an experimental research program testing various treatment approaches to alcoholism, one against another on a variety of patients that were there. And this became a book. It became a book that was one of the very first books Basic Books published. They were a new publishing firm. The book came out in the 1950s.

VH: What was the exact name of your book on alcoholism?

RW: *Hospital Treatment of Alcoholism* (1957), and I was the principal author and editor. It was the first book that I was involved with. The book I did with Ekstein was the second book. That alcohol project, even before the book was written up, caught the eye of some of the people in the research department at the Menninger Foundation, particularly, George Klein. He went to Gardner Murphy, who was Director of Research, and said to Gardner, "You're looking for a psychiatrist in your research department; there's the guy." And so Gardner Murphy asked me to come over to see him. I did, and he offered me a job at the Menninger Foundation, half of the time in the research department, half of the time doing clinical work. I was scared at becoming suddenly a psychiatric researcher. I was in my analysis then, in my analytic training. But I was going to be *the* psychiatrist in the Research Department, and I would be responsible for developing a clinical research program, which didn't really exist. Even in Rapaport's day, other than Merton Gill who worked with Rapaport, there were no psychiatrists involved in the research program at the Menninger Foundation, and they weren't doing any clinical research. Well, Gill was in hypnosis research then.

VH: But you had no training in research!

RW: That's right, but I had done this alcohol project. The alcohol project was well conceived. It'd be a digression to go into it now, but, anyway, it caught their interest, and so I quit the VA job with trepidation. I went over, I found when I got there that I had a title, Assistant Director of Research.

VH: Did you feel like an imposter?

RW: I felt awed. I was 33. Murphy was a man maybe 20 or 25 years older. We developed a very, very close relationship. He and I would meet together 1 or 2 hours every week, sometimes more. He'd go over all kinds of things, and he'd ask my advice about them, and off the top of my head I would say whatever came to my mind. Then I realized, suddenly, whatever I'd say he was acting on. He actually just went ahead and did all the things I suggested, which made me quickly realize I better not just speak off the top of my head because this guy takes me seriously. I developed a number of things; for instance, a program in psychosomatic research and we published a bunch of papers on it. The psychotherapy project at the Menninger Foundation was my creation, with a couple of other people whom I had pulled together, and it's been the big research program of my life, which I don't want to describe because it's all been written up—basically it was about 15 to 20 people working over a 10- to 15-year span with varying amounts of time, out of which about 70 papers and seven books were produced. My book *Forty-Two Lives in Treatment* (1986a), that's sort of the final clinical accounting and overall summary of a 30-year span for that project, which started in 1954. It studied patients whose treatments went back to 1952. I wrote up the book in 1981 or 1982, some 30 years later. There were very long-term follow-ups with a significant number of the patients. The book got published in 1986, and it's become quite a big thing.

VH: A wonderful thing. I'm curious now, back to your childhood if that's okay. Your father left your mother and you in Germany when you were 1.

RW: She had a little money, and she, I think, was working. She was a textile designer. She would design, hand paint the fabrics for drapes and things which she also did in America. I don't know if she started then, but she was also an artist.

VH: Did she do it at home?

RW: That I don't know.

VH: You seem to have a very curious, extraordinarily organized mind that somehow got what it needed in order to be able to speak clearly, to organize, to systematize, to relate one system to another very precisely. And yet it sounds as though you were a working mother's baby, your mother had a loss when you were a baby, and then there was a move.

RW: As I grew up I never looked back at that as a traumatic time. I had one dream in my analysis, a recurring dream, of being in the street and looking up at a facade of an apartment house and my mother in the window. The picture of that building, that was like no building that I knew, only I felt I would recognize it if I saw it, and I reconstructed it. Was that the memory of the apartment house in which I lived in Berlin between 1921 and 1923 up to the age of 2? I don't know. I didn't go back to Germany until 1985 when we had the Hamburg Congress. That was now some 62 years later that I went to Germany. I went over to Berlin. We had a colleague who guided us through East Berlin, and I found the street on which I had lived those first 2 years. I grew up knowing the name of that street. It's a rather short street about three or four blocks long with a rundown row of dilapidated apartment houses—just like the house in my dream. It's called Schumannstrasse, after the composer Robert Schumann. It's right near where the Berlin wall was. It intersected with a street where my father's hospital was, which was a few blocks from his medical school. I saw those places.

VH: What was your mother's story about what you were like from birth to age 1?

RW: I don't know her story. I didn't ask or she didn't tell me. I kept speaking German until I was about 3 or 4, and I taught German to other kids on the block.

VH: Were there any siblings?

RW: I had a brother born afterwards, in the United States.

VH: What happened to him?

RW: He's a very famous professor in sociology, today. He's in New York half the year and in Paris half the year. In his field, a world renowned figure.

VH: What do you think accounts for your special ability to organize?

RW: I was always an organized kid. In 1991, we went to my 50th college reunion of the Columbia College Class of 1941. It's the most remarkable college class that's ever come out of any college in this country, because it's the only one I know that's had a reunion every single year for 50 years. When I went to this reunion, and I hadn't been to one for the 50 years, I was startled by a number of things. First, the warmth and the recreation of old days, including—I knew most of them. It was rather a small class. One guy, a family practitioner, greeted me like his long-lost brother. He reminded me of all the time we had spent studying together at my house. It's something I'd forgotten about. In that sense I have always been the organized character wherever I've been. It goes back to high school.

I was kind of a troublemaker in elementary school. My mother came to school once because she was sent for, by the teacher, because I'd gotten a D in conduct. An A in work and a D in conduct and always making trouble, and my mother says, "Is he the worst one?" And the teacher says, "No, the one who sits next to him is the worst one. The two of them together are always up to a lot of mischief." So my mother says, "Why don't you separate them?" It hadn't occurred to the teacher to put me at one end of the room and him at the other end of the room.

VH: Do you remember feeling mischievous?

RW: I was bored by a lot of what was going on. At the end of that term, in the fifth grade, that teacher gave me a book that she inscribed. It was *The Last of the Mohicans*. The inscription was for my excellent scholarship or something, with her love and affection. In those days you could skip, and I was being skipped through school. I actually got out of high school at 15½, and my mother was smart to say, "You're too young to go to college." She sent me to live in Mexico City with her brother, a pediatrician, for a year. That was the Winter of 1936–1937. I learned some Spanish and got all caught up in the Spanish Civil War.

VH: You make it sound as though you didn't have any input in the decision.

RW: I didn't have a lot. I mean, put it another way, they talked me into not applying for college because they said I was too young. I was not only young, I was small. I graduated from a high school that was the largest high school in the world. It had 10,000 students, which is huge and had two graduations a year.

VH: Interesting.

RW: They lined them up in size places to march across the stage to get diplomas. I was the fourth smallest. That year in Mexico, I grew 6 or 7 inches. And suddenly I was just about my present height.

VH: How did that home compare to your New York home, emotionally and dynamically?

RW: That was a great time because I had a bachelor uncle who was sort of a romantic figure in Mexico City. He had a mistress who was from one of the leading conquistador families that had come over with Cortez.

VH: Did your mother know this?

RW: No, not especially. She just knew that her brother was an important pediatrician in Mexico City. I was an artist at the time also. I used to paint, and I took art lessons in Mexico.

VH: What were you painting?

RW: I started doing pastels and charcoal drawings, a little bit of still life, mainly figures.

VH: Do any of them still exist?

RW: There are some that still exist. One watercolor and one oil that I have actually on the wall at home. My mother wanted me to be an artist. She didn't have any ambition for me to go to medical school. I felt I wasn't a good enough artist. I wasn't good enough to make a career at that, but I did during the year in Mexico take lessons from the man, who was an old man at the time, who had been Diego Rivera's teacher.

VH: Did you meet Tamayo?

RW: Tamayo was a youngster who was unknown. The people I met in the 1930s, the people I met through my uncle's mistress, and she knew them all, were Orozco and Siqueiros, a whole generation older than people like Tamayo. I was a kid, and I was taken to meet them in their studios. Orozco was a very famous man; he had one arm. I never met Rivera but met several of his ex-wives. He had many before he got to be with Frida Kahlo. I would attend meetings of LEAR. LEAR was the League of Revolutionary Writers and Artists. They were all Communists. Rivera wasn't allowed to be there because he was a Trotskyite. I didn't understand all the Spanish; but there would be these long talks in Spanish, and almost every other word would be "Yanqui Imperialismo." And then pandemonium would break loose, they'd all applaud. That's when I started to smoke, in Mexico, which I hadn't dared to do at home. When I came back I was suddenly bigger and older and went to college and gave up the idea of being a painter.

VH: How would you characterize your mother?

RW: My mother was a remarkable woman. She was always a very lively, energetic woman. She lived until her mid-70s. She had, until the day she died, jet black hair, and it wasn't dyed. She lied about her age and got a job, in the last 10 years or so of her life, in a home for old folks. She was in charge of the occupational therapy program, in her 70s. They thought she was 10 or 15 years younger, and she carried that off. She tried to promote both me and my brothers into artistic careers, me as a painter, my brother as an actor; and he was a child actor. He appeared in plays, one play that had been on Broadway.

VH: Which one?

RW: Lillian Hellman's *Watch on the Rhine*. There was a kid with a big part in that.

VH: Somehow when you said your mother decided you would go to Mexico, you said it rather pointedly that it was her decision. Your father didn't seem to be there.

RW: She ran the house.

VH: That's the impression I had, that she had a lot of power and a lot of control.

RW: My father was a wonderful guy, but he was no businessman, and his medical practice was always something that was just keeping things together; but she was controlling the money, and those were Depression years. We lived through the worst of the Depression, when a lot of patients didn't pay, and in those days when they visited the doctor's office, the fee was 2 dollars. What we had that other families didn't have was a car. When I was a kid, even though it was hard times and all, I could sort of give the other kids the treat of a ride with our family on Sunday. We would go out for a drive out of New York City. So in that sense we had family status in the Bronx.

VH: What were those rides like?

RW: Oh, my mother and father would be sitting in the front and the rides were very monotonous, actually.

VH: It seems as though there was some sort of controlling and rigidness and maybe even a lack of emotional communication in the family.

RW: No, between them there was a distance, because they had different interests and values, and my mother was always upset with my father for not handling the business aspects of his medical practice well enough. From her point of view, the family wasn't well enough provided for, and she was always having to make sure there was money to pay the rent and things like that. And his interests were really in medicine and his friends from Germany, especially after Hitler came into power, and friends began to come over. There was constantly political talk.

VH: Not at the temple?

RW: No, he was not a religious man, but he was a very learned man. He was a Hebrew scholar, and he wanted me to learn Hebrew as a language; and he had a substantial library of Hebrew that he read.

VH: Was your mother interested in the Hebrew language also?

RW: No, her interests were really in the kids, and promoting me and my brother, and in her career as an artist. At first when I was growing up she was a textile designer, but then later on she began to paint, sculpt, and do ceramics and do different kinds of sculpture, with clay and casting it—but also doing wood sculpture and the kind of things that modern sculptors do. And she was a very creative person.

VH: Whose style?

RW: Her own.

VH: Do you have some of her things?

RW: Yes. She did sell some things. She never really got the recognition I felt her sculptures should have. She was a lot better than many people who have established names.

VH: When did she die?

RW: She died in the early 1970s, 1972 I think. She got a heat stroke in her apartment in New York in the middle of a heat wave in the summer, and her cardiovascular system wasn't that stable, and she didn't have air conditioning.

VH: You use the word promote. "My mother was promoting my brother and me." It's rather an unusual word to describe as a mothering thing.

RW: She was a promoter. My brother was very serious about an acting career, or she was very serious about that career for him as a child actor. She enrolled him in a special school in New York called Professional Children's School. Children who were going to be ballet stars or child actors went to that school; then they could be on the road with a show and send their homework in. When he went on the road, as he did for several years, she traveled with him. A 9-year-old, and she would be with him, and she worked out all the contracts, and to her great disappointment he grew into adolescence and broke away from that and wasn't going to go on with that career either.

VH: How do you think her need to promote you affected you psychologically? What were the good things and bad things about it?

RW: She had a lot of confidence in me. She was disappointed I didn't want to be a painter. She, unlike most Jewish mothers, was disaffected with medicine as a career. She didn't especially think it was so grand and glorious.

VH: It sounds as though you couldn't please either parent.

RW: I didn't do exactly what either parent wanted, and neither one really understood, well, what I finally did. But they were both always very proud.

VH: What effect do you feel your mother's disappointment in your father, which it sounds like he sort of accepted passively, had on you?

RW: He was kind of a passive guy in a lot of ways.

VH: How does it all fit together? In your analysis, what did you come up with?

RW: A lot of times one goes into analysis thinking one's going to find out, like what really went on in me, that made me shift from internal medicine into psychiatry or psychoanalysis. I'm not sure I ever found out anything special about that.

VH: Well, you must have wondered in some way, what would it take to make Mom happy? What would it take to make Robert successful?

RW: I didn't think in terms of what it would take to make Mother happy. I really always thought in terms of this is my life and what's going to make me happy. Where my mother and I had a difference of opinion I went my way, at least by the time I was in my college years.

VH: It doesn't sound like when you went to Mexico you had achieved that.

RW: No, I hadn't, then I was a kid. I felt I was a kid.

VH: Were there areas, besides that fifth grade, where you were rebellious?

RW: A lot through elementary school. When I went to high school, I was an assiduous student. I did extracurricular things. I used to play chess, and I was, for a while, on the track team; but basically I was a student, and I was going to get into a good college of my choice. When I was in that class of 1,000 people who were graduating, I wasn't the valedictorian. I had the third or fourth highest grade average in the high school. I planned to get into the medical school of my choice, and I wasn't going to have the problems everybody else had. When I came to apply, when people would be applying to 10 or 15 medical schools, my premed advisor said where do you want to go; and don't apply to more than three places.

VH: Who was your analyst?

RW: I had two. One ended up in Los Angeles, that's Robert Jokl. He died a long time ago. He was part of, not the first generation, but the second generation around Freud in Vienna. I went into analysis in 1951. He was already a man in his 60s.

VH: Did you pick him or was he assigned to you?

RW: In Topeka, you were assigned but told that if it doesn't work out between you, you can ask for another assignment; but you didn't go around looking. He was one I wanted, actually.

VH: Because?

RW: Because I had reasons for not wanting others, basically.

VH: What were those?

RW: Oh, you wouldn't know these men, but I thought Jan Frank, who was a charismatic figure, was just a crazy character, and I had gone through enough of his craziness. I didn't want to spend time talking about it. Rudi Ekstein was a close friend. Hellmuth Kaiser was caught up in his being a disciple of Wilheim Reich and "defense analysis," and I didn't like what I heard about what went on with his analysands. So I went to Jokl, who was an interesting man. He was a Viennese who had never really learned English that well, and I remember a friend of mine who was also in analysis with him came out one day, and he said, "Fifteen dollars an hour I pay him." That was the standard fee then. He says, "Fifteen dollars an hour I pay him, and I give him English lessons besides." And when I was with him, which was only for about a year, every once in a while he would say some things to me like, "At a time like this, in response to what you are saying, the professor would say to me . . . " and he gave me one of Freud's interpretations. The professor was Freud, he was Jokl's analyst, that made me a symbolic grandson. I, at times, felt that what he told me that the professor said to him wasn't really applicable to me.

Then he went to Los Angeles. I had the decision to make of—do I follow him there, as some of my friends were urging, and finish my analysis with him and transfer to the Los Angeles Institute or do I stay in Topeka and finish there. I went back and forth over that for a while and for lots of reasons, including the fact that we had a child then, my wife was going to be going into analysis, I had a good job, I had started the psychotherapy project; we chose to stay. And then I switched to a woman I don't know if you've heard of, Nellie Tibout, who was from Holland. She was in that first group in Holland around Jeanne Lampl, and her analyst had been a man named Karl Landauer who was one of the few analysts who got killed in a Nazi concentration camp. He was from Frankfurt, Germany, and he had fled Germany during Hitler's time and gone to Holland; but then when the Germans overran Holland, he was picked up. When I was in Frankfurt visiting in October 1990, I went to the Institute there, and there's a plaque they had just put up. To Karl Landauer who was one of the founding members of the psychoanalytic group there, and there had been a big, big fight over the plaque because the way the bronze plaque was first written it said his date of birth and death and it said born and then died. And there was a revolt in the place. They said, "He didn't die. He was murdered." They got it to say he was murdered. They sent it back and had it redone to say, born and then murdered. Anyway, that was her analyst. Nellie was a wonderful lady, and she lived out—her professional life—she worked in Holland during the war. She was not Jewish, and she was allowed.

VH: You went four times a week to both of them?

RW: Five. Topeka was always five.

VH: How long did you see her?

RW: About $4^1/_2$ years with her and a year with Jokl, $5^1/_2$ years altogether.

VH: Have you ever had any psychotherapy or analysis since then?

RW: No.

VH: Who were your supervisors?

RW: My first supervisor was a man named Otto Fleischmann, who was a Hungarian, who had survived during the War in the Swedish Legation in Budapest. My second supervisor was another Hollander, H. G. Van der Waals, who wrote one of the first and best articles on narcissism that nobody ever quotes anymore. It long predated Kohut's. But, anyway, he was from a very famous medical family in Holland with an uncle who had been a Nobel laureate. His life-long ambition to become the first analyst to be professor of psychiatry at a medical school in Holland had been dashed. He was denied that. In his bitterness, he came to Topeka. One of his students then became the first analyst to become a chairman of psychiatry. He was very close to the Van Gogh family. And then my third supervisor was Karl Menninger, who was, in many ways, a remarkable man. There have been two authentic geniuses I have worked with in my life, worked with closely, got to know well; and Karl Menninger was one.

VH: Who was the other?

RW: Erik Erikson. Karl was a remarkable man with all kinds of flaws.

VH: It sounds like he could be a real jerk to people.

RW: Well, he could be an awful man. I got to know Karl well when I was assistant director for research. I ultimately became director of research there after Gardner retired, and I had a very close working relationship with Karl. It started there when I was a resident, and he was the great figure, and I was one of the residents. Every resident, when he graduated, had to write a paper, and he was the one who was the reader of my paper. He called me in one day; he talked to me about my paper. He always had a barrel of apples there. And if he liked you, he'd give you an apple. And he gave me an apple. That was a good sign, and then he said, "I liked your paper." And that was a good sign.

VH: What was the paper about?

RW: What the paper was on was the treatment by sodium amytal and psychotherapy of a psychotic guy with a syphilitic brain. It was the first analytic paper I wrote. I was finishing the residency. He said, "I liked your paper." I said, "Thank you, sir." But he said, "But you know I do have to talk to you about your style." I said, "What about it?" He said, "You know, it's so Germanic. I mean these sentences. Look at them. Look at how complicated they are." And I said, "My sentence structure is pretty complex with lots of dependent clauses strung out." "Yeah, but you don't know how bad it really is. Let me read you something," and he flipped open the paper and read a sentence. And I looked at him; I was then about 30 years old. They called him Dr. Karl in those days, I did too. So I said, "Dr. Karl, you know what you say about my style, that's true. But that sentence I didn't write." He said, "What do you mean you didn't write it? It's right here in your paper." "Yeah, but that's a quote." "Yes, there are quotation marks. Let's see where you got that." And he sits back, and it's the one thing I had quoted from a book of his. That he had found!

VH: How did he react to that?

RW: He got embarrassed, and he flushed and he said, "Well, the point stands anyway." That was one of my first encounters with him.

VH: Were you scared of him?

RW: Not especially, no. I mean, I had all kinds of situations with him when I'd be at the VA Hospital and wanting to go over to the Menninger Foundation two miles across town. He'd be there in his car, and he'd see me standing there and say, "Come on in if you're going over, I'll give you a ride." I'd go for a ride, and he comes into the parking lot and he sees somebody's car. He had an old beat-up Ford, and he'd see somebody's shiny new Buick or something. He'd say, "Who has a car like that?" I'd say, "I don't know." He said, "Well, let's ram it." And so he just plows into it and dents the fender a little bit.

VH: That must be envy.

RW: He wouldn't call it envy. He'd say, he's having fun, and he's the boss, and he's letting everybody know he's the boss.

VH: Was he a narcissistic personality disorder?

RW: A narcissistic personality disorder? He didn't do that kind of thing often, but just a little bit. But when he supervised a case, he was also a very impatient man, and his attention span was not long. He recently died at 96, and he was bright as a bell.

VH: Lawrence Friedman had a field day with Menninger.

RW: I know that book. I looked up what they said about me in the book. Two-thirds of it is accurate, and one-third of it is just "off." But anyway, I knew he was an impatient man, and I had two possible control cases, I'd been given the charts on, to bring to him. I read them both, and one's an obsessional character. Both men, and the other one's kind of a hysterical character. And I picked the hysterical one. I just figured that if I brought the obsessional character case to him he'd lose patience with it. The guy would just be going on, obsessionally hour after hour, and Karl would have begun pressuring me to do things I wouldn't have wanted to do, and there would have been big fights coming. So I took the other case, and it all went very well. So he and I had a good relationship, and when I wanted to bring Kernberg to Menninger, he made it possible.

VH: You seem to have figured out pretty early in your career who was influencing what—how it might very dramatically effect a case, and how your patient was going to influence the supervisor.

RW: That didn't take a lot of figuring out. I knew Karl Menninger well by that time, and he's a man of tremendous breath of interests. Everything from the plight of the Indians, which he knew an awful lot about, the environmental movement, and the earthworms in Kansas and the history of Kansas, and prison reform which was another of his big things, and the way the society treats the elderly—all of that. He was getting impatient specifically with psychoanalytic psychiatry. His horizons kept getting broader and broader in the final decades because he lived so long. When I first met him in 1949, he was a 56-year-old man. He had a quickness of intelligence that could see to the heart of issues in a seemingly very naive way; that is, he could naively ask the penetrating question that sort of brought the whole house of cards tumbling down. It was Karl Menninger's great gift!

VH: How would you characterize the analysis you had?

RW: It was all classical ego psychology. There was nothing else. There was no other analysis. People knew that there were people called Kleinians, but they lived in England, and they were crazy; and Rapaport had a very famous comment which is possibly a footnote in his 1960 monograph saying, "The difference between us and the Kleinians is that we have an ego psychology and they have an id mythology."

Heinz Hartmann was the ideological dean of American psychoanalysis; and Rapaport was his chief systematizer. It was his job to systematize the theoretical structure being created by Hartmann and inherited from Freud and Anna Freud. Theoretically, you know, there are major differences between analysis as I understood it then, when everything was built around the structural model and instinct theory basically, and now.

I mean it was really a drive psychology we're talking about. That is, the vicissitudes of the instincts and the ways they're defended against and warded off and managed and coped with, in order to make an adaptation to reality. Instincts meant the sexual and aggressive impulses and how they were managed. That was the theory and from that flowed a particular technique. There was a meeting of the American Psychoanalytic Association about 15 years ago. We had a discussion group, at which Merton Gill, who has always played Peck's bad boy said—we were talking about all of the theoretical advances over the preceding 25 years, everything from Kohut's work, Kernberg's work, Mahler's work, and all, and everybody said they felt we had so much expanded theoretical understanding, and Gill said, "Well, can anybody here specify how his or her own work with patients is any different technically on the basis of all of this expanded theoretical perspective we all talk about?" People were very hard put to say that there was anything very different in what they were doing, and they were groping for it.

VH: Do you agree with that?

RW: To a much larger extent, yes, a lot. Not totally. Obviously, I think, for instance, to take Kohut, who was a good friend and with whom I had a special relationship. He was different. I was never one of his followers. But I'd known him for a long, long time.

VH: Did you go to his birthday party?

RW: No. I never lived in Chicago. One thing many people don't know about Kohut—he was probably, in many ways, after Rapaport, the country's best Freud scholar. In the days before I had the Concordance available and I wanted to find out where Freud said something, if I asked everybody else and no one knew, I could always write or call Kohut, and he would know, off the top of his head. He had Freud memorized from beginning to end and was that much of a classical scholar; but, anyway, Kohut always saw me as somebody who's not one of his people but somebody who was sympathetic to him personally and friendly to him and therefore would be a friendly critic.

VH: So you weren't one of the ones who no longer recognized him in the halls?

RW: No, we were friends. I think Kohut has made a major clinical contribution. I wrote a bunch of papers about my differences with self psychology (Wallerstein, 1969, 1970, 1975, 1976a, 1976b, 1977, 1978, 1980, 1980–81, 1981a, 1981b, 1983a, 1983b, 1983c, 1983d). Basically what I said can be summed up in, "I think he made major clinical contributions. I think he needn't have and shouldn't have gone off to develop a whole new theoretical structure and a separate kind of psychology to encompass this. The clinical contribution that I felt that he made was in the much closer attention than had been paid before and making much more explicit the whole concept of what he first called narcissistic transferences and then later selfobject transferences, and the characteristic countertransferences they evoke. The conception of the idealizing transferences and the mirroring transferences people had been intuitively aware of before. He gave it a substance and a name. He said these are important issues. They come up particularly with these narcissistic characters, but they come up with everybody as well, and we should pay more attention to them." And that, I think, was a major contribution, and in that sense that's something I'm aware of today that I wasn't aware of in the same way, 20 years ago.

If you asked me how I analyzed. How I was analyzed was in a very American classical analysis. Interpretations given by my analysts were in terms of this is your impulse, and this the defense against it, and this is the anxiety that it evokes.

VH: It sounds very hands off.

RW: Not really. I mean, it can be made into that. That depends on the analyst, and the empathic resonance with which they try to feel themselves into your psychological world.

VH: How did you feel your analysts' empathic resonance, both of them, how did they compare?

RW: Actually I felt, I was more distant from Jokl. He was more distant from me. There was a kind of austerity about him, whereas Nellie Tibout, I don't think she'd ever been married, she was very grandmotherly, you sensed that. And what you sensed also was her real interest in you, although I think that she had certain naive ways about the American scene. She came here as a woman in her 50s, and there were times when she and I just disagreed because I felt she didn't understand the way American politics, or society, was structured. On the other hand, I went haywire, too, because in 1956 I remember I was in analysis, and it was the Eisenhower–Stevenson campaign. And I had it all figured out that Stevenson could win, and I had her convinced on the basis of the way I had everything lined up for it to be narrow, but he was going to just make it. And I had her almost talked into believing it.

VH: It's interesting, I don't think I've ever heard anybody say I had my analyst almost convinced about political probability.

RW: Politics was important in my life. It was the vehicle of a lot of things, and there was a time, when I was a kid, I thought I was going to grow up to be a United States senator. I could never be president because I wasn't born in this country. I had a great hero and that was the famous Robert Wagner in New York, whose son has been the recent Mayor Wagner, Robert Wagner.

VH: You were going to be a doctor, a senator—

RW: No, I was going to be a politician. I didn't know how one got to be a politician, but I was going to be one. When I was a kid I used to go—as a 12-year-old I would stand on the street corner and listen to Norman Thomas give speeches. He was the perennial socialist candidate for president.

VH: It sounds almost as though you were—you know this is a wild interpretation. It sounds as though you were saying, "Mother, I really know how to run the world. Can't you see I know how to?"

RW: You can see it that way, sure. And actually she was in that sense like my mother. My father understood politics. My mother wasn't really interested in that world. She paid no attention to it, so I had to educate her too.

I've come, through my life in analysis, to know the analytic communities literally around the world. I've spoken in them everywhere from analytic societies in Japan, in Australia, in Israel, in half a dozen in Europe and half a dozen in Latin America, in Canada, in Mexico, and all over the United States and England; and I taught in a Kleinian Institute in Latin America for a week. And I've come to, I think, a real grasp of the varieties of psychoanalysis, seeing them through those people's eyes as I do, which is what sort of led me to pick the themes for my presidential addresses in the International.

VH: You've been very successful in politics.

RW: I think I did have a political career, but it was in analysis.

VH: How do you feel about the psychologists winning the suit?

RW: Well, psychologists didn't *win* the suit.

VH: How would you put it?

RW: The suit was settled in the interests of analysis, and I was very central to that because I was one of the people siding for settlement in the lawsuit. That suit came up just before I became President of the International, and it went on over the first 2½ years of my presidency; and I was the central figure in working out the final settlement that came.

VH: So you felt good about it?

RW: I felt good about it. I have had a very special career in psychoanalysis; and it's a two-fold career. I've always been in the establishment. When I started in Topeka, when I became a training analyst. I became a member of the American in 1960. As I was becoming a member, I was invited to come on to one of the committees of the American; and I started on a committee which I became chairman of within a year or two.

VH: Which committee?

RW: It was then called the Committee on Training for Research. It happened to be the committee through which the waivers for all nonmedical training were being processed, and I was the guy sitting on that pipeline and shepherding those waivers through, for nonmedical people who were going to get analytic training under what was then a small, but very significant, exception to the general rule that only medical people—

VH: Those are the ones who still had to sign saying they weren't going to be primarily clinicians?

RW: They didn't have to sign.

VH: In L.A. they had to sign.

RW: In some institutes, yes. That was never required for the American. The American just said that there was an understanding that people who were going to be trained analytically in that program were being trained for the purpose of better serving their scholarly, academic, and research careers and that they would commit themselves to maintaining their scholarly work and do only so much psychoanalysis as was consistent with their scholarly pursuit, and they would monitor that themselves. The American never said you've got to sign this thing. Different institutes did.

VH: But there was clearly from that phraseology an implication that you were not to be a clinical—

RW: You were not to go into full-time practice. That was the way it was set up. That was understood from the start. I know this history very well; I've been planning to write a book on it, about the original way in which the Thirty-Eight Rule was set up, the famous Thirty-Eight Agreement, which took a year short of 50 years to be reversed. The first opening in that was the creation of this Committee on Training for Research. It was created in 1957 or 1958. It had met once or twice when I joined the committee in 1960, so I was in on the very origin of it. Within 2 years I was chairing that committee and guiding the whole process through which these people were getting trained. I was always central in the establishment, the American. I became president when I was 49. I wasn't the first but one of the first who was not from New York. Up until then New York, which was the largest, had sort of a hammerlock on the presidency. Before me, Roy Astley of Pittsburgh had been president. I became president in 1971, and ever since then I've been centrally in the establishment there. I was the champion of the nonmedical training issue. That was always identified with me.

VH: I'm not going to those meetings until I can go to the clinical meetings. You've done such wonderful research.

RW: The research is what made my scientific reputation. I always got my way, in that, what I wanted to go after, I got. It would take 2 or 3 hours to tell the whole story of the lawsuit, how it came about. The fact was that a number of us knew that it was coming before it came. We warned the then officers of the American about it. Anyway, it happened; and when I became president of the International, basically the lawsuit was by psychologists, on behalf of a class, a class-action suit, on behalf of several thousand.

VH: Well, we all contributed.

RW: It was an anti-trust action. They said that here is a way of earning a livelihood that you people are monopolizing and depriving us of. That was the charge. The defense of the American was that the economic issues aren't the real issues, it's a matter of a professional organization setting its standards, and all professional academic, scientific bodies do so. The American was sued as the primary defendant. The International was sued secondarily; as you allow your component organization to do these bad things. And then for some reason I never understood, the plaintiffs never explained, they also added two institutes in New York. I think the suit was filed in New York. But basically the American was the chief target. They didn't sue Columbia, which was at the time the most anti-nonmedical training group of the three in New York. But I was the new president of the International. We were being sued for letting our component society do these bad things. The position of the American was that every component organization in the International has a right to set its standards and you, the International, have to support the component groups. If we're caught in a lawsuit, you've got to stand by us. You can't let the organization fragment and fall apart. On the other hand, Europeans and the Latin Americans were saying, "Look, we allow nonmedical people to be trained. It's not our problem. The American's in trouble over this issue. We don't want our dollars that we pay for dues to be used to defend a lawsuit that we don't believe in."

I, as the president, was caught between these, and I was putting together a way of working out of the suit. Ultimately, with the help of very good lawyers, both in London and in New York who were fastening the legal aspects of it, we were putting together a proposal that 2 years later was ultimately accepted. When the proposal was first brought forth, by me, on behalf of the International, the American didn't want to buy it, and the plaintiffs didn't want to buy it. The American's lawyers told the officers of the American and the firm the psychologists had hired were telling them, "Let this process go on, let the depositions unfold, let the discovery process happen, we'll find out things that will put us into such a good position when it comes to trial that we'll win." Both sets of lawyers were telling their client that we'll win. Obviously one had to be wrong.

VH: All the attorneys were getting wealthy.

RW: But all the attorneys, they were winning on both sides because the longer it went on—and the American had some attorneys who were real litigators, who wanted to carry this through and fight to preserve—to them it wasn't just a fight on behalf of the psychoanalysts, psychiatrists against psychologists, it was a fight of medicine against all those who had encroached on medicine. And then next it would be the nurses and everybody else would be cutting into our prerogatives, and we were fighting for the sanctity of the medical profession. There were big, big fights between me and the lawyers for the American. There was one very famous, bitter scene when the American called a special Executive Council meeting—I was flying to New York every other weekend during this time.

VH: That was when?

RW: That was 1986, in the Fall of 1986. There was a 5-week period in which I spent three weekends in New York. I was seeing my patients during the week. But, at one of those meetings, an Executive Council meeting, at the American where proposals were on the table, well, I got into an open fight with the lawyer of the American, and one point after I said something on the floor—I was a guest, I wasn't an officer of the American, I was president of the IPA. He said, "If Dr. Wallerstein will stop practicing law, I'll promise to stop practicing psychoanalysis." What happened, finally, the American changed its lawyers and brought in another firm which was much more committed to negotiating with whom I could get along and with whom my lawyers could get along.

VH: How did that stand you with the American?

RW: There were tense times, and longstanding friendships almost got fractured. It took 2 years to repair. When I was going to be elected president of the International, although that was unofficial because you're not elected until the election, it wasn't clear whether anybody would run against me. No one ran against me. But, anyway, people expected I would be the next president. Customarily, the president picks the secretary. The secretary is an appointed position in the International. The president picks the secretary, someone he or she can work closely with, usually in the same city so you have a close team. But there were people who were making noises about the fact that maybe I should depart from tradition and pick a non-American, a European as secretary, because I'd have a conflict of interest between my membership in the American and my presidency of the International. Actually, it turned out I didn't listen to that advice. I picked a secretary right here from San Francisco, Ed Weinshel, who was a close friend and colleague; and it was lucky in a lot of ways. Only an American president of the International could have fought with the American and fought with the officers of the American, in a way, to bring them around. No European would have dared to do it. The organization could have been split apart. The lawsuit wasn't settled until 1988. Members of the British Society through some of its most respected members, members like Hanna Segal, Nina Coltart, Ron Baker, Betty Joseph, and others, had signed a petition to bring something to the floor at the next International Congress in 1987. They were calling for a vote on a resolution that if any component organization gets into trouble with the legal authorities in its own country, it would have to handle this alone and hold the International harmless in the sense of covering all legal expenses the International is dragged into on behalf of the organization. The Americans, of course, would have fought fiercely against it, and the Americans would have been about half the people there at the business meeting, although they're only about a third of the world membership. But the vote would have determined it. That would mean the International isn't standing by any of its component groups. It would have led to a major fight on the floor, possibly in the secession of the American. It was important to us, to me, to head that off, to get the British to withdraw the resolution. This came up in October, 1986, and we wanted to get a counterthing in place, as a proposal, to come up on the floor, which would have to be published 6 months in advance.

We had until January first to fashion something that the British would accept as a basis for withdrawing their proposal. We worked out the famous change of the Thirty-Eight Agreement. The Thirty-Eight Agreement had two basic component parts. One was that it broke up the International Training Commission; and it said that the American would no longer be under the jurisdiction of the ITC but would have total internal autonomy, set its own standards for admission, selection, progression. And the IPA would accept what the American did.

That was one part of it, and the second part was the exclusive franchise, that the IPA would recognize no other groups in the United States except the American. Now the Americans had brought that to the floor in 1938 as a proposal. It created pandemonium, and they never took a vote on it. It was just put off to the next meeting, the next Congress. Everybody would go home to his or her own societies, think about this, talk about it for 2 years, the issue would be settled at the 1940 International Congress. Well, there was no 1940 International Congress; World War II was on. The next Congress was in 1949, 11 years after 1938, after this hiatus. When the Congress got together in 1949, it was clear that the Americans were in the majority, and they were insisting on this; and so a compromise was worked out. Ernest Jones was in on it, Anna Freud was in on it, and the leaders of the American. They acted as if it had been voted in, in 1938, and we were now abiding by it. It was never voted on officially, but it was understood that we were living in accord with the

Thirty-Eight proposal. What we wanted in 1987 was to get the Americans to agree to revise that.

VH: I'm sure this shows my paranoia more than anything. But in your book on *Becoming a Psychoanalyst* (1981c), my fantasy in terms of why there was a Ph.D. supervisor studied and a nonmedical supervisee, was that, in the event it didn't come out well or didn't look good, there wouldn't be medical people exposed.

RW: That's a true paranoia.

VH: I hear you, that it is.

RW: The supervisor happened to be one of my best friends. He was a member of the group, and he made the material available; and he said it would be on his next supervisee, whoever that was; it turned out to be this guy.

VH: I had some mixed feelings, some of them obviously negative about this person being studied without their knowledge.

RW: You have to put yourself back into that time in history. Informed consent was not a doctrine that was around then.

VH: Even to another professional?

RW: Supervisions are done in analytic institutes all the time without it—and there are continuous case conferences where a case is presented to a group of colleagues without informed consent.

VH: But everybody knows your case is being presented, you know.

RW: The supervision was being presented by the supervisor to a small group of seven or eight colleagues who are studying supervision. At the point at which we decided to make a book (Wallerstein, 1981c) out of it and go public, it was my job, I undertook it, to write to the candidate that had been supervised. He was one of my close friends.

VH: The young man who wrote the wonderful paper about being the person who was studied was a close friend of yours?

RW: Oh yeah, he and the supervisor are among my closest friends.

VH: Still?

RW: Still, sure. When I wrote to Howard Shevrin, I said there's been a study group that's been studying a case Herb Schlesinger provided, and you were the supervisee and there's a lot in this that we think can make a book, and since you were the supervisee, we want to tell you about it and invite you into it. And he was delighted.

VH: His paper didn't sound like that was his first reaction.

RW: Well, there are some different memories about the way he presented it. He was delighted, and, he said, "Of course, I'd like to see then what you're saying." I said, "Of course, we want you to see what's being said, and we want then to get you to comment on that." It's only when he saw the material and the way in which he felt things had been put by the supervisor, that his anger erupted. We almost had a lawsuit over that, and that friendship got very strained. But there's a certain amount that's self-serving in the way he wrote that up, as I'm sure there would be with anyone. His first reaction was one of surprise and delight at being a part of this book.

VH: Why did you all pick someone who was not the darling of the Institute to study?

RW: Because he was one of the darlings of the Institute.

VH: As I read the book, he felt that he had been put on hold and made to wait for a case because his work was questionable.

RW: Not really. What happened was everybody had to wait for cases.

VH: He was not medical in the days when that still wasn't very popular.

RW: At Menninger, more than half of the people were nonmedical. The supervisor said I'll pick the next case. It is true, he had trouble with an earlier case with the person, one of my supervisors, Van der Waals, the Hollander, who thought his work was kind of very stiff and very intellectual. Herb Schlesinger felt Howard was a very bright guy, and he was very highly regarded. Herb said, "Well that chemistry didn't work between the two of them, but Howie's a great guy, and he's the next one I'm having coming up; and it'll be a good case and he does good work." And the supervisor was dedicated promptly to showing how good his own work was, but also he was picking somebody he thought very highly of.

VH: You had an experience with the same supervisor that young man had an experience with. How did your perception of that supervisor compare to his perception of that supervisor?

RW: He was kind of an authoritative type, that supervisor. That is, he made up his mind about something, that's the way it was, and a group discussion couldn't sway him very much. He liked me. He liked my work. I presented a case, for a while, to a case seminar where if anybody was questioning things I did, he would be too quick to jump in and say how good it was, because he approved it. I learned a lot from him, but he wasn't somebody you could argue with a lot.

VH: What do you remember learning from him?

RW: Something that wouldn't make people very popular, but a patient of mine, he supervised, was a young woman of 20, an extraordinarily gifted young woman, who was in endless fights with her father, bitter knockdown, physical, drag-out fights. She had been brought up on a ranch with thousands of head of cattle and punctuated by the oil wells that her father owned, a big rancher family. She was the first child. Her father taught her, as a 3-year-old, to run this huge tractor. Then her brother came along, she was bounced out of everything, because now, all attention was focused on the brother, and so she would get in endless fights, the biggest fights; and her father was always putting her down. She came home one day from school, just had an IQ test in class; "Gee, you know, I got 139, and it was the highest in the class." And her father said, "That's pretty good, mine was 142." This went on all the time. When she went to college, her characteristic way of doing things was to enroll in a class no other girls took—chemistry class, she was one out of 100. She got the highest grades. So high that, at the end of the semester, she was asked to be a lab assistant for the next semester. She had proven to herself that she was better than all of them. She then lost interest, fell apart and flunked out. She flunked out of three colleges in a couple of years, punctuated by a lot of promiscuity, usually with guys who could make any girl.

VH: That wouldn't usually get you to Menninger's.

RW: I'll tell you how that happened. A guy would say he was such a charmer he could have any girl on this campus. She heard that, and so she went out with him on a dare; and she fought him off like a tigress when he tried to—and it was really an attempted rape.

VH: Sort of a black widow spider thing.

RW: When he came to school the next day, he had scratches all over him, and she let the story go around or she made sure that everybody knew that he hadn't succeeded. She was in such trouble being thrown out of colleges, and she was now the black sheep of this family and was seen by the minister of the church whom the family went to. Her parents were almost fundamentalists. The minister of the church sent them for psychiatric consultation. She was seen by an analyst who sent her to the Menninger Foundation where they recommended analysis. The family didn't want all that "hifalutin" treatment, but she was looked at as such a good case that she was offered a reduced fee, even though it was a rich family. And the family couldn't pass up a bargain.

VH: So they hospitalized her?

RW: No, she wasn't hospitalized. She became an outpatient. She was a schoolgirl. She was 20, she hadn't finished college yet. She was at the university, she went and enrolled in college there. She was an analytic case of mine. In the analysis, the same kind of things went on obviously, the same kind of acting out. She had a boyfriend who was trouble from the word "go" and who was one of these ne'er-do-wells who was always in trouble with the law and a motorcycle type; and finally he made her pregnant. Then she doesn't want to have anything to do with him. Of course, he skips out anyway at the point at which she was pregnant. She was going to get an abortion, which was illegal. There were legal abortions, and she wanted to know how to go about getting a legal abortion. I told her she would have to get two or three physicians, at least one of them a psychiatrist, who would certify what the risks were of her carrying this baby to term to her physical and emotional health. And as she listened to it, she said, "I'd never qualify," and in the way the law was being interpreted, she never would. So she got herself an illegal abortion in a back alley someplace. This was butchered, and she called me the night that it happened, and she was bleeding, and I gave her the name of a gynecologist. She was hospitalized, and it was completed and she recovered.

VH: She wanted to have that abortion with your consent.

RW: Well, I wasn't involved one way or another.

VH: But you were involved in telling her what the law was. You had to be somewhat involved.

RW: Oh yeah, I told her what her options were, how to go about trying to get a legal one and what the law was; and then she said she had made this decision, and we talked about it.

VH: How did you do that?

RW: She was doing what everybody was doing. That was the way people got abortions, and usually they worked out well enough, and this one didn't; but she recovered from it. Nine months later, at the point at which the baby would have been born, she went into a depression and in a fury at me. And the fury at me was that I hadn't stopped her from doing this terrible thing, that I hadn't stopped her from murdering her child and all of her childhood fundamentalist upbringing was now back. She was going to be punished forever for this murder she had committed—to which I was an accomplice because I hadn't prevented it when I could have said, "Don't do it. Carry the child." If her family ever heard about it, of course, they would have disowned her. She knew that too. That was the dilemma she was caught in.

VH: And you? And disowned you equally.

RW: It was Van der Waals who said, "You know, in this country abortion is so hard to get, and that's a terrible social policy. We have to live with it. But, you know, even if people can just get abortions, it's not an inconsequential thing. It always has psychic reverberations," and he had said, "Something's going to happen at the time this baby would have been due." He said, "It'll either be a depression or it'll be an anger at you." It turned out to be both. He said, "Because it has its consequences. It's not a meaningless act." Women's lib wouldn't like to hear that kind of talk.

VH: What he said is certainly true.

RW: But it's true. Now she got past that, it was a successful enough analysis. A year after the analysis ended she married. There was a guy whom she had met during the final days of the analysis. I've lost track of her, but things seemed to be going very well for her at that point. Anyway, it was Van der Waals who steered me through the handling of this thing without getting either moralistic about it or pushing her one way or another but being ready, not only to help her if she wants to get the abortion, in a sense of not stopping her, but also then being willing to realize that there might be consequences and to be able to deal with those.

VH: Wasn't it possible as a psychiatrist or an analyst to say it would be damaging to her mental health?

RW: It had to be something that would drive her to suicide or would make her psychotic. In fact, it would be upsetting to her.

VH: Was she mad when you said that?

RW: What?

VH: Was she mad at you?

RW: I was never going to be the psychiatrist.

VH: Was she mad about that?

RW: No, she was realistic about that. She said, "You know, that's not true of me."

VH: She was a reasonable person.

RW: She was really a reasonable person, and her reality testing was very much intact. She was a healthy, neurotic individual. She wasn't in danger of a psychotic decompensation, and she wasn't going to be suicidal, but her life would have been—if she had the illegitimate kid it would have been something to live through with her parents and with unknown consequences for her future. And yet she was by no means going to marry this guy either.

VH: It does sound like a tough spot to be in if you were the psychiatrist. Analytic or not, you could save her from a dangerous abortion. She's going to have an abortion either way. With a statement she's safe.

RW: If I collude, at lying, to get her a safe abortion, then I have played the role of being the promoter of the abortion.

VH: It's a tough one, isn't it?

RW: Yeah.

VH: A real tough one.

RW: It was Van der Waals who had the judgment to steer a course in this. He kept things on course.

VH: What was your own inclination? Here you know you were right.

RW: I was troubled either way, and I turned to him as a senior person. Howard Shevrin and he really didn't get along because he thought of Howie as a very intellectualizing guy who was full of theory that he would give in big, complicated interpretations to patients who would say, "Yeah, that sounds okay or that sounds sensible." And he never felt that Howie could enter really into somebody's psychological world in a kind of sympathetically understanding way. He felt that Howard was a much better researcher than clinician, I think, although he's a well established analyst now, and I'm sure he's had his successes too.

VH: But not a training analyst?

RW: No, not a training analyst as far as I know.

VH: Those kinds of calls like you described with the girl are the toughest; whether you're an analyst or not, really does matter. The neutral position, the value of it, always emerges victorious somehow.

RW: That was my second case. About that book, if you go back to that, what you said was your paranoia. Yeah, it is a paranoid idea. Besides Schlesinger, Ekstein was on the committee, studying this case and, of course, Ekstein's whole career had been built up on studying material that there was never informed consent about. What existed then was that it was your responsibility as a clinician to only do, you cannot do anything that would be hurtful to your patients. And if you were writing about them, to do it, in a way it wouldn't violate their privacy, that would protect them, but you didn't have to get their consent to do this.

VH: But how about the student? The student has rights too.

RW: It was looked at as the same. Nothing was being said in the group that in any way impacted hurtfully on his supervision with Schlesinger; and if he knew it was a case under scrutiny, then that could make him more self-conscious.

VH: Can you do it today?

RW: Today, no.

VH: You wouldn't be allowed.

RW: To the other extreme. Suppose you wanted to write up a case of a child analysis, a 4-year-old who had analysis until the child was 7. Well, do you get formal consent from a 7-year-old or a 5-year-old?

VH: Or the parents.

RW: That's ridiculous. A little child like that can't give consent. Do you go to the mother? The mother doesn't know what goes in that treatment. If you really follow the full consent doctrine out to its logical conclusion, there is no way to write up a child case. Furthermore, when patients of mine have given, for legal matters, informed consent; that is, it's okay to open their records, I've refused. I'd said, "It's not the patient's record, it's my record." It's my record about the patient, the patient doesn't know what's in the notes. How can she give informed consent for me to release things, the contents of which she doesn't know and that have to do not only with her but with the people in her life?

VH: What do you do when they come with a court order?

RW: I've never handed a record over on a subpoena. I've said to the attorney if there are legitimate questions at stake here, if the patient has said, "You have the rights to look into my records about," you ask me the question, I'll have the record in front of me, I'll answer it.

VH: You've always had success with that?

RW: I said I will not give you the record for a fishing expedition. If they said, "Well, I'll go to a judge and get a subpoena," you go to the judge, and I'll explain to the judge that I don't want to do this because neither you nor the patient knows what's in that record. Suppose the patient, this young woman, has had a homosexual affair with somebody else who's an innocent third party. I should give you the record to expose somebody like that? No judge would say that's sensible to do as long as I make a commitment to answer the questions relative to this case, and I'll give the record to the judge and let him check on it. If you want to argue that in front of a judge, I'll go and do it with you. At that point they've always backed off. They've always accepted that position. My records are useless to anybody.

VH: Could you summarize your main interests?

RW: I call it a discipline, which psychoanalysis is, partly an interest in it as a science and partly an interest in it as a profession, and they are distinct. As a science, my commitments are really twofold. One is obviously, psychoanalytic research. I want it to mean something very specific. There are varieties of psychoanalytic research, and what to me is central, is research into the nature of the psychoanalytic treatment process and basically what happens in it, which can be divided into two questions. What changes take place in the unfolding psychoanalytic treatment? Then how those changes come about or how they're brought about through the interaction of the patient and the treatment and the life situation. Which doesn't mean there aren't lots of other kinds of psychoanalytic research. There's baby watching, developmental research, and there's psychosomatic research, and all the kinds of correlations you can get into with that. There's experimental research using psychoanalytic propositions of different kinds.

What to me has been the central issue and my interest is the search in the treatment process for two things. One is to find out more about treatment, how it works, what makes it work, under what circumstances it works, with whom, towards what end, basically so it can be better in the end. But also as a way of finding out more about the mind. That is, basic knowledge about how the mind functions through a treatment process that's geared to change that function; and that is, you know, has been my lifetime commitment that I've written about it endlessly. It represents the basis on which I got known in the psychoanalytic world, very early, in the 1950s actually.

Then, alongside of that, another commitment that grew out of that is if there is such a thing as psychoanalytic research and if it is finally coming into its own today in the 1980s and 1990s as a burgeoning enterprise, not just in the United States, but other places around the world as well, then that means it's something that can be researched, that means it has the attributes of a science; and that was an easy commitment for me to have. In fact, you can't do research except in the framework basically of some kind of scientific activity where you're applying a method; however you define it, a scientific method is a way of looking at phenomena.

So then I got interested in the issues of the nature of psychoanalysis as a science. In what ways is it a science? How much akin is it to the natural sciences? Is there a difference between a natural science and the social sciences? And to me what defines a science is not a content, but a method that is a way of looking at phenomena. And so I don't make the kind of distinction that some people make between saying that natural science is fundamentally different from the social or behavioral sciences. The arena of observation is very different, and the ways in which you have to put your observations together may be different because they have to be tailored to the phenomena; and we're dealing with very subjectivistic phenomena. But nonetheless, to me, what a science is, is something—again I can repeat what I said—where you have a way of making observations and in a way that others can look at the data so they can say yes I agree or I don't agree. And that you marshal evidence that makes the conclusions you come to on the basis of those observations more likely than any other alternative anybody can think of. This is an incremental process, and it builds.

And so I got involved and interested in the nature of science, nature of psychoanalysis as science, the philosophy of science literature, and I got into the hermeneutic literature and what I think—and I read some but certainly not all. I've read obviously, in America, Spence's books, and I wrote the foreword to Spence's first book (1982a) though I disagree with him. A lot of the ultimate to which he drives his argument, he really has a lot to say that I like, and you can see in the foreword I wrote to his first book how I put that, and Schafer and in Europe people like Gadamer, Lorenzer of Germany and others. But, anyway, I take my own positions on that. If you want to see how it all evolved, I had two main articles on "Psychoanalysis as a Science" (1976b, 1986b) to both of which I've added a subtitle. And then I had another 10 years later, which was the Freud anniversary lecture at the New York Institute, which is their big honor. They invite somebody to give a lecture. That's the only time I gave a lecture in a tuxedo in my life (which I had to rent). The second one I called *Psychoanalysis as a Science: A Response to the New Challenges* (1986b). The challenge is sort of from the left and the right. On the one side, the hermeneutic challenges and on the other side, the positivist challenges, like Adolf Grünbaum and a few who know his work. Grünbaum is an important philosopher of science who's written articles and a book on the scientific potential of psychoanalysis, and there are books written in response to that. So that's been another strand of my interests.

As a profession, I've had a lifelong commitment to the identity of psychoanalysis as an autonomous profession distinct from medicine and psychiatry but allied to it and standing in a kind of interface between the biological sciences and social sciences and the humanities and with linkages to each but separate from them. In 1969, I was invited to give a paper chairing an opening, a big plenary session at the International Psycho-Analytical Association Congress in Rome on psychoanalysis and psychotherapy, similarities and differences, which came out in an article in the *International Journal of Psycho-Analysis* and which was, incidentally, the first time ever that the International had that as a topic on a panel. Up to then, the word psychotherapy as an enterprise, linked to, but very distinctive from psychoanalysis had never entered International discourse. That was an American phenomenon. We worried about what's psychoanalysis and what's psychotherapy and how do they relate and how are they different. That didn't exist as a set of considerations in other parts of the world for a long time.

In 1969 the International had a panel on that, and on the panel with me was Tom Main. He's dead now, and Pierre Luquet of France, and Clemens de Boor of Germany, and from America, Jerry Oremland. That was my first big paper at the International. In 1973, Serge Lebovici, who was then president of the International, asked if I would co-chair the pre-Congress on training, which is always a 3-day event before the

International Congresses for training analysts to discuss training issues. And I was asked to co-chair it in 1973 for the 1975 meeting in London, which I did, and then to take it on by myself for the 1977 meeting in New York—no, the 1977 meeting in Jerusalem, and then the third time for the 1979 meeting in New York. So I was running the pre-Congress three times running, which was unprecedented until then. Anyway, he put me in a very central, visible position in the International. I was elected as vice president in 1977. I was vice president for 8 years before I became president, and in the course of that I literally went all over the world for meetings, partly because the Congresses were in different parts of the world; headquarters are in London. We had a lot of trouble in one institute in Latin America, which was in ghastly trouble and had just literally fallen apart and ceased functioning; it was caught up in the political turmoil of the country including even the tortures that were going on in that country at that time, and some of the people were implicated. When Adam Limentani was president of the IPA, this came to a head, and I was asked to chair the Site Visiting Committee that went there. Since it was a very strongly Kleinian institute, he put Hanna Segal on the Site Visiting Committee with me so that whatever we did about them and to them, they couldn't say it was persecution because they were Kleinians. Anyway, she and I had to go to that particular city in Latin America four times in 2 years, together with a third member of our committee, Ramon Ganzarain.

VH: Where?

RW: Well I'd rather not say. It's fine now. It was one of the institutes in Latin America that has now worked its way out of the trouble. It's resumed functioning; everything is okay; they've been reinstated in good standing, and the chief protagonists on both sides of the struggles there are out. It's a whole new group running things: The constitution has been rewritten; the curriculum's been refashioned; everything's been changed.

I've got a perspective on worldwide psychoanalysis, and I suppose the main theme of my work in the International at least over the last 8 years and during my presidency was to bring together and hold together all the disparate trends within psychoanalysis by trying to define what we have in common. That's the whole search for the common ground, which is really two questions. One question is that there are so many theoretical perspectives and presumably different ways of understanding the mind and how it works and how it hangs together and how you can do something about it, and yet they all call themselves psychoanalysts. The first question is, what do they have in common that makes them all psychoanalytic, and the companion question is what differentiates them from other things that are not psychoanalytic because not everything is psychoanalytic? And that became the theme of not just my Presidential addresses in Montreal and Rome but became the theme of the Rome Congress, and all the papers that were written there were in relation to that. Not everybody agrees with me on how to define the common ground, or where it is, or whether there even should be.

In my Montreal paper I tried to trace out Freud's history where he tried to maintain the unity of psychoanalysis, and he tried to do it within a unified theoretical perspective. But that fell apart. It fell apart really with the rise of the Kleinians and the fact that they said we differ from those others, but we are also Freudians. That is, we're also the heirs to the legacy of Freud, but we have a different metapsychology, and we have different ways of working technically based on our different metapsychology.

VH: Boy, how would you prove some of those fantasies?

RW: The point I came to in my article was you don't prove those fantasies ever because all the metapsychologies are in the present state of development—really metaphoric expressions. The Kleinians are not unique. And then I followed a distinction made by George Klein and Rapaport, before him, into a what's called the clinical theory and the general theory. Although the dividing lines are not all as sharp as that and the edges are always fuzzy. I look for the commonality and the common ground in the experience—near-clinical phenomena. And the divergences are there in the theoretical explanatory structures that create a particular language in which to explain the clinical phenomena, and those are still not scientific but metaphoric languages whether we're talking ego, id and superego, whether we're talking part objects and whole objects, or depressive and paranoid positions, or cohesive selfobjects and fragmenting selfobjects.

But like ego psychology, Kleinian analysis has changed a good deal; and if you hear Hanna Segal's and Betty Joseph's presentations today, they are quite different from our stereotypes of the Kleinian work they were brought up in under Melanie Klein. And with the three groups in the British Society, by their interacting with each other as much as they have over the years, listening to each other's presentations at scientific meetings, sitting on committees with each other, the clinical work of each has been influenced by that of the others enough so there's a lot more clinical common ground than is theoretically acknowledged.

VH: It sounds like you've had so much to do with the keeping it one discipline, psychoanalysis.

RW: I hope it can be kept one discipline, and I think—you see, Freud felt, for reasons maybe suitable to his time in history and all that, that he had to maintain the absolute purity of a purified theoretical structure and that anybody who deviated from it would feel they had to leave or be pushed off starting with Adler, Jung, and Stekel back in the teens of the century, going all through his lifetime. There are people who are saying today, and I think they're right, if the Jungian viewpoint had arisen today, it would be accommodated within the body of psychoanalysis the way Kohut has been, rather than Jungians feeling they had to leave.

The kind of unity that Freud tried to impose was an impossible one because it demanded a real orthodoxy. You had to subscribe to the articles of faith established by the seven ring holders, and that could last just so long, before people said we have other points of view; and, of course, even in his lifetime. If you want to really read the history of this, Riccardo Steiner has written a series of very brilliant articles: They're long, they're furiously detailed. But the history of the controversial discussions that were in the International and are contained in a big fat thousand-page book which just came out about that last year, edited by Pearl King and Riccardo Steiner (1991), on the whole controversial discussions during the 1940s and all the detail of all the papers given, all the discussion remarks made at the meetings that have been gathered from the archives and minutes of those meetings, and the famous Gentlemen's Agreement at the end of it that sort of created the structure of the British Society. And the British Society has been, in many ways, the bell ringer for the IPA. It's the only society in the world in which three separate theoretical strands have existed side by side, in mostly a good working truce. It has problems right now and there are forces that might try to break it apart at this moment, and there are troubles that they're trying to cope with. But I'm sure it'll hold.

VH: Thank you so much.

Case Discussion

Dr. Wallerstein, an ego psychologist, recognizes that the patient has a hysterical character structure with quasipsychotic disorganizing episodes. He goes on to say that Roselyn was severely traumatized by her mother, and she feels chaotic inside. Further, Dr. Wallerstein says that there are times when Roselyn cannot tell fantasy from reality.

This case discussion with Robert Wallerstein took place in his San Francisco Bay home Saturday morning, October 7, 1991. He began sharing his own training experience. He said that when he graduated in 1958, analysis was defined quite narrowly. All he had known then was ego psychology. He had never read a Kleinian paper and only a few of the British middle-school writers. In those days, you weren't expected to read any others except the ego psychologists. "Reading other psychoanalysts' theories would be like reading a novel. They wouldn't be psychoanalysis. Analysis was quite narrowly defined, and anything that departed from the analyst's role being that of the listener who tries to understand had to be undone. If it was not undone, it was not really an analysis, or it was certainly not a complete analysis and thereby a species of psychotherapy. Today, I have a somewhat similar but modified position that is partly the outcome of the psychotherapy project in Topeka. There is no such pure product. There are not such pure lines distinguishing psychoanalysis from an expressive psychotherapy, from a more supportive psychotherapy. There is a kind of a more fluid movement; there is infiltration across borders, and there are all kinds of things that go in any analysis that could be looked at as, by narrow criteria, 'nonanalytic.' Eissler would say that it is unnecessary to have a process between two people that cannot be carried out with a kind of austerity. It is not just Eissler's model, but it is Charlie Brenner's model, and to a certain extent, Jake Arlow's. In effect, the Kleinians say we're analysts because we are thinking of what's going on unconsciously, so everything we do is analytic in analysis, even if they do things that to us would be looked at as quite unanalytic. So it's partly a clinical question of how one defines analysis."

Wallerstein noted, "In regard to this patient of yours, sure, I would say it's analytic in the sense that you're working with the framework of a psychoanalytic understanding trying to understand meanings and symbolic things and widen the patient's understanding and control over her world. It's not, to me it's *not* psychoanalysis because it encompasses a lot more than having a patient lying on the couch. I don't know, does she? I would doubt it."

I replied, "Sometimes Roselyn lies on the couch, and sometimes she sits on it. Years ago, she even sat on the Oriental rug at times of great distress."

Wallerstein went on, "But having a patient lying on the couch and free associating. . . . To give you an idea of the austere model of analysis, you had a training analyst in Topeka, who later left, who is now dead, who first disclaimed any kind of therapeutic interest in the patient, 'I'm not here to treat you; I'm here to analyze you.' " I asked if this were an occasional view. He reiterated, " 'My job is to listen to you and tell you what I think it means. As long as you want to keep coming, lie on the couch, and keep talking, I'll listen, and I'll try to tell you what I think it means for as long as you can take me and that. Anytime you want to get up and go and say, "I've had enough," that's fine. Anytime you think you feel better, or you're cured, that's okay too; that's up to you; that's not my intent. My intent is only to listen to you and tell you what I think it means.' Now it's that kind of model people can have in mind, which I think partly comes from Freud's famous mirror analogy and his surgical analogy."

I responded, "But Freud really didn't treat people that way. It makes me angry just to hear you say so."

Wallerstein countered, "Well, it shouldn't make you angry. Freud didn't do that; he wrote that."

I said, "He also wrote about feeding people and lending them money."

Wallerstein replied, "Of course. It's out of those statements of his that models got created. I don't know if you've read Sam Lipton's papers." I said that I had.

Wallerstein began, "The patient's a lot sicker than the ones I usually treat. These are the patients, exactly a patient like this, that all Americans in the 1950s and 1960s, and most Americans today would still say, 'She cannot be analyzed.' They would say, 'She needs to be treated by analytic psychotherapy.' Kleinians and mainly object people in Britain would say, 'She's a good patient for analysis'; and how much they would do different things or how much they would call what they do by different names is to me the big question mark in the American way. I had one patient similar. By the way, nosologically, these are the patients whom I feel fit a category that doesn't exist anymore. It doesn't exist in the *Diagnostic and Statistical Manual of Mental Disorders, Third Edition* (American Psychiatric Association, 1982). It's the concept of, to me, the hysterical psychosis. People with basically hysterical character structures, with all the attributes, including the histrionic attributes, the clairvoyant ones, which I think are there, and also with the hysterical type of defenses. They can easily regress into directions where reality goes out the window, and they can have quasi- or temporary psychotic disorganizing episodes.

"I had one patient very much like this, who happened to be my first analytic case. It happened to be a case that was given to me because she was going to be such a good analysand for a first control case. And I wrote her up—I'll give you the reference. It's in my bibliography; it's called *Reconstruction and Mastery in the Transference Psychosis* (Wallerstein, 1967b), and it describes two cases, that one and another one. It came out in the *Journal of the American Psychoanalytic Association* in 1967. It was a long clinical case in which the one patient I'm thinking of was described in length and another one more briefly."

I asked, "What do you mean by transference psychosis?"

Wallerstein replied, "What I meant by transference psychosis, not the transferences of psychotic patients, because psychotic patients have psychotic transferences, is the kind of patients Margaret Little wrote about: people who are delusional and act delusionary in relation to the analyst, but people who are, on the surface, well enough put together so you classify them as normal neurotic people who have neurotic problems who come into intensive analytic treatment. In the course of the unfolding of the treatment, and under the pressures of the transference, they have shorter or longer decompensating periods in which the 'as if' quality of the transference disappears, where the patient is no longer reacting to you as if he had a father who is always disdainful, but at the moment, identifies you with the father and feels that you are the father. This is, by the way, one of the hazards of our field. The biggest hazard we have is suicide. Patients we're treating get depressed and get out of control, and they commit suicide. A much lesser hazard but a real one are those patients who will absorb the therapist, and even on a rare occasion you read about therapists being shot."

I said, "My lady is not that sick."

Wallerstein concurred, "No, of course not. But those are people who are in a transference psychosis, where at that moment the analyst is not being seen as someone who is like the father but who becomes the diagonized father; and the patient now feels, 'I'm an adult, and I'm really going to get back at you' and pulls out a gun and shoots him in a psychotic rage. But the patient I'm talking about, who was such a good analytic case, was a woman whose father committed suicide when she was 4. I won't go into any part of the whole history, but this was in the early 1920s, at a time when children were supposed to be spared such things. She wasn't told that her father was dead. She didn't participate in the funeral or any part of it. She was told her father was away on a trip, and she kept going to school and she kept asking for her father and her mother said he was still away. And it wasn't until several months later, when she was a 5-year-old, that other kids said, 'Your daddy is dead; your daddy is dead,' and she went home and confronted her mother. Her mother acknowledged that was so. She tried during the course of analysis to reconstruct the father's death through dreams, fantasies, and things put together. She acted out and that got interpreted, in various ways. The daughter had two visions of the way he died. One was that he jumped out of a third-story window in that big frame house in the city in the East, out onto the street—out the window, came crashing on the ground, on the trolley car tracks. The trolley car came by and ran over his body, chopping it up into many pieces. That was one vision she had. The other one was that she and her mother were home and somebody came and knocked on the door. There was a policeman at the door, and he said, 'I have bad news for you,' and then told the mother and the child this story. The patient didn't know which, if either, was true. She searched through newspapers at that time. It was a socially prominent family, and there would have been an article in the paper, but she couldn't find the records.

She went off in various psychotic directions so that she broke up her marriage although she remarried her husband later. She gave up the care for her kids completely; she just couldn't take care of them and just handed them to neighbors. And I carried through her analysis, the whole analysis with substantial periods of sitting up and of extra appointments and of all kinds of things; but what I had then that most people who treat patients like this don't have, and I admire their courage, is I had a hospital back of me. And although she was an outpatient, she had two periods of hospitalization. During those periods of hospitalization, she was quite crazy; I had her hospitalized, and I went to see her there everyday. This was the predrug era, so there was no temptation to be giving her antipsychotic medication of any kind. It was in the 1950s still, but I didn't have unlimited resources. She didn't have enough money to pay for hospitalization, so the Menninger Foundation was just sort of carrying her, but one time they kept her in for a few days and one time for a month. With patients like this, like your lady, your two episodes you call psychotic episodes—the time she's sitting in the closet after her house had been vandalized or the time she's going in for surgery—it's not always clear that one session with a therapist is going to sort things out in such a way that life can go on. And what do you do if she's still sitting in a closet?"

I said I would hospitalize her then. Wallerstein continued, "And there are people in this country—you've mentioned one, Giovacchini is one—there are some who have treated people this sick in outpatient settings without any recourse to a hospital. But you see, you don't have what we had in Topeka. I could hospitalize her. I could have some say about her hospital management, which I wanted; and I could see her there everyday without interrupting my schedule because the hospital was literally across the street. I could see her in the same hour that she was ordinarily my patient without having to make a trip a half-hour away to get there and disrupt the rest of my day. These are the patients who will wake you up at night with emergencies, who intrude on your life in all kinds of ways."

I replied, "Roselyn didn't really trust me enough to act in those ways yet. She usually puts control on herself."

Wallerstein went on, "What you have going for you is the fact that most patients, in a way, are considerate of their therapists."

I replied, "Maybe this one's too considerate."

Wallerstein went on, "It may be. When I am going to be away for a month, many of my patients have no idea where I am, and whatever fantasy they want to have, they can have. I have a patient who's a candidate. She shows up at the same International Congress I'm at. I have other patients to whom I give the name of somebody else who can see them in the interim, or I tell them where I will be and give them the telephone number where they can reach me during the time I am away. I've never had a patient abuse that. They don't. And the fact that they had the number, in a way, is often enough to hold them. If they know they can get in touch with you, then they can somehow manage. So I think the people who are always afraid of being taken advantage of by patients, and are always on guard against that, are being too paranoid or too stand-offish."

I said, "Those analysts know what they are going to give."

Wallerstein responded in a reassuring way. "But then they shouldn't be treating those patients. I don't have patients like this mainly because I've always also had an academic life. I've been chairman of the Department of Psychiatry, I've had teaching obligations as well as a clinical practice, and I haven't sought out patients who can be the kind of patients who intrude upon things and make you disrupt your schedule when I've had the kind of schedule that couldn't make those disruptions."

I said, "She hasn't done disruptive things, except two or three."

Wallerstein continued, "I had one such patient here in San Francisco who's in the professional field, a very well-known family therapist, who was referred to me by a colleague, a very senior colleague, who said, 'This patient may need to be hospitalized sometime. I wouldn't treat anybody who needs to be hospitalized.' And he was a guy who functioned well professionally, who at times would be bitter at me when talking about his marital difficulties by saying he makes his living dealing with marital situations. He makes his living at the things I avoid doing. But anyway, he never did have to be hospitalized; but it could be touch and go very often. When he walked out of the door, I would sometimes wonder what's going to happen between now and the next time he comes. And I had one patient in Topeka—I won't say anything about the one who actually went psychotic because you can read that whole case. Just one other was a guy who was a severe alcoholic and a predatory homosexual. . . . He was from one of the wealthiest families in a major city in the South and went back 200 years; they had been a big slave-holding family and now some minor industrial empire, but the Southern nobility. And, of course, the people he sought out for his homosexual escapades had to be blacks from the ghetto. This was in the 1950s when homosexuality was in the closet, for one, totally; and his involvements were under the most sordid circumstances, usually with the blacks in a way that would really have disgraced him if it ever came out. His father disappeared when he was young. He was one of three or four children. His father disappeared when he was a latency-age kid. It was a major, major scandal, and the mother collected millions in insurance because the father was dead. The insurance company didn't believe he was dead, and they wanted to recover their money, so they put private detectives on it. And years later they picked up the father in Texas living a new life with the secretary he had run off with. And then the insurance company sued the family; they wanted their life insurance money back. That hit *Time* magazine; it was a big thing. Of course, all the bitterness between his parents was then front-page news all over the country. He had been treated by two people before me, both of whom gave up after a year or two; and he was then put on a list for a third therapist. He was one of those patients who always knew what was going on behind the scenes. He knew that three or four people subsequently looked at his chart. He knew they said, 'So and So tried to treat him, and So and So did, and they were good people. I don't want him.' He knew he had been turned down by three or four people, and then I took him. He had two reactions to me. One was regret: 'You'll undertake me, no one else has.' And the other: 'What a fool you are, all the smartest people have said no. What kind of jerk are you to try and treat me?' He'd always be polite in the hours, differential. But he would go out on drunken binges, and then he'd call me in the middle of the night. Two in the morning when he was tossed out of a bar after getting into a barroom brawl with somebody, and then he could pour out things, which were not quite so differential, in his drunken state. Always at 2 in the morning with, 'I'm sorry to be interrupting you.' Now the interrupting—his fantasy was always that he was interrupting me and my wife in intercourse, getting in between. But one day—it was the first time he came into the office drunk. He had never done that before—he proceeded to tell me off, under cover of being in this drunken state, for all the things that were wrong with the therapy, with me, and on and on and how despairing he was. And this was after about 2 years of treatment. He was now going to leave my office and give up on the treatment. I hadn't helped him, nobody before me had helped him, nobody *could* help him; he was going to go down to the State Capitol building and go climb up on the top and jump off, and it would be a suicide.

"He was well known, a prominent name, and there would be a headline in the paper the next day about him. And everybody would know who his therapist was. With saying that, he got up, and was walking out the door; and I didn't know if he might just do that. He was a bigger person than I was; I couldn't really physically restrain him. And I didn't know what to say; I was kind of stunned, and I just looked at him and said as he was going out the door, 'You can't do that.' He said, 'What do you mean?' I said, 'You can't do that.' He said, 'What can't I do?' 'You can't go out of here and kill yourself because I'm not talking about what you owe yourself, that's between you and yourself; you owe me more than that. You owe me something for the 2 years I put in with you and all the calls you made in the middle of the night, and you just can't do that to me.' This is really tugging on the transference. He had this powerful attachment to me because he might have said, 'Fuck you,' and walked out. He didn't. He said, 'You're perfectly right,' and he sat down and began to cry. He never came drunk again after that. But that was a maneuver, sort of, out of desperation."

Wallerstein continued, "There was one other like it that I had when I was a resident. I had a patient in psychotherapy, before I was in analytic training, who was a neurological patient because he had grand mal epilepsy. I never wrote this up. And he wouldn't take his medication for the epilepsy because the medication he's supposed to take, Dilantin, can sometimes swell your gums so it can disfigure your face a little bit. It's a relatively rare complication, but it can happen. He was a very handsome guy, and he wasn't going to take anything that would or could mar his beauty. He wouldn't take the medication; he had these seizures that really incapacitated him because he had them rather frequently. The neurologist had the guys crazy getting psychiatric consultation to make him take his medication. So I saw him for consultation. An outcome of this very unhappy story, and the kind that makes you feel what a dreadful person he is—is this: He made his living as a blackmailer. And what would he do? He was in his 20s, a handsome young guy. He would go into a small Southern town; he would join the local church, usually a Baptist church, get active in the church's cause and activities and attend services, meet some of the older widows who were lonely, get into an affair with them, then threaten to expose them to the congregation unless they paid him off—$1,000,

$2,000, whatever it was—which they were always happy to do. They would dip into their life savings and give him money, and he would promise to get out of town, which he did. He made his living this way.

"You listen to more of this story. He was brought up in an orphanage, in a day when they still had orphanages in the South. He was a bedwetter, and when he wet his bed in the orphanage, the women who ran the orphanage would beat him because they had to clean, wash the sheets and the mattress, and air everything out; and he just created problems for them. So he, as a 6- and 7-year-old kid, would stand at the side of the bed holding onto the bedrails, trying not to fall asleep—so that he wouldn't fall asleep and wet his bed—and try to stay up all night and ultimately collapse. And this was his childhood. When you hear that childhood, you can get some idea of what he was revenging himself for with all these women.

"Anyway, I had him in treatment on a once-a-week basis. And he came in one day very, very agitated. He said he'd been downtown, on Kansas Avenue, the big, broad avenue in the middle of downtown Topeka. There was a crowd on the sidewalk, and he went up to it curiously. 'What's going on?' And somebody there said, 'Oh, it's just someone having a fit.' There was a man having an epileptic seizure, and he was fascinated, morbidly fascinated; he wanted to see one of these; he'd never seen a seizure; and he saw the man writhing on the ground and frothing at the mouth. It horrified him and revolted him to see a seizure, and there was a tremendous anger at the man who had said, 'It's just someone having a *fit*.' I asked what the anger was about. He said, 'He called it a fit. Dogs have fits. People don't have fits. He called him a dog. That's me.' This is a powerful man. He said, 'I wanted to hit him. I wanted to hit him and send him sprawling. I controlled myself. 'Dogs have fits. People don't have fits.' I said, 'What do people have?' 'People have seizures. People have spells. Dogs have fits. You never use the word fit.' And I said, 'You're right. I never use the word fit, but you know, what would have happened if I had used the word fit?' He said, 'If you had said fit, I would have done one of two things. I would have either gotten up and walked out of here and never come back again or I would have gotten up and sent you crashing into that wall and then walked out of here and never come back again. I would have done one of those.' And I just looked at him and said, 'You mean everything was riding on the word I chose to use?' He said, 'Yes.' I said, 'How was I to know that?' And then he began to cry, and he said, 'You're right, you had no way of knowing.' At that point the therapy really began. Those are the patients who are closer to the kind of patient I mean. He was a guy who thought in psychotic rages. At any point, he could have just lost all control."

Wallerstein continued, "My first patient really had delusional and psychotic states—the one I wrote up in the article whose father committed suicide and whom I hospitalized. I told you about the fantasy of the father jumping out of the third-story window. The patient lived in an area of town where there were many houses with third-story windows. One of them was a house of a colleague of mine. She walked by there one day, and she said she saw my colleague up there at the window; and she said there was a penis in the window. I said, 'What do you mean, a penis in the window?' 'He was standing up there in the window, and he had his penis out as if he was going to urinate out the window.' And then she revealed her childhood fantasy of when it rained that was God urinating on the world, and this colleague was somebody she identified with me and so that was me up there. She came into the analytic hour with me one day with a hammer, shaking it. What was the hammer for? Either to hit me in the head or to break the window of my office and make me jump out to recapitulate the father's jump. At the end of the hour she left the hammer with me, never asked for it back. I don't have it anymore, but I kept it for quite awhile.

"This is obviously a story about a patient who was also traumatized by a mother, whom I recall as a functioning psychotic. Your patient had a mother who was suicidal, at least one major episode of attempted suicide, and the child was involved in this. Her father suffered from bleeding ulcers and nervous breakdowns, and she had a feeling, I guess, that life at home was out of control. The parents are out of control. They don't take care of themselves or each other, and they certainly can't take care of me. Growing up in this kind of fright; how can I function and survive in this world if I don't have a nurturing, protective contact in which to live? But she nonetheless is apparently well-educated and functions well in a job and is married. And yet she is constantly living in a world where what's real and what's unreal are never quite clear. It must be a struggle for her to maintain her appearance of normalcy."

I agreed and said, "It isolated her."

Wallerstein continued, "Because inside she feels so chaotic, and inside she feels she's never learned to tell the difference between what's fantasy and what's reality. It's a little bit like the 4-year-old who bursts into the parental bedroom and sees the parents having intercourse, and the mother screams at the little kid, 'Get the hell out of here; you didn't see anything.' And the child has to remember to say that what she saw she didn't see. She's not sure; was it real or was it not real? Therefore, her task in treatment is to be able to establish firm boundaries and to tell illusion or fantasy from reality. You never say things in a sort of stereotypical way, but basically the format of interpretation is, 'Here is an instance in which you're reacting to me as if I were your mother who smothered you so much and wouldn't let you alone and always hovered over you. Here's a way in which you're responding to me, to this situation, as if I were your father who was always buried in the newspaper, was never interested in you, always sarcastic with you, whatever.' It's always here; it is a way in which you're reacting to us as if we were a transference figure and it's always got the 'as if' quality. And with a neurotic patient, they understand the interpretation, in that sense, because they know that at the same time you're not that person from childhood. You are who you are, but they're reacting to you as if you were someone else. With patients like this, they don't always know that difference. It's the kind of situation where one has to convey, not necessarily in words, 'Here you are acting towards me as if I were So and So. But you know, really, that I'm not; and you know that I'm Wallerstein.' One has to, almost, reaffirm."

I said, "Roselyn often knows something intellectually, but it does not change her feelings."

Wallerstein agreed, "You have to convey that, where there's this discrepancy. I have a patient now, an analytic patient, who will say—how would he put it—'I know this is so, but just because I say it doesn't make it so. I need you to say it and not only to say it but to say it very loudly and to yell at me; otherwise I don't hear it.' We have to be constantly aware of the interpretative task."

Wallerstein wondered how Roselyn understood her regressed state the time when her house was broken into and scattered and spilled. I said, "She felt her boundaries had been assaulted and nothing connected anymore."

Wallerstein responded, "This would be the interpretative act that, to her, being vandalized was being trooped upon, all the boundaries violated, and the whole world disintegrated rather than its being a terrible loss. But to other people, it's a terrible loss but it's not the end of the world. My house is still here, I'm still here, it's only money, we can make it up."

I said, "The house was her container, her skin; so to have even that violated was awful. She'd already had a feeling of no skin."

Wallerstein said, "What I would have conveyed to her is something like that she feels, at this time, everything is destroyed, the world is ended, the house which is her life and her skin is gone, it is as if there's nothing left even though she knows at the same time that she's here, her husband's here and despite this terrible loss, things can be rebuilt. She may know that, but that doesn't cut into her feelings at all; and her feelings, which are so real, it's as if everything is gone. It's sort of that which I think would hit at—what is going through her mind; she's wrapped herself in, 'I'm retreating back into the womb where I don't know about the world at all. And it's all come apart.' "

I said, "My feeling is that at that point that she was so regressed that you had to treat her as you would any child who has been devastated."

He agreed, saying, "Which is a way of saying there is more to life in this world than what's just happened to you. You can rebuild from here, and there are people who care and will help you and help protect things and help you rebuild. And then after a while, she can begin to sort out what terribleness it was; it wasn't everything; it wasn't all of life."

Wallerstein recalled, "When we had that earthquake in 1989, and I came home, especially down at the bottom of the hill when you passed the Bon Appetit, the supermarket—during that earthquake, 10,001 bottles were thrown off the shelves and crashed. And I knew that, and I came up the hill to this house and it was intact. A couple of pictures were off the wall, so I knew the house had shaken. One small object over there had fallen over and broken; one small object; but I know how I would have felt if I'd come in to destruction. I wouldn't have done as your patient, but I would have been devastated."

I went on, "The anger of knowing somebody had done this deliberately and maliciously would be difficult."

Wallerstein agreed, "And at that moment, it's hard for her. It's as if somebody was out just after her—which can be the case sometimes, that somebody has something in for her, or it can be a random burglary that somebody's coming through and just happened to hit her house. But to her, she doesn't make those distinctions at that point. And, again, those are things one has to both understand and understand the feeling that it's as if everybody was conspiring to do this to you."

I said, "I'm doing psychotherapy. To the best of my knowledge I'm keeping the frame, the psychoanalytic frame, as close as I can hold it to her. But sometimes that frame, she pushes against it and I move with it."

Wallerstein said, "I would call it psychoanalytic but not psychoanalysis. It may become psychoanalysis, if by psychoanalysis we mean that we're reconstructing the infantile neurosis or psychosis, the infantile interactions and tracing out developmentally the path through which they have influenced every aspect of life, after which you bring her to where she is now and in effect fill in that whole biography. To me, one of my definitions of psychoanalysis is it's rewriting your autobiography. You come into analysis and you say, 'I'm this kind of person; I've got these kinds of troubles. It's because I've had this kind of upbringing, this kind of mother. If you had a mother like that, you'd be like me too, or father, or these experiences,' and you present them. And you use what you create of your past as a way of justifying who you are at the present. And to me analysis is a process thing: 'Yes, all that's true, and let's find out more about it.' And whatever the patient says, in a way you could say, well the customer's always right; that is, you're trying to see the patient's psychological world through her eyes. But also the customer's always wrong in the sense that, 'You say you're mad, but what more is there and what else is there and can we find out more?' It's always, 'That isn't quite enough; that isn't the whole story.' And analysis becomes an effort to fill out as much as possible the whole story so you have a much more three-dimensional autobiography. You now can say, 'When I came to analysis, I saw my mother or father or brother or uncle in this light; but there are all these additional perspectives on them that I was less open to then. They give me a more realistic picture of them, my way of interacting with them, and my contribution to the way I interacted with them, and made me see them in a particular way at a particular time in my life.' If you're reaching for the fullness of that process, it becomes analysis."

Wallerstein continued, "You're dealing with all the resistances too. And in this, I think what you're really dealing with is trying both to stabilize her life unchanged at present, to contain her disintegrating tendencies. You're trying to give her a firmer grasp today of her emotions and the relationships of her feelings to her interactions that push her one way or another; to give her a better way of distinguishing fantasy from reality and knowing—and whether to take people's words at face value and whether to take them concretely or more metaphorically. Whether that necessarily involves recreating the totality of her life or whether one can recreate her life in a classically analytic way, her whole life, I don't know; and I would leave it open as to whether this could ever be a complete analysis, although you're doing as much analytic work as you can with patients like this."

I asked if he had some thoughts about Roselyn's migraines. Wallerstein said, "Her migraine has, must have, many, many meanings. I think one of the meanings, though, of her somatic symptom is something like this: It gives you a sense of reality. You feel something painful here, and that's real." He went on, "I was just reading a piece by somebody, apropos of some of these issues, in which the point he makes is there are many different ways in which something is real or is a reality. We can have a lot of somatic symptoms that have no physiological basis, and to the chemist there's no reality to them. Yet to the patient, the headache is a something; it's not a nothing. It's a something in a different sense than if you had a brain tumor in there, which is also a something of a different kind. It causes headaches, and they continue. It's that kind of something to her—a sense of reality. The pain in her head makes her feel she really has a head, and she's a real person. It has a lot of other meanings. The rages that are expressed."

I said, "Roselyn feels that when she was physically abused, she pushed all her feelings back into her head."

Wallerstein continued, "And then they press against her head and cause pain. Then the other meanings come to mind; they press against her head; they're trying to get out. They're trying to get out, but she doesn't have a way to bring them out that's manageable. She's afraid they'll get out of control, they'll overwhelm her, and so she tries to keep them in; and that is reflected in the headache where she's working hard to keep in feelings that she doesn't know how to express in a modulated way. It's like she has never learned how to express feelings in the appropriate way without just overwhelming herself or overwhelming the other person."

I asked if he had any technical ideas that might help. He replied, "In effect, I'd say to her that what she struggles with, in her migraine, are the pressures of all of these feelings that just bubble all through her that are so powerful. She'd like to express, but she's afraid to express them. She's afraid to express them because it would overwhelm her and because she doesn't think she can control them in the way she expresses them. She feels they would overwhelm and maybe destroy the other person, and so her only alternative—and it's a dreadful alternative—is to hold it all in and have this terrible headache instead of having a way to really articulate her feelings appropriately, whether to the husband, to friends, to coworkers."

I replied, "I've done it, I've done it. I know we have a good treatment relationship. What she says to me is, 'I don't know how to do it. I know I have to do it. I know and we both know, but I don't know how to do it.' "

Wallerstein said, "There's a place for some role playing of a particular kind. I had a patient in Topeka, a young teenage girl, who had two older sisters. She came from a Southern family which was very proper and prominent and conscious of their social position. The daughters were being brought up to be perfect ladies. The two older sisters were kind of rebellious toward the very controlling mother. They rebelled at the mother's smothering. They got off to college, and they wanted to get as far away from her as possible. The patient couldn't bring herself to rebel against mother. She was more dutiful, guilty about the thought of even the idea. But she had something of a psychotic breakdown and was hospitalized at the Menninger Foundation. I had her in psychotherapy three times a week. The first time she was supposed to go home, over the Christmas holidays for 2 weeks, her mother said, 'We all look forward to your coming home; your sisters are coming home, you're coming home; it will be a wonderful reunion. You've had a lot of social invitations.' The mother listed them, saying, 'I rejected these. I've accepted these because they're appropriate for you, and these are the parties you'll go to. We'll go shopping together, and I'll buy you clothes.' Mother always insisted on buying her clothes because Mother had a better sense of style, and so my patient felt completely smothered. Her mother was even telling her which friends she could see and which not to see. How could she handle this? She just collapsed then. If she didn't go, what choice did she have? Later, a similar kind of thing was coming up. We went through role playing such things as, 'What is it that your mother is going to say to you, and what would you like to be able to say? What would your sister say to your mother?' And she would go through that. 'Well, what would happen if you said what your sister said or what your sister would say? What would mother do?' And then she went through various scenarios. 'Well, suppose mother said that. How would your sister respond to that?' And it's kind of a role playing and coaching and kind of working through in her own mind scenarios of how she would try to deal with each situation. I said,

'Remember, also, it's 2 weeks; but the airlines fly, the telephones work; you don't have to stay the 2 weeks. You can call me at anytime during that 2 weeks, and you can always get on a plane and come back early. You don't have to stay.' But with the kind of role playing of what she would like to be able to say, if she could say it, and calling on the fact that her sisters somehow had been able to say things like this and get away with it, her mother couldn't do anything. And it may be that that kind of role playing and coaching of what is the scenario out there that is so dreadful would help. 'What would happen if, instead of having a headache, your feelings really came out? How would you express this? What would you like to say? What are you afraid you might say, and what would keep you from saying what you'd like to say?' "

I thanked Dr. Wallerstein for his generosity in allowing me to have this case discussion in his home on a Sunday morning. As we concluded, he offered me a piece of fruit "for the road." He escorted me with my equipment up the steep stairs to my car.

Arnold Modell

Dr. Modell is known for his writings regarding the treatment of primitive mental states. Recently he has turned his interest toward the need for "states of aloneness" in an analysis.

This interview took place in Modell's home in Waban, Massachusetts, on October 12, 1991. Modell has an outwardly calm, but clearly lively mind. His interests range from psychoanalysis to neurobiology. He practices yoga and enjoys his role as grandfather. Besides writing, which is a passion of his, he also enjoys movies and museums. At my request, he allowed me to see the room where he writes, which is not the same room where he sees patients. The writing room had clearly lost the fight or any claim it may have once had to order. Order had graciously surrendered to creativity; books and periodicals were everywhere, even covering the floor.

Dr. Modell and his wife seem to enjoy guests, good wine, and food along with their many other interests. They are lively conversationalists and enjoy history and current events. They were very interested in the Anita Hill–Clarence Thomas hearings which were ongoing during my visit. Dr. Modell seems to possess both contemplation and candor.

Dr. Modell has published many clinical papers. His books include *Object Love and Reality: An Introduction to a Psychoanalyst Theory and Object Relations* (1968b), *Psychoanalysis in a New Context* (1984), and *Other Times, Other Realities: Toward a Theory of Psychoanalytic Treatment* (1990). *Private Self* (1993), which Dr. Modell was thinking about during my visit, has since been published.

Interview

Virginia Hunter: How did you come to be interested in psychoanalysis?

Arnold Modell: Well, I am one of those people who wanted to be an analyst as a teenager. I don't know precisely how I got to him, but I was reading Freud, I guess, when I was 14, 15, something like that. And I went to college with this in the back of my head, somewhere. And I didn't quite get off that track. I toyed, perhaps, with being a psychologist, studying anthropology but that didn't get very far. Somehow I thought psychoanalysis was for me even before I went to college. Actually, I guess I felt, in myself, that I had some interesting psychology and came across Freud's *The Interpretation of Dreams* (1900).

VH: What did your parents think about your being interested in psychoanalysis?

AM: They weren't very happy about that. They didn't know what to think about it. I think they thought people interested in psychiatry are crazy.

VH: Could you tell me about them and your childhood?

AM: I was born in 1924, in Manhattan, an only child; we later moved to Brooklyn. My father was essentially a businessman, with his ups and downs. Sometimes up and sometimes down, but totally unintellectual. Some of my patients think that I must have had intellectual parents. That couldn't be farther from the truth.

VH: What kind of business was your father in?

AM: Various businesses. He had a knack of seeing things coming, and he got into the radio business when radios just came out and did very well. Then that didn't quite work out, and he went into a whole variety of other businesses. He ended up in the art business. He was kind of an entrepreneur of making portraits, having people's portraits made.

VH: But not the artist?

AM: No, he wasn't an artist; but he had many businesses.

VH: How would you describe his character?

AM: A very nice man. I was lucky in that. A very fundamentally nice man. Smart. I think a basically good businessman, perhaps a little passive in some ways.

VH: You make it sound as though there were a lot of mean men in those days.

AM: I guess I am extrapolating from my experience with patients, many of whom have mean fathers.

VH: And your mom?

AM: My mom was also kindly, but not terribly intelligent. Sort of limited.

VH: Then where did you get your intelligence?

AM: I don't know, maybe grandparents. My father's quite bright. There isn't any intellectual heritage, as it were, in the family other than my grandmother's brother, who's reputed to have been a professor at the Sorbonne. If it's true or not, I have never found out.

VH: Your papers on "Whose Reality Is It" (1968a, 1968b) make me wonder if your mother's reality and your reality were quite different.

AM: Right on. Quite right on. That's true. I guess I am very sensitive to that issue. I will say, which I'll talk about further, that I firmly believe, and I think most people do, most psychological discoveries are self-discoveries.

VH: How were you as a student, as a child?

AM: Good, not extraordinary; I was a good student, not brilliant, good enough.

VH: You were certainly said to be brilliant. I've noticed it said in several different places. Did that come after your analysis? I don't mean did the innate intelligence come after the analysis, I mean was your own analysis helpful to you in being able to organize or use it in a different way?

AM: Oh yes, very much so. I have a funny, uneven kind of mind. I think I'm good at what I do. I'm not being modest about it; but I'm bad at languages and terrible at mathematics; so it's a very uneven kind of intelligence.

VH: How do you understand this?

AM: I think that's the way intelligence is. It's kind of scattered. There are people that are good across the board. I don't happen to be one of those kinds of people.

VH: I guess, since I was a dyslexic child, I'm particularly interested.

AM: I'm not dyslexic, but I have a son who might have had a dyslexic problem. I have a stutter, which is partly related to a neurological genetic pattern.

VH: You think stuttering is mostly related to neurological patterns?

AM: My father stuttered too, and he had it before I knew him, as a young man. Stanley Cobb, who was a very famous professor of psychiatry here, was a stutterer and studied his family tree and found he could trace the origin of his stutter. I'm fairly convinced it's genetic and neurological.

VH: It raises an interesting question, for me, in terms of where's the object, do you think not at all in this? It's an interference of language certainly in the production of language.

AM: It's the expression of language.

VH: Expressional. You don't think the object plays a part?

AM: Like many symptoms, stress will bring it on. It also has psychological significance.

VH: Could you tell me about your schooling and training?

AM: I went to Columbia College in New York in 1944, and then went to medical school, during the War, at the Long Island College of Medicine. It's now called Downstate. After graduating and internship, I had a year at Worcester State Hospital, which was very interesting in those days, back in 1948. It was still a research hospital, and a very good one. Then I went to Yale. The thing that was wonderful about those days (I guess I can tell our hidden audience); you were not overwhelmed with service functions. We had all the time needed to study our patients; and in those days, psychotherapy with schizophrenia was an "in" thing. People didn't know its limits: One found an interesting case and simply immersed oneself in the treatment. Also, in those days, there were no drugs to speak of. So you saw schizophrenia as a pure culture, and it was very educational. If people had any question about primary process and the meaning of the unconscious, all they had to do was have one schizophrenic patient and they were convinced. Today, this doesn't happen. I suppose now all schizophrenic patients are on some kind of medication. It was very different. I remember a schizophrenic patient having a postpartum psychosis; and the content was very clear that she really felt that this baby was a penis that was taken out of her.

VH: A good penis or a bad penis?

AM: I couldn't say, I wasn't thinking along those lines in those days. But that connection stuck in my mind. The point is, one was not overwhelmed with service functions. Unfortunately, that's not the case today.

VH: You were primarily doing talking cures without electric shock?

AM: There was electric shock. We used that, and there were patients who were on shock and insulin, which did some good. I don't think it was necessarily a bad form of treatment. Then we had patients we chose for psychotherapy, and we could do whatever we wanted.

VH: Who supervised you?

AM: That's interesting. There wasn't any supervision. There wasn't any supervision because nobody knew anything, which in some ways was wonderful, because you could be your own explorer. People at Worcester didn't know much about psychotherapy then. We were taught basic psychiatry. The people knew a good deal about interviewing, about making diagnosis and that kind of thing; but in terms of psychotherapy, no one knew anything. The analysts came later. The hospital was primarily a biological research hospital and a place where actually the birth control pill was discovered—not at the hospital but at the Worcester Foundation. When I went to Yale, it was different. I did get supervised there. There were people in analytic training and experienced analysts, and that was a very different picture.

VH: So you went straight from one place to the other?

AM: Yale was just beginning to develop a really high-powered analytic service. It was a very, very good place to be. Fritz Redlich was the head of it, and this was kind of a high point of combining psychiatry and psychoanalysis.

VH: Do you know who his analyst was? Do you remember?

AM: I don't know. The person that's outstanding, in my mind, in those days was Robert Knight, who was then at Stockbridge but came down to supervise at Yale. We were all frightened of him. He was of the old school of psychotherapy. I picked up some of his traits as a resident, but he was very imposing and a little scary. If you presented to him he'd grill you.

VH: Kind of like Menninger's rumored to have been?

AM: Yes, he was working there, but he was a very dedicated therapist with sick people, and he was a kind of role model, for a while.

VH: Was he tough with patients, as well as residents?

AM: No, very tender with very sick people. And Merton Gill was there for a while when I was there. We were neighbors actually. David Rapaport would come down and Loewenstein and Kris—we had quite an array of people in those days. Then I became busy as a chief resident my second year. I didn't spend as much time with these people as I wished I had. But Kris was known to be a wonderful teacher. So I had some excellent supervisors. It was the first time that I came to have good supervision.

VH: Did you have several different supervisors or just one primary one? Who were they?

AM: One I'm thinking of is Alfredo Namnum. He was a young man then. He's now at Menninger's. He's a training analyst there. He was a few years older than I was. Dick Newman, who was in analytic training, was the head of the outpatient clinic. His wife, Lotte, was a respected psychoanalytic editor for many years, a friend of Anna Freud's.

VH: You had to finish your medical residency before you could apply to become an analyst? So what was that little period like? How many years were there?

AM: I had some Navy service in between. I became a Navy psychiatrist. Actually, I got out a bit sooner than I would have for unfortunate reasons. That is, my wife, then, became ill with multiple sclerosis, and I came to Boston in 1951. I started my analytic training in 1954. My wife and I had two children, a boy and a girl. My wife was later hospitalized in a nursing home for 10 years before she died.

VH: It must have been hard raising two kids under those circumstances. What did they end up doing? If I get too personal—

AM: That's okay. I'm proud of both of them. My daughter is a neurology resident at the moment, and it's her daughter, who's in college, whom you met. My son, who lives in Missouri, is a plant engineer and also has a child.

VH: You entered the Boston Psychoanalytic Institute in 1954. Who was your analyst?

AM: Elizabeth Zetzel. I saw her four or five times a week. As analyses go, it was typical—5 years or so. She died fairly young, when she was about 64 of a heart attack. I think she was an excellent analyst.

VH: What makes an excellent analyst?

AM: Oh, she was "with it." She just could follow all the material very carefully and compassionately, a little too compassionate—one of her faults. I think she got too involved with her patients, in the sense that she got involved in their lives and this kind of thing. If someone had trouble, she'd be there in the flesh, which has its good points and bad points.

VH: Could you share your memories?

AM: All right. I could share this with you. At one point there was some question whether my wife, my first wife that is, was developing some brain damage, and Elizabeth volunteered to see her in consultation. I wouldn't do that myself. I think it's a little intrusive, too much involved. At the time I was grateful to her. But there could have been another consultant, but this was her style. She had that reputation. Well, I guess, it didn't hurt me. But, I don't think it's a good thing to do.

VH: Are there other ways, where you feel she conducted an analysis in a very different way than you would?

AM: Oh yes, I have a very different outlook on analysis. Of course, this was in the 1950s. My analysis started in 1954 and ended around 1960. It's very different now. I have a very different idea about analysis than she probably had. I think she was much more classical. She was analyzed in England by Ernest Jones. She concentrated on the oedipus complex. I practiced that way, for a while, and I gradually evolved as a different kind of analyst.

VH: Could you describe the evolution, the process, where you came from and where you moved to?

AM: I couldn't map it out in great detail, it's hard to say. These things happen so gradually. It isn't only the way I've changed. I think the whole field has changed in many ways. I think it's changed in terms of theory and technique. How technique and theory have changed is really what you're asking. I've been influenced by Winnicott's idea of establishing a climate in which things will happen and not be too intrusive or interpretative. I've become less interested in content, as I've gotten older. The whole field has changed. The patients have changed; technique has changed—the whole business has changed. It's an interesting question; if you try to spell out, in detail, how it's changed, but I don't think I could do it off the top of my head.

VH: It is a difficult question. But it's an interesting question since you've been doing it since the 1950s; in terms of what you were aware of in yourself. I spent some time with Ernest Wolf and he talked about Gitelson and how he had to leave that analysis because of his unresponsiveness, and Giovacchini talked about how he felt attacked—the fault was found and it was consistently attacked.

AM: I don't have any complaints about my analyst really. Whatever she did, I felt as if I had a good analysis. As a person, she's reputed to have been difficult, and I can imagine that this was true. It was true. She was a rather difficult lady socially, picked fights and was arrogant. She had very strong opinions. But behind the couch, she was fine.

VH: Who were your supervisors?

AM: I think my favorite supervisor was Beata Rank. She supervised my first case, and I think she was great. She had a gift of seeing the whole person. My second case was with Felix Deutsch, and he was in a totally different ball game. I liked Felix because he was an extraordinary fellow, but I don't think he was a very good analyst. I don't think he was a very good supervisor. I don't think I had very good treatment with my patient. In fact, I'm sure I would never treat a patient with his technique. He was of his own school. I suppose in those days you could call it the id school. Felix was married to Helene Deutsch, and he originally was an internist, and he actually was one of Freud's doctors. He's the one who diagnosed Freud's tongue cancer in April 1923. That's a separate story. Freud fired him as a doctor because he did something which was common in those days—he withheld the diagnosis from Freud. They did a biopsy and discovered cancer, and they didn't tell Freud about it.

Anyway, to come back to Felix as a supervisor—he was not my type. The Deutsches and the Bibrings were the ruling analytic families in Boston. Felix was a kind of a master of fantasy—of discovering fantasy. He had an extraordinary grasp of fantasy material. He lived in fantasy material.

VH: Personally?

AM: No, not personally, with the patient. And so his way of conducting analysis was to elicit fantasy. He was not interested in object relations and the relationship you had with the patient, the patient's life—it was all fantasy. If a patient came in and said, "I went to a cocktail party," Felix would say, "A cocktail party?"

VH: But he wasn't a Kleinian?

AM: No, he wasn't a Kleinian. He hated the Kleinians. They were the opposite camp.

VH: Well, now I know I'm lost in terms of theory because I thought that much interest in fantasy usually came from Kleinians.

AM: Well, she got to it later. Felix was an analyst of the 1920s. It's true that the Kleinians are known for their interest in fantasy, but they didn't have a corner on that market. When ego psychology came along, people like Felix were very much id psychologists. Now, this was not good analysis, as I subsequently learned, and I also knew it at the time. It wasn't good analysis because it was one sided. You can't do analysis looking at just the patient's content. But he was a master of this, and it was quite an extraordinary experience to be supervised by him.

VH: How did that work for you? I mean, were you chomping at the bit all the time?

AM: I didn't—I was a dutiful student. I did what he told me to do, and it didn't work too well. I learned something. I was interested in fantasy, but I later realized that this was not the way to conduct an analysis. I'm sorry for the patient. The patient didn't do that well.

VH: Were you uncomfortable at the time?

AM: I think so. I think I felt that I was missing something. In those days you did what your supervisor told you, more or less. He was conducting the analysis. It wasn't like today where you act as a kind of consultant to your students and let them do the analysis their own way and tell them how you differ. But this was different. There was an authoritative aspect. One of his supervisees told this to me. Apparently at one point, when you went into supervision with him, he'd give you a checklist of what to do with dreams. He'd have the thing checked out and you'd get a dream and do this and this and this. Felix was an old man when I saw him. He was in his 70s. He would fall asleep sometimes during supervision. He wasn't too well physically.

The next one was Eleanore Parenstedt, and she was a lady who was nice and sound, and I had a good patient in analysis—it went on its own steam.

VH: Did you pick her or was she assigned to you?

AM: I really can't recall. I think she was assigned to me. I think in those days lots of cases were assigned. My last supervisor was very good. We had a tough case of a homosexual man. I didn't cure his homosexuality. We tried to do that in those days. But the supervisor, Gregory Rochlin—he's still around. I guess he's the only one of these people who are still around. He was very good. He was a child analyst. He wrote about depression in children, and he wrote a book, several books, on aggression. He was a student of Helene Deutsch. She was also his analyst.

VH: Was that couple, the Deutsches, aligned in their beliefs, or were they different?

AM: They were aligned in their beliefs but probably not their technique. There was a feud here between the Deutsches and the Bibrings. This was pretty much before my time. When I came on the scene, this had died down a bit. But I think the Bibrings were more associated with ego psychology, and the Deutsches more associated with an earlier so-called id psychology. There might be a distinction like that, really a silly distinction. Felix practiced a kind of wild analysis, that if you see content, you interpret it. I guess the Kleinians took this over. The thing I recall, if the patient's name was Anna, Felix Deutsch might say, "Anna, that's like anus. She has an anal complex of some sort because her name is Anna."

VH: So there was sort of a wild association and the evacuation of the mind, by the analyst.

AM: That's right. It was a wild association to the patient's speech, the patient's utterances.

VH: Your paper on "Whose Reality Is It?" (1991a) comes to mind. It sounds as though the analyst's associations were imposed as "truth." Was is out of that kind of wild free association on the analyst's part that we got to such a later withholding, nongratifying, nonresponsive style?

AM: I think it's probably safe to say that there was a reaction to the wildness, that people became very constrained—this was in the 1950s perhaps, and the caricature of the analyst—the patient comes into the analyst. The patient says, "Good morning." The analyst doesn't say anything. We went through that phase; then we had to work our way out of that. Leo Stone comes to mind, as a very important person who had this way of seeing that in analysis there was a human relationship. Analysts lost sight of that for a while. This did a good deal of damage and further hurt psychoanalysis. Some of the people who were analyzed then became anti-analysis. It was not too good.

VH: How do you think your training compares to training now?

AM: My training was much more authoritative. Now, I think the training is better at the Institute. The courses are better, they're more flexible, there's more openness.

VH: What was that early atmosphere when you were at the Institute like? Was there a camaraderie?

AM: Well, there was amongst people in one's class, but it was a kind of spooky atmosphere, a paranoid kind of atmosphere. The old Boston Institute—I'm talking about around the 1950s and the 1960s, 1970s too perhaps—was one in which there was a lot of infighting amongst the training analysts group. There were a lot of animosities. And it just sort of filtered down throughout the organization.

VH: Based on theory or based on politics?

AM: Personality. There weren't any real theoretical controversies.

VH: The splits do interest me, and they seem to be in almost every institute. It puzzles me.

AM: I don't think psychoanalysts are any wiser or better than other people, unfortunately. In spite of the fact they've been analyzed.

VH: What was your first published paper?

AM: My first published paper, in 1949, was a paper using figure drawings as a way of differentiating psychosomatic patients. There was a figure drawing test usually administered to hospitalized patients—a draw-a-person test. What I did was to apply the test to patients in the hospital for various diseases such as hypertension, ulcers, and asthma; I think, those were the three groups. At that point, psychosomatic medicine was very much in the foreground. There was a theory that there is some linkage between character types and certain illnesses. It's never worked out too precisely. There were certain patterns that could be discerned from figure drawings, differentiated into groups. I haven't looked at this paper in years, but something like the hypertensive was more involved with helplessness and powerlessness, and I forget how I differentiated the other groups. I've lost contact completely with this kind of research, and I don't know whether it's valid. I think there's something to it actually, but it's hard to discern.

Then I wrote a review paper on schizophrenia, psychoanalytic theories of schizophrenia. And then I went into my one and only formal research project where I tried to systematically look at the meaning of hallucinations. And in those days, remember that there weren't any drugs, so the symptoms were florid. So I went around tape recording patients' accounts of their hallucinatory experiences. That took a while, and I wrote up a research project. One of the things I learned was that a lot of the voices were very helpful and not persecutory. But that was an isolated research project. That's all the formal research I think I've done.

I was very interested in treating schizophrenics for a while, and I did a lot of psychotherapy, but I think the results were so disheartening that I gradually gave it up. Of course, with the advance of drugs it became very complicated. I learned a lot. Then I gradually got interested in borderlines. Actually, my first paper on borderlines was trying to differentiate the borderline from the schizophrenic because that was a muddy area in those days. Robert Knight wrote a paper on the borderline, but he was talking about schizophrenia. You see, the term borderline originally was not differentiated from people who were, let's say, incipient schizophrenics or kind of mild schizophrenics. One of the things that was very prevalent in those days was the notion that a patient may look neurotic, may present to you with a neurosis; but he or she might have an underlying schizophrenia. So it was quite important, especially for analysts, to be careful diagnosticians because one of the catastrophes would be to take somebody into analysis and precipitate a psychosis, and people worried about that. My paper was directed to the idea that the borderline concept was a character illness with stable defenses and should be differentiated from incipient schizophrenia.

VH: Do you think an analysis, as you would conduct it today, would precipitate a psychosis? That theory, to me, seems more appropriate with that id attack stuff, but not as we generally practice today.

AM: I think my technique has changed, so I'd probably be safeguarding that. We've learned a lot. Our experience has accumulated over these years so that most people, I think, are much more experienced than the average good analyst was back in the 1950s. So this is not likely to happen. It could happen, if we treated patients the way Felix Deutsch did. That is, if you paid no respect to the relationship with the patient, or defenses or the ego processes and simply went after content. You could simply push someone over the edge.

There are tremendous changes in the whole field. Since we are all part of the process, and since we are seeing this happen gradually, it's very hard for us to recognize. The kind of patients I saw as a candidate are very rare today, so-called good neurotics are very, very rare.

The whole spectrum of neurotic character, I think, has changed in a very curious way. Neurosis is, in some ways, responsive to cultural change. Some people have said it's only surface phenomena. The oedipus complex, I don't think, is very central anymore, at least to my patients. I think that could be a cultural change. The old analyst wasn't manufacturing this stuff. I think for them, as with many of my earlier patients, as well as with my own, the focus was on the oedipus complex.

VH: I was interested in your recognition that theoretical convictions really influenced what your therapeutic aims are, and I wonder if you could say something about that.

AM: It is perfectly obvious that if your aim is to make the unconscious conscious, you're going to be doing one thing; but if you have another kind of aim, if your aim is to integrate the self, let's say as an example, or the aim is to enable an individual simply, to unflower and develop his inner core—one way of looking at it—one will do different things. I'll think about this probably again tomorrow, in relationship to your case, but one of my more recent interests has been the theory of self. I'm going off in a different direction than self psychology people, and I'm very much interested in the private self, what Winnicott called the true self. But the point I'm getting at is that one of the aims, as I see it, in analysis is to enable the individual to experience a kind of protected solitude; that is, to let the analytic setting and yourself in that setting, be a presence, be a benign, protective presence that allows the individual to be by himself.

VH: This sounds similar to Bollas's work.

AM: I suppose it is in some ways. We both were influenced by Winnicott.

VH: So you have a feeling that perhaps in the past there was so much intrusion or so much activity or so many preconceived ideas that a space wasn't allowed.

AM: It goes further than that though. It is the fact that there are generative forces in the self and that you are a facilitator, midwife, as it were. You're not the person who does it. It's different from that of the self psychology people.

I was at Chicago about 2 weeks ago, giving this paper on the private self; and the self psychology people simply didn't show up. I think their point of view is different. I think their point of view is that the self is fundamentally defective, and you have to provide that which is missing.

VH: A function.

AM: Yes, a function. There are patients for whom you provide certain functions, I think about processing affect, for example. But there are also internal processes that are self-generating, and you're simply there to allow the person to get in touch with them. Some people suffer from a kind of decentering of themselves. Something happened in their development so that they're cut off from the core of their inner experiences. One of the aims of analysis would be to allow them to rediscover this, the inner core, as it were. How you do it is another problem.

Wolf, Kohut's colleague, recently, in his book said our need for a selfobject is akin to a need for oxygen. So the notion that we are always dependent is not entirely wrong, but one-sided.

VH: You've written a lot about dependency yourself.

AM: We are always dependent to some extent on affirmation from others. No one is totally self-sufficient, and nobody can live without some kind of affirmation, but it's overdone, overstated. When I gave this paper, my discussant was John Gedo; and he and I were pretty much in agreement. He used the analogy that, yes, you need vitamins; but you don't need to take them every day, and I think that's right.

VH: Could you give an example of a patient and how self psychologists would be viewing it, thinking of it and interpreting it with a patient; and here is how you would be doing it?

AM: I couldn't do that because I don't know enough of what they do. If I worked with a self psychologist or supervised one or heard the case, I would be better able to do that.

I don't want to misrepresent their position because the way people practice and the way people say they practice may be two different things; so I'm not saying that this is necessarily the way they practice, but at least what they say they do in practice. Now their position is that the self is defective. I agree that patients will report the fact that they may feel defective, they feel something missing or something like that. But it would be a mistake to be so identified with the patient's experience that you will take that as a so-called objective statement. That is, the patients may, to themselves, appear to be defective, and yet you'll see, in terms of their life and their life experiences, that they're pretty damn resilient. It's a different position. If you say that they're defective, then you have to provide what's missing. The notion being that people suffer from parental relationships that are out of synchrony or unempathic or unsupportive of the self, things like that. I'm not saying that doesn't happen. That does happen, but you can make a case for something quite different. That is, that people who were exposed to trauma and violence of one sort or another, may develop, as a consequence, a great inner strength and a greater inner resiliency. This is not something self psychology people are emphasizing.

VH: I think Wolf would agree with that specific point, however.

AM: He would? But they haven't emphasized that, and they haven't emphasized the fact that this leads to a need for a private self, that there's a certain organization within the self—this is from Winnicott. That there's a need not to communicate. There's a need to have experiences that one has only for oneself.

VH: For autonomy.

AM: That's right. I've said elsewhere that empathy can be a double-edged thing. I have had patients tell me this rather specifically; they're rather threatened sometimes by empathic people because they can get right in, and they can see what's going on inside of them, and they don't want that.

VH: So respect for nonintrusion.

AM: I guess self psychology people would agree it's empathic not to be intrusive. There isn't any difference between my position and theirs with regard to intrusion. Kohut was very sensitive about the issue of intrusion. But I think there is a difference, a real difference, in terms of the idea of there being a self that's defective and is cured by the selfobject. They need some kind of holding environment, but they don't always need your doing something for them. Sometimes you have to simply let patients be, to simply let them be and let them find what's there.

VH: Your primary thrust there is that the self psychologist is assuming too much responsibility?

AM: Yes, it's putting the patient in the passive position, as far as I can tell. This is what I gather from what they write.

VH: And they do attack in terms of, what did you do to make the patient feel that? And you think, my Gosh, didn't this patient have some aggression before I failed to say the right thing?

AM: That's the important part. It's very clear this issue of the analyst's mistakes. That is, of course, there are times when you'll make a mistake and maybe the best thing to do is say, "Look I made a mistake." But there are other times where the patient needs you not to understand something. They are developmentally recreating something they have to create, recreate a situation in which you don't understand because they're working through some earlier trauma. And this is not something that the self psychology people see, or at least they don't say that they see. One's theoretical position will influence how you approach a case. If the analyst believes that misunderstandings are his own fault, then the urge is to be as empathic as possible, recognizing that one can never be totally empathic. That, I think, is in some ways putting the patient in a very passive position. That is, the analyst has that responsibility. Rather than seeing that the analyst will be caught up at times in a process that emanates from the patient. The patient is the active one!

One of the things I'm very sensitive about is the issue of the analyst imposing his or her ideas on a patient. A lot of people are very sensitive about this issue. But I'm also aware of it presenting a paradox, which I think is an interesting paradox because there comes a point in many treatments where the analyst has to be aware, becomes aware, that—let's say that the patient isn't functioning as well as he or she could be within the context of the therapy. You think the patient can be doing more or be using this treatment in a little more advanced way. As I said, this raises a very interesting problem because this means that you have a hidden agenda as to how you think the treatment should proceed. This is at variance with another position that you simply want things to unfold and want the patient "to be." There are paradoxes in the therapeutic set-up that we simply have to accept. That's the way it is. I think we're conscious of it and know this is the way it is, and are able to cope with it. But in some ways there's a problem. Because you don't want to be intrusive, yet there are times when you know that you have to be intrusive and you have to intrude your ideas and beliefs. You presume to know something that they don't know. It's a very interesting problem.

VH: You've written that countertransference is the total response, whether neurotic or not neurotic, to the patient; and that was in that same paper on paradox relationships.

AM: I think countertransference is a problem, it still is a problem. It especially becomes a problem when you have issues such as Winnicott has described. That is—the objective aspect of countertransference. If you experience the patient as obnoxious, maybe they are an obnoxious person. In most cases, countertransference experiences are somewhere related to an objective-like identification. I'm supervising a case where I initially interviewed the patient. In my estimation, the patient was much healthier than my student's estimation, and moreover my student told me, after we got started, that she finds this woman repulsive. And I couldn't quite figure out what was repulsive about her. Maybe she is repulsive, but I did not find her so.

VH: Usually does the training analyst see the patient?

AM: Not always. I do sometimes when there's a question about their analyzability. I prefer not to because it simply complicates things a little bit, but in this case I did see the patient. There were some uncertainties to it. I thought she was a good prospect for a case even though she was not very sick. In the first couple of weeks it became very clear that my student was caught up in a projective identification. This woman's mother had rejected her, thought that she was disgusting—why and how we don't know, but I think this is a fact. And this was repeated. As a male, I probably didn't get whatever simulated this thing in the countertransference; but my student was at first simply being honest with me and saying, "I don't like this person."

VH: So a reenactment.

AM: In an unconscious way. Communication of something. I think with beginning therapists, inexperienced therapists, it is probably the major thing that screws the therapy up.

VH: Could you say more about that?

AM: I think people don't recognize projective identification, and they're treat it as an objective aspect of the patient's character. I've been caught up in this, too. The more inexperienced you are, the more likely it is to be a major problem and cause impasses.

VH: What makes a case suitable for analytic treatment?

AM: I suppose my criteria are pretty broad these days because we don't have these ideal patients. I think of somebody who can stay, can maintain himself or herself within the analytic set up, that is without killing himself, without getting too depressed, and also is of good moral character. I think Freud said this also. He said, "People in analysis should be of good moral character." I think there are all kinds of problems in this area. People may lie and do antisocial things as a neurotic defense, but there's also such a thing as moral character. And I think, in my best judgment, if somebody simply has values that are not—I'll have to say good values, who simply have bad values—I don't think that can be altered by psychoanalysis, I really don't. I think that people's value system develops quite early in life and can be quite personal and idiocentric. And I don't think that's an issue that can be altered by psychoanalysis, which is different from saying he or she has a problem with a superego or lies or steals. There are people who steal and lie who might be treatable. This is my opinion. And I also think we derive moral values from ourselves.

VH: Ourselves?

AM: This is part of my interest in the self. I'm writing a book on the self called *Private Self and Public Space* (1993). I've been thinking a good deal about this. Obviously we're influenced by our parents, and we accept our parents' values up to a point or it's maybe the opposite of our parent's values. There are people whose fathers may be thieves, and they turn out to be very righteous people, so it isn't a simple thing. But I do believe in people having a private morality that they create themselves. This is part of my notion of the created self—I think value is self-created. How they're self-created is a different problem. But what people are interested in, what they think is good, what they think is right is largely self-created.

One of my notions of private self is related to Winnicott's "true self." I've also been very supported by recent work by neurobiologists. Gerald Edelman has a notion of the self, based on brain functions—that of freeing the individual from the tyranny of current time. So his notion of the self is something that's self-creative and autonomous; but more than that, his notion of the central nervous system is something that's self-created. And he's convinced me that he's right. I think he's right. The brain, to some extent, is self-generating. It may sound crazy but it's not.

VH: We make ourselves hyperactive?

AM: It would be silly to infer that all influences are self-creative. But the brain appears to be individually tailored.

VH: What do you mean?

AM: Our brains are selectively individualized. That is one of Edelman's main points. One of my recent excitements is helping in starting a study group with psychoanalysts and neurobiologists, and I have learned about Edelman's ideas firsthand. The complexity of our nervous system is such that there are many things that are not prewired in our genes but develop idiosyncratically in environmental interaction.

VH: Not as Chomsky thought?

AM: Well that's another matter. But there's a great deal that is individually created and developed starting in the embryo, and going on throughout our life. What I'm convinced about is that there is a function of the self that is homeostatic, it's unconscious, like an organ, as it were. One of the functions of the self is to create a sense of coherence by modeling the inputs of the external world as well as the internal world. And this is done in a highly individualized creative manner.

VH: Please, say it one more time.

AM: One of the functions of the self, the biological self, is a kind of homeostatic process in which it creates a model of events of what's meaningful; and by doing that, it frees itself from the inputs of current time—it doesn't have to react to everything coming in because it can create a coherent model that creates distance, as it were. This is Edelman's theory, and I think it's a very powerful idea.

From my point of view, it indicates that the self has autonomous self-generating functions from the very beginning; and what's exciting about all this is that these ideas fit in very well with what the people who study infant behavior have noticed. They notice that the infant isn't just responding to the mother, it's creating something in its own period of time, of time out from responding. It's creating things, within themselves. I'm quite excited about these ideas because there is a convergence in the fields of infant psychiatry, neurobiology, and psychoanalysis.

VH: I've seen mothers with manic defenses who run their children from one stimulation to another and watched how disruptive that is to intimacy or a sense of calm.

AM: That's what I'm talking about. One needs private time for survival.

VH: It's hard to find in the society.

AM: We're talking about this. Actually in two weeks I'm going to New York. There's a conference there on solitude, and this is what I'm going to be talking about. One needs solitude. One needs time for solitude.

VH: I wonder if we even have it as a value, because it seems to me, I see more and more people who have no space of their own that's not filled with TV or something. When I think of my childhood and I think where patients are today, there's so little time and space for it, now.

AM: That's right. That's a very major problem. I can think of one patient of mine who suffered from what she felt to be kind of intrusiveness, and she feels out of touch with her own thoughts. She feels she doesn't have any thoughts. She can't think. She means she can't have contact with her thoughts. She's never had the time or the solitude to have private space so she can be in contact with her thoughts.

VH: Boy, you know, I certainly see more and more children with learning difficulties who have attention deficits and concentration deficits that would lead you to think along those lines. That they don't have that space. Is the space between the object, the space, is it a transitional space?

AM: No, it's a private space.

VH: It's a private space, not a transitional space?

AM: Having a benign presence there, I think, is useful, and may be necessary; but it's private time, private space.

VH: Do you have the feeling we've lost this in our society, somehow?

AM: It's a very interesting problem. The history of privacy is very implicit. The idea of having one's physical space is pretty new. Up until the 16th or 17th century, nobody had any privacy. Even the king slept in his bed and had a few servants around the walls and so forth. Literally, nobody was ever alone. So one wonders what they did for private space. I suspect this is one of the good things about religion in those days. You could have private space in your prayers. I do think that self psychologists have not cornered the market on the subject of the self, and I think there's a lot in addition to be said. I'm trying to put the subject of self in a broader perspective, and it needs to be put in a broader perspective. My thinking was pretty obviously influenced by Winnicott. His notion of self, I think, is quite different from other self psychologists, in that, he does acknowledge this private core of the self that needs to be secret and uncommunicative. He didn't elaborate on it very much, but he was thinking very much along these lines.

I'm talking, now, about something that has to do, not with object relations, but the opposite of relatedness, solitude, time for oneself, a mirror image of relatedness. I think it requires a presence. There are all kinds of qualities of solitude. There's a quality of solitude when one's actually alone. There's a quality to the comfort of solitude, to have a companionable solitude in the presence of the object which is one of the aspects of psychoanalysis. I think we give our patients a companionable solitude.

VH: I'm silent because I'm thinking of how much my father would agree with you and yet how little. I see or hear about that kind of relatedness. I think of it, as that kind of relatedness of two people fishing and not talking or two people walking a road and looking at leaves and not talking. It does seem to me there is less and less—

AM: There's less and less, that's very unfortunate.

VH: I hear patients with their schedules, where they go from event, to event, quite rapidly. You're focusing on the necessity to allow these peoples' own innate organic potential to develop to become their own, to have ownership.

AM: That's precisely right. I think we got lost on the subject of relatedness. We need to go back a bit. I'm speaking as a person who's devoted his life to the theory of object relations, but I also acknowledge the fact that, for me, it's a different kind of space. It has to be safe, and that's the point. They have to learn that this is safe. There are people who grow up in environments that are so impinging, in Winnicott's terms—*that* isn't safe. And they retreat to their private self and do all kinds of things to survive; fantasy or daydreams or illusions or ideas about themselves, all kinds of ways. This is different from somebody who is in the protective set-up where he can be free to explore himself.

So for individuals who have been very traumatized, they may have to experiment and experience a great deal before they recognize that the environment is relatively safe and that they can have this kind of companionable solitude. So they have to achieve that, as it were. And usually before getting to that point, they have to learn that they don't need their emergency measures, as it were, to cope, that these are no longer necessary. They're grandiosities.

VH: Thank you, Dr. Modell, for this time. I have one last question. Do you call yourself a Winnicottian?

AM: I don't think so. I'm very much influenced by him, and there's very little I disagree with—with what he said.

VH: What do you call yourself?

AM: A Modellian!

Case Discussion

Dr. Modell, known for his work with primitive mental status, states that Roselyn experienced a kind of psychic death as a child. He goes on to say that since she has internalized faulty psychic attunement she has faulty affect processing. He believes that as a child Roselyn was helpless to leave a nongratifying mother and turned to herself to create a separate, internal world. He pointed out that her internalized objects are constantly attacking her.

This case discussion with Dr. Modell took place in his home outside of Boston, October 13, 1991. He began by saying that borderline people have trouble in shifting from ordinary life to transference; they cannot differentiate, and they really confuse transference with ordinary life. Winnicott's conception was that the benign presence of another is necessary to create fantasies. "But in some cases, like yours, the presence is not benign; it's very complicated," he said.

He continued, "I can tell you how I'm trying to think about it. That one function of the self would be not only to process meaning but to create meaning, generate meaning. If we think of the homeostatic function of self as a kind of biological given, one aspect of this function is to match meaning; that is, to match the memories of past experiences with current experiences. We assume that if all goes well, if this process goes well, there has been an adequate holding environment. Now where there is interference in this process, the self, in a sense, doesn't generate meaning, and people feel a sense of absence—taken to an extreme, a 'black hole.' They have a feeling of an absence in a process that is normally present, so the absence is experienced as emptiness as some meaninglessness and a sense of futility. I said this is very complicated because what also enters into this is the process of containing affects. I can tell you of some current material of a patient I have in analysis who doesn't speak of the 'black hole.' But life is futile; nothing has any meaning. Now this is linked with failure to process affect."

I asked, "All affects?"

He replied, "Positive affects especially, but she has no problem getting angry."

I said, "My patient can process fear, fear of annihilation, but only in the last 6 months has she been able to process longing, deprivation, needs for tenderness. All she could report was this fear of annihilation, fear of attack, fear of danger, the survival—actual survival needs but not the dependent needs."

Modell said, "I think this is true of my patient too; deficiencies exist in an area of acknowledging dependency and acknowledging love. The point being that there is some interference in the processing of affects. This interferes with the capacity to be in touch with the affective center in herself."

I asked if he could talk about some of his writings regarding the child's fear and difficulty in separating in that situation. He said, "I've talked about two separate aspects. One is the fact of helplessness—that the child can't pick up and leave. If the child is in a situation that is nongratifying and not protective, then the child has to turn to the internal self to create an alternative world. So here . . . your patient has the capacity to live in a world of fantasy. I see it as a very positive thing. One can recreate a separate internal world in the presence of an unsupportive environment. This allows children to maintain themselves."

I said, "When my patient, as a little girl, had made up little people in her mind, that kept pieces of her safe and alive in her mind."

Modell replied, "It doesn't totally substitute for getting something good. I have a patient who is not anywhere near as sick as your patient, but whose mother was psychotic, and her father suffered some head damage and . . . became a functional psychotic. She spent her days daydreaming, creating people and situations, and she lived on two levels all the time. So she could do what she had to do in school and later on in a job, but she kept a second life going, because the problem is you can't turn that off. She has no problem with separating fantasy from reality, but what's happened in the transference is that I've become essentially a subjectively created person. And she has me as a fantasy object. She has relations with men, has affairs with men, but they're never as good as her fantasies about me. So this kind of living is a handicap, in some ways."

I asked, "Could you elaborate some more about the gratification that is implicit in the psychoanalytic relationship? I was trained in the years when nongratification was the word, and I think people got that all confused."

He replied, "Well, as I've said, where in the world can you find somebody who is totally focused on you and who, at least for the hour that they're seeing you, puts aside their own needs, and can be self-reflective as to what's going on? This is a unique situation."

I asked, "If you have a training case, do you ever lend them a paper if they ask for it, or a book?"

He answered, "Oh, I wouldn't hesitate. I don't think it's a technical error to shift from ordinary life to the frame and back to ordinary life. It's a technical error if one stays either within ordinary life or just within the frame. This was the error that analysts made in the 1950s and 1960s. They didn't act like ordinary human beings with their patients."

I said, "It's an interesting road to walk."

He agreed. "Yeah, that's right. I think most experienced therapists do that. They learn to do just enough."

We returned to my case. Modell wondered what had happened since the material I sent him was written. I said, "Where [Roselyn] is now? In the last 6 months there's been a dramatic change in that I'm getting more good memories of her mother. I'm getting a lot more longing and a lot more need. She's closer to me. It's not a clinging, but it allows for a separation."

He replied, "So then, this very stark picture is being changed."

I agreed. "It's changing rather dramatically, actually. Even her dreams have changed. The dreams have changed from this maze and monsters, things trapping you, to where she's found her way out of them. In one of the most recent ones she was arguing with some people who had congregated in order to kill themselves; and she was horrified. And she didn't want to be there; she thought they were wasting their lives. It was the first time she had ever had a dream where it was not unconsciously correct, inside of her, to want to die. In this dream, she was disgusted with them; she was horrified; she didn't want anything to do with them. When she told me this dream, we were both in tears, because even though she had not even started to interpret it, it was so clear to both of us that it was different. There was a part of her that was not totally combined with her mother, which was a whole different thing."

Modell commented, "She has to take her time. I think this is the kind of patient that you can't ever stop with. I don't think you can ever do that. I have people like that. What I thought about is how healthy she is that in one sense she has a serious illness, but the illness is really subtle. Her mother was suicidal; her father is described as having been occupied

occupied with his ulcers. Despite the fact that she has had minimal parental support, she has done well in her life. I gather she got herself educated . . . I don't know what her work is, but I assume that she's doing something that's fairly responsible. So this points to what I've been talking about as the capacity to generate oneself from within, to create oneself. You indicate this, in part, in terms of these little people. That is very striking. So this woman, who's gotten so little from her family, was able to survive."

He continued, "She has this image of falling out of space, symbolizing the absence of support. The other thing that interested me in the material were two other metaphors that relate to immunology. One is the response to her associations to this dream where she speaks of the daughter living on poison. There are two sides to this image. One is that if you are exposed to poison in small doses, you become strengthened. The other side to the metaphor is that you take the poison in yourself, and like somebody with an immune deficiency disease, you attack your own tissues . . . I think both metaphors are operating in this material that you sent me. To carry this further, this dream of this old witch-like lady with the cage and chickens and cats attacking each other—I would interpret that dream as a representation of her internal objects. What's happened is something like this, whether real or fantasy: The paradigm is that there's a poisonous mother and herself as the child; and she internalizes both of these images. This interaction is continual, in itself, within the self. So I think this dream, where she talks about the chickens and cats—two animals attacking each other—I think this dream is a representation of internalized objects. That the metaphor of immunology has these two sides. One is that if you take the poison in small doses, you immunize yourself like getting snake venom. The other side of it is that the attack by the poison goes on internally. So on the one side you immunize yourself. On the other side, there is a sense that your own tissues are going to get attacked. She says that, in effect, when she speaks about defense systems. 'Sometimes when I hurt myself, it feels like I'm hurting my mother. Sometimes when I feel hurt, I really feel unhurt.' "

I wondered if the migraines also expressed this internal attack attacking herself. Modell said, "I think so, but this is very difficult to know with certainty. Where you have a pathological relationship that's internalized itself, it's very, very difficult to sort out. I don't see this ending with treatment, or treatment ending. I see her as an ongoing patient. Also, she'll gradually get better. I can't quite see her actually totally well. I may be mistaken."

"Why?" I asked.

He said, "Some functions just don't get internalized. I think certain things, certain functions have to do with processing affects. If they don't happen at the right time, they may not ever happen. I have a patient, and my sense of her is that I function as a kind of prosthesis. In other words, I provide something that's missing."

I asked him to say more about affects not getting processed at the right time. Modell went on, "I'm thinking of a patient, who when she got anxious, the mother would get more anxious; and who, if she were depressed, the mother would minimize it and so forth. Her mother seemed to be always out of sync with her. And consequently, this person is unable to process her own affects; that is, when she gets anxious, she gets flooded with anxiety. She felt the mother to be a persecuting object. The mother, instead of making things better, was making them worse. There may be some truth to that. The tragic thing about it is that this interaction, with the mother, is internalized in oneself so that if she does something good, let's say, if she's proud about something, the mother would say, 'What about so and so?' This is constantly what she does to herself. I'm somewhat pessimistic about this kind of fundamental interaction being really erased. I think it goes on. Not that one cannot see movement."

I said, "I have some bears that have to do with this case that I would like to show you and hear you comment on. You may feel very critical about the way these bears were used in treatment. In the very beginning of treatment, when I went on a long vacation to China, she (Roselyn) brought this bear and asked me to take it with me; it was in a little bag like you would carry a ring in. And she made it a Chinese hat. And we talked about it and analyzed it. I took the bear."

He replied, "Sure, I would have, too. I think it was a transitional object. You carried it, and this was a connection."

I said, "I brought her back a bear from a later trip. I didn't put them together. I left them separate. She then eventually put them together and made them similar hats for traveling. Now when she goes away, she now takes the bears."

Modell asked, "So these are now with you because you're traveling?" I concurred. "They're with me because I'm traveling. But these bears have been play, amusement, and amazement as well. This summer when I was painting, I did a painting of the bears, thinking maybe if I give her something showing that when I'm away, I have an image of her in my mind, that she could let me leave the bears at home because then she would have something to hold on to, something concrete."

Modell said, "She needs to have some concrete intrusion in your life, to indicate that she's become part of your life while you're gone. It is an acting out. It reminds me of the 'emotional symbolic realization' I wrote about in *Object Love and Reality* (1968b). The example I gave was of a woman therapist treating a schizophrenic adolescent girl by giving her little gifts that she thought were symbolic. This patient needed a concrete symbol of something."

Transcription follows:

AM: It's a very, very nice example here of how she tolerates the separation. A piece of her goes with you.

VH: It's such a little piece.

AM: Therefore, it's no burden to you.

VH: Someone else said, "Suppose she'd given you a brick?"

AM: But she wouldn't have.

VH: Exactly. But someone else felt that it should have only been interpreted and not acted on. I get confused sometimes. I should or I shouldn't.

AM: This reminds me of a case I'm supervising. Within the first week of analysis, the patient asked my supervisee whether she could bring a blanket for the hours, and the analyst should keep the blanket for her so she could use on the couch. The supervisee didn't know quite what to do. I told my student: "Okay, do it and then see what it means." We alter the frame at times to allow the meaning to develop and emerge.

Modell showed an example where a patient of his wanted and was given a paper clip when terminating. I asked what he thought about my having broken the frame when Roselyn became psychotic. He said, "I think people are confused about imaginary rules that come from misunderstandings. If a patient of mine who had a serious illness were in the hospital and wanted me to visit, I certainly would do so. That is, if one breaks the frame, as it were, it doesn't mean that it's broken forever. These are flexible frames that we deal with."

I asked, "If I were your student, what would you be saying to me?"

He replied, "I'd probably say you're doing very well with this lady. The fact that she's continuing to grow—you're doing the right thing. Your patient experienced a kind of psychic death in childhood. Her urge to suicide may be looked upon as a need to actively recreate the experience of psychic death and bring it within her control, as it were. My sense and my experience is that if people lose out, in terms of psychic attunement with their mothers at crucial stages in their developments, it may not be able to be undone in psychotherapy. They may need to maintain contact with somebody who can process their affects. And hopefully that carries over; they pick it up, as it were. But whether they can truly internalize this process remains to be seen. Obviously some people can, but some people can't. We have to accept that we're dealing with chronic illnesses."

I asked if he felt that the "black hole" were a dead center. Modell said, "I think the feeling of deadness can be modified when people come in better contact with themselves. I'm not too pessimistic about that, but I am more pessimistic about questions of processing affects. It becomes part of temperament, in a sense. So we're dealing with complex factors. We're dealing with the environmental influence, and we're dealing with probably the biological issues as well, some of which can and some of which can't be undone. I don't wish to give a wrong impression that I'm always pessimistic, but I think one has to consider the possibility that some of this is not reversible in psychoanalysis or psychotherapy."

Jacob Arlow

Dr. Arlow is the leading theorist of ego psychology. He is known for his many theoretical and clinical contributions to our field, especially regarding fantasized as contrasted to concrete thoughts, as well as for his generous contribution to education in psychoanalysis; he is respected for his generosity to many students, writers, and researchers in the field.

Jacob Arlow is known not only for his many contributions to theory and technique, but also for his high standards in scholarship, his activities in the development of a psychoanalytic community, and for his involvement in the growth of psychoanalytic education. He is also known for his warmth, devotion to family and students, and for his generosity as a mentor. He has strong attachments and a deep sense of commitment.

I was a personal witness to both his warmth and his commitment. In my experience as an interviewer a few experiences stand out. My encounter with Jacob Arlow was the occasion for one of these. When I arrived in Great Neck, New York, for our interview, I could not have known that Arlow had only just that day returned from his daughter-in-law's funeral. She had lost a valiant and painful fight against leukemia. What is more, Arlow's wife had been unable to accompany him because she was recovering from her own surgery. They had barely had a chance to spend time together following his arrival, as he had arrived home late the night before. He was concerned for all involved. I arrived at the railroad station early the next morning, and he picked me up there. Although I had spoken with him the night before, he made no mention of these events.

Arlow merely assured me we would proceed with the interview, though there could be some interruption with incoming telephone calls and needs to check on his wife. Family members would be arriving around noon. I was grateful, as I was looking forward to our time together, but I also felt uncomfortable. I was conscious of thinking he was very much like my deceased college professor father, who I believe would have acted in much the same manner.

Later, I was to think, "This ego psychologist had a very well functioning ego." Of my own ego functions I became less certain. On the second day of our interviews, when Arlow again picked me up at the train station, he generously detoured for a short drive to show me some of his community on the way to his home where we would have our case discussion. He explained that people would be coming and going because of the death and his wife's illness. As he drove into his garage I discovered, to my great embarrassment and alarm, that I had left my purse on the train. All my money, tickets, credit cards, checkbook, and address book were in the purse. My husband was already returning to Los Angeles with our luggage. I was alone. Since it was Sunday, I received only recorded messages when I telephoned the train company. I have traveled the world, and had never, before this, lost a single thing!

Out loud, I questioned what in the world was going on in my mind. Dr. Arlow kindly wondered if perhaps I had punished myself for going on with the interviews now that I was aware of his other obligations. He knew I was upset about the circumstances under which they were taking place. But he was not content with analysis alone; he was determined to help me solve my problem.

He drove me back to the train station, and we learned that the same train I came on would be returning any minute on its way back to New York City. Arlow went one way on the platform, and I went the other; we each informed all the waiting passengers of our need to locate the conductor. The train stopped, people got off and on, the train hissed and moved forward. My heart sank. Then there was a screech and the train stopped. The conductor hopped off waving my purse. Only $50 were missing. Arlow teased me about what a nice place New York is. Throughout this experience Arlow was patient, kind, and appeared unruffled. Days later I had a dream that clearly indicated my wish to be adopted and become a part of his family.

Arlow is a clear thinker. He has many interests, including sculpting. One of his bronzes, a bust of Jeremiah, is in his home. Jeremiah was a fierce Jewish prophet who was charged by God to admonish his people. Freud's last book was a study of the contribution of Moses to the world, *Moses and Monotheism* (1939). Much earlier, he wrote an essay, "The Moses of Michelangelo" (1914), focusing on Michelangelo's statue and the representation of the power of Moses. Freud compared himself to Moses, saying he had "struggled successfully against an inward passion for the sake of a cause to which he had devoted himself" (Freud, 1914, p. 233). Arlow, surely, could rightly make the same claim in relation to his long devotion to the cause of psychoanalysis.

Arlow has an unusual gift of sensitive intuitiveness. He is extremely aware of people and seems quietly to support and encourage them. Eleanor Galenson told a story to La Farge (1991) that rang very true to my own experience with Arlow. She felt that in her early career her mentors had not picked up any weakness in her grasp of theory, but she herself had little confidence in her own intellectual abilities. She doubted her intellectual gifts. Galenson said, "I owe my first serious attempt at analytic writing to my good friend Jacob Arlow. I had been invited to discuss a paper on a panel. Afterward, Jack came up to me and said, 'I always thought you were beautiful, but I never thought you could think so well.' I had a lot of respect for Jack. I decided to write and wrote my first paper on play."

The following interview is, in its intelligence and its warmth, a good representation of Arlow's character and ability. Perhaps above all, the interview shows his close attention to detail and his ability to make salient connections that are so much hallmarks of his work and his personality.

Interview

Virginia Hunter: Would you tell me about your parents and what kind of people they were? I know they were very into civic things, but tell me more about what the family was like.

Jacob Arlow: My parents came from the Ukraine. My father was born in Rostov on the Don. He lost his mother fairly early, and he and his father and an older brother wandered through various cities of the Ukraine. My grandfather was an unsuccessful cap maker. My father had two older sisters but, because of the death of his mother, they were separated from him and his brother. Both sisters apparently went on to academic work and did well. One reputedly got the Czar's Gold Medal. More than that I do not know about them. My father finally ended up in Odessa with his father. There he met my mother. She was from a large family. She had been apprenticed to a seamstress at the age of 8. She never received any formal education. My father preferred to take the route of Russian education rather than the traditional Jewish education that was offered to him, partly as a reaction, as I learned very late in his life, to competition with his older brother. The older brother was a fine scholar, as my grandfather had been. The two of them seemed to have formed a league against my father, one that excluded him. I didn't discover this until perhaps a few years before my father's death. It helped me understand a good deal about my relationship with my father, which two analyses had not completely made clear.

VH: Can you elaborate on that?

JA: I always had the feeling that I couldn't get as close to my father as I had wanted. He got along very well with my older brother. The two of them were practical men, businessmen. I was the bookish one in the family. I learned about my father's relationship to his father in an interesting way. One Sunday afternoon I was about to pick up my oldest son at Sunday School. I said to my father, "Let's go together to pick him up." When Michael was in the car, my father said to him, "Well, what did you study this week? Did you study the Sedre (the weekly portion of the Torah read in the synagogue, which was the traditional way in which studies were conducted in the Old World)? My son responded, "Uh." He had never heard of that. I said to my father, "Come on, Dad, you know he didn't receive the kind of intense Hebrew education that you and I received." My father said, "Perhaps what you received, I did not." At this point he began to tell me all about his competition with his older brother for his father's affection. He felt that the two of them had made a league that excluded him. (This was striking, because I was my grandfather's favorite. Whenever I visited him, he would feed me some line from the Prophets, and I was expected to complete the line.) On this occasion my father went on to talk about his father in a way that I had never heard before. At this point his father had been dead some 25 years, but the hurt was so strong; he was so angry he sounded like a patient on the couch.

VH: How old was he when he lost his mother?

JA: He must have been 2 or 3, very young.

VH: A lot of exclusion.

JA: Even before I became an analyst, I was sensitive to that factor. My father was a very active, very busy man—business during the day, community concerns in the evening. But he had a habit of taking naps. If he had 30 minutes to spare, he could lie down anywhere and sleep. When I was a high school or a college student, I reflected on this readiness to fall asleep. Even without any analytic background, it occurred to me somehow this must have something to do with his yearning for his dead mother. He had been raised by a stepmother who indeed had been very good to him, and she was also very, very partial to me. I never discussed this aspect of my father's life with him. Only in later years does one realize so many things.

VH: The subject of intimacy was not really a subject people talked about in those days, I don't think.

JA: My father was a busy man, and I really didn't see very much of him. I saw a good deal more of my older brother and, of course, my mother. But the kind of intimacy of talking freely about personal affairs was not entirely absent, especially when I was younger. However, as I grew older, I became pretty much a private person as far as my parents were concerned. But I always knew that they were there, and they were completely dependable. As I have gone through life and listened to the stories of colleagues, friends, and above all, my patients, I have come to realize how unusual my family relationship was. It was a very stable, calm, unconflicted family. My mother was quite neurotic. She had obsessional symptoms, and she did have two minor depressions in the course of her life.

VH: What was she obsessed about?

JA: I have a theory I think is correct. It was elucidated for me by my first analyst. My mother had a compulsion about the number three. If she put sugar in her tea, it would have to be three teaspoons. She would count everything in threes. Somewhere growing up, she told me—I can't recall the occasion, it was a long time back, I was quite young—she told me that, after my brother and sister had been born, she became pregnant and had an abortion. That was the third child, the third pregnancy. Then I was the third child, but the fourth pregnancy. My analyst, Dr. Wittles, felt that the number three might have been connected with her guilt over that abortion. I feel that that view was confirmed by the following. My mother devoted most of her life, after I was 6 or 7 years old, to working for an orphan's home. She was one of the founders and served on the Board of Directors most of her life. She was active all the time, raising funds, selling tickets for theater benefits, soliciting merchandise for bazaars, and even going with a truck with some other people to the food markets in Brooklyn, where generous dealers would make donations of food. The institution, The Pride of Judea Orphan's Home, for several years maintained a summer place in Long Beach. One year they took the children who resided at the home to Long Beach for an outing. Apparently there was a sand bank on the beach. Some great waves suddenly came and swept the children off the sand bank. Seven of them were drowned.

VH: How awful!

JA: She became quite depressed and after that developed a compulsion for counting seven. Whenever she saw children playing in the street, she used to count seven children. So I think my analyst's intuition about the relationship to the number three and the number seven to the compulsions was very much on target.

VH: I'm struck—in what I read about you, it seems usual to say how congenial, how warm, how reciprocal, how endearing, how nice—and I don't mean nice in a derogatory way. But that seems to run through everything about you that anybody's written about you personally. And I'm struck by two things: that the father apparently didn't share or let you in, in today's language, and that you came clearly after a child that was not wanted, which has to cause some feeling of was I wanted, can I make myself wanted, can I deserve to be wanted; something in that neighborhood.

JA: You are very right on target. My earliest memory, as I recall it, and it is probably a distorting one, consists of my mother saying to me in

Yiddish, "God grant me this child," and I would answer, "Forever and a day." That is probably the accurate version but, as I recalled it, I thought she had said, "So long as he is here, let him be," to which I would respond, "Forever and a day." My version of the memory must be incorrect. It must have been recast with feelings of hurt or disappointment that I had.

VH: You were sickly as a little boy, from what I've read. Is that connected? Were you sad about that? Are you aware—was it organic? What do you understand of your childhood illnesses?

JA: You are very intuitive. When I was about $4^{1}/2$ years old, I developed a case of measles with complications in the form of bronchopneumonia and bilateral otitis media.

VH: Dizziness?

JA: I was dizzy. Apparently I ran a very high fever because I remember one night lying in bed having a kind of delirium. I imagined I saw paper Christmas bells.

VH: The angel bells?

JA: I saw them but I knew that they weren't there. My mother was sitting at the bedside crying. I said to her, "Are you afraid I'm going to die?" or "Am I going to die?" She began to cry some more. So I said to her, "You know, maybe you better fetch Aunt Fanny (who lived down the hall) and have her come to take care of me."

VH: You didn't trust her caretaking?

JA: Not at that moment, but other times it didn't seem to be a problem.

VH: Was this after the seven children died?

JA: This was before.

VH: So even before then there was some feeling—mother was not the ultimate as a caretaker. Aunt Fanny was.

JA: She was the backup. But so were all of my mother's sisters and brothers. She was one of eight siblings. By the way, I am one of 28 first cousins. My Aunt Fanny was the youngest one of the lot, but she was very practical, very dependable and very, very outspoken.

VH: So not given to confusion or depression, sort of like—

JA: She was a takeover person—a "can do."

VH: And lived right down the hall? What do you mean, right down the hall?

JA: In a tenement in New York City. The section is called East New York. Currently it has the highest crime rate in the city.

VH: At the point your father had come to America, how many years before you were born?

JA: He came to America in 1905. I was born in 1912.

VH: So there was already your brother and already your sister.

JA: He brought my mother over the following year. They were married in 1906, and my brother was born in 1907.

VH: And she came from a very large family.

JA: She came from a very large family, all of whom came to this country, including her parents.

VH: Which one was she?

JA: She was number six. There were two after her. We have a big chart, a family tree, which I can show you later if you are interested. Every year we have an annual cousins' club reunion. It is held here because we can accommodate the numbers.

VH: I'm trying to piece out, how the heck did you get to be so wonderfully able to pull together information, sort it out in your mind, and organize it? It doesn't sound like you got that from your mom in terms of interrelations. It doesn't sound like your father shared enough with you that you would have gotten it from him. Where did it come from?

JA: I have no idea.

VH: Just a high IQ. What's your theory about it?

JA: My father was a very intelligent man and so was my brother.

VH: That wouldn't necessarily give you that ability.

JA: No. His life experience was very different from mine, but he was very enterprising—very courageous.

VH: Was your mother hurt when you said get Aunt Fanny?

JA: I don't remember. I don't know.

VH: What would you guess?

JA: I think she was just overwhelmed. She was easily overwhelmed.

VH: Is that the major illness of your childhood or were there others?

JA: That was the major illness of my childhood.

VH: Were there recurring ones with the lungs?

JA: Sore throats, respiratory infections. As a result, I spent a lot of time in bed. I went through my brother's Bar Mitzvah gift which was the *Book of Knowledge*. I must have gone through the *Book of Knowledge* half a dozen times, knew what was in each of the volumes.

VH: But Freud probably wasn't in there.

JA: No, I came upon Freud, I don't recall exactly how, when I was in high school. I don't know if this led to my wanting to do my senior study in psychology or whether my senior study in psychology made me find Freud. I think it was the former. What impressed me about reading Freud was that his description of the family constellation, the conflicts among us, seemed to coincide so closely with what I observed in my own family.

VH: Can you elaborate on that, what you've just said?

JA: Well, I felt there were three of us children. There was my older brother, who later was close to my father. I was definitely my mother's favorite, and my sister was very much involved with my father. My older brother, I felt, had been left out and not given a fair deal. He had all the typical so-called anal characteristics. He was excellent in mathematics. He kept a record of every penny he spent. He was very careful about earning money, very enterprising in that respect. He became a CPA. He was on the math team of his high school, which was the leading academic high school in the city. He spent hours doing puzzles, frequently in the bathroom. This was so striking when I read it in Freud. I read the *Introductory Lectures on Psycho-Analysis* (1916–1917) when I was 15 or so.

VH: Did you tease him about that or did you keep it all in your head?

JA: I kept it in my head. However, I did see in my mother some of the symptoms that corresponded to what Freud called neurasthenia. I didn't have a very good idea what it was at the time, but I recognized some of the symptoms.

VH: For example? What did you see exactly?

JA: Persistent anxieties. I mentioned that in the family, and it became the subject for teasing my mother. My father in particular used to tease her. That wasn't very nice.

VH: Did her anxiety annoy him then?

JA: Not really, but as I grew older I recognized a certain pattern that she pursued—a gentle, masochistic form of provocation. She would offer my father something to eat, which he would accept. The next moment she would ask, "Would you rather have something else?" My father would respond that he was satisfied. She would persist: "I could give you something else if you want." Thus some irritation would arise between them, but there was never any great scene or a persistent pattern of quarreling. Quarrels were between my sister and my mother or my sister and my father mostly.

VH: You mentioned your first analyst. Who was that?

JA: Fritz Wittles.

VH: And who had been his analyst?

JA: His analyst was Wilhelm Steckel.

VH: Was he chosen for you or did you choose him?

JA: At that time you could choose your analyst. I chose him.

VH: Why?

JA: I was a resident at that time at the Psychiatric Institute, Physicians and Surgeons Columbia. I consulted with Dr. Hinsey, who was the Assistant Director of the Institute. He recommended Dr. Wittles.

VH: You don't know why he recommended him?

JA: I think he may have been his analyst. I am not sure. That's the best of my recollection at the present time. It may not be the only reason.

VH: How long was that analysis?

JA: I really don't know. It was at least 3 or 4 years.

VH: Five times a week?

JA: Five times a week.

VH: I know that you and Brenner and some of your buddies all went to have second analysis, and yet it seems that earlier, when you were speaking of your first analysis, you got some good stuff out of it. What were its deficiencies? Can you compare, here, the good things about your first analysis and where analytic knowledge was then; some of the deficiencies, and where theory and analysis was then? Is that too difficult?

JA: My first analysis with Dr. Wittles reflected the early teachings of technique. It centered on dream interpretation and "making the unconscious conscious" in the form of recollection or reconstruction, and so forth. Very little attention was paid to character defenses. It was sufficient, for example, to point out something about the transference without going very deeply into it.

VH: Give me an example.

JA: I had a dream, I recall, in which I saw a utensil, one that is used to display cakes in bakeries. It consisted of a stand with a circular platform. On the top of it was a bicycle. Wittles said, "The bicycle is a bisexual symbol." He was relating it to bisexual identification. Now that sounded interesting to me but it didn't affect me. The following day, Dr. Wittles brought in a lingam, which is a bisexual symbol from Hindu mythology.

VH: He brought it in?

JA: He brought it in.

VH: What did it look like?

JA: It looked very much like what I saw in my dream. It was very interesting, but I felt it didn't have anything to do with me. Many years later, after my second analysis, I went to the movies—this must have been at least 10 or 12 years later after my second analysis. I was watching the picture *The Life of Lon Chaney*. In the film a scene from *The Hunchback of Notre Dame* was reproduced. There is a scene in the movie where the hunchback is being punished. He's placed upon a circular platform in the middle of the square and is beaten. I had seen the original movie, perhaps when I was 7 or 8. I remembered being struck when I saw the movie at that age when the hunchback says, "I thirst," and Esmeralda gives him a drink. When I saw this scene in *The Life of Lon Chaney*, I knew immediately that my dream of the platform with the bicycle was connected to this experience, to this movie. What had been missed was the intervening mediation of the beating fantasy, a representation of the feminine component ultimately connected with a tendency towards moral masochism.

VH: You had identification with your mom and her masochism. He didn't allow you to associate?

JA: He allowed me to associate, but this is how he handled the material. The point is that he didn't correlate the idea of a feminine identification with the beating fantasy. It may seem unbelievable but he never mentioned the word masochism throughout the analysis.

VH: It sounds like in those days—

JA: They didn't do that. They just analyzed the depths. The intermediate representations were just taken as evidence to prove that the depths existed.

VH: It sounds much more "analyst active," much more analysts deciding what it means than is practiced now.

JA: I don't understand that.

VH: He seems to have come up with the meaning, your meaning. If you look at it in terms of "Whose analysis is this, whose mind did it come from?" As I hear you, his interpretation came from his mind, not based on association or evolutions from your mind. And, therefore, it was sort of presumptuous, if nothing else.

JA: Well, it was a correct interpretation, but it was premature. It had not depended on working through the intermediate representations, which is what you were saying. The intermediate representations have to be analyzed first.

VH: So, in those days, the analyst was really on the spot to come up with a "guesstimate" interpretation pretty fast.

JA: Well, that's what he did. That was quite different from my second analysis, which was with Dr. Loewenstein. So the point is that I ended my first analysis considering it only a training analysis. My second analysis I entered because, for the first time, I was experiencing anxiety.

VH: Why did you have anxiety for the first time?

JA: It was part of a conflict that was generated by unanalyzed transference.

VH: Do you mean as an adult? Because, truly, when you felt that the aunt down the hall was a better caretaker than your mother, you must have had some awareness of anxiety, for example? Wouldn't you think?

JA: I think you're trying to put this in the context of mother–child relationship. No, it wasn't that at all.

VH: What was it?

JA: It was more a father–son relationship. It had to do with passive submission, and it's interesting that it comes up when you say to me, "You know, you have a reputation of being a nice guy." This is one of the roots of it.

VH: Passive?

JA: Yes, pleasing others.

VH: How much later did you have the second analysis?

JA: It must have been 2 years.

VH: Fast.

JA: Maybe even less.

VH: Maybe even less. Was it generally known at your institute?

JA: Oh, I think so.

VH: Was there a split in the institute between the first analyst's orientation and Loewenstein's?

JA: No. The split that took place in the New York Institute was just before I became a student. It had nothing to do with issues of this kind. They were not really ideological issues. They're more political and personal.

VH: Aren't they always?

JA: Of course, as far as I know.

VH: Was there something about Loewenstein himself or what was it about Loewenstein?

JA: I was doing supervision with him, and when I needed help, I came to him. He was my supervisor.

VH: Who were your other supervisors?

JA: Sally Bonnett and Herman Nunberg.

VH: All adult cases?

JA: All adult cases. Yes. I did have experience with children. For 5 years I was the consultant psychiatrist at the orphan's home that my parents were involved with. When Margaret Mahler first came to the United States, she was the consultant to the Child Division of the Psychiatric Institute of Columbia. She supervised one of my case presentations. Years later she said to me—you can take this as boastful or not—she said to me, "You were the best student I ever had. Why didn't you go into child analysis?" I said to her, "If you had told me, I would have done it."

VH: What does that mean, if you had told me, I would have done it?

JA: If she had said, you know, I think you're talented in this particular department of psychoanalytic work, I might have considered this might be something for me to do. But as it was, I was getting into my career. I was satisfied with the way things were going.

VH: How much do you think our choices, career-wise—how much are our choices analytically in career or theory based on someone saying, "I like you, I admire your work, I'll take you under my wing, I'll respond to you, I'll be your mentor?" That sounds as though, if she had embraced you with affirmations, you would have gone that way relatively easily.

JA: I can't be sure of that. I have never worked under the protective wing of any such figure. I did conduct a Kris study group. I had assisted Kris in the group for several years with Dr. Brenner. Ultimately I became head of one of the sections. Kris kept one and Brenner kept one. Later Loewenstein had one. But I was never a protégé. I was never strictly identified with any one leading figure.

VH: Do you think that was because you were an independent thinker?

JA: In that respect I think I am rather independent.

VH: Do you connect that to the dynamics with your parents? It sounds like you might have been one of those children who out of safety would have thought for himself.

JA: It's possible. I really don't know. However, even when I was very young, in whatever group I was—and I was always affiliated with some group activity—I almost always moved into the position of leadership. From that point of view, I became self-reliant. At age 16 or 17 I was president of a youth organization, boys and girls, connected with a religious institute. We had about 200 members. They ranged in age from 6 or 7 up to 19, 20, and that was a responsibility I took on.

VH: The impression I had from reading about you was that you somehow, very early, had a very powerful and meaningful sense of ethics and morality.

JA: Yes.

VH: Very, very early, and I wondered—one of my fantasies was that you had become a leader partly to be sure that some of those values got in place.

JA: That happens to be true. A thought suddenly came to me that might be of interest. I lived for a while in a two-family house—a "taxpayer," you know, stores downstairs.

VH: A "taxpayer" is what you called it?

JA: Yes, "taxpayers," stores downstairs, two apartments above. I was a studious youngster. I did very well in school easily, but I was always short and not very strong athletically. Also, because I skipped a number of classes, I was usually the youngest and the smallest in my classes. When I graduated from public school, I was the second shortest boy in the class, and that was a big issue. In our house there was a boy who was half a year older than I. He was a tough kid, one who was always in trouble, often with the police. I remember on one occasion—my mother used to make my clothes—I was wearing short pants, not knickers as the other boys had. This neighbor made some derogatory remark, and I felt that he was right, that I wasn't sufficiently masculine. I went to my mother to complain about my clothes. She, of course, took care of it; that was no problem. But his taunt made me attach myself to him. For a short period of time, perhaps 2 or 3 weeks, he taught me how to steal. For example, in the playground, you kick away someone's school book and then you take it. The things I stole were petty ones, like pens—not fountain pens but the kind in which you put pen points. I'm not sure you remember them or even know about them. But they were petty things that I took. The climax came when I stole a book belonging to someone in a higher grade. As I was reading it, my brother came home and said, "What have you got there? Where did you get it?" I took the hint. I returned the book. That ended that relationship, but about that time another youngster on the street said that there was a club connected with the local Hebrew school which I attended. The club was a Youth Congregation. I joined shortly, and that was an extraordinary, enriching time in my life, from the ages of 11 to 17. In the meantime, the study of the Bible was very important. And at home principles were taken for granted. My father was in business, and

I have heard about business people talking about sharp deals they made. I never heard anything of the sort, anything about cheating or getting away with anything. My brother was also a very hard worker. So those values were the ones we lived by. Later, when I heard what went on in other families, it was hard for me to believe.

VH: Someone said to me recently that one of the contraindicators for psychoanalysis is based on values, and if the patient's values were unalterable or if the patient's values—maybe that's not the right word—that if the patient's sense of right and wrong was so off from what was acceptable to the analyst, that they thought it was usually unalterable. We certainly know that with some character disorders and perversions, I guess, some of them. But do you think that's a reasonable—

JA: I think it would be a problem. My own experience has been limited on those cases. Those cases that I did have would fall into the generalization that you're quoting, namely, a pregenital character.

VH: Why do you think that it's so hard to alter? How do you understand it theoretically, that those early—?

JA: As far as its relationship to—

VH: Is it a lack of identification with other people?

JA: As far as treatability is concerned, I think the commitment to undergo an analysis is a moral commitment. The person has to reach that stage in life where he feels that he cannot go on the way he has in the past, that he has to confront himself with complete honesty and truth; and that really is a moral decision that a person makes, and I think it's a prerequisite, really, for undergoing analysis. But how people get to organize their moral code is a great issue that I wouldn't dare summarize or epitomize in a few sentences. I did write about it recently as a contribution to a volume honoring Leo Rangell. I spoke about "The Quest for Morality" (1990c).

VH: You have written a lot about morality. It seems to me that society, at least from my standpoint, seems to become less and less moral. Do you have that feeling too or not?

JA: By what standard does one judge that?

VH: That's a good question. How would you judge it?

JA: Morality is a reflection of the status of the society at a particular time. As the society's vision changes, what is considered moral and immoral changes too. I have discussed these issues in my paper "The Poet as Prophet" (1986). In general, I would say that what we have been seeing in recent times is an extension of what is permissible, what is thinkable and, therefore, what becomes doable. The poet acts as a harbinger of the changes that are evolving. He is the first to sense what society will consider permissible in keeping with its changing values. My writing about morality is deeply influenced by my very special Hebrew education.

VH: You've written also about charismatic leaders, and I think of Lacan or Hitler.

JA: I had occasion to talk about Sandor Rado. He was a charismatic leader. He was the founder of the Columbia Psychoanalytic Institute. In regard to charismatic leaders, three papers influenced me: one by Freud, namely, "Group Psychology and the Analysis of the Ego" (1921); the second, by Annie Reich, entitled "Narcissistic Object Choice in Women" (1953); and then a paper by Christine Olden entitled "About the Fascinating Effect of the Narcissistic Personality" (1942). Olden's paper is very fascinating. Unfortunately rarely quoted.

VH: Would you elaborate?

JA: All three describe the interaction of the charismatic leader with the mass. The charismatic leader exudes an unqualified sense of omnipotence. He is free of ambivalence. His self-esteem does not depend in any fashion on the reaction or the approval of others. He is certain of his mission and seems to be free of any doubt. This quality appeals to individuals who are beset by doubt, insecurity, and ambivalence. They are frequently emotionally depressed and realistically oppressed. They would love to be free from doubt and ambivalence, in the fashion that they seem to recognize in the charismatic leader. Accordingly, he becomes their ego ideal. He represents to them the freedom from anxiety and doubt that everyone would like to achieve.

VH: Who would you say stands out in psychoanalytic literature or psychoanalytic history that would fit that?

JA: Lacan, I think, would be an outstanding example.

VH: What others come to mind?

JA: What other person? I already mentioned Sandor Rado. These are two outstanding examples of narcissistic personalities in the analytic world.

VH: It seems in the history of psychoanalysis there have been an awful lot of splits in institutes related partially to a split between narcissistic personalities and a sort of charismatic style versus a more down-to-earth, ethical, realistic one. Is that your impression, too?

JA: There were such. I have written on the subject but not published it. I did refer to these issues in my farewell address as Chairman of the Board on Professional Standards. It's entitled "Group Psychology and the Analysis of Institutes."

VH: As yet published?

JA: I did not publish it because it was a report to the board, but copies have been requested by so many people that the office of the American Psychoanalytic Association has reproduced it several times.

VH: Were you one of those definitely against the nonmedicals becoming trained or were you for them being trained?

JA: At what time?

VH: In the early fight, in your history.

JA: At first I was uncertain about my position, but later I felt that qualified nonmedical people should be accepted and trained. Recently, as you know, Dr. Brenner and I wrote an article for the *Psychoanalytic Quarterly*, entitled "The Future of Psychoanalysis" (1988). In this article we said that in the future psychoanalytic practice will be in the hands of nonmedical people. This is almost true already.

VH: That's because it's become financially unprofitable.

JA: That's one of the main reasons. I feel that it behooves the well-trained medical analysts to see to it that the nonmedical analysts get the best possible training. I also advise young people against studying medicine as an introduction to psychoanalysis. I suggest that they rethink their priorities. When my daughter-in-law was finishing medical school, she thought of entering analysis as a career, but I directed her away from this choice. Medical education today is not the best introduction to psychoanalysis at all. It has become too technical.

VH: What would you say would be the best approach?

JA: The humanities.

VH: You've written a lot about wish-fulfilling fantasies and games and what little boy's play means. What are your thoughts about the video games?

JA: I discussed that issue specifically in a symposium that I participated in entitled "Psychoanalysis and Folklore." Nowadays children are hearing fewer fairy tales. I introduced my presentation with an illustration taken from the life of my second son.

VH: The attorney who just lost his wife?

JA: Yes. He was visiting here 2 weeks ago to see his mother. I was delighted to show him my description of him when he was 5 years old. I used to watch him slouch over his tricycle, his head turned skyward, blissfully preoccupied in his daydreams. It was not hard for me to surmise the contents of his fantasy world. First of all, he had earlier announced, with full candor, that he was going to eat lots and lots of marble cake so he could become like Captain Marvel. He used to run down the street, stop suddenly, raise two little pudgy fists in a gesture of exultant triumph and proclaim at the top of his voice "Mighty Mouse!" But most of all, day and night, he insisted upon wearing the remnants of an old brown bathrobe pinned to his shoulders. That was his Superman cape, with which he could fly through the air to perform heroic deeds in pursuit of right and justice. The major challenge to my wife was to seize an opportunity to detach the magic cape from my hero so she could put it into the washing machine for a much-needed cleansing. This was all before the time of television and computerized programmed gamesmanship that electronic progress has made possible. It has become a middle-class American commonplace.

Now I watch one of my grandsons. He is now $5^1/2$ years old also. He sits in front of the television screen, his Nintendo control firmly grasped in his hand, defiantly fending off multiple challenges as they appear on the screen. It made me think, does he feel that they are threatening him or just his computerized representation on the television screen? The assaults come from every corner of the perceptual field. Most of the games, it seems to me, appear to be variations of high-technology, state-of-the-art, Star Wars type of aerial combat. The game demands precise, split-second decisions. Give yourself over to daydreaming just for one moment, and your television persona gets zapped into a thousand fragments of light, sinking ignominiously beneath the lowermost boundary of the television screen. As I watch my grandson, I think, is he being discouraged from looking skyward? Is he being diverted from looking inward? And above all, does it make a difference?

VH: One of your primary contributions is your concept of unconscious fantasy. What do you think of video games and the use being made of them now, in families and family life, what do you think it means? What does it make you think of?

JA: I really can't say at the present time what I think the ultimate effect will be. It is a game, it is distracting, it is kind of narrowing. It narrows the field of interests, but in and of itself it is neither an incentuative of anxiety or necessarily an alleviator of anxiety, primarily I would think castration anxiety. Now suppose the youngster becomes very adept at zapping down the enemies. That is one kind of experience that may be transitorily gratifying. Is there a carryover to the real world? At least it affords an opportunity to master the opposition in fantasy. But suppose the child develops no great skill, and his friends are much better than he at the Nintendo game? The other elements enter. There is always something that someone can do better than one's self. In other words, I am not in any position to make a generalization about the psychological effects of deep involvement in the Nintendo games.

VH: I do child therapy as well as adult psychoanalysis. I find they're often used very, very defensively. A child can bring one of those things in, and they isolate the child in large measure.

JA: Don't forget your sample consists of children who need therapy. Video games are isolating and repetitious. The fantasies that they project are common ones, but the experience is not one of sharing fantasies unless you have two youngsters playing together or competing against each other and emphasizing the fantasies that they are sharing in common. There is no doubt that most of these games are really variations of ideas of killing somebody. The question is, is it any better than what is often on the television screen? It's too small an issue of the totality of the mental experience for me to be able to generalize. Intense preoccupation with computerized games, I would feel, is more a symptom than a cause of emotional conflicts.

VH: But then there are an awful lot of symptomatic children. There seems to be less and less space created for the interpsychic experience.

JA: Of course. These are isolating devices. It's not like playing ball or other games together.

VH: You seem to have had an unusual ability to be nonisolated. I'm thinking of your relationship with Brenner and the work that you shared, apparently your entire lives. How do you account for that?

JA: I think it's an exercise in brotherhood. If you notice the wall behind me, there is a picture of a group of friends that I've had since the age of 10. We see each other frequently. We used to celebrate every New Year's Eve together. Every Memorial Day they come here. I have a way of keeping almost all the friends that I've made throughout my life.

VH: How did your mother relate to all the cousins?

JA: In my mother's family, the ties were very strong, and the cousins related to each other quite well. We lived close by each other during our childhood. We were well acquainted with each other, and we liked each other. There was little of the competitiveness that sometimes ruins family relationships. Fortunately, nobody was outstandingly rich, and that always helps.

VH: And yet from your paper on "The Only Child" (1972), my impression was that you felt an only child could be as healthy or as pathological as anybody's child.

JA: That's right.

VH: There seems to be something in what you're saying; that these early experiences of accommodation and affiliation and security somehow affected your political ability or your ability to help institutions, education, and psychoanalysis.

JA: It seems like a valid supposition, but I have never really thought about it. At our annual cousins' club meeting, we usually invite one of the cousins to tell some story about the family background. This year I spoke because I think it is probably the last year the group will meet. Interest is beginning to flag. People have spread throughout the country, and few people wish to take the initiative or have the kind of home that could accommodate so large a group. My wife has been most forthcoming in this respect.

The presence of so many cousins was a source of great security for me. For example, during one of my mother's frequent hospitalizations when I was young, I stayed at the home of one of my older cousins. In the morning an uncle picked me up and took me to public school. During lunchtime at public school, I went to the home of another cousin, who lived nearby. At the end of the day, I went to an aunt who I lived around the corner from, where I had supper, and in the evening I went back to the cousin where I had been sleeping. There was a complete network of support.

It also had a stimulating incentive to match up to the expectations of the cousins. For example, during one of my mother's illnesses, when I was about 6½, I slept over at the home of an older cousin, who had been my babysitter. I was very fond of her. She was very beautiful. Having been raised in a cold-water flat, in the wintertime I used to get dressed from under the covers, and my mother would come in and put my shoes and stockings on. As a result, at the age of 6½ I didn't know how to make a bow for my shoes. I felt humiliated if I had to reveal to my cousin that I was unable to do so. Necessity was the mother of invention. I had no trouble tying my own shoelaces from that point on. As I tell you the story, I realize in many respects I had a very fortunate childhood, emotionally speaking.

VH: If you'll forgive me for saying, it's unusual in a Jewish analyst. The story I have usually heard has been one of terrible things happening to the family. And yet your family seems to have all been safe, here, when the terrible things were happening abroad.

JA: Yes, both sides of my family came over, except for my father's brother. He was a political activist. In 1905 my father asked his brother if he wanted to come to the United States. The brother said, "No, big things are about to happen here." It was the 1905 Revolution, and he stayed on. My father and his brother kept in contact throughout the years. During the New Economic Policy period, my father sent his brother some money, which was confiscated on the way, but he did send him a sewing machine so he could do some private work. The contact continued until the outbreak of World War II. After that we never heard of him. When I went to the Soviet Union in 1961, I asked my father when he had last heard from his brother. He said he didn't know. When I came back, my father greeted me at the airport, and that was the last time I saw him alive. He died shortly afterwards.

VH: Of what did your father die?

JA: He must have had a cardiac arrest. He was 79 years old. My sister told me that my father didn't want me to make any inquiries about his brother. He was afraid I might get into some difficulties with the authorities. His brother probably perished at Babi Yar. Except for that, both sides of the family moved to the United States.

VH: In the last psychoanalytic newsletter of the American, they were talking about your having made a speech at the San Francisco Institute at the graduation (1990a). Apparently you said that, basically, if Freud had been presenting his four cases to the American at this time, he would not be accepted for full membership. As a nonmedical person coming and bringing you a case tomorrow, I have some anxiety, so I'm very interested in what you said about Freud's cases.

JA: You must read it.

VH: I would like to. It must be quite clever.

JA: It was very funny. I thought it was funny. The group thought it was funny.

VH: You've written some about borderline cases.

JA: What is commonly called a borderline character really represents very sick patients who have many defects in the way they organize their compromise formations. They're unusual, and they are maladaptive, and they're maladaptive also in the social sense.

VH: You started out very early in your career writing papers on psychosomatic illnesses. In that area, what is of particular interest to you now?

JA: I got into that interest in psychosomatic medicine in an unusual way. What happened was that Flanders Dunbar, who had started a psychosomatic department at Columbia University, offered a fellowship for someone to work at Columbia. She offered it through the New York Psychoanalytic Institute. They asked me if I would be interested. Again, I found it interesting, and I went there. And that is how I got into the field.

VH: But you had mentioned that your mom had all kinds of illnesses. What kinds, of all kinds?

JA: She had gall bladder disease, she had fissure in ano, pancreatitis adhesions. She had kidney stones that could not be removed except by surgery. With all of this, she survived to 89, whereas my father, who had been well all the time, only made it to 79.

VH: Do you have any psychoanalytic theories about that?

JA: No.

VH: None at all? Do these illnesses reflect some expression of unconscious fantasy that may have kept her alive?

JA: Her relatives were all long-lived. They all lived well into their 80s. Her father had lived to be one 100.

VH: And how about you? What age are you going to live to?

JA: Well, you know, I have a pacemaker. Did you read my article on "The Analytic Attitude of the Service of Denial" (1991)?

VH: No, I didn't.

JA: You'll have to read it. Essentially this is what happened. I was in the middle of a telephone conversation with my wife when suddenly I found myself on the floor, sleeping. I awoke with a dream that I was tired and I decided to lie down on the floor to rest, a strange place to sleep, on the carpet of my own consultation room, I thought. With that I became fully awake. My next reaction was to recall what I had been thinking just before I awoke. It was a sense of the deepest, most pleasant kind of relaxation I had ever experienced, and at that point I said, "Well, if death is like this, there's nothing to fear about that." As I was coming out of the cardiac arrest, I was aware that I had had a confrontation with death, but I was denying it by saying, "Who's worried? It sounds great." Secondly, I denied it further by saying "I didn't have a heart attack. I just was tired." In the ensuing 2 or 3 hours I had many such denying experiences as a result of further cardiac arrests until I finally received a temporary pacemaker. If you want to see how an analyst can use his skills as a denier, you should read that paper.

VH: It's also a coping mechanism.

JA: That's right, it was a defense against overwhelming anxiety. It is very much like what happens in states of depersonalization. People in the middle of an accident become depersonalized and act as if they're just observers to what's going on affecting someone else. This enables them frequently to do the appropriate things to protect themselves. Denial serves to master the overwhelming anxiety that otherwise might have paralyzed them. That is the essence of my article on "The Analytic Attitude in the Service of Denial."

VH: What do you regard as your most important contributions?

JA: I would say the role of unconscious fantasy. Maybe it's being understood a bit too narrowly, but what I really meant by the concept is a description of the nature of unconscious mentation. We speak about unconscious processes, but what is really going on? How do we understand it? To what kind of metaphor can we translate it? The metaphor I began with was the moving-picture screen. It's as if we're watching an internal movie flashing before our eyes all the time, and as a result we are being influenced all the time. It's part of the input, combined with current perceptions and as altered by memory, which determines what an individual does.

VH: I was shocked as I was reading your work to see how easily you have handled the big hoopla about countertransference and its uses that has raged so hotly for so long. As I read much of your work, what you seem to be saying in different ways, and very sensibly, is that the analyst uses everything that comes to his mind, maybe not verbalizing his own mental experience, but uses it in order to formulate interpretation and to sort out the experience of what's transpiring between the analyst and the analysand. The whole debate over countertransference doesn't mean much to you; you don't take sides, you cut right through it.

JA: Yes, that's right.

VH: What do you think when you see all this hoopla going on about use of countertransference versus nonuse?

JA: It is terribly misused. One must remember not to focus on the analyst's affect without realizing that this affect, just like any other aspects of the analyst's mental experience—his thinking, his ideas while listening to the patient—all represent his reflections on a patient's material. One has to be disciplined in one's responses in keeping with what has been going on in the session. I refer to these issues in my paper on "The Genesis of Interpretation" (1979). The analyst's affective response, I point out, is an aspect of the aesthetic phase of the interaction with the patient. That response has to be subjected to disciplined, cognitive examination.

VH: I won't presuppose you. What is your reaction when you see all this focus on it as though it's ah-ha, we've suddenly seen the Holy Grail?

JA: I think the idea is wrong. I was in Boston on a panel with Dr. Schwaber on the subject of countertransference. She presented some clinical material. Essentially what happened was the following. The patient, apparently an intellectually gifted man, suffered from intense anxiety about examinations and about making progress in his life. He was in a conflict over doing graduate study and had been working as a hillbilly singer. Among his other symptoms were difficulties with alcohol, drugs, sexually perverse trends, and so forth. At some time in the treatment, she suggested that if he applied to graduate school, more might be learned about his sexual problems. The patient did decide to apply and immediately became tremendously anxious and many of his symptoms recurred. He began drinking, having sexually perverse fantasies and so forth. He was beside himself with anxiety. When he complained in the session about feeling badly, she said, "If you felt so bad, why did you apply at this time?"

VH: That sounds so attacking.

JA: As we know, there are no questions in psychoanalysis. The patient took the analyst's question as a suggestion. At the next session he announced that he had withdrawn his application for graduate school. To this Dr. Schwaber said, "What made you do that?" The patient's response was "At least I no longer have the feeling that I'm being led to my execution." Schwaber's concern in this context was her own reaction. Was it countertransference? Had she influenced the patient unduly as a result of her different view of reality as distinct from his view, and so forth? I said to her, "In response to the question, why did the patient have this response, namely, 'Now I no longer have the feeling that I'm being led to my execution.' This is what we have to analyze." Ultimately, some sessions later, after a number of weeks, the anxiety related to competitive fighting and murder was taken up, but I believe that this is a case where focusing on the analyst's feelings derailed the interpretive process. It interfered with viewing objectively what was going on.

In order to illustrate my point with students, I suggest to them that they have to listen in the same manner as they would in an ordinary conversation. I suggest that they take the conversation out of the analytic consultation room to the local bar. Suppose the patient now is talking to his best friend, one whom he trusts, and he says, "I withdrew my application from graduate school." The friend asks, "Why did you do that?" to which the patient responds, "Well, I was so anxious, but now I feel better. I no longer feel as if I'm being led to my execution." Surely the friend would say, or certainly think, "Being led to your execution? What has that got to do with it?" I focus on the dynamic evolution of the patient's associations. What people lose sight of is that, basically, psychoanalytic therapy is a form of conversation. Different from the usual form of conversation, but it is conversation. There is a reality that serves as the context for the treatment. The patient comes because he wants to get better. Those elements that he selects to tell the analyst are those which in some way he feels are significant in the pursuit of that goal. He may not know why at the time. This is the frame of reference of the treatment. Some people believe free association is talking right out of the system unconscious or right out of the id. They think that disjointed, unconnected associations are more relevant than other thoughts that come to one's mind. As a rule, patients do not talk in that disjoined way. They talk to the analyst.

VH: It's been my impression that some analysts in the United

States focus blame on New York, that if we are rigid and if we make too many interpretations or we're not empathetic, somehow we got it from New York. I don't hear that at all from you. What I hear is a fluidness, a receptiveness, and a deep respect for listening to the patient.

JA: But that reputation of New York is well deserved, it's true.

VH: But not about you?

JA: I haven't said that I'm typical. I've been on the outs with the Education Committee of New York for at least a generation.

VH: Apparently you have some strong feelings about it.

JA: Oh, yeah.

VH: Well, let's hear them.

JA: Do you know how I came to write the article for the graduating class of the San Francisco Institute? I did not write it for that occasion.

VH: Why?

JA: I wrote it as a form of emotional discharge. What happened was the following. I had been invited to a meeting of the Curriculum Committee of the New York Institute. I hadn't been teaching there for years.

VH: Is there a story there as to why you weren't teaching there?

JA: I was not persona grata with the people who control the Education Committee, and for a long time neither was Brenner. All of that has changed recently. You didn't know that?

VH: No, I didn't. I was amazed to hear Giovacchini say he'd never been allowed to be a training analyst. I was outraged by the whole thought, and yet I understand a lot of that has to do with personality.

JA: I think it was personality. I don't think it was plots. I think it was more personality, but I was much more open about certain issues of practice.

VH: Like what?

JA: I'll tell you. To continue with my meeting with the Curriculum Committee of the New York Institute, they wanted to know if I had any suggestions about the organization of the curriculum. I felt that the curriculum was wrong. It was mostly a historic recapitulation of psychoanalysis, and I did not think that that was the way to teach it. I said there should be three tracks. The first track should be an overview of the basis for psychoanalytic concepts, a historical overview of Freud's contributions, specifically the findings and the problems that led him to his theories. I said I would not study the case histories in detail. They could be used as part of the training program, but not more. I got no further than that suggestion. I never got to the two other tracks that I was going to suggest. They had to do with development and methodology. For $2^{1}/2$ hours, the members of the Committee kept asking me questions such as, "You would leave this out?" "Why not this paper?" "What about that paper?" I replied that what Freud describes in the early writings doesn't resemble anything of how we practice analysis or how we think about analytic problems today, that methodologically some of his clinical presentations are flawed. For example, one of the cases in *Studies on Hysteria* (Breuer & Freud, 1895) was just a conversation he had on a walk with a waitress. It is introduced into the book as a case report. What about the Dora case? That is a case in point. It illustrated Freud's discovery of transference, but it should not serve as a method for how to conduct an analysis. Do you know how many papers have been written doing and redoing the Dora case? There was no budging the members of the Committee. There was no real exchange. When I got home, I was very angry, and in the next few days, I took out my frustrations by dashing off the spoof that I wrote about Freud's applying to the American Psychoanalytic Association. It was sometime afterwards, when I was invited to give the talk in San Francisco, that I thought that this would make a good commencement address. I hope you will read the article as reprinted in the *American Psychoanalyst* (1991b).

VH: I would love to read it. Have there been repercussions?

JA: There have been many repercussions but only one unfavorable. That has appeared in the *American Psychoanalyst*. It was respectful, of course, but I have a letter here just received from someone in Spain who liked my talk so much she had it translated into Spanish and distributed to the students.

VH: I always think of you as getting to have your say.

JA: People will listen to what I say? That's interesting.

VH: You don't think so?

JA: I'm not aware of it. It certainly isn't so in the New York Institute.

VH: But there are many institutes in New York.

JA: I get a much more favorable reception at Columbia and at the New York University Institute.

VH: If something like Section 39 of the psychologists asked you to come on board as a consultant, would you consider that?

JA: I talk to them next year.

VH: Will the American hate you?

JA: I never thought of that.

VH: What makes for power in psychoanalysis? I've read Kernberg on group dynamics and Bion, and I've read some of your writings, but one of the things that's been hardest on me in doing these interviews was learning so much about the politics. It's hard for me not to idealize the field.

JA: In such a case, you should read my address to the Board of Professional Standards (1970), which I entitled "Group Psychology and the Analysis of Institutes." There too I was letting off some steam. I had been Chairman of the Board on Professional Standards. I am not sure that you know the story of the fight in the Cleveland Institute. If you have any illusions about how strong my influence is, you can see what happened there. I came out on the losing end.

VH: What were you involved in?

JA: I had been Chairman of the Board of Professional Standards. I had also been vice president of the International Psycho-Analytical Association. In this time I learned a great deal about splits, fights, and break ups at various institutes. There is one syndrome—it's not the only one, but a characteristic one—that is frequently the background of such splits. In a situation in which three analysts form an institute under the rules of the American Psychoanalytic Association, it's a husband and wife team and they get a third person as a training analyst. Usually he had been an analysand of one of the couple. They start an institute, and inevitably the students get involved in transference and countertransference struggles. Not all the transferences are positive, and there is a great deal of sibling rivalry. A good deal of it has to do with an unconscious fantasy or who will inherit the mantle of leadership. Frequently enough, the candidates or graduates break into two groups and war against each other. In Cleveland there was an idiotic situation. Not only were there originally three primary training analysts, but all the members of the institute worked for the Department of Psychiatry at Western Reserve University. They had their offices down the same corridor, they would go to conferences together. Some were analysands of the very people with whom they sat at committee meetings. And, of course, there was also the situation of currying favor with the head of the department. It was an incestuous setup which inevitably led to a fight.

According to the rules of the Board on Professional Standards, when there is a split in an institute the procedure is as follows. Each fragment of the former institute is considered a new training unit, which enables the American to place it under the aegis of the Committee on New Training Facilities and to have each body evaluated for its quality, in order to qualify for recognition as an accredited institute. Clearly this should have been the procedure to be followed in this instance. The group behind the Katans wanted to be recognized immediately as the old institute without any supervision or investigation from the Board. This was most undesirable inasmuch as I had asked members of both factions to keep their dissensions within the faculty and not to take it up with the students. They did not follow my advice. Each side called in each student and laid out the claims against the other party, including charges that ranged from embezzlement of money to murder. The fight went on in the Board for many years. It was aided and abetted by procedural peculiarities of the Board, namely, that a two-thirds majority was necessary to carry any vote. No one even remembered that this was the rule until the protagonist of one side brought it up in the discussion. Accordingly, no one wanted to offer a resolution, since the Board was almost equally divided and no one's proposal could carry two-thirds of the vote. In addition, there was endless filibustering by the group supporting the Katans. For 2 years the work of the Board was completely hampered. Finally I decided it wasn't worth the fight. I threw in the towel, and the group became an accredited institute without any supervision or help that the American Psychoanalytic Association Board of Standards offered. It was all done on a personal level, with complete disregard for the interests of the candidates or for the standards of psychoanalytic training.

VH: They needed your power.

JA: They got along very well without it. I have no illusions about having power. I write my papers and, if people read them and use them, that's the only criterion that I prize. I was asked to be president of the International twice but after the experience of the Board and with being president of the American, where my task was to clean up the mess of the accreditation fight of 1959–1960, I had no interest in being president of the International.

VH: Do you think we will survive as a field? In Los Angeles, we're seeing a sort of "war of theories."

JA: Well, that's been going on in the International all the time without any reconciliation or real exchange. The International is a hybrid organization, to use a respectable term.

VH: Are there trends now, that you see, that distress you?

JA: The most significant trend that disturbs me, and one that we will be discussing in connection with your case material, is a departure from methodological discipline, the imposing of meaning onto the material on the basis of empathy, intuition, or countertransference alone. One has to stick to the fundamentals of what the psychoanalytic method is about and what the psychoanalytic situation is founded on. We who call ourselves psychoanalysts have to agree upon a common ground. Here I differ with Wallerstein very strongly. There may be many different approaches, but the common ground is the use of the psychoanalytic situation and the psychoanalytic method of interpretation. Unless we follow that, we're not talking about the same data.

VH: Define the method.

JA: To me the method is clear. The principles were enunciated by Freud when he devised the psychoanalytic situation, namely, we put the patient in a position where what is presented to his consciousness is the result of intrapsychic forces in conflict. What comes to the surface are derivative manifestations. It is on the basis of these presentations we infer the nature of unconscious process. Our conclusions must depend upon how we read and understand the text of the patient's associations, guided, of course, by our knowledge and by the patient's reaction to our responses. The latter, of course, is secondary. The primary point is the methodological analysis of the patient's productions as they occur in sequence and in context. These are the same criteria used for understanding any communication. What we should do is to demonstrate to the patient how his mind works. We analyze his productions. Understanding how his mind works is what the patient is coming for. Freud's original idea of the goal of treatment was to have the patient give up his repressions in order to recover the traumatic memories. He repeated that as late as his very last papers, for example, in "Constructions in Psychoanalysis" in 1937. Other people say that psychoanalysis is a form of repair, that in the treatment we compensate for certain experiences and deficits in the patient's life—for example, if a mother wasn't sufficiently empathic, didn't smile at the patient, or didn't appreciate the patient's productions.

VH: You're thinking of Alexander's "corrective emotional" experience or the Kohutians?

JA: Both! They have been correctly characterized by Friedman (1978) as replacement therapy. The treatment is supposed to replace what the child had missed in the course of development. There had been a deficit of experience and, according to these theories, this is what had produced the defective ego. In the course of treatment, the patients reflect upon what they have been thinking and saying and upon the things that have been pointed out to them. They are aware that somebody has been listening for a particular reason. He professes that he can uncover things for the patient that will be useful to him. The analyst has one goal in mind and that is to present to the patient's consciousness the inferences to be drawn from the patient's thinking. The patient should be influenced as minimally as possible by any extraneous influences.

VH: Which your analyst violated immediately when he brought in this idea, this representation of what he had in his mind?

JA: Yes, you are right. The analyst was presenting me with a bit of his experience. He wanted me to confront an idea, the similarity between the image in the dream and his knowledge of a bisexual symbol from Hindu mythology. This was the way the correct interpretation came into his mind, but he was interested in getting me to recognize the objective similarity between my visual presentation and the sexual symbol he had in mind. Now he was right, but I didn't do anything with the suggestion he made. In effect, he said, "You are rejecting the idea," and I was, in effect saying, "Yes, I do." But there was a dissonance there. It was not that I was rejecting the similarity between my dream and the symbol that the analyst had brought in. I was really rejecting the idea of bisexuality and that is what he should have focused on. What he should have analyzed was the flow of the associations. Whether I said yes or no was irrelevant. The objective similarity of the dream representation and the lingam was irrelevant. What was relevant was the next association, that I didn't want to deal with the idea of bisexuality.

VH: Do you think we're doing a better job with that now than we used to?

JA: Yes, much better.

VH: That's my impression when I hear someone like you talk about his early analysis. Some say your mind should be absent of any preconceived ideas. I have trouble imagining how you could go in with no idea. What do you think about the notion of the analyst beginning a session with no ideas?

JA: That's self-delusion. How could you treat a patient under those circumstances? When the patient walks in, you look at him. You have a reaction to everything that you see—what he might be communicating, his body language, and so forth. Immediately you get a set of associations. You may not be conscious of them but you are put in a certain frame of mind. The frame of mind is part of the context. What happened last session? What is the nature of the man's problem? Each session is not a tabula rasa. That is how the mind works. There is a constant interplay of perception, fantasy, and memory. This is the frame of reference that I bring into my thinking. It's there all the time and creates the mental set against which we selectively perceive, interpret, register, and react to stimuli.

VH: On both sides.

JA: Well, of course.

VH: So do you think this is something we're doing better than we used to?

JA: Much better.

VH: Are there other things that come to mind that you think we're doing better?

JA: Oh, a lot of things, especially defense analysis.

VH: I know that the unconscious fantasy is one of your contributions that you value, but in terms of technique, which is what we're really into now, what do you feel your valuable contributions have been?

JA: Methodology of psychoanalytic interpretation. These are all laid out, but I realize much too sparsely, in my two papers, "The Genesis of Interpretation" (1979a) and "The Dynamics of Interpretation" (1987a). They deserve much more elaboration and, of course, I always feel I could do it much better with actual clinical material. In the paper I wrote with Dr. Beres, "Fantasy and Identification in Empathy" (1974), I described a dream I had while listening to a patient. The dream was identical with the dream that the patient was reporting to me. It's a classic example of something in my own experience that I can use as a model of what happens while we listen to a patient reporting a dream. I gave the background of what the patient's dream was about. I had a visual fantasy of my own at the same time. In this fantasy, I was at a European airport, and I saw my father coming towards me in a bus, as happens in several European airports. Now the truth of the matter is that the last time I saw my father was at an American airport where he was waiting for me to come in. This was a reversal of the situation depicted in the dream. My father was dead at the time, and this dream expressed the wish to reverse the situation between life and death, the wish to have a reunion made possible in a never-never land, a twilight zone between life and death. I had been listening to the patient describing his dream. In the dream he had been calling to an uncle, who had been a father surrogate during the years when his father was in the United States and the patient was left in Europe with his mother and siblings. He loved that uncle very much. When he was separated from him on coming to the United States, he longed for a reunion with the uncle. He was sure that the uncle was still alive, although this was after the war, and they had not heard from him. As he discovered in time, the uncle had been killed the very first day that the Nazis came to the town. In the patient's description of the dream, he was in a house. It was neither daylight nor nighttime, but it was getting towards evening. He was calling out his uncle's name and his uncle was calling his name back. Both of them were using the Yiddish equivalents of the names, ones that they used in the patient's childhood. As I was having my fantasy, I thought, this is the twilight zone between life and death, where people can meet once again. I can see my father again. At that point I woke up, and I heard my patient saying, "Last night I was watching the 'Twilight Zone,' et cetera. Now the content of his dream and the content of my visual dreamlike fantasy were identical. They represented a wishful event in the never-never land between myself and my father and between himself and the father surrogate. I had identified with the patient but, when I realized that my dream represented a comment on the patient's material, I had passed from identification to empathy. This was how the interpretation was forming itself in my mind.

VH: I think we've used our time for today. You've been very generous. Thank you.

Case Discussion

Dr. Arlow tells us that the patient's fantasies and many concrete thoughts are very important to focus on. He argues that Roselyn was abused by a critical mother and a passive father with serious consequences to her ability to share emotions. He was interested in Roselyn's conflict between feeling that her mother hated her and that she hated her mother, along with her wish to protect her mother and herself.

This case discussion took place October 20, 1991. Dr. Arlow opened the interview with a discussion of some principles of psychoanalytic research, which I will save until my conclusion. He then proceeded to ask some penetrating questions about the case. "Now, she's an only child, and her earliest memories at the age of 2, her mother's bloody attempt to kill herself. What does that consist of? What did the patient see? What did the patient experience?" I said, "She heard screaming. She was sleeping and she heard screaming, and she got out of her little 2-year-old bed and went down to the bathroom and saw her parents struggling when her mother had just apparently—some of this we have to assume—we don't know the exact details, but there was blood all over." He said, "That was the story she told you. That's what we want to hear."

I said, "And she, in trying to bring it closer to her consciousness and connect to the feeling, she's even brought colored pencils and drawings. She always makes them red and white."

JA: But that is not the answer to my question. Exactly what did she relate? She came into the bathroom in the middle of the night when she heard screaming.

VH: She didn't know who was killing whom.

JA: No, she saw blood.

VH: First.

JA: Blood all over the place. At the age of 2, it's improbable that she understood what killing was.

VH: No.

JA: What we know is that she had a memory at the age of 2 coming into bathroom, seeing blood all over the place, and her parents seemed to be involved in some violent, muscular activity. Then what happened?

VH: She went and hid in her closet.

Dr. Arlow asked if the mother had made other attempts at suicide, and I reported the known history. Dr. Arlow said, "I want to separate fact from interpretation. I want to understand what the patient's experience was when she came to treatment and talked to you. Now, you say her mother was a functional psychotic. What does that mean?"

VH: What it meant to me was that she never figured out her rage, her hate, her displacement.

JA: These are technical terms. You mean the mother had very limited insight.

VH: Very.

JA: But those technical terms don't belong at this point in a description of the case history. We have to know what the mother did in addition to having made a number of suicide attempts. How did she behave in general? What did the patient observe and how did the mother react to the patient? What we are trying to find out is what was the patient's experience with this mother.

VH: Her father had many siblings. Her mother, through the years, managed to somehow get all of them into an enemy position so that the family became totally isolated. She had grievances against everyone.

JA: Justified or unjustified?

VH: How's a child to know?

JA: How did the patient report it to you when she was interviewed?

VH: When she reported it to me, she felt that before the mother had made them into enemies, she would go to a summer picnic with the family, and she liked them. She found it to be the happiest time of her life when she could go visit those relatives. They became enemies, to her, in her mind, the mother had destroyed something that was good and made them into enemies.

JA: And deprived her of her family.

VH: Or anybody who might have helped her.

Dr. Arlow wondered how the mother treated the child. I said, "She hit her a lot, physically attacked her a great deal. Her experience was that anything that happened that could be blamed on anybody would be blamed on her. If the grandmother, who lived with them, was nasty to the mother, then the mother would say, 'Well, if you hadn't upset your grandmother, she wouldn't have been nasty to me.' The father would say, 'Well, just ignore your mother,' even though he would come in and see her swinging the child by her hair. Literally, swinging her around by her hair." Dr. Arlow said, "It's an important detail, and so is the extreme form the mother's anger or violence took."

I went on, regarding the father. "His later reply always was, 'Oh, well, you know your mother's very nervous.' And he always defended the mother. He never said, 'You were bad and you deserved it,' which is what the mother was saying to the child. But he did say, 'We just won't talk about it. She's a nervous mother.' So there was a conspiracy or he wanted to avoid talking about it, to deny it, to not deal with her outbursts. That incident where the child witnessed the suicide attempt was never discussed. In her memory, no one ever said, 'That must have been pretty scary for you.' "

Dr. Arlow asked about what the father's nervous breakdown had consisted of. I said, "The child remembered ambulances coming and strait jackets. There was also an occasion when he had bleeding ulcers and had thrown up and again ambulances came."

Dr. Arlow said, "Violence and blood were part of her experience as a child." I emphasized that no one ever talked about these occurrences. Dr. Arlow wondered how the father treated the little girl. I replied, "He never attacked the child. He basically got ulcers or had to go to the hospital—his nervous breakdowns were not evidenced by screaming or hollering. They were more apparently a collapse into depression where he was just almost catatonic. You had the feeling he just couldn't deal with anything."

JA: But if he had to be put in a strait jacket, then he must have been physically violent.

VH: I somehow question if that was real, but he was put on a gurney. I question her description of what —

JA: But that's what she told you?

VH: Yes. She questions it too.

JA: This is the kind of material which one would have to have placed. Now, she created a world of little people who kept her company and contained pieces of herself until about age 8. What does that mean?

VH: Well, I can tell you how she described it. Her memory is that she would have in her mind a little person who her mother couldn't impact, and that little person would be somewhere placed in the room, maybe behind the book, behind the rug; and she would have another person that could not feel pain. And that little person would be somewhere, and she would think, okay, I have a little person. It's not like a multiple personality. It was more like an imaginary game.

JA: Oh, I understand what you're saying. But why do you put it in terms of containing *pieces* of herself?

VH: How would you put it?

JA: She had fantasies.

VH: They would split off. They carried certain functions.

JA: She had fantasies of little people with whom she identified, and these little people could hide in places where her mother couldn't reach her, where the mother couldn't hurt her. That's what was happening. These aren't literally pieces of herself. They were thoughts that the patient had. She had concretized a thought. She visualized it very much as one visualizes a thought in a dream.

VH: She concretized it actually. But, I do too.

JA: You put it down as "contained pieces of the self." These aren't pieces of the self. These are the thoughts that she had. If only I were a little person, and I could hide somewhere where my mother couldn't hurt me. If only I were a little person who had the ability not to be injured physically by blows. That's what she was thinking.

VH: And there was also one that could wish ill on the mother.

JA: Of course, I'm not doing it, this little representative of mine is thinking that.

VH: She stuck her tongue out.

JA: Because she must once have stuck out her tongue at her mother and gotten a good spanking for it, she would fantasize that there was a little person somewhere, who represented her, who could stick the tongue out at the mother and get away with it. These were various fantasies of how to get revenge on the mother, how to handle the dangerous situations. These are responses to a situation which the patient knew very realistically that she could not control. You know, to put it in terms of pieces of herself, doesn't really capture what was going on. It's inaccurate. It's a different level of discourse.

VH: Okay. If it had been pieces, or do you think pieces would never be accurate?

JA: People don't think that way unless it's part of some psychotic mentation.

VH: She has a lot of psychotic thoughts.

JA: But the question is: Is she expressing the idea as material pieces of herself? That is why I asked the question. It is possible that she had a fantasy of having been cut up into little pieces and that she thought of these little pieces acting independently. That is not the fantasy that she had.

VH: No. You're right.

JA: She was thinking of her thoughts and her wishes. These "people" are representations of her wishes.

VH: It's a very creative way, really, of keeping a thought of herself this way.

JA: These are fantasies. That's what I concentrate on. You begin to see how I work. She's an excellent student, and so forth. She felt that she was two selves, one trying to learn and another one begging for her dismal unreal life and self to end. Meaning really that she, at times, had the wish to die, to get out of her misery. It was too much for her to handle.

VH: I have always been struck with the degree of her humiliation.

JA: Of course. Let me tell you how I listen to a summary. A summary is not the same as process notes of a session. A summary represents an edited version of what you feel you want to convey to the listener so that he may understand the case. Anyone who writes a summary hopes to convey that kind of information to the reader. That's the conscious process at work. But I believe that, in addition to the conscious selection of material, there's an unconscious element that enters into the arranging of the material. The text, the sequence, the contiguity of elements, as they appear, even in the summary, not only in the patient's associations, have certain significance to me, and it demonstrates how I work. For example, the patient felt deeply distressed. She couldn't share her feelings with anyone. And then you add that she often suffers from migraines. What it suggests to me is that the juxtaposition of these two elements may indicate that the suppressed feelings became manifest in the form of the migraines. The fact that you juxtaposed the two represents some connection you have made, whether you are aware of it or not.

Dr. Arlow pointed out that the material regarding Roselyn's brief psychotic episodes should have been fuller and greater detailed and should have been included in the presentation. I said that during the hospital episodes she had thoughts that her mother would kill her during the surgery. Dr. Arlow went on to say, "You went down to the hospital to visit her and she felt better. What was it that you did or said?" I replied, "I walked into the hospital room, her husband was standing beside the bed, the doctor was standing over here. I walked in, she reached for my hand. I took her hand and I held it. I sat down by the bed and I said, 'The doctor asked me to come.' Roselyn replied, 'I know; I'm crazy right now. I think he's going to kill me, and I know he's not going to kill me but I think he's coming to kill me. And I'm afraid I've wished to be dead so many times that if my mother doesn't get me, when I'm unconscious, God will, because I wished it.' And so I sat there listening and holding her hand. I asked if she had any particular idea why at this particular moment she was having so much trouble with reality, and she repeated basically the same thing. She had wished to be dead so many times, God might take her seriously. She wanted somehow for me to let her know that someone wanted her to live, and it was sort of like I was a magician." Dr. Arlow said, "Your presence was the magic. So the question becomes, 'Why was your presence so therapeutic?' This gives us a clue. It's not hard to imagine that a patient under these circumstances would feel overwhelmed, frightened, and angry. As she grew older, I would imagine, she quite correctly believed that her mother would want to kill her. After a while, she would also have the idea that she would want to kill her mother. Even if she couldn't actually do it, because she was a child, she could wish it. Now the child believes in the omnipotence of his wishes or possesses a hope that these wishes could be omnipotent. She could think that the mother would die as a result of her wishes. Helene Deutsch describes the mechanism called the protector under protection. You were the protecting presence. You represented the mother. When the patient could see that you (the mother) were still alive, she could feel reassured. Her wishes had not killed her mother, and she didn't have to feel guilty or anxious any more."

Dr. Arlow did not like my use of the word "containing." He said, "It's a concretistic image, and you revert to a concretistic expression: 'My presence or containing seemed to help her reconstitute herself.' She didn't reconstitute herself. She calmed down. These are two different levels of discourse."

We passed from her psychotic episodes:

VH: And she stopped thinking psychotic thoughts mostly.

JA: She calmed down. She improved. She stopped having psychotic thoughts. You suggest a certain theory of psychopathology and pathogenesis. And you incorporate your theory into what should be description. Actually it should read, I came, I sat with the patient, she told me what she was thinking, she held my hand, she said she felt guilty, maybe God would punish her. She knew that the ideas weren't real and, after a while, without further intervention, she felt better. My being there seemed to help her. She calmed down. That's how we have to listen, with a minimum of preformed paradigms to impose upon the data.

VH: I have another question when you're talking about this. Theoretically I agree with you, and I have looked, and I have probed, and I have tried to find evidence of her wishing to kill her mother. In all these years, I have not seen it until the last 6 months. I've always been puzzled by it. I had the theory that the migraines had to do with her rage and hate. That's not what has been in the material.

JA: It's in the material.

VH: Her fear of her feelings sure is.

JA: We'll come to that. It's in the material, and it's there beautifully.

VH: I hear more her terror of the mother.

JA: Oh, that's there, of course. That she knows. What terrifies her is her fear of violent murderousness, that she could be like her mother. She even gives us an idea of how she would kill. We'll get to that as we examine the material. I will try to demonstrate how the material suggests these ideas to me. The problem in analysis is to listen in such a way as to obtain either confirmation or disconfirmation of a hypothesis that suggests itself to us. Since you put January 1990 first, let me proceed from there. We begin with the idea that her basic problem, as I see it, is a struggle with her violent rage against her mother, her wish to kill her, and her fear her rage will get out of control and that she will actually carry out wishes. She will do all these terrible things, her wishes will make her mother die, and so forth. We have also surmised, among other things, that the mechanism of protector under protection was generating. Now she has a repeated fear of going insane. Did you ever ask her what going insane seems to her?

VH: Yes. Having no power over her own mind, having no control over her own thoughts.

JA: Going insane means losing control. Is that the picture?

Dr. Arlow brought up Roselyn's mentioning "unreal space" and wondered what is real space. I said, "To her, real space would be to be under one's own motivations, one's own passions, to be the one deciding I am, I feel, I want, I decide, to have a sense of, I'm doing what I want with my life, and I'm not being always governed by my past interjects. That is the way she would say it. But the memories, the thoughts of my previous experiences have always dominated me." Dr. Arlow felt at various times she must have felt unreal. I agreed, saying her feelings were never responded to. He felt that was an ideological consideration, and we were now just at the descriptive level. He went on, "She must have felt that she wasn't quite herself. She had been depersonalized. She had a sense of herself as being unreal. She had the sense of her perceptions, of the external world, at various times, not being real. She had little sense of herself. We've already mentioned it as being split in two. One part of her was actually involved doing things and another part of her, off at a distance, observing her other self-representation doing things, but feeling not connected to it. Do you know my paper on 'Structure of the Dèjá Vu Experience' (1979b)?" I said I did and he went on, "It's one of the characteristic ways of handling great danger. And, of course, she has quite a bit of that. I'm here, my mother's beating me, but there are little bits of me, representations of me out there that are immune from what's happening. That's part of the process of depersonalization. Many psychological dangers are responded to with depersonalization and derealization. For example, a tremendous upsurge of a violent impulse may induce the reaction, 'This is not happening to me. I am just watching that other person.' As one can see, it is a split in the self-representation and this patient seems to have had it many, many times."

I said, "Nothing that happened to her was ever validated. The father would act like he hadn't seen it. The grandmother, with whom she shared a room, would act like she hadn't just witnessed the child abuse." Dr. Arlow responded, "It also suggested one way of handling unpleasant situations. A lot of the defense mechanisms that are employed are borrowed from the interpersonal relations with the important primary objects."

I went on to explain the technical problem, "It's been a real problem with the treatment because if I say anything like, 'You must have felt,' she's real quick to say, 'I did not feel it. It happened.' And then she will tell me how she spent so much of her childhood trying to sort out whether what she had experienced or seen or gone through was real because nobody was acting like it was real." Dr. Arlow responded, "That's right. But there's no question about the reality of the bad things that happened to her. But that's not her problem. Her problem is that she's struggling with what she conceives are the bad things happening within her. That's where the problem is.

"She begins a session and she feels terrible and then she's silent, and then you ask quite appropriately, 'Physically or mentally?' and she says, 'Both.' And then she elaborates further, 'I have a headache.' That could be both physical and mental. And you say, 'It seems difficult for you to talk today. I'm unsure if my silence is helpful or not.' Again, going back to what I was telling you yesterday about taking the conversation to the local bar. 'You have a headache. You feel it's both physical and mental. Tell me about it.' What are her thoughts about it? She begins the session saying that she feels bad and that she has a headache. That has to be the theme of the session. The first thing the patient says is the theme for the session. That's why she's coming, she's coming for the purpose of telling you what's on her mind, to get well, and she picked that out. Consciously or unconsciously, the reality of the therapeutic relationship is always part of the framework of the treatment situation. She responds to what you said. You said, 'You know, it must be tough for you to talk,' and she says, 'I know what I must work on, but I am terrified.' 'Well, what is it that terrifies you?' And yet you go on with the silence and you say, 'The silence may feel something like it felt when you were small and overwhelmed with so many feelings and no one there to contain you.' "

Dr. Arlow was firm regarding countertransference. He queried me on "contain."

VH: I know. I should have said comfort.

JA: And then you said, "I wish I had said 'hold you.' "

VH: Or comfort.

JA: You, yourself, knew that this was a stilted way of talking.

VH: I did.

JA: What happened at that moment tells me something about your countertransference. What happened at that moment is you wanted to say "hold you," but you felt "this is going to be too intimate, too close," so you took refuge in technical language. You are tremendously attached to this patient. You're very sympathetic; you want desperately to get her well because you feel so sorry for the really terrible things that happened in her life. You were struggling against an impulse. I am not.

VH: But I didn't want to interfere. I was also feeling that would interfere in her thoughts, in her learning that she can deal with these feelings and remember that I'm there.

JA: It's interfering with your listening. Instead of listening to what was terrifying her and what was giving her a headache, you were thinking, what can I do to alleviate this poor woman's suffering. She's talking about something that's giving her a headache and that terrifies her, and she knows she must work on it. And you're saying, "Let's not work on that. I wish I could hold you." Of course, you gave her an interpretation about the terrible things that happened to her in childhood. Absolutely true. You're saying, "I can understand how you might feel that way. It was terrible." She said, "Yesterday I felt I had a glimpse about something about the migraines. It seems that when I get closer to expressing my real feelings I get migraines." In other words, what's really troubling me, that's what gives me migraines. And now what's the next thing she says? You remember my talking about implosions. Black holes in the universe where stars exploded inwardly, inward. "A black hole containing all my back into myself-self." Words seem inadequate. What is her profession? Is she in the sciences? . . . Implosion. What's an implosion?

VH: Violence inward.

Dr. Arlow pointed out that an implosion is an image of tremendous violence, and she had talked about that 5 years earlier. She turns it back on herself and gets headaches from the suppressed rage and turning her feelings back into herself. He asked if I had asked her to explain "black hole." I said she had given me many different versions, and they change as she gets better. He was insistent that here the black hole was the implosion.

VH: And she's described it as, like this, where it squishes, squishes, squishes all her feelings down, sort of like if you were—

JA: Which feelings?

VH: The negative ones. For a long time it was only the negative ones.

JA: What are negative feelings?

VH: Negative feelings are hate, destruction, fear of being destroyed, fear of retaliation. What they are now are longing for comfort, longing to have a good mother; they're different feelings now.

JA: She's talking about inhibiting, repressing, containing feelings of great violence. She's sitting on a tremendous rage.

VH: Dr. Arlow, give me some examples. I have raised the question of that rage. At times I raise it if I get even the slightest glimpse of it. It just seems to encourage her to seal it up. Sometimes I think when you were as terrified as she was as a child, that rage is almost inconceivable.

JA: How to handle this is another matter. Your question is, how do I look upon this material? In spite of your speaking about holding and your feeling along with the patient and her childhood, the patient kept speaking all the time about the migraine, to which she then said, "Migraines feel like they are me in a container inside myself of pain and pain that would destroy me if it came outside. It would explode my mind, myself. It'd be like little molecules going any and everywhere." First of all, you have here a contrast between implosion and explosion. I saw the same thing in the 1985 material. She has the idea that she is ready to explode.

When you have in mind exploding, what do you think of? How do you conceive of it? She tells you. It would be like molecules going anywhere and everywhere. Where are there molecules that go anywhere and everywhere in connection with explosion? A nuclear bomb, an atom bomb. These molecules are little things, they are tiny but they can kill. You don't even see them but they kill everything in their path.

VH: And, of course, she's correct. The image of the mother inside as a destructive mother and the image—it is both inside and outside.

JA: Well, of course, we'll get to that. But if you feel your real feelings and trust them, trust me with them, are you afraid you will go mad and cease to exist? So you're suggesting something about the transference that may or may not be correct, but at this particular time, the latter part of what you said was to the point. You are so afraid that, if you go mad, you will release that explosion and kill everything in sight. That's what she doesn't know. She doesn't know she wants to kill.

VH: And it's not that I haven't suggested that that is a possibility.

JA: It's not a possibility. You've got to tell it to her as if *you* believe it. If you don't believe it, she won't believe it. I remember somebody told me about a supervisory experience reported to him about somebody who was in supervision with Dr. Isakower. Dr. Isakower had pointed out something that the supervisee had missed. The supervisee was struck by it, and he said to Dr. Isakower, "Should I tell that to the patient?" Dr. Isakower said, "No." The student said, "Why not?" Dr. Isakower replied, "Because I believe it and you don't." Now I am not recommending this as a technique of supervision, but there is a point there. To return to your patient, she said I told you once about crystals being formed in a centrifuge. That's a very strange association.

VH: You know, she corrected that. Just recently, about a year ago, when I decided I was going to share this case. I let her read this. One of her primary responses was that I had that incorrect, that she hadn't said the crystals were formed in a centrifuge. That she had said that the crystals were formed in a violent environment and that she wasn't sure where I had gotten the idea of the centrifuge. And I still don't know where I got it—but it is true that she felt she had been formed in a violent environment.

JA: Let's go on. We'll leave that centrifuge out. It doesn't make any difference because the real point is what she said next. She said, "When things are formed in a chaotic environment, it can't hold together." So she's saying, "You know why I feel like exploding and killing everybody, because of what happened in my chaotic and violent childhood." This is how I hear it, namely, her fear of her violence. She recognizes that she has violence so powerful in her that, unless she contains it and turns it upon herself, she would kill. Now back to the 1985 situation, the long dream. Is she the first patient in the morning?

VH: No, she's midafternoon.

JA: Anyway, a long dream like that, but you recall the details of the dream and, of course, you can't.

VH: I was struck by her literary style. I wrote that one down most particularly because I like the literary symbolism, and I thought it fit her very well that she felt she had been raised on poison. I thought it symbolized her very well.

JA: You look back. I'm departing from the way I work to go to the way I teach. If you look back upon that whole session, what was she talking about? What would be the central theme? Let us suppose a friend of yours asked, "You saw a patient today?" "Yes." "What was the patient talking about? What was on her mind?"

VH: That she had been fed, nurtured on poison, and it had made it impossible —

JA: Poison and what else?

VH: Made it impossible for her to make a new world for herself.

JA: Well, that sounds very—I'm your friend now, you see. Well, that sounds very interesting, but you know, you're an analyst. I hear that you analysts get really interesting, deep kind of stuff. Did she have anything of that sort?

VH: That she wouldn't be able to leave the father.

JA: She was talking about people who eat dogs.

VH: In the transference she was saying I was a fool because I was like those Americans who will try to save those animals from being destroyed. And they are already destroyed, and the inevitability of their destruction is already there.

JA: That's all very nice.

VH: So you're a fool to try to save them.

JA: That's all very nice, but how do you feel about dogs being devoured for food?

VH: She knows I like dogs.

JA: She doesn't like the idea of dogs being devoured for food. She thinks of this in terms of cannibalism. Dogs are pets, little things to be loved. Children are loved, little things to be loved. She speaks here about the parent poisoning, poison goes through her mouth; she speaks about a witch who feeds Snow White a poison apple; and then she has a transference reaction to you. She says, "You wanted death, you got it." Did you want her dead? She's not talking about you. She's speaking about someone who wanted her dead. She realized her mother wanted to kill her. Her mother is the witch. And how did her mother want to kill her in her childhood mind? She thinks of the mother's cruel mouth. Think of the situation of any 2-year-old. The mother is raging at her. The 2-year-old is fascinated by the mouth that is calling violent names, saying wild things. She thinks, mother wants to eat me up. That's the way people are killed, of course, and that's how she wants to kill me. If I want to kill her, that's what I will do. I will do the same thing.

VH: She once was drawing the mother during a session. She's a very artistic person.

JA: The figure in the drawing, did it have a big mouth, big teeth?

VH: It was like a Mexican thing with—basically the whole drawing ended up with sharp points, like a geometric design, with all the teeth and the sharp points and the fingernails.

JA: The idea of being poisoned by the mother's food and being eaten up by the mother involves an identification with the aggressor.

VH: But it doesn't work very well.

JA: It doesn't work at all because she's terrified. She thinks she is potentially psychotic like her mother. The Kleinians would say that she has introjected the violent, destructive mother. It is a matter of language here. She has a fantasy that her mother would want to eat her up, and she wants to do the same thing to her mother. That is what terrifies her. She is afraid of losing control and cannibalizing her mother. Finally, she says, "I am convinced I will alienate anyone I love, and they will let me do it." Of course, she's talking about her mother.

VH: She's always afraid, too, that I will decide that she's untreatable and give up.

JA: That's a mild way of attacking you, that you'll ultimately get so annoyed that you'll get rid of her. That's a form of hostility. Then she says, "It makes me think of those one-cell animals that have these stinging capsules all over and all around them." Does it sound familiar? Those are the molecules, and if you're a kid, and you've got this great big monster trying to kill you, you'll think, oh boy, there are certain little things, some of them are so small, you can't even see them. Some of them you have to use a microscope to see, but they can kill. This is where she thinks of killing. She's thinking of killing all the time. Sometimes she says, they are called paramecium. They can even sting themselves. "Sometimes when I hurt myself, it feels like I am hurting my mother." An example of aggression turned against one's self. The aggression consists of a fantasy of devouring the mother and the fear of the devoured mother retaliating inside. Many suicides really represent combinations of suicide and murder. The suicide kills the object with whom he or she is identified, the object that he or she has introjected. She has a fantasy that her mother is in her and that, in killing herself, she would at the same time be killing her mother.

VH: She equally has the fantasy that she's escaped the mother. It seems to alternate pretty rapidly.

JA: One doesn't negate the other.

VH: No, it doesn't.

JA: You just have to think of her as a little girl about to fall asleep. She is lying in her bed and thinking of the day's events. She thinks, "My mother is trying to kill me and I would like to kill her. She wants to eat me up. I would want to eat her up. But if I eat her up, I'll have her inside me. I could kill her but maybe she would kill me inside me."

VH: The mother was apparently suffering from insomnia because frequently in the middle of the night she would wake this child up by grabbing her up and accusing her. Even in her sleep she was not allowed to sleep peacefully. Because the mother was a night stalker.

JA: Her mother couldn't sleep at night because she was disturbed by this wish to kill the patient.

VH: She would go in and practice by grabbing the kid up and giving her a few whacks.

JA: Give her a few whacks but didn't kill her.

VH: No. Left her terrified.

JA: The beating that she gave the child was a compromise between letting her sleep in peace and murdering her; she simply beat her. When the patient speaks of the woman in the dream destroying dogs, she is thinking of her mother. They sold puppies in cages.

VH: I sell time.

JA: They sold puppies in cages. They were the ones, the parents, not you. "They eat people." she says, "but you would have bought the puppies, Ginger." She calls you Ginger. Other times she calls you Virginia. Ginger is an affectionate variation. It's more intimate than Virginia. She is saying, "You wouldn't do anything like that." She senses your affection for her. She says, "You wouldn't be like my mother. She is a cannibal, and she would eat me up." She goes on to say, "In that country they eat young puppies." Then she says, "You don't think people should eat young things, do you?" She is against cannibalism. It wasn't about dogs that she was concerned. It was about eating people. The next thing she says is, "I remember my mother's mouth." Context, contiguity, juxtaposition, one thing right after the other. Those are the criteria that I use. That is how I make my inferences. "I remember my mother's mouth. I was so afraid." She is saying she was afraid her mother was going to devour her, and that is what she should have heard from you at the time.

VH: I wish I had said that.

JA: Of course. It's right here in the material. This is something one cannot dispute, no matter what theory of analysis one entertains. You cannot dispute that, when she is talking about eating puppies, she is thinking that people shouldn't eat young things. She says, "I remember my mother's mouth. I was so afraid." To me it cannot be any clearer. As I said before, there are certain interpretations that we can be sure of, others that are only probable. This is one, I think, that you can be sure of. She was afraid her mother was going to kill her and eat her. She says, "I felt like somehow her mouth was going to get me. I always felt that. Sometimes I feel that way here." And then she says, "So unreal. I protect myself when I have this tremendous fear of being afraid by becoming depersonalized." Then she begins to cry and says, in effect, "You know, it is really a horror, this feeling of being poisoned by your own parent." How much clearer can this be? It is really a horror. Inferences become possible by examining the sequence of thoughts. She has the dream about the puppies and the old witch. And then she thinks about people in Asia who devour young things. She then makes the connection of young things with people, and from there she goes on to the idea of her mother's cruel, cannibalizing mouth. She says that she is afraid that her mother would eat her, "poison me." There is another compromise. Then she says, "It's a terrible thing to think that your parent would want to kill you and eat you up. It's a real horror." The next association is, "You know, about your painting, when I feel I need protection and I feel I cannot stand reality, I go into the painting and move behind it, and you don't know where I am." It's transference. These were the thoughts that she had when she felt her mother was going to kill her.

VH: The fantasies of hiding.

JA: The little people who could hide. They're not pieces of her, these are ideas. How can I get away from this monster and how can I get back at her? "I feel torn between the real world and the temptation of the unreal world." She never had a definition of what it's like to depersonalize. The material just cited illustrates it beautifully. The patient goes on to say, "This is not my Catholic stuff. All this feeling of being devoured and wanting to devour, I begin to think of my catechism." And this is something that deserves to be explored. It would seem that it refers to the eucharist, because she is talking about devouring, and the eucharist involves ideas of incorporating the body of what was once at least a living person. She says, "I feel poisoned." In reality, the eucharist should have the opposite effect, but she feels that, if she eats her mother, her mother is going to retaliate when she is inside the patient. "I must keep talking. It's how I got here and where I want to go." In the treatment she is always reexperiencing the possibility that she may have a confrontation with her crazy mother all over again. Whom can one trust? What grownups can you trust? People who eat dogs and children? Do I want to live or not? How did my conscience get me? She answers her question: her Catholic upbringing. Can someone be born poisonous? She expresses it in the passive mode. She is both active and passive all the time. "There's a time when I think of falling off the earth or falling off, I think about running into a barrier like the painting. I want to disappear." She fantasies getting out of this world. She says, "I want not to have to be real and deal with real feelings." In all of this she was feeling a bit cornered. The wood grain makes a cow. "I would like to disappear there too. I wish I were back in my mother's womb. I wish I were never born. I wish I'd enjoy peace and quiet and nurturing instead of this violent interaction." This material makes her think of Solomon and the idea of cutting the child in two. The *real* mother surrenders the child. In other words, the love for the child is greater than the wish to have the child for herself. Well, that's not how her mother responds. Her mother is ready to cut her in two. "I don't know whether I have to stay poisoned with my parents." Of course, it's no longer the real issue. She's talking about them as if they are really alive and wondering if there is some way you and she can get her out of this. This is her family romance. When she was a child, she must have thought, "I wish I were in another family. I wish I had other parents. I wish somebody else would be raising me. I don't want these parents. They're crazy, they're cruel, and they don't love me." So one of the transference fantasies is that you would be that rescuing abductor.

VH: You know what would happen with that. It's so difficult to deal with technically because, in this particular patient, if you say anything like that, she has a phobia about even the word "mother." If I make a mistake and say, "You wish I were a better mother," or "You wish you had." "No, you're not my mother, you'll never be my mother, you cannot be my mother, and I don't want a mother. Think of another word," she says. She is phobic about the word mother.

JA: Instead of killing her mother, she's killing the word.

VH: She really is.

JA: And then she goes on. "I want to believe there's a way out, but it is so hard to believe." Of course, there was no way out for her when she was a child. "The other thing it makes me think of is my little people. My little people who go back and forth into the mirror or the painting or into the world. Some of them, when I was a child, wanted me to go into the unreal world, and some of them also, in my mind, wanted me to stay in the real world." In other words, what she is saying is, when I was a child, I had two sets of thoughts. Let go and let my fantasy world take over; let my wild impulses to murder take over. She also had another set of thoughts connected with the little people. She had personified, she had appersonated, I think is a technical word. She had personified her ideas. She could always use this to comfort herself. I think this gives you an idea of how I listen to material. I listen to everything the patient says, and I pay particular attention to the context, the sequence, the contiguity, the figures of speech, and so forth. She spoke repeatedly about implosion and explosion. We have already covered the ideas. The explosion would release destructive particles. They would behave like Pandora's box, releasing destruction upon the entire world. These are all fantasies of how a weak person can kill, and she is afraid that she may really kill. She has to contain or avoid any idea of violence.

VH: In the early years, I was often afraid; that is, the first 6, 7 years. I would raise the question of hospitalization. Probably I would handle it very differently now because now I feel like what we're doing does contain her, but there were years when I didn't trust it. And I still don't know whether it was I who couldn't stand the anxiety, maybe she'll kill herself. Maybe I should have been able to stand it because it felt to her like a betrayal when I would raise the possibility of—did she need to be hospitalized.

JA: There's a lot to be said about that. First of all, your reaction was a correct perception of what was going on in the patient. She was involved with the idea of killing and your emphasis always came down on the defensive side of the equation. You were afraid she would kill herself. But you were also afraid, and at first you brushed it aside, that she might kill others, indeed, that she might kill you.

VH: I've never really feared that, not consciously. But she could kill me by killing herself.

JA: She kills your reputation. That's a nice compromise.

VH: Then I'd have to deal with the guilt, which would be killing for me.

JA: Intuitively you sensed that she wanted to kill you and that may be another element that contributed to the particular therapeutic stance that you took, namely, you were pacifying in addition to having this tremendous sympathy for her. In so doing, you were also pacified. Now, did you do the right thing or the wrong thing? You did the right thing if she's still with you after many years.

VH: Twelve years.

JA: Twelve years, she's still living, she hasn't killed herself, she hasn't killed. But you can do a great deal more for her, I think, if you can get her gradually to see her fear of being killed by the introjected object. Her fear of killing, her wish to incorporate, her fantasies of being little subatomic particles, her fantasy of paramecia, her fantasy of opening Pandora's box have become clear.

VH: Or the fantasy of needing.

JA: Does she have any children?

VH: No, because she was afraid, as we've analyzed it, she was afraid she would be as destructive as the mother was.

JA: She's killing the mother in her.

I mentioned Roselyn's fear of sleeping. Dr. Arlow corrected me that she is afraid to dream, and sleeping means she loses control. He agreed that she is afraid to lose control. I went on, "Her migraines were so bad at one point that I had written to England trying to find out more about migraines and treatment of migraines. Did anybody have a better idea than her neurologist, her internist, all the people who had seen her through the years and not been really helpful? And I wasn't being very helpful. Somewhere I found that there had been a sleep treatment. I had the fantasy that, if she could just be able to sleep peacefully, she could change something. I know, it's a fantasy. It turns out there was such a cure in England that was apparently successful with some migraines." Here I resume verbatim transcription:

JA: That's right.

VH: It's illegal here.

JA: That's beside the point. The point is, what are your thoughts about the countertransference? You want to be able to soothe her, take her in your arms, and to lull her to sleep. You were so struck by the picture on the wall of my house, the picture of me holding my grandson.

VH: How can you do this analytically? This person has no internalized soothing mother, and I've tried words, I've tried words, I've tried words.

JA: You've been there.

VH: That's true, but how do you fix it?

JA: I think you have some work to do with interpretation too.

VH: Some people have said when it's not gotten early—there is only a certain period in life when you can get that soothing stuff and if you don't get it, you don't get it. What do you think about that?

JA: That's the deficit theory. If we invoke the concept of deficit, we are departing from interpretation by way of conflict and context. I think that conflict is always there. It is inexorable in human psychology. It is something that one can deal with therapeutically. She has this conflict over implosion-explosion that she hasn't mastered. She still does not have insight into it. The analysis has to deal more effectively with that aspect of her problem—her fear of losing control, her fear of her rage, and her fear that she will kill.

VH: I don't think she would ever kill anybody else, I really don't think that. But I feared that she would kill herself.

JA: I tell my students, when a patient says, "I don't think I will ever do or ever want to do this or this," we have to think of it in two steps. First, she may kill somebody, and secondly, she thinks to herself, "No, I don't think so." If you put it that way, it means they can actually think of wanting to do it. This is what Freud said about the negative. Certain ideas can only come into consciousness if preceded by the negative sign. I believe you are afraid of her potential for violence.

VH: Not for myself, I don't think. Maybe professionally. I heard what you said, and I know I'm arguing.

JA: I said that before, that you were afraid originally that she might kill you, but you focused on the idea that she might commit suicide. You're afraid for your life. When you have such an idea, you may be inclined to think, "That's an unreasonable thought for me to have. I shouldn't be anxious. I'm a neurotic analyst." But that is incorrect. One should really think, "This is an important reflection on my patient's material. She really wants to kill."

Dr. Arlow confronted me about my reaction to his interpretation, saying that I was using denial or projection. Dr. Arlow said I deny my fear of being killed. I am more comfortable thinking that she wants to kill others, which, of course, is true, and that she wants to kill herself. But the fear of the patient killing the analyst is something one must think about. Dr. Arlow said, "You told me at the very beginning of our interviews that you have not been able to get the patient focused on her wish to kill. You've dealt effectively with her fear of being killed and her wish to kill herself." I replied, "You're absolutely right. This patient has never been able to express much rage at me or hate at me or enough hostility to make me feel I'm just like her mother, and she hates me and wants to kill me. It's never been so powerful that I felt the least anxiety on that level, and I always think it's got to get there. But it doesn't get there."

Dr. Arlow concluded, "The point of our discussion was to get an idea of how I deal with the material, and in this case, the last session gave me ample opportunity to demonstrate my approach. What I try to emphasize is context, the importance of contiguity, sequence of events, the basis on which you make inferences in order to interpret the emerging unconscious fantasy. We are dealing here with an unconscious fantasy of a wish to kill her mother. Her basic fear is losing control. One of her defenses is to depersonalize. One could say to her, 'You've become depersonalized because you cannot countenance that part of you that wishes to kill.' I think we got most of the important points into our discussion."

Synoptic Chart

Interviewee	Main focus	Genetic focus	Dynamic Focus	Comments on dream
André Green	Splitting between external and internal world.	Patient had extreme pain from a violent and dead mother.	Patient has no psychic formations to express her painful affects.	Childbirth and how to expel self from witch-mother who may devour.
Hanna Segal	Attack on functions of analyst.	Identification with destructive, suicidal mother. Split between something totally idealized and totally cruel.	Lacks a container. Patient is afraid of sanity and the realization of her mad mother.	Rappaccini dream is picture of a bad mother, full of bad children who have come out.
Frances Tustin	Autistic bits.	No control over her mother. Overwhelmed by undifferentiated feelings. No maternal container.	No space for the expression of feelings and consequent fear of feeling.	None.
John Bowlby	Helping patient sort out what is real and what is fantasy.	Childhood abuse leading to mistrust in attachments.	Internal conflict between the patient's wish to express her feelings and the fear of doing so.	None.
Ernest Wolf	Faulty selfobject relationship.	Terrible relationship with mother leaving patient in a psychologically crippled state and leading her to think she cannot have good relationships with others.	Still feels dyadic relationship cannot be lasting, secure.	Patient is identified with Rappaccini's daughter who has been poisoned. She feels she has been so altered by this poisonous, poisoning mother that she herself is poison to everybody else.
Peter Giovacchini	Patient is very vulnerable, experiencing frequent states of disintegration.	Mother unpredictable, psychotic, and assaultive; father gave her no protective barrier.	There was no continuity, hardly any holding environment. Can't hold mental representation without symbol.	None.

Comments on transference	Comments on countertransference	Treatment recommendations	The expected audience for the comments
Patient trying to give up bad mother but not sure she is safe with analyst to be an individual without revenge.	None.	Needs to feel analyst can tolerate anger and not be destroyed by it.	Any advanced clinician.
If analysis is successful, patient feels envy, spite, and revenge.	Makes analyst feel terror, guilt, helplessness, and hopelessness of separation. Makes analyst wish to reassure her.	Do not allow patient to destroy analyst's containing analytic function. She must separate from mother and grieve.	A case commentary, as in a seminar.
No comments.	The patient's states of undifferentation can make us feel we're going mad.	Establish a state of trust and security.	Clinicians of many levels of training.
Mother transference and consequent fear that analyst will not respond to her needs with comfort and protection but condemn her for them.	Analyst has to live with the discomfort of the responsibility of treating such a patient.	Make it absolutely plain analyst knows just how the patient did feel. Express all the feeling you know she did have. Keep helping her see that she treats herself just as her mother did. Help her remember some good things about her mother.	Any trained clinician.
Feels analyst relationship will not be lasting and is humiliated by her needs.	Postpone all thoughts of her getting out of treatment.	Relax.	Ordinary clinic[illegible] and psychoa[illegible]
Patient is giving analyst parts of herself and making a symbolic relationship where she can feel cared for.	Do not worry if you see her all your life.	Continue to [illegible] develop m[illegible] resenta[illegible]	

Interviewee	Main focus	Genetic focus	Dynamic focus	Comments on dream
Arnold Goldberg	Need to develop an idealizing transference.	Early inability to idealize malevolent mother; consequent development of psychotic system of thinking.	Longing for protection and for an omnipotent merger.	None.
Rudolf Ekstein	Patient wishes to die if she cannot be helped. Must liberate self from poisoning mother.	Patient was in constant fear of being killed or dropped. She was traumatized by her mother's attempt at suicide.	Patient wishes analyst to give her a reason to live. Help her feel safe.	She is trying to get out of the mother. She feels poisoned and wishes to be poisoned because mother made her wish to die.
Robert Wallerstein	Patient has hysterical character structures with quasipsychotic disorganizing episodes.	Patient severely traumatized by mother.	Patient feels chaotic inside and cannot tell fantasy from reality at times.	None.
Arnold Modell	Faulty psychic attunement internalized, resulting in faulty affect processing.	As a child, patient was helpless to leave nongratifying mother, so turned to self to create a separate internal world. She experienced a kind of psychic death as a child.	Her internal objects are attacking constantly.	A poisonous mother and herself as a poisoned child became internalized and continually interact.
	Importance of fantasies and concrete thought.	Abused by critical mother and passive father with consequence of inability to share emotions.	Conflict between patient's feeling that her mother hated her and she hated her mother and a wish to protect her and herself.	Resents feeling that her mother would eat her up or she will eat up her mother.

Comments on transference	Comments on countertransference	Treatment recommendations	The expected audience for the comments
Sees therapist as omnipotent erratic mother whom she must remember to protect herself against.	Analyst, like every therapist, has trouble being idealized.	Analyze each failure of idealization and the rage that ensues.	Clinicians, especially psychoanalysts.
She wants you to be mother even as she wishes you to be different from mother. There is an internal struggle between her and her suicidal mother. Must tolerate self. Hurt self—hurt mother.	She creates in analyst a wish to prove you can be a valuable mother and cure her quickly.	Continue on.	Any advanced clinician.
She needs to feel secure and safe and develop feeling of having skin and safe container.	None.	Help her express negative affects.	Any advanced clinician.
She wants to be sure a piece of her goes with analyst. Needs concrete intrusion in analyst's life.	None.	Prepare to be a kind of prosthesis for processing her affects forever.	Advanced clinicians and psychoanalysts.
Inability to trust mother and analyst.	Use of concrete images and language in order to keep her from going too deep.	Help this woman regress appropriately and deal with her rage.	Any psychoanalyst.

Bibliography

Adler, G. (1981). The stance of the analyst and its effects on regression. *Issues in Ego Psychology*, *4*, 17–25.

Aichhorn, A. (1925). *Wayward youth*. Lepzig, Vienna, Zürich: International Psychoanalytic Publishers.

Allport, G. W. (1961). *Pattern and growth in personality*. New York: Holt, Rinehart & Winston.

American Psychiatric Association. (1982). *Desk reference to The diagnostic criteria from the Diagnostic and Statistical Manual of Mental Disorders*. Washington, DC: Author.

Arlow, J. A. (1958). Psychoanalytic scientific method. *Psychoanalysis, Scientific Method, and Philosophy*, 2, 201–211.

——— (1969). Unconscious fantasy and disturbances of conscious experience. *The Psychoanalytic Quarterly*, 38(1), 1–27.

——— (1970, May). *Group psychology and the study of institutes*. Unpublished farewell address to the Board of Professional Standards, American Psychoanalytic Association, New York.

——— (1972). The only child. *The Psychoanalytic Quarterly*, *41*(4), 507–536.

——— (1979a). The genesis of interpretation. *Journal of the American Psychoanalytic Association*, *27*(Suppl.), 193–206.

——— (1979b). Structure of the déjà vu experience. *Journal of the American Psychoanalytic Association*, *7*, 611–631.

——— (1981). Theories of pathogenesis. *The Psychoanalytic Quarterly*, 50(4), 488–514.

——— (1984a). Disturbances of the sense of time—with special reference to the experience of timelessness. *The Psychoanalytic Quarterly*, 53(1), 13–37.

——— (1984b). The psychoanalytic process in regard to the development of transference and interpretation. In G. H. Pollock & J. E. Gedo (Eds.), *Psychoanalysis: The vital issues* (Vol. 2, pp. 21–44). New York: International Universities Press.

——— (1986). The poet as prophet: A psychoanalytic perspective. *The Psychoanalytic Quarterly*, *55*(1), 53–68.

——— (1987a). The dynamics of interpretation. *The Psychoanalytic Quarterly*, *56*(1), 68–97.

——— (1987b). Trauma, play, and perversion. *Psychoanalytic Study of the Child*, *42*, 31–44.

——— (1990a). Psychoanalysis and character development. *The Psychoanalytic Review*, *77*(1), 147–166.

——— (1990b). Psychoanalysis and the quest for morality. In H. Blum, E. Weinshel, & F. R. Rodman (Eds.), *The psychoanalytic core* (pp. 147–166). Madison, CT: International Universities Press.

——— (1990c). The psychoanalytic process. *The Psychoanalytic Quarterly*, *59*(4), 678–692.

——— (1991a). The analytic attitude in the service of denial. In H. J. Schwartz & A.-L. Silver (Eds.), *Illness in the analyst* (pp. 9–26). Madison, CT: International Universities Press.

——— (1991b, June 16). Address to the graduating class of the San Francisco Psychoanalytic Institute. *The American Psychoanalyst*, *25*(1), 15–16.

Arlow, J. A., & Brenner, C. (1963). *Psychoanalytic concepts and the structural theory*. New York: International Universities Press.

——— (1988). The future of psychoanalysis. *The Psychoanalytic Quarterly*, *57*, 1–14.

——— (1990). The psychoanalytic process. *The Psychoanalytic Quarterly*, *59*, 678–692.

Atwood, G. E., & Stolorow, R. D. (1984). *Structures of subjectivity: Exploration in psychoanalytic phenomenology*. Hillsdale, NJ: Analytic Press.

Baudry, F. (1991). The relevance of the analyst's character and attitudes to his work. *Journal of the American Psychoanalytic Association*, *39*(4), 917–938.

Benedek, T. (1950). Climacterium: A developmental phase. *Psychiatric Quarterly*, *19*, 1–27.

Beres, D., & Arlow, J. A. (1974). Fantasy and identification in empathy. *The Psychoanalytic Quarterly*, *4*(1), 26–50.

Berger, J. (1989, September 21). *Manchester Guardian Weekly*, pp. 143–144.

Bick, E. (1968). The experience of the skin in early object relations. *International Journal of Psycho-Analysis*, *49*, 484–486.

Bion, W. R. (1959). *Experience in groups*. New York: Basic Books.

Bion, W. R. (1975–1979). *A memoir of the future*. Rio de Janeiro: Imago Editora, Ltd.

Bion, W. R., Rosenfeld, H., & Segal, H. (1961). Melanie Klein. *International Journal of Psycho-Analysis*, *42*(1–2), 4–5.

Bollas, C. (1987). *Shadow of the object: Psychoanalysis of the unthought known*. London: Free Association Books.

Bowlby, J. (1940). The influence of early environment in the development of neurosis and neurotic character. *International Journal of Psycho-Analysis*, *21*(2), 154–178.

——— (1944). Forty-four juvenile thieves: Their characters and home life. *International Journal of Psycho-Analysis*, *25*, 19–52, 107–127. (Reprinted [1946] as a monograph. London: Bailliere, Tyndall & Cox)

——— (1984). Psychoanalysis as a natural science. *Psychoanalytic Psychology, 1,* 7–21.

——— (1985). *The role of the psychotherapist's personal resources in the treatment situation.* London: Archives of the Tavistock Clinic, unpublished.

Breuer, J., & Freud, S. (1895). Studies on hysteria. *Standard Edition, 2,* 1–32.

Briggs, J., & Peat, F. D. (1984). *Looking glass universe: The emerging science of wholeness.* New York: Simon & Schuster.

——— (1989). *Turbulent mirror: An illustrated guide to chaos theory and the science of wholeness.* New York: Harper & Row.

Britton, R., Feldman, M., & O'Shaughnessy, E. (1989). *The oedipus complex today: Clinical implications.* London: Karnac.

Campbell, J. (1982). *Grammatical man.* New York: Simon & Shuster.

Chasseguet-Smirgel, J. (1983). Perversion and the universal law. *International Review of Psycho-Analysis, 10,* 294–300.

Chiarandini, I. C. (1992). A conversation with Riccardo Steiner. *The American Psychoanalyst, 26*(1), 28–30.

Chrzanowski, G. (1989). The significance of the analyst's individual personality in the therapeutic relationship. *The Journal of the American Academy of Psychoanalysis, 17*(4), 597–608.

Dilthey, W. (1926). *Meaning in history.* London: Allen & Unwin.

Edelman, G. (1992). *Bright air, brilliant fire.* New York: Basic Books.

Edwards, B. (1989). *Drawing on the right side of the brain.* Los Angeles: J. P. T. Archer.

Einstein, A. (1905). *Relativity: The special and the general theory.* New York: Crown Publishers.

Ekstein, R. (1966). *Children of time and space, of action and impulse.* New York: Jason Aronson, 1983.

——— (1971). The challenge: *Despair and hope in the conquest of inner space.* New York: Brunner/Mazel.

——— (1974). *Speaking of the truth behind fairy tales.* New York: McGraw-Hill.

——— (1980). *Clinical use of dreams.* Ego Psychology Training Workshops, Laguna Beach, CA.

Ekstein, R., & Motto, R. L. (1969). *From learning for love to love of learning: Essays on psychoanalysis and education.* New York: Brunner/Mazel.

Ekstein, R., & Wallerstein, R. S. (1973). *The teaching and learning of psychotherapy* (rev. ed.). New York: International Universities Press.

Feynman, R. (1988). *What do you care what other people think? Further adventures of a curious character.* New York: Norton.

Fine, R. (1990). *The history of psychoanalysis: New expanded edition.* New York: Jason Aronson.

Fleming, J., & Altschul, S. (1959, March 24). *Activation of mourning and growth by psychoanalysis.* Paper presented before the Chicago Psychoanalytic Society. (Also in *Bulletin of the Philadelphia Association of Psychoanalysis, 9,* 37–38, and *International Journal of Psycho-Analysis, 44,* 419–431.)

Fraiberg, S. (1982).The adolescent mother and her infant. *Adolescent Psychiatry, 10,* 7–23.

Fraiberg, S., Lieberman, A. F., Pekarsky, J. H., & Pawl, J. H. (1981). Treatment and outcome in an infant psychiatry program: I. *Journal of Preventive Psychiatry*, *1*(1), 89–111.

Freud, A. (1937). *The ego and the mechanisms of defense*. London: Hogarth Press.

Freud, E. L. (1969). Some early unpublished letters of Freud. *International Journal of Psycho-Analysis*, *50*, 419–427.

Freud, S. (1900). The interpretation of dreams. *Standard Edition*, *4–5*.

——— (1914). The Moses of Michelangelo. *Standard Edition*, *13*, 211–236.

——— (1916–1917). Introductory lectures on psycho-analysis. *Standard Edition*, *15–16*.

——— (1921). Group psychology and the analysis of the ego. *Standard Edition*, *18*, 65–143.

——— (1937). Constructions in psychoanalysis. *Standard Edition*, *23*, 255–269.

——— (1939). Moses and monotheism. *Standard Edition*, *23*.

——— (1950). *Beyond the pleasure principle* (Trans. J. Strachey). New York: Liveright.

——— (1953–1974). *The standard edition of the complete psychological works of Sigmund Freud* (24 vols.). London: Hogarth Press.

Freud, S., & Jung, C. G. (1974). *Letters*. Princeton: Princeton University Press.

Friedman, L. (1978). Trends in the psychoanalytic theory of treatment. *The Psychoanalytic Quarterly*, *47*, 524–567.

Friedman, L. J. (1990). *Menninger: The family and the clinic*. New York: Knopf.

Fromm-Reichmann, F. (1943). Insight into psychotic mechanisms and emergency psychotherapy. *Medical Annual District of Columbia*, *12*, 107–112.

——— (1955). Clinical significance of intuitive processes of the psychoanalyst. *Journal of the American Psychoanalytic Association*, *3*, 82–88.

——— (1958). Basic problems in the psychotherapy of schizophrenia. *Psychiatry*, *21*, 1–6.

Gedo, J. E. (1983). Saints or scoundrels and the objectivity of the analyst. *Psychoanalytic Inquiry*, *3*(4), 609–622.

Gedo, J. E., & Pollock, G. H. (Eds.). (1976). *Freud: The fusion of science and humanism (Psychological Issues, Monograph 34/35)*. New York: International Universities Press.

Gedo, J. E., & Wolf, E. (1970). Die ichthyosaurus briefe—Psyche. *Zeitschrift für Psychoanalyse und ihre Anwendungen Herausgeben*, *24*, 785–797.

Gill, M. M. (1963). *Topography and system in psychoanalytic theory*. New York: International Universities Press.

Giovacchini, P. L. (1960). On scientific creativity. *Journal of the American Psychoanalytic Association*, *8*, 407–426.

——— (1965). Some aspects of the development of the ego ideal of a creative scientist. *Psychoanalytic Quarterly*, *34*, 79–101.

——— (1971). Creativity and character. *Journal of the American Psychoanalytic Association*, *19*, 524–542.

Giovacchini, P. L. (Ed.). (1972). *Tactics and techniques in psychoanalytic therapy* (Vol. I). New York: Science House.

Giovacchini, P. L. (1973a). Character disorders: With special reference to the borderline state. *International Journal of Psychoanalytic Psychotherapy*, *2*(1), 7–36.

——— (1973b). Diagnostic and technical factors in treating the borderline adolescent. *International Journal of Psychoanalytic Psychotherapy*, 2(1), 47–63.

——— (1974). The difficult adolescent patient: Countertransference problems. *Adolescent Psychiatry*, 3, 271–288.

——— (1975). *Psychoanalysis of character disorders*. New York: Jason Aronson.

——— (1978). The borderline aspect of adolescence and the borderline state. *Adolescent Psychiatry*, 6, 320–328.

——— (1979). *Treatment of primitive mental states*. New York: Jason Aronson.

——— (1981a). Countertransference and therapeutic turmoil. *Contemporary Psychoanalysis*, *17*(4), 565–594.

——— (1981b). Creativity, adolescence, and inevitable failure. *Adolescent Psychiatry*, 9, 36–59.

——— (1981c). *The urge to die . . . why young people commit suicide*. New York: Macmillan.

——— (1982). *A clinician's guide to reading Freud*. New York: Jason Aronson.

——— (1984a). *Character disorders and adaptive mechanisms*. New York: Jason Aronson.

——— (1984b). The quest for dependent autonomy. *International Forum for Psycho-Analysis*, *1*(2), 153–166.

——— (1985). The borderline adolescent as a transition and object: A common variation. *Adolescent Psychiatry*, *12*, 233–250.

——— (1986). *Developmental disorders: The transitional space in mental breakdown and creative integration*. New York: Jason Aronson.

——— (1987a). *A narrative textbook of psychoanalysis*. Northvale, NJ: Jason Aronson.

——— (1987b). Treatment, holding environment, and transitional space. *Modern Psychoanalysis*, *12*(2), 151–161.

——— (1988). Bewilderment and the borderline phenomenon. *Psychoanalytic Inquiry*, 8(3), 398–421.

——— (1989). *Countertransference triumphs and catastrophes*. Northvale, NJ: Jason Aronson.

Giovacchini, P. L., & Boyer, L. B. (Eds.). (1980). *Psychoanalytic treatment of schizophrenic, borderline, and characterological disorders* (2nd ed.). New York: Jason Aronson.

Giovacchini, P. L., & Boyer, L. B. (1982). *Technical factors in the treatment of the severely disturbed patient*. New York: Jason Aronson.

Giovacchini, P. L., Boyer, L. B., & Flarsheim, A. (Eds.). (1975). *Tactics and techniques in psychoanalytic therapy* (Vol. II). New York: Jason Aronson.

Gleick, J. (1987). *Chaos: Making a new science*. New York: Penguin.

Gleick, J. (1992). *Genius: The life and scienc of Richard Feynman*. New York: Pantheon.

Glover, E. (1924). Lectures on psychoanalysis. *International Journal of Psycho-Analysis*, 5, 269–311.

——— (1931). The therapeutic effect of inexact interpretations: A contribution to the theory of suggestion. *International Journal of Psycho-Analysis*, *12*, 397–411.

Goldberg, A. (1978). *The psychology of the self: A casebook.* New York: International Universities Press.

Goldberg, A. (Ed.). (1984). *How does analysis cure?/Heinz Kohut.* Chicago: University of Chicago Press.

Goldberg, A. (1988). *A fresh look at psychoanalysis: The view from self psychology.* Hillsdale, NJ: Analytic Press.

——— (1990). *The prison house of psychoanalysis.* Hillsdale, NJ: Analytic Press.

Green, A. (1986). *On private madness* (pp. 142–173). London: Hogarth Press/The Institute of Psycho-Analysis.

Greenspan, S. I., & Lieberman, A. F. (1988). *Clinical implications of attachment.* Hillsdale, NJ: Lawrence Erlbaum.

Grinberg, L., & Grinberg, R. (1989). *Psychoanalytic perspectives on migration and exile.* New Haven: Yale University Press.

Grosskurth, P. (1986). *Melanie Klein: Her world and her work.* London: Manesfield Library.

Grünbaum, A. (1984). *The foundations of psychoanalysis: A philosophical critique.* Berkeley: University of California Press.

Hamilton, V. (1985). *Beyond Freud: A study of modern psychoanalytic theorists.* Hillsdale, NJ: The Analytic Press.

Hanly, C. (1992). *The problem of truth in applied psychoanalysis.* New York: Guilford Press.

Hartmann, H. (1939). *Ego psychology and the problem of adaptation.* New York: International Universities Press.

——— (1958). Psychoanalysis as a scientific theory. *Psychoanalysis, Scientific Method and Philosophy, 2,* 3–37.

Hawkings, S. M. (1988). *A brief history of time: From the Big Bang to black holes.* New York: Bantam.

Hawkings, S. M. (1990). *A brief history of time.* New York: Bantam.

Hedges, L. E. (1983). *Listening perspectives in psychotherapy.* New York: Jason Aronson.

——— (1992). *Interpreting the countertransference.* Northvale, NJ: Jason Aronson.

Heimann, P. (1950). On counter-transference. *International Journal of Psycho-Analysis, 31*(1–2), 81–84.

Hunter, V. (1990). An interview with André Green. *The Psychoanalytic Review, 77*(2), 157–173.

——— (1991). John Bowlby: An interview. *The Psychoanalytic Review, 78*(2), 159–175.

——— (1992a). An interview with Frances Tustin. *The Psychoanalytic Review, 79*(1), 1–24.

——— (1992b). Ernest Wolf: An interview by Virginia Hunter, part I. The early years. *The Psychoanalytic Review, 79*(3), 309–326.

——— (1993a). An interview with Hanna Segal. *The Psychoanalytic Review, 80*(1), 1–28.

——— (1993b). Ernest Wolf: An interview by Virginia Hunter, part II. The analytic years to 1990. *The Psychoanalytic Review, 79*(4), 481–507.

——— (1993c). Clinical clues in the breathing behaviors of patient and therapist. *Clinical Social Work Journal, 21*(2), 161–178.

Hurwitz, M. R. (1986). The analyst, his theory, and the psychoanalytic process. *Psychoanalytic Study of the Child, 41*, 439–466.

Ishiguro, K. (1990). *Remains of the day*. New York: Random House.

Jacobson, E. (1964). *The self and the object world*. New York: International Universities Press.

James, W. (1963). *Pragmatism and other essays*. New York: Washington Square Press, 1968.

Karen, R. (1990). Becoming attached: What children need. *The Atlantic, 265*(2), 35–70.

King, P., & Steiner, R. (Eds.). (1991). *The Freud–Klein controversies*. London: Routledge.

Klein, G. S. (1976). *Psychoanalytic theory: An exploration of essentials*. New York: International Universities Press.

Klein, M. (1930). The importance of symbol formation in the development of the ego. In *Love, guilt, and reparation and other works* (pp. 219–232). Hogarth Press, 1975.

Klein, M. (1932). *The psychoanalysis of children*. London: Hogarth Press.

Klein, M. (1946). Notes on some schizoid mechanism. *International Journal of Psycho-Analysis, 27*(3–4), 99–110.

Klein, S. (1980). Autistic phenomena in neurotic patients. *International Journal of Psycho-Analysis, 61*(3), 395–402.

Knobel, M. (1990). Significance and importance of the psychotherapist's personality and experience. *Psychotherapy Psychosomatics*, 53(1–4), 58–63.

Kohon, G. (Ed.). (1986). *The British school of psychoanalysis: The independent tradition*. New Haven: Yale University Press.

Kohut, H. (1959). *The search for the self: Selected writings*. New York: International Universities Press.

——— (1971). *The analysis of the self*. New York: International Universities Press.

Kohut, H., & Wolf, E. S. (1978). The disorders of the self and their treatment. *International Journal of Psycho-Analysis*, 59, 413–25.

Kris, E. (1975). *Selected papers of Ernst Kris*. New Haven: Yale University Press.

La Farge, L. (1991). A conversation with Eleanor Galenson. *The American Psychoanalyst, 25*(3), 11–13.

Lieberman, A. F., & Pawl, J. H. (1984). Searching for the best interests of the child: Intervention with an abusive mother and her toddler. *Psychoanalytic Study of the Child*, 39, 527–548.

Lipton, S. D. (1943). Dissociated personality: Case report. *Psychiatric Quarterly, 17*, 35–56.

——— (1948). Dissociated personality: Status of a case after five years. *Psychiatric Quarterly*, 22, 252–256.

——— (1957). A clinical note on the occurrence of malingering in a case of paranoia. *Bulletin of the Philadelphia Association of Psychoanalysis*, 7, 91–95.

——— (1961). Aggression and symptom formation: A panel presented at the Fall meeting of the American Psychoanalytic Association (New York, 1960). *Journal of the American Psychoanalytic Association*, 9, 585–592.

Little, M. (1945). The wanderer: Notes on a paranoid patient. In *Transference neurosis and transference psychosis: Toward basic unity* (pp. 3–31). New York: Jason Aronson, 1981.

——— (1950). Countertransference and the patient's response to it. In *Transference neurosis and transference psychosis: Toward a basic unity* (pp. 33–50). New York: Jason Aronson, 1981.

——— (1951). Countertransference and the patient's response to it. *International Journal of Psycho-Analysis, 32*, 32–40.

——— (1957a). The analyst's total response to the patient's needs. *International Journal of Psycho-Analysis, 38*, 240–254.

——— (1957b). "R"—the analyst's total response to his patient's needs. In *Transference neurosis and transference psychosis: Toward a basic unity* (pp. 51–80). New York: Jason Aronson, 1981.

——— (1957c). On delusional transference (transference psychosis). In *Transference neurosis and transference psychosis: Toward a basic unity* (pp. 81–91). New York: Jason Aronson, 1981.

——— (1959). On basic unity. In *Transference neurosis and transference psychosis: Toward a basic unity* (pp. 109–125). New York: Jason Aronson, 1981.

——— (1964a). Transference in borderline states. In *Transference neurosis and transference psychosis: Toward a basic unity* (pp. 136–153). New York: Jason Aronson, 1981.

——— (1964b). Transference/countertransference in posttherapeutic self-analysis. In *Transference neurosis and transference psychosis: Toward a basic unity* (pp. 247–263). New York: Jason Aronson, 1981.

——— (1981). *Transference neurosis: Transference psychosis*. New York: Jason Aronson.

——— (1985). *Winnicott working in areas where psychotic anxieties predominate: A personal record*. London: Free Association Books.

——— (1987). *On the value of regression to dependence*. New York: Jason Aronson.

——— (1990). *Psychotic anxieties and containment: A personal record of an analysis with Winnicott*. New York: Jason Aronson.

Little, M., & Flarsheim, A. (1964). Toward mental health: Early mothering care. In *Transference neurosis and transference psychosis: Toward a basic unity* (pp. 167–181). New York: Jason Aronson, 1981.

Loewald, H. W. (1975). Psychoanalysis as an art and the fantasy character of the psychoanalytic situation. *Journal of the American Psychoanalytic Association, 23*(2), 277–299.

Lorand, S. (1946). *Technique of psychoanalytic theory*. New York: International Universities Press.

Milgram, S. (1975). *Obedience to authority*. New York: Harper & Row.

Modell, A. H. (1963). Primitive object relationships and the predisposition to schizophrenia. *International Journal of Psycho-Analysis, 44*, 282–292.

——— (1968a). A psychoanalytic interpretation of delusion. *International Journal of Psychiatry, 6*(1), 46–50.

——— (1968b). *Object love and reality: An introduction to a psychoanalytic theory of object relations*. New York: International Universities Press.

——— (1970). The transitional object and the creative art. *The Psychoanalytic Quarterly, 39*(2), 240–250.

——— (1975a). A narcissistic defense against affects and the illusions of self–sufficiency. *International Journal of Psycho-Analysis*, 56(3), 275–282.

——— (1975b). *Amore oggettuale e realta*. Torino: Boringhieri.

——— (1976). The holding environment and the therapeutic action of psychoanalysis. *Journal of the American Psychoanalytic Association*, 24, 285–308.

——— (1978). The conceptualization of the therapeutic action of psychoanalysis: The action of the holding environment. *Bulletin of the Menninger Clinic*, 42(6), 493–504.

——— (1984). *Psychoanalysis in a new context*. New York: International Universities Press.

——— (1990). *Other times, other realities: Toward a theory of psychoanalytic treatment*. Cambridge, MA: Harvard University Press.

——— (1991a). A confusion of tongues on whose reality is it? *The Psychoanalytic Quarterly*, 60, 227–244.

——— (1991b). The therapeutic relationship as a paradoxical experience. Symposium: Reality and the analytic relationship. *Psychoanalytic Dialogue*, *1*, 13–28.

——— (1993). *Private self*. Boston: Harvard University Press.

Modell, A. H., & Potter, H. W. (1949). Human figure drawing of patients with arterial hypertension, peptic ulcer and bronchial asthma. *Psychosomatic Medicine*, *11*(5), 282–292.

Money-Kyrle, R. (1978). On cognitive development. In D. Meltzer (Ed.) (with the assistance of E. O'Shaugnessy), *The collected papers of Roger Money-Kyrle* (The Roland Harris Educational Trust Library No. 7, pp. 691–698). Pentshire, Scotland: Aberdeen University Press.

Motto, R. (1990). In honor of Rudolf Ekstein. Special issue honoring Rudolf Ekstein, Ph.D. *Los Angeles Psychoanalytic Bulletin*.

Natterson, J. (1991). *Beyond countertransference: The therapist's subjectivity in the therapeutic process*. New York: Jason Aronson.

Olden, C. (1942). About the fascinating effect of the narcissistic personality. *American Image*, 2, 347–356.

Pribram, K. H., & Gill, M. M. (1976). *Freud's "project" research*. New York: Basic Books.

Rangell, L. (1982). Transference to theory: The relationship of psychoanalytic education to the analyst's relationship to psychoanalysis. *The Annual of Psychoanalysis*, 10(I), 29–56.

Rapaport, D. (1960). The structure of psychoanalytic theory [Monograph No. 6]. *Psychological Issues*, 2(2), 7–158.

Reich, A. (1951). On countertransference. *International Journal of Psycho-Analysis*, 32, 25–31.

——— (1953). Narcissistic object choice in women. *Journal of the American Psychoanalytic Association*, *1*, 22–44.

Reich, W. (1933). *Character analysis*. New York: Institute Press.

Rochlin, G. (1961). The dread of abandonment: A contribution to the etiology of the loss complex and to depression. *Psychoanalytic Study of the Child*, *16*, 451–570.

——— (1973). *Man's aggression: The defense of the self*. Ipswich, MA: Gambit.

Rosen, J.N. (1965). *Acting-out.* New York: Grune & Stratton.
Schafer, R. (1976). *A new language for psychoanalysis.* Connecticut: Yale University Press.
——— (1978). *Language and insight.* New Haven: Yale University Press.
——— (1980). Narration in the psychoanalytic dialogue. *Critical Inquiry, 7,* 29–53.
Schneiderman, S. (1980). *Returning to Freud: Clinical psychoanalysis in the school of Lacan.* New Haven: Yale University Press.
Schreber, D. P. (1903). *Deukwurdigderten lines Nervenbranken.* London: Hogarth Press.
Schwaber, E. (1981). Narcissism, self psychology, and the listening perspective. *Annual of Psychoanalysis,* 9, 115–131.
——— (1983). Psychoanalytic listening and psychic reality. *International Journal of Psycho-Analysis, 10,* 379–391.
Sechehaye, M. A. (1951a). *Symbolic realization: A new method of psychotherapy applied to a case of schizophrenia* (Trans. B. Wursten & H. Wursten). New York: International Universities Press.
——— (1951b). *Autobiography of a schizophrenic girl* (Trans. G. Rubin-Rabson). New York: Grune & Stratton.
——— (1956). *A new psychotherapy in schizophrenia* (Trans. G. Rubin-Rabson). New York: Grune & Stratton.
Segal, H. (1962). Symposium on curative factors in psychoanalysis: III. *International Journal of Psycho-Analysis,* 43, 212–217.
——— (1978). *An Introduction to the work of Melanie Klein.* London: Hogarth Press. (1988) London: Karnac/Institute of Psycho-Analysis.
——— (1979). *Melanie Klein.* London: Fontana.
——— (1981). *The work of Hanna Segal.* New York: Jason Aronson. (1986) London: Karnac/Free Association Books.
——— (1990). *Dream, phantasy and art.* London: Routledge.
Sharpe, E. F. (1968). *Collected papers on psychoanalysis.* London: Hogarth Press.
Sherwin, H. (1981a). The supervision and treatment as seen from the analyst's perspective. In *Becoming a psychoanalyst: A study of psychoanalytic supervision* (Monograph of the study group on supervision of the Committee on Psychoanalytic Education, American Psychoanalytic Association, pp. 227–268). New York: International Universities Press.
——— (1981b). On being the analyst supervised: Return to a troubled beginning. In *Becoming a psychoanalyst: A study of psychoanalytic supervision* (Monograph of the study group on supervision of the Committee on Psychoanalytic Education, American Psychoanalytic Association, pp. 311–329). New York: International Universities Press.
Silverman, M. A. (1987). Clinical material. In S. E. Pulver et al. (Eds.), How theory shapes technique: Perspectives on a clinical study. *Psychoanalytic Inquiry,* 7(2), 147–165. (Includes commentary on the case by twelve analysts, along with concluding responses by Silverman and Pulver to case comments. Both the case and comments upon it were presented in writing.)
Spence, D. P. (1982a). *Narrative truth and historical truth: Meaning and interpretation in psychoanalysis.* New York: Norton.

——— (1982b). Narrative truth and theoretical truth. *The Psychoanalytic Quarterly*, 51, 43–69.
Stolorow, R. D., & Atwood, G. E. (1979). *Faces in a cloud: Subjectivity in personality theory*. New York: Jason Aronson.
Tausk, V. (1919). On the origin of the influencing machine in schizophrenia. *The Psychoanalytic Quarterly*, 2, 519–556.
Ticho, E. (1966). The effect of the analyst's personality on psychoanalytic treatment. *Psychoanalytic Forum*, 4, 135–172.
Tustin, F. (1966). A significant element in the development of autism. *Journal of Child Psychology and Psychiatry*, 7, 53–67.
——— (1972). *Autism and childhood psychosis*. London: Hogarth Press. (1973) New York: Jason Aronson.
——— (1980). Autistic objects. *International Review of Psycho-Analysis*, 7, 27–38.
——— (1984). Autistic shapes. *International Review of Psycho-Analysis*, 11, 280–288.
——— (1986). *Autistic barriers in neurotic patients*. London: Karnac. (1987) New Haven: Yale University Press.
——— (1989). The black hole—a significant element in autism. *Free Associations*, 11, 36–50.
——— (1990). *The protective shell in children and adults*. London: Karnac; New York: Brunner/Mazel.
——— (1991). Revised understandings of psychogenic autism. *International Journal of Psycho-Analysis*, 72(4), 585–591.
——— (1992). *Autistic states in children: Revised version*. London: Routledge.
Tuttman, S. (1982). The impact of the analyst's personality on treatment. *Issues in Ego Psychology*, 5(1–2), 25–31.
Von Eckardt, B., & Grünbaum, A. (1985). *Beyond Freud: A study of modern psychoanalytic theorist*. Hillsdale, NJ: Analytic Press.
Wallerstein, R. S. (1957). *Hospital treatment of alcoholism: A comparative, experimental study*. New York: Basic Books.
——— (1967a). An approach to the quantitative problems of psychoanalytic research. *Journal of Clinical Psychology*, 23(3), 243–291.
——— (1967b). Reconstruction and mastery in the transference psychosis. *Journal of the American Psychoanalytic Association*, 15, 551–583.
——— (1968a). A talk about the psychotherapy research of the Menninger Foundation. *Nederlands Tijdschrift Voor Psychologie en Haar Grensgebieden*, 23(3), 138–164.
——— (1968b). The challenge of the community mental health movement to psychoanalysis. *American Journal of Psychiatry*, 124(8), 1049–1056.
——— (1969). Introduction to panel on psychoanalysis and psychotherapy: The relationship of psychoanalysis to psychotherapy: Current issues. *International Journal of Psycho-Analysis*, 50(1), 117–126.
——— (1970). Panel on "Psychoanalysis and psychotherapy." *International Journal of Psycho-Analysis*, 51(2), 219–231.
——— (1975). *Psychotherapy and psychoanalysis: theory—practice—research*. New York: International Universities Press.
——— (1976a). Introduction to symposium on "Ethics, moral values, and

psychological interventions." *International Review of Psycho-Analysis*, 3(4), 369–372.

——— (1976b). Psychoanalysis as a science: Its present status and its future tasks. *Psychological Issues*, 9(4), 198–228.

——— (1977). The contribution of child analysis to training in adult analysis. *Revista Brasileira de Psicanalise*, *11*(2), 225–242.

——— (1978). The mental health professions: Conceptualization and reconceptualization of a new discipline. *International Review of Psycho-Analysis*, 5(4), 377–392.

——— (1980). Psychoanalysis and academic psychiatry— bridges. *Psychoanalytic Study of the Child*, *35*, 419–448.

——— (1980–81). Diagnosis revisited (and revisited): The case of hysteria and the hysterical personality. *International Journal of Psychoanalytic Psychotherapy*, *8*, 533–547.

——— (1981a). The bipolar self: Discussion of alternative perspectives. *Journal of the American Psychoanalytic Association*, *29*(2), 377–394.

——— (1981b). The psychoanalyst's life: Expectations, vicissitudes, and reflections. *International Review of Psycho-Analysis*, 8(3), 285–298.

——— (1981c). Preface. In *Becoming a psychoanalyst: A study of psychoanalytic supervision* (Monograph of the study group on supervision of the Committee on Psychoanalytic Education, American Psychoanalytic Association). New York: International Universities Press.

——— (1983a). Reality and its attributes as psychoanalytic concepts: An historical overview. *International Review of Psycho-Analysis*, *10*(2), 125–144.

——— (1983b). Self psychology and "classical" psychoanalytic psychology: The nature of their relationship. *Psychoanalysis and Contemporary Thought*, 6(4), 553–595.

——— (1983c). Some thoughts about insight and psychoanalysis. *Israel Journal of Psychiatry and Related Sciences*, *20*(1–2), 33–43.

——— (1983d). The Topeka Institute and the future of psychoanalysis. *Bulletin of the Menninger Clinic*, *47*(6), 497–518.

——— (1984a). Anna Freud: Radical innovator and staunch conservative. *Psychoanalytic Study of the Child*, *39*, 65–80.

——— (1984b). The analysis of the transference: A matter of emphasis or of theory reformulation? Special Issue: Commentaries on Merton Gill's analysis of transference. *Psychoanalytic Inquiry*, 4(3), 325–354.

——— (1985). The concept of psychic reality: Its meaning and value. *Journal of the American Psychoanalytic Association*, *33*(3), 555–569.

——— (1986a). *Forty-two lives in treatment: A study of psychoanalysis and psychotherapy*. New York: Guilford Press.

——— (1986b). Psychoanalysis as a science: A response to the new challenges. *Psychoanalytic Quarterly*, *55*(3), 414–451.

——— (1988a). One psychoanalysis or many? 35th International Psychoanalytic Conference (1987, Montreal, Canada). *International Journal of Psycho-Analysis*, *69*(1), 5–21.

——— (1988b). Psychoanalysis, psychoanalytic science, and psychoanalytic research: 1986. Annual Meeting of the American Psychoanalytic

Association (1986, Washington, DC). *Journal of the American Psychoanalytic Association*, *36*(1), 3–30.
——— (1989a). Followup psychoanalysis: Clinical and research values. Fall of the American Psychoanalytic Association—Evaluation of outcome of psychoanalytic treatment: "Should followup by the analyst be part of the post-termination phase of analytic treatment?" (1987, New York). *Journal of the American Psychoanalytic Association*, *37*(4), 921–941.
——— (1989b). Psychoanalysis and psychotherapy: An historical perspective. *International Journal of Psycho-Analysis*, *70*(4), 563–591.
——— (1989c). The future of psychoanalysis. *The Psychoanalytic Quarterly*, *58*(3), 341–373.
——— (1989d). The psychotherapy research project of the Menninger Foundation: An overview. *Journal of Consulting and Clinical Psychology*, *57*(2), 195–205.
——— (1990a). Psychoanalysis: The common ground. 36th International Psychoanalytical Congress (1989, Rome, Italy). *International Journal of Psycho-Analysis*, *71*(1), 3–20.
——— (1990). The corrective emotional experience: Is reconsideration due? *Psychoanalytic Inquiry*, *10*(3), 288–324.
Wallerstein, R. S., & Sampson, H. (1971). Issues in research in the psychoanalytic process. *International Journal of Psycho-Analysis*, *52*(1), 11–50.
Wallerstein, R. S., & Smelser, N. J. (1969). Psychoanalysis and sociology: Articulations and applications. *International Journal of Psycho-Analysis*, *50*(4), 693–709.
Webster. (1989). *Encyclopedic unabridged dictionary of the English language*. New York: Gramercy Books.
Winnicott, D. W. (1945). Primitive emotional development. In *Through paediatrics to psycho-analysis* (pp. 145–156). London: Hogarth Press/The Institute of Psycho-Analysis, 1975.
——— (1947). Hate in the countertransference. In *Through paediatrics to Psycho-Analysis* (pp. 194–203). London: Hogarth Press/The Institute of Psycho-Analysis, 1975.
——— (1948a). Paediatrics and psychiatry. In *Through paediatrics to psycho-analysis* (pp. 157–173). London: Hogarth Press/The Institute of Psycho-Analysis, 1975.
——— (1948b). Reparation in respect of mother's organized defense against depression. In *Through paediatrics to psycho-analysis* (pp. 91–96). London: Hogarth Press/The Institute of Psycho-Analysis, 1975.
——— (1949a). Hate in the countertransference. *International Journal of Psychoanalysis*, *30*, 69–75.
——— (1949b). Mind and its relation to the psyche-soma. In *Through paediatrics to psycho-analysis* (pp. 243–254). London: Hogarth Press/The Institute of Psycho-Analysis, 1975.
——— (1949c). Birth memories, birth trauma, and anxiety. In *Through paediatrics to psycho-analysis* (pp. 174–193). London: Hogarth Press/The Institute of Psycho-Analysis, 1975.
——— (1950). Aggression in relation to emotional development. In *Through*

paediatrics to psycho-analysis (pp. 204–218). London: Hogarth Press/The Institute of Psycho-Analysis, 1975.

——— (1951). Transitional objects and transitional phenomena. In *Through paediatrics to psycho-analysis* (pp. 229–242). London: Hogarth Press/The Institute of Psycho-Analysis, 1975.

——— (1952a). Psychosis and child care. In *Through paediatrics to Psycho-Analysis* (pp. 219–228). London: Hogarth Press/The Institute of Psycho-Analysis, 1975.

——— (1952b). Anxiety associated with security. In *Through paediatrics to psycho-analysis* (pp. 97–100). London: Hogarth Press/The Institute of Psycho-Analysis, 1975.

——— (1954a). Withdrawal and regression. In *Through paediatrics to psycho-analysis* (pp. 255–261). London: Hogarth Press/The Institute of Psycho-Analysis, 1975.

——— (1954b). Metapsychological and clinical aspects of regression within the psycho-analytic set-up. In *Through paediatrics to psycho-analysis* (pp. 278–294). London: Hogarth Press/The Institute of Psycho-Analysis, 1975.

——— (1956a). Primary maternal preoccupation. In *Through paediatrics to psycho-analysis* (pp. 300–305). London: Hogarth Press/The Institute of Psycho-Analysis, 1975.

——— (1956b). Clinical varieties of transference. In *Through paediatrics to psycho-analysis* (pp. 295–299). London: Hogarth Press/The Institute of Psycho-Analysis, 1975.

——— (1958). *Collected papers of D. W. Winnicott*. New York: Basic Books.

——— (1960a). The theory of the parent–child relationship. In *The maturational processes and the facilitating environment* (pp. 37–55). London: Hogarth Press, 1965.

——— (1960b). Ego distortion in terms of true and false self. In *The maturational processes and the facilitating environment* (pp. 140–152). London: Hogarth Press, 1965.

——— (1960c). Countertransference. In *The maturational processes and the facilitating environment* (pp. 158–165). London: Hogarth Press, 1965.

——— (1961). The effects of psychotic parents on the emotional development of the child. *British Journal of Psychiatric Social Work*, 6, 12–20.

——— (1962a). Ego integration in child development. In *The maturational processes and the facilitating environment* (pp. 56–63). London: Hogarth Press, 1965.

——— (1962b). Dependence in infant-care, in child-care, and in the psycho-analytic setting. In *The maturational processes and the facilitating environment* (pp. 249–259). London: Hogarth Press, 1965.

——— (1962c). Communicating and not communicating leading to a study of certain opposites. In *The maturational processes and the facilitating environment* (pp. 179–192). London: Hogarth Press, 1965.

——— (1962d). The aims of psycho-analytical treatment. In *The maturational processes and the facilitating environment* (pp. 166–170). London: Hogarth Press, 1965.

——— (1962e). A personal view of the Kleinian contribution to the theory of

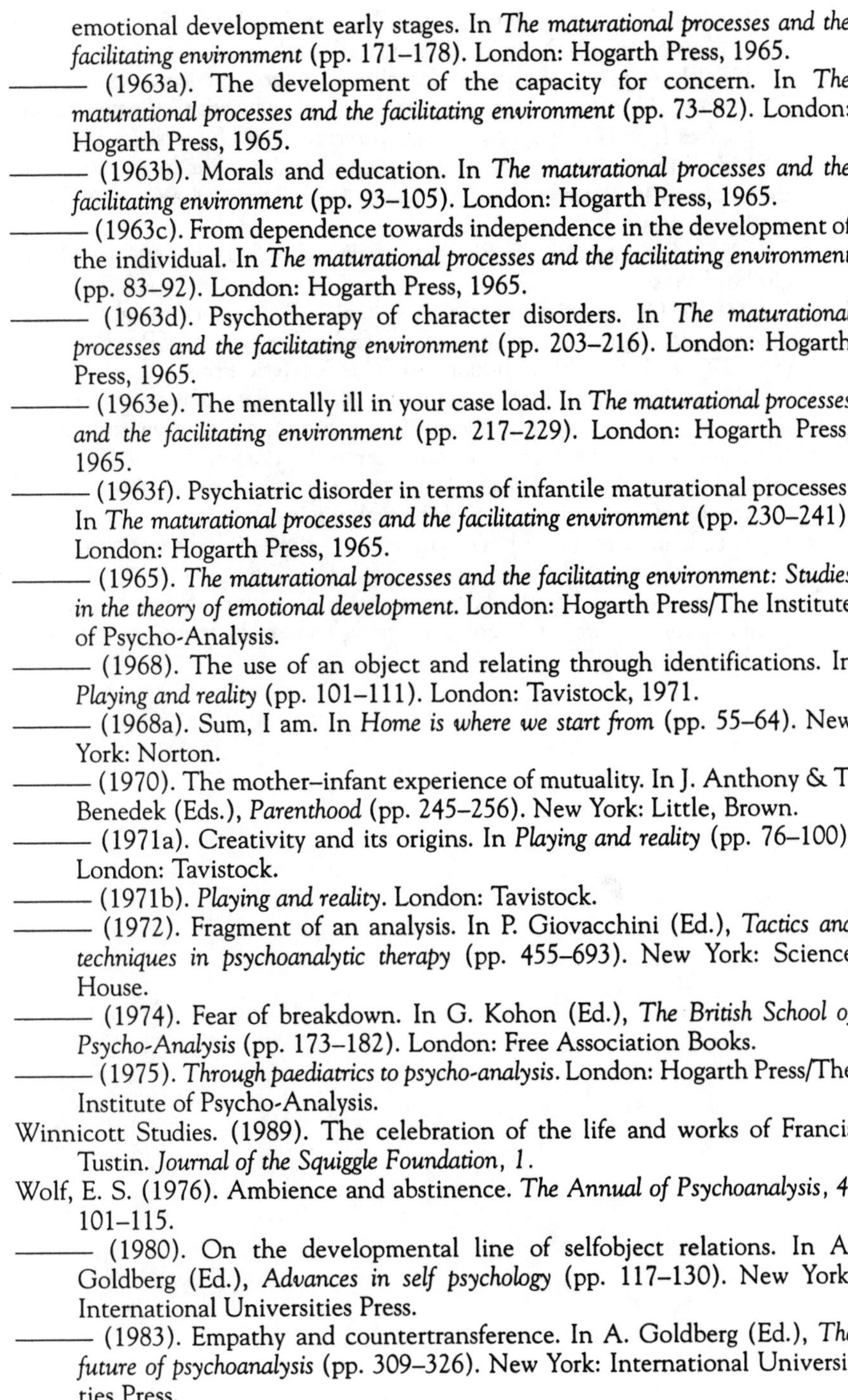

emotional development early stages. In *The maturational processes and the facilitating environment* (pp. 171–178). London: Hogarth Press, 1965.
——— (1963a). The development of the capacity for concern. In *The maturational processes and the facilitating environment* (pp. 73–82). London: Hogarth Press, 1965.
——— (1963b). Morals and education. In *The maturational processes and the facilitating environment* (pp. 93–105). London: Hogarth Press, 1965.
——— (1963c). From dependence towards independence in the development of the individual. In *The maturational processes and the facilitating environment* (pp. 83–92). London: Hogarth Press, 1965.
——— (1963d). Psychotherapy of character disorders. In *The maturational processes and the facilitating environment* (pp. 203–216). London: Hogarth Press, 1965.
——— (1963e). The mentally ill in your case load. In *The maturational processes and the facilitating environment* (pp. 217–229). London: Hogarth Press, 1965.
——— (1963f). Psychiatric disorder in terms of infantile maturational processes. In *The maturational processes and the facilitating environment* (pp. 230–241). London: Hogarth Press, 1965.
——— (1965). *The maturational processes and the facilitating environment: Studies in the theory of emotional development*. London: Hogarth Press/The Institute of Psycho-Analysis.
——— (1968). The use of an object and relating through identifications. In *Playing and reality* (pp. 101–111). London: Tavistock, 1971.
——— (1968a). Sum, I am. In *Home is where we start from* (pp. 55–64). New York: Norton.
——— (1970). The mother–infant experience of mutuality. In J. Anthony & T. Benedek (Eds.), *Parenthood* (pp. 245–256). New York: Little, Brown.
——— (1971a). Creativity and its origins. In *Playing and reality* (pp. 76–100). London: Tavistock.
——— (1971b). *Playing and reality*. London: Tavistock.
——— (1972). Fragment of an analysis. In P. Giovacchini (Ed.), *Tactics and techniques in psychoanalytic therapy* (pp. 455–693). New York: Science House.
——— (1974). Fear of breakdown. In G. Kohon (Ed.), *The British School of Psycho-Analysis* (pp. 173–182). London: Free Association Books.
——— (1975). *Through paediatrics to psycho-analysis*. London: Hogarth Press/The Institute of Psycho-Analysis.
Winnicott Studies. (1989). The celebration of the life and works of Francis Tustin. *Journal of the Squiggle Foundation, 1*.
Wolf, E. S. (1976). Ambience and abstinence. *The Annual of Psychoanalysis, 4*, 101–115.
——— (1980). On the developmental line of selfobject relations. In A. Goldberg (Ed.), *Advances in self psychology* (pp. 117–130). New York: International Universities Press.
——— (1983). Empathy and countertransference. In A. Goldberg (Ed.), *The future of psychoanalysis* (pp. 309–326). New York: International Universities Press.

——— (1984a). Selfobject relations disorders. In M. Zales (Ed.), *Character pathology* (pp. 23–38). New York: Brunner/Mazel.

——— (1984b). A psychoanalytic selfpsychologist looks at learning. In B. J. Cohler & G. Wool (Eds.), *Learning and education: Psychoanalytic perspectives* (pp. 377–393). New York: International Universities Press.

——— (1986). Discrepancies between analysand and analyst in experiencing the analysis. In *Progress in self psychology* (Vol. 2, pp. 84–94). New York: Guilford Press.

——— (1988). *Treating the self: Elements of clinical self psychology*. New York: Guilford Press.

——— (1991a). On being a scientist or a healer: Reflections on abstinence, neutrality, and gratification. In J. Winer (Ed.), *The Annual of Psychoanalysis* (Vol. 20, pp. 115–129). Hillsdale, NJ: The Analytic Press.

——— (1991b, October). *Disruptions of the therapeutic relationship in psychoanalysis: A view from self psychology*. Paper presented to Symposium on "Disagreements between patient and therapist," Boston.

——— (1993, June 10–13). *Varieties of disorders of the self*. Paper presented at 3rd International Symposium für Selbst Psychologie, Dreieich.

Wolf, E. S., & Kohut, H. (1978). The disorders of the self and their treatment. *International Journal of Psycho-Analysis*, *59*, 413–425.

Wolf, E. S., & Wolf, I. (1979). We perished, each alone: A psychoanalytic commentary on Virginia Woolf's *To the lighthouse*. *International Review of Psycho-Analysis*, *6*, 37–47.

Index

DRAKE MEMORIAL LIBRARY
WITHDRAWN
THE COLLEGE AT BROCKPORT